Theosemiotic

Theosemiotic

Religion, Reading, and the Gift of Meaning

MICHAEL L. RAPOSA

Fordham University Press
NEW YORK   2020

Copyright © 2020 Fordham University Press

All rights reserved. No part of this publication may be reproduced, stored in a retrieval system, or transmitted in any form or by any means—electronic, mechanical, photocopy, recording, or any other—except for brief quotations in printed reviews, without the prior permission of the publisher.

Fordham University Press has no responsibility for the persistence or accuracy of URLs for external or third-party Internet websites referred to in this publication and does not guarantee that any content on such websites is, or will remain, accurate or appropriate.

Fordham University Press also publishes its books in a variety of electronic formats. Some content that appears in print may not be available in electronic books.

Visit us online at www.fordhampress.com.

Library of Congress Cataloging-in-Publication Data available online at https://catalog.loc.gov.

22 21 20   5 4 3 2 1

First edition

for Murray G. Murphey
in memoriam
and for Tobin Conway Raposa
in hope,
with my love

Contents

	Preface	ix
	Parenthetical References	xv
	Prolegomena	1
1	A Brief History of Theosemiotic	15
2	Signs, Selves, and Semiosis	43
3	Love in a Universe of Chance	75
4	Theology as Inquiry, Therapy, Praxis	107
5	Communities of Interpretation	155
6	Rules for Discernment	192
7	On Prayer and the Spirit of Pragmatism	227
	Postlude: The Play of Musement	259
	Acknowledgments	265
	Notes	269
	Index	301

Preface

In 1989 I published a book-length study of the religious thought of Charles S. Peirce (1839–1914), one of America's most important philosophers, scientists, and mathematicians.[1] "Theosemiotic" was the title of the last chapter of that book; I coined the word to serve as a label for Peirce's distinctive worldview (from which he perceived the universe as "a great work of art, a great poem"). That chapter was also prospective in nature. It seemed clear to me that Peirce's theosemiotic had historical roots that run deep in the American philosophical tradition and beyond. It seemed equally clear that Peirce's articulation of that perspective supplied a uniquely promising framework for the contemporary reconsideration of certain classical issues in philosophical theology. Within that framework, the relationship between religious experience, belief, and practice might be productively reconfigured. These Peircean insights established the agenda for a line of inquiry that was initiated but could not be pursued within the limited confines of that earlier study (which was primarily exegetical in intent, designed to interpret Peirce's writings, rather than to trace his historical predecessors and successors or to develop his ideas for constructive philosophical or theological purposes).

If that chapter was a promissory note, indicating my commitment to the future development of these insights, this book is intended to supply payment in full. Partial payment has already occurred in a series of essays published since 1989, dealing both with theosemiotic's historical trajectory and with its contemporary significance. During the same period of time, in two books published just before and soon after the turn of the millennium, I explored in a limited fashion the utility of some of Peirce's ideas for analyzing certain aspects of religious experience and practice.[2] I am grateful, also, for the attention directed by other scholars to my idea of a Peircean theosemiotic, even in instances where their interpretations of Peirce's thought may have differed somewhat from my own.[3] Such individuals have worked creatively to develop Peircean resources for contemporary projects both in theology and the philosophy of religion. Yet this group of scholars remains distressingly small, with the good news about Peirce's relevance for the scholarly investigation of religious topics still somewhat muted. Moreover, my own previous explorations of the theosemiotic terrain hardly constituted a systematic exploration of its breadth and depth; that is the central purpose of this book.

From the vantage point supplied by Peirce's theosemiotic, the world is "perfused with signs." Conceived as semiosis, our human experience of the world is always a matter of interpretation; even the simplest perceptual judgments take the form of interpretive inferences, albeit often ones that are unconscious and not subject to immediate self-control. Finally, human beings are themselves properly to be regarded as complex symbols, with interactions between them consisting at least partially in acts of reading.

The implications of such a view for theology and the philosophy of religion are profound. As with the other classical American pragmatists, there is continuity rather than a gap between theory, experience, and conduct on Peirce's account. Experiences and practices labeled as "religious" are not simply raw data, then, to be subjected to careful philosophical scrutiny; they themselves have an essentially interpretive dimension and function, so that the meaning of religious ideas is signified by and embodied in certain habits of feeling and patterns of behavior. In particular, for the pragmaticist Peirce, our disciplined practices display a logic that more effectively exposes the meaning of religious beliefs and ideas than any carefully articulated verbal argument or explication ever could.

Peirce's claim that human experience and conduct are best understood as forms of semiosis is radical in itself, with important consequences for philosophers engaged in the task of understanding religious phenomena. Any detailed elaboration of theosemiotic must also take into account Peirce's synechism or doctrine of continuity; his theory of evolutionary love; his defense of a somewhat idiosyncratic form of anthropomorphism; his rich semiotic conception not only of the self but also of community; his complex and nuanced classification of the various types of signs; his characterization of interpretation as a pragmatic, experimental, and highly fallible process, with interpretive skill manifesting itself as a certain kind of self-control; and finally, his extraordinary development both of the logic of vagueness and of the logic of relations, with all of logic being portrayed as consisting essentially in semiotic. My project will require drawing these elements together in order to provide a clear sketch of theosemiotic, not simply as Peirce conceived it, but as it might be understood and further developed by contemporary philosophical theologians.

Among other advantages, I will claim that a theosemiotic perspective expedites the task of understanding what makes a community worth caring about, enabling one who adopts it to formulate morally meaningful answers to the question "Who is my neighbor?" At the same time, it facilitates comparative work in theology and religion studies, exposing certain continuities among various religious ideologies and communities (a consequence, in particular, of interpreting diverse religious utterances and behaviors within the broad framework supplied by Peirce's logic of relations). And since it is an essentially pragmatic perspective, its adoption inspires a healthy suspicion regarding the alleged sharpness of a whole series of historically prominent contrasts: tradition/experience, thought/feeling, body/soul, subject/object, self/other, internal/external, theory/practice, contemplation/action, faith/works, roots/fruits, natural/supernatural, nature/culture, nature/grace, individual/community, and theology/spirituality. With regard to the last of these, the distance between philosophical theology and a theology of the spiritual life is dramatically reduced from this point of view.

This constructive project is the edifice for which my historical inquiries (especially in Chapter 1 of the book, but then interwoven throughout) supply the foundation. Such inquiries originated with but are not limited to my study of Peirce. I propose that theosemiotic is a distinctive tradition in American religious thought that can be traced back through Ralph Waldo Emerson to Jonathan Edwards as an early exemplar. It achieves full flower in the philosophy of Peirce and then bears fruit in the work both of William James and Josiah Royce, as well as in some of H. Richard Niebuhr's writings. Edwards and Royce are particularly important for the account that I provide. Certain aspects of the former's *Treatise on Religious Affections* and the latter's *The Problem of Christianity* each receive extended consideration in the following pages; indeed, Royce's work represents the first deliberate attempt to develop Peirce's ideas for specifically theological purposes.

Venturing beyond the confines of American religious thought, I shift my gaze briefly toward the Iberian Peninsula, to the thought world flourishing there in the sixteenth and early seventeenth centuries, in order to engage both John Poinsot and Ignatius of Loyola in this conversation. Pressing back even further, I want to suggest that theosemiotic has some medieval roots, most especially in the thought of the thirteenth-century Franciscan John Duns Scotus. The influence of Scotus on Peirce is direct; but a more general consideration of the link between medieval scholastic and American philosophy would also require attending to intermediary figures like Spinoza and Schelling. Nor does the medieval story begin with Scotus. Although only occasionally mentioned here, Augustine represents a towering figure in the early development of semiotic theory.

Duns Scotus, a notoriously difficult and subtle thinker frequently ignored because of the serious challenge that his writings represent for any careful interpreter, has received at first sudden and then considerable attention since the last decade of the twentieth century. Much of it has been negative, as certain conservative theologians have blamed Scotus, his doctrine of the univocity of being in particular, for precipitating the "fall into modernity," identifying him as the remote cause not only of much that they find problematic in Western philosophy since Descartes, but also of many of the ills afflicting modern culture and social life. Here I argue that, if one traces the legacy of Duns Scotus to its modern development in Peirce's thought, rather than through Ockham and the Reformation or as terminating in Gilles Deleuze's postmodern musings,[4] then a different picture of Scotus's relationship to modernity emerges. Scotus was somewhat idiosyncratic among the medieval schoolmen in his characterization of theology as a "practical science." At the same time, and much like the classical American pragmatists writing centuries later, he conceived of theory and practice as being essentially continuous. Peirce read Duns Scotus carefully and regarded him as one of the most important philosophers who ever lived. His theosemiotic has a Scotistic dimension that I think it would be useful to expose, even if most of the other thinkers in the American intellectual tradition to which I am attaching this label were never directly influenced by medieval thought.

Consequently, a secondary feature of this inquiry will be a repositioning of Duns Scotus with respect to modern Western religious thought. Scotus emerges as one of the heroes rather than as a villain in my narrative. His philosophy, when supplemented by insights gleaned from the American pragmatists, yields invaluable resources for the contemporary reconfiguration of philosophical theology as theosemiotic. Moreover, since I link both Edwards and the later Royce to Peirce as "pragmatists," while distancing all of them from certain other philosophers usually so labeled, there is a somewhat unorthodox account of the nature and meaning of American pragmatism embedded in the story that I propose to tell in this book. Theosemiotic is not "pragmatic" in just any way, but most especially in the peculiar sense that Peirce intended to convey when he articulated the meaning of his "pragmaticism." I will also attempt to show that while both the thought of Simone Weil and the deliberations of certain Latin American liberation theologians (especially the "father" of that movement, Gustavo Gutierrez) are not typically linked to pragmatism, they further extend the trajectory of theosemiotic reflection across the twentieth century and now into the twenty-first.

Despite the historical musings with which I begin here, the purposes of this inquiry remain primarily constructive and philosophical; moreover, even such musings are not intended to be strictly historical. I aim to think *with* and *through* these historical figures, Peirce in particular, rather than simply *about* them. The connections that I establish among them, consequently, are not always causal connections displayed as actual lines of historical influence but, rather, are often relations among ideas—disparate in point of origin—that nevertheless resonate with one another. Even in cases where the historical influence is real and significant, as in Scotus on Peirce, I am not concerned with its demonstration.

I *am* concerned with the act of reading broadly conceived, with the kind and quality of attention that specific forms of reading require, and with the discernment of meaning as it is conveyed by and embodied in various signs and symbols. When that meaning is judged to be "religious," then the task of discernment becomes an explicitly theological task. Peirce and his intellectual kin, I hope to persuade *my* readers, are invaluable guides for anyone who engages in that kind of theology or philosophically reflects on its proper exercise.

System of Parenthetical References to Editions of Peirce's Writings

Collected Papers of Charles Sanders Peirce, edited by Charles Hartshorne, Paul Weiss, and Arthur Burks, 8 vols. (Cambridge, Mass.: Harvard University Press, 1931–58). [Reference is with the designation *CP*, followed by volume and paragraph number.]

The Writings of Charles S. Peirce: A Chronological Edition, edited by the Peirce Edition Project, 7 vols. to date (Bloomington: Indiana University Press, 1982–present). [Reference is with the designation *W*, followed by volume and page number.]

The Essential Peirce, edited by Nathan Houser, Christian Kloesel, and the Peirce Edition Project, 2 vols. (Bloomington: Indiana University Press, 1992 and 1998). [Reference is with the designation *EP*, followed by volume and page number.]

New Elements of Mathematics, edited by Carolyn Eisele, 4 vols. (Atlantic Highlands, N.J.: Humanities Press, 1976). [Reference is with the designation *NEM*, followed by volume and page number.]

Semiotic and Significs: The Correspondence between C. S. Peirce and Victoria Lady Welby, edited by Charles E. Hardwick (Bloomington: Indiana University Press, 1977). [Reference is with the designation *SS*, followed by page number.]

Charles Sanders Peirce: Contributions to The Nation, edited by Kenneth Lane Ketner, 4 vols. (Lubbock, Tex.: Texas Tech University Press, 1975–87). [Reference is with the designation *N*, followed by volume and page number.]

Reasoning and the Logic of Things: The Cambridge Conference Lectures of 1898, edited by Kenneth L. Ketner and Hilary Putnam (Cambridge, Mass.: Harvard University Press, 1992). [Reference is with the designation *RLT*, followed by page number.]

Pragmatism as a Principle and Method of Right Thinking, edited by Patricia Ann Turrisi, (Albany: State University of New York Press, 1997). [Reference is with the designation *PPM*, followed by page number.]

The Charles S. Peirce Manuscripts (Cambridge, Mass.: Houghton Library of Harvard University), catalogued by Richard Robin, *Annotated Catalogue of the Papers of Charles S. Peirce* (Amherst: University of Massachusetts Press, 1967). [Reference is with the designation *MS*, followed by the number assigned by Robin.]

THEOSEMIOTIC

Prolegomena

". . . all this universe is perfused with signs, if it is not composed exclusively of signs."

(CP 5.448, NOTE 1)

"Perfusion" is the process of pouring a liquid over or through something, like blood through the organs and tissues of a human body. In a world "perfused with signs," semiosis is the life-blood flowing through the universe, giving it meaning and life. That we inhabit such a world, moreover, that we stand in a relationship to the universe as potential readers capable of discerning fragments of its meaning, are fundamental hypotheses of any theology conceived as theosemiotic.

The state of being "perfused" with signs, in point of fact, is quite different from that of being "composed exclusively" of them; indeed, from the perspective to be occupied here a claim about the former possibility represents the more plausible hypothesis. That anything can be or can become a sign does not entail the conclusion that semiosis is ubiquitous in the universe.[1] To insist on the latter is to erect a theoretical Tower of Babel that no reasonable line of argumentation could hope to sustain. It is salient for the purposes of any theosemiotic inquiry that there can be real growth of meaning in the universe, that human beings can contribute to this process—also, that they can fail to do so. Semiosis waxes and wanes, even as living things are born and die. There are spaces empty of meaning, just as there are regions of the world devoid of life. Still, "there lives the dearest freshness deep down things," so that even in places without meaning there is always a real potential, the possibility of becoming meaningful.[2] Here the line between discovery and creation is blurred; interpretation is a complex phenomenon that involves both finding and making meaning.

Human experience is always already a matter of interpretation. Even the simplest sensations and perceptions take the form of hypothetical judgments, nevertheless frequently consisting of inferences that are immediate (although not unmediated), unconscious, and (at least as they occur, if not upon further reflection) indubitable. In order to make sense out of this claim about human experience as semiosis, one needs to develop a generously expanded and carefully nuanced understanding of what it means to give an interpretation.

One can interpret a sign or symbol with language, by talking or writing about it, in the process hoping to explain its meaning. Yet, on the account to be delineated here, what I feel when I encounter some symbol is also constitutive of its meaning. This is most especially the case if my feeling responses are not anomalous or episodic—that is, if some pattern of feeling (however complex) becomes habitually associated with a particular symbol. The same is true with regard to specific patterns of behavior. My unthinkingly running a red light on some isolated occasion tells us much less about the meaning of that sign than does the habitual stopping behavior that it elicits from me at intersections. Interpretative activity is organized around habit responses, then—habits of thought, feeling, and conduct.

At the same time, interpretation cannot be reduced to habit. When I first encounter a sign and commence to interpret its meaning, no habitual way of doing so may yet have been established. To recognize anything at all is to apply a familiar class concept to it, perceiving that thing encountered, by virtue of some inveterate way of thinking, as being of a certain kind. Yet one may also chance upon something curious or strange, fail to recognize it immediately, and so need to cast about for appropriate classifications. Here is a form of interpretive activity, the upshot of which may prove to be the formation of a habit, but the early stages of which can be a good deal more playful and free.

These qualities of playfulness and freedom can also characterize interpretations that occur even beyond the point when some patterned response to a certain sign has already become well entrenched. Such a response can suddenly become problematic for any number of reasons, pushing interpretation in new directions, as suspicion grows that this may not be exactly the kind of thing or situation that one had thought it was all along. In some cases, one simply becomes *bored* with the habitual response elicited by the thing in question, and so one begins to explore novel ways of thinking or feeling about it, imagining new possibilities for interaction with it.[3] In the extraordinarily complex semiotic interactions that constitute our relationships with other persons, for example, this can take the form of falling in love all over again with somebody already well-known and beloved—the discovery of an entirely new depth of meaning in that relationship.

Finally, habits can be more or less rigid in the control that they exercise over our interpretive behavior, allowing less or more room and freedom for play. A lock or a safe with a set combination is a sign the interpretation of which must occur within fairly narrow parameters if it is to be regarded as correct or successful (and for unlocking to occur). Like the red light at a traffic intersection, such a sign is likely to elicit the same interpretive behavior on repeated occasions except in those cases where mistakes happen. In contrast, many signs and symbols, artworks for example, invite an interpretive response that is shaped by habits a good deal gentler in their effects.[4] Some interpretations, to be sure, will simply be ruled out as incorrect or inappropriate, but a wide range of possibilities remains open on any given occasion. Like the driver at an intersection in reaction to a traffic light, the dancer at a recital interprets a piece of music by performing certain physical actions; but in the latter case, the creativity of the performance will be significantly greater than in the former, the range of possible (and yet still felicitous) performances considerably more broad.

Human beings are themselves complex signs, conversations and interactions among them constituting a kind of living intertextuality. In an important but somewhat vague and limited sense, community already exists whenever such interactions occur—that is, whenever persons direct attention to one another for the purpose of communicating or discovering meaning. *Consensus, complementarity*, and *critique* are all features of interpretation that presuppose the existence of community; none of these interpretive goals can be achieved apart from the sorts of interactions among persons being alluded to here (except in the truncated sense in which every individual person represents a kind of community in miniature and so might gradually achieve, as an individual, greater accuracy, complexity, and self-awareness in interpretive behavior). Whether our thinking is something that we do together in conversation or that we appear to pursue more privately, "we have no power of thinking without signs" (*CP* 5.265; *W*2: 213). Indeed, Peirce portrayed thought as consisting "in the living inferential metaboly of symbols whose purport lies in conditional general resolutions to act" (*CP* 5.402, note 3). Here, also, he supplied in shorthand a useful characterization of any philosophical theology conceived as theosemiotic.[5]

All religious symbols are necessarily vague, typically determining a range of possible meanings, yet with their interpretation left indeterminate to some extent and in certain respects. The process of determining meaning is a central task of theosemiotic. As with all properly scientific modes of inquiry for which the logic of induction has a normative status, success in executing this task is at least partially judged by the ability of interpreters to achieve consensus about what symbols mean and how they are to be used for various religious purposes. At the same time, if theosemiotic is to flourish as an enterprise, no rigid criterion of sameness or insistence on consensus can be invoked to circumscribe narrowly the set of meanings a religious symbol will be permitted to have. Two interpreters in conversation may discover that the different meanings of a symbol, as they each construe it, complement one another in interesting and important ways. Taken together, these interpretations themselves form a complex symbol, its own meaning enriched by such complementary elements and itself subject to further interpretation. The logic of relations supplies useful resources for resisting the false idol of the univocity of meaning. This is accomplished by moving beyond talk about logical "classes," the members of which all share characteristics that make them the same kind of thing, in order to pursue the analysis of logical "systems," the elements of which are linked together in a meaningful pattern by some general purpose or idea.

Recognizing the multivalence of symbols does not reduce to a claim that meaning is arbitrary. To say that a symbol has potentially many meanings is not to say that it can mean just anything at all (as if meaning were always something purely external, attached to a symbol as if by a code). For the theologian to be able to regard an array of complementary interpretations as permissible does not preclude the possibility of critique, of arguing for the superiority of one interpretation over another, or of insisting that some specific construal of meaning is altogether illegitimate.

Theosemiotic will require a properly scientific method for the purpose of evaluating and fixing beliefs; consequently, it will also be considered "experimental." But here again, as with one's understanding of interpretation, it is important to employ an expanded, subtle notion of what it means to conduct an experiment. Guided by such a notion, it becomes possible fully to appreciate Jonathan Edwards's agenda for an "experimental religion," as well as to make sense out of the claim that Peirce intended the practice of what he called "musement" to constitute a kind of theologically meaningful experiment.[6] Many religious practices that may appear to have clearly identifiable and obviously nonscientific purposes may also be perceived as experimental from the special perspective that theosemiotic provides. For the classical American pragmatists, the scientific method was considered too powerful and important for its exercise to be restricted to the laboratories of natural scientists. In their view, everyday human life is a laboratory, our lived experience involving a steady stream of interpretations and an ongoing process of testing their validity. Consequently, theological reflection will quite frequently begin with our lived experience and should continuously return to it as a touchstone.

To the extent that its practitioners display an experimental *habitus*, theosemiotic will be readily distinguished from any type of philosophical theology that operates primarily in a deductive mode. At the same time, deductive reasoning will figure prominently in the sort of inquiry being envisioned here, albeit located at the midpoint rather than as the upshot of any line of reasoning. Its primary purpose will be considered as explicative rather than as strictly demonstrative. That is to say, deduction establishes a necessary link between the formation of any hypothesis and the experimental testing of its validity by clarifying the consequences that would necessarily be entailed if the hypothesis were shown to be true. This "showing" is an inductive process, but it is a blind one if not shaped by valid deductions.

In semiotic terms, hypothetical inference or abduction, at least in its incipiency, constitutes a form of "contemplation" resulting in the "fixation of attention," as Peirce described it, the use of self-control in order to facilitate the process of considering "the interesting bearings of what may lie hidden in the icon" (*CP* 7.555). Yet all of these modes of inference or stages of inquiry flow seamlessly one into another, since a preliminary deductive assessment will already be involved in hypothesis formation or selection—that is to say, making explicit in consciousness what the affirmation of some hypothetical idea might further entail involves directing attention to selected features of that hypothesis, resulting in the even fuller exposure of what may now "lie hidden." Moreover, the repeated "contemplation" of hypotheses and of their implications can become a disciplined practice that (it will be argued here) has real inductive value. Such repetition can result in the formation of distinctive habits of thought that will then facilitate future inquiries, gently, perhaps even unconsciously helping to generate greater insight.

Theosemiotic entails a commitment both to empiricism and to pragmatism. Yet, these words are fuzzy labels for a broad range of perspectives, not all of which will be considered congenial for theosemiotic purposes. As indicated, the type of empiricism most relevant to these purposes is one that incorporates a conception of experience as always already interpreted—that is, of experience-as-semiosis. Since theosemiotic falls within the range of disciplines that Peirce designated as "cenoscopy," it will be especially concerned with the kind of "normal experience" that occurs "for the most part in every waking hour" of human life. Observations of such experience frequently "escape the untrained eye precisely because they permeate our whole lives" (*CP* 1.241). Rather than requiring some special revelation or equipment, success in making these observations requires a certain discipline.

The species of pragmatism most suitable for theosemiotic will much more closely resemble Peirce's "pragmaticism" than it will many contemporary forms of neo-pragmatism. In the first place, this means that pragmatists *should be* empiricists, so that the concept of "experience" is not one that they can dispense with in their philosophies.[7] In addition, it means that the genuinely pragmatic inquirer will emphasize results that can be generalized and that form patterns; she must be attentive to any evidence of a certain consistency or continuity in experience, even if it does not always need to manifest itself as a uniformity. Emphatically, it requires that the pragmatist resist the temptation to assume that semiosis must always be linguistic in form, while also insisting that the meaning of a sign will to some extent be determined by its object and not merely be socially constructed.

"By their fruits you will know them" was Peirce's scriptural warrant for the claim that Jesus was pragmatism's first philosopher.[8] But the question of how one proceeds to assess "fruitfulness" from within the framework supplied by theosemiotic is a challenging one. Acting on religious ideals or engaging in religious practices may, but also may not, cause one to flourish in any common or worldly sense; indeed, doing so may appear as "foolishness" in the eyes of the world. One's commitment to pragmatism should never blind one to the tragic sense of life, to the nobility of some terrible failures, to the often-violent conflict of purposes. Moreover, the vagueness of religious ideas and the extended or "long run" character of what may be regarded as meaningful religious "experiments" make the task of assessment delicate and formidable. Finally, theosemioticians should not oversimplify their task as involving a concern with the "fruits" *rather* than the "roots" of some belief or idea; instead, they need to conceive of fruits and roots as standing in an often-complex sign-object relation.

That relation is always mediated and irreducibly triadic; every sign will both refer back to its "object" and elicit an "interpretant." The latter (a response that consists in some thought, feeling, or action) itself constitutes a sign, one that not only refers in this mediated fashion to the same object, but also invites further interpretation. "Meaning" is not a property of the sign, then, nor does it consist exclusively either in the sign's semantic relationship to its object or in its pragmatic determination of some interpretant (what Peirce called its "significate effect"). Meaning is an event, generated in semiosis and merging with other events in the continuous flow of signs. For theosemiotic purposes, it makes less sense to talk about the meaning of any given idea or thought-sign than about the gradual emergence or development of meaning in thought, such meaning being always "in a state of incipiency, of growth" (*CP* 1.615).

If it is correct to argue that semiosis is pervasive but not ubiquitous in the universe, then it becomes important to recognize the necessary limits of any theosemiotic—indeed, to include reflection on those limits as a part of the process of inquiry. This is one of the reasons it is appropriate to consider theosemiotic as also embracing a form of apophatic or negative theology, a theology of mystery. Peirce once suggested, with regard to any philosophical discussion of the divine attributes, that "we only wildly gabble about such things" (*CP* 6.509). In part, this remark was informed by Peirce's deliberations concerning the logic of vagueness; on his account, all talk about God must be necessarily and exceedingly vague. For Peirce, the logic of vagueness appeared to occupy a role similar to that played by the doctrine of analogy in Aquinas's philosophical theology, allowing each thinker to explain how the same term appearing in different contexts could display continuity without identity of meaning. Yet the truly apophatic moment in Aquinas's theological career occurred at the end of it, when he allegedly lapsed into silence.

One of the paradoxical features of any theosemiotic inquiry is the obligation to talk about such silence, somehow to gesture toward whatever dark realities may elude semiosis altogether, lurking beyond even the vaguest forms of representation. The roots of thought may lie deep in the unconscious, if not directly accessible or subject to self-control, nevertheless bearing fruit (either bitter or sweet) in the conduct that our "occult nature" determines (*CP* 5.440). It is important to consider how deeply these roots of thought might reach, how fully enshrouded in darkness they actually are, and thus the extent to which their mysterious content can be mediated to consciousness by determinate signs and symbols. When the indeterminate puts on determinacy in the flow of semiosis, meaning grows; but what else (is it some alternative meaning or meaning's more primordial "other") might be lost in or occluded by this process?

This proposal for theosemiotic incorporates a kind of "natural theology" in a post-liberal era when many have become convinced of the impossibility of such an enterprise. In part, this possibility remains open for theosemiotic because it preserves a space for deliberation about human beings as a sign-using species—that is, about our special capacities and experiences as *homo symbolicus*. Such deliberations are legitimate even apart from or prior to consideration of how individual human experiences are also shaped by a great variety of linguistic, social, and cultural differences. They presuppose a mode of abstraction, a generalizing tendency, characteristic of most natural theologies, but one that need not be conflated with a failure also to recognize how we are always already thoroughly enculturated and socialized beings. Despite important differences, at a certain level of vagueness it should be possible to discern the similarities or continuities among our experiences that derive from the fact that we are the same kind of creatures, with similar brains and bodies, that we share certain natural capacities and predispositions, some of which may prove to be religiously significant.

Theology as theosemiotic can also be characterized as "natural" to the extent that it is informed by a pragmatic refusal to endorse any kind of sharp or rigid nature/culture distinction. Flourishing in societies, creating cultures, and using languages are all precisely the sorts of things that, from a pragmatist's perspective, it is thoroughly natural for human beings to do. The building of dams is no less natural an activity for beavers than their eating or sexual behavior. Likewise, participation in many different forms of semiosis is something to which humans appear to be naturally inclined. Recognition of these facts involves embracing a kind of religious naturalism (but only of the sort that conceives of "nature" quite broadly, much as Emerson or Spinoza did). Tracing natural continuities across diverse cultures and communities will also require engaging in some form of comparative theological inquiry.

Theosemioticians will want to emphasize both the primacy of praxis and the extraordinary significance of a community of inquiry for theological purposes. The former emphasis should not be conflated with just any claim about the relative importance of practical activities vis à vis purely theoretical ones; rather, it amounts to yet another pragmatic refusal to drive a deep conceptual wedge, this time between theory and practice. The dichotomy is false because thinking is itself a kind of doing, deliberate theorizing a mode of praxis. Nowhere is this insight more perfectly illustrated than with Peirce's brief but vivid portrayal of the practice of musement in his essay on "A Neglected Argument for the Reality of God" (*CP* 6.452-91). Moreover, it is important to remember that logic was dependent upon ethics in Peirce's treatment of the normative sciences, as he was persuaded that any theory of thinking correctly must be framed by a theory of right conduct in general.

Attending to the primacy of praxis is another strategy for underscoring the crucial role that habits play in both the production and the interpretation of meaning. Habits can be generated in multiple ways, but most reliably through practice; it is only insofar as they represent the upshot of such deliberate behavior (as opposed to being the result of a sudden, traumatic experience, for example) that they can be properly regarded as self-controlled. So even where there is no direct and immediate impact of theory on practice, the former can be perceived as gradually shaping the latter in the long run, via the mediation of habit.

Our practices can be pursued in solitude, but they are typically social in origin, as well as socially significant in their long-term effects. And so attention to praxis also places the spotlight back on the community. Interpreters will engage others in conversation for all of the reasons that induction flourishes best in a communal context; comparison with the conclusions of others will serve both to check and to complement one's own. This much has already been observed. What needs to be added is the insight that one's hypothetical or abductive inferences—the construal of a sign's meaning prior to any intersubjective exchanges that may result in the modification or even the abandonment of that interpretation—are dramatically shaped by one's habits of cognition. A great many of these habits are inculcated in community, acquired by exposure to traditional teachings or through participation in traditional practices.

Practice takes time, shapes behavior over time. This is how Peirce understood self-control, not merely as a flexing of one's volitional muscles on the spot and in the moment, but rather as the self's gradual, gentle shaping through habit formation of future versions of itself. This is also the kind of voluntarism that a Peircean pragmaticism entails and that theosemioticians will be eager to endorse. It is one that features as central to its doctrine the Scotistic ideal of *firmitas* or steadfastness, exposing not only those acts of will involved in the making of new choices, but also those displayed in the constancy of commitment to certain ideals, to choices already made. On this view, human beings are living symbols in the sense that each of their thoughts and actions can be significant, but most especially insofar as their lives as a whole take on a certain shape and character. It is the continuity of purpose evidenced in one's deliberate, ongoing commitment to ideals—even as those ideals may evolve and purposes may undergo development throughout the entire process of interpretation—that fully signifies the meaning of a human life.

Such a view entails a distinctive understanding of human freedom. This concept cannot be explained exhaustively in terms of some measure of one's autonomy, the range of options available in any given situation, and one's capacity to select among them. The ability to make such choices surely constitutes part of what it means to be free, yet only a slender fragment of its meaning. Freedom will also be exercised and displayed, as just indicated, in the reaffirming of choices already made—moreover (and somewhat paradoxically), in the choosing or affirming of certain life events and experiences that would occur *willy nilly*, apart from one's ever having chosen them at all. Here the freedom exercised may not affect the actual occurrence of some event but can nevertheless dramatically transform the quality and meaning of one's experience of what occurs (as when one chooses to accept that fact that one must die). Even when one's choices really do effect a difference in outcome, this is still to be regarded as a freedom *within* rather than *from* constraint. Peirce tended to characterize it in aesthetic terms, as an "affair of *form*" rather than of the "*matter* of life" (*CP* 4.611). Such a portrayal of freedom is worth exploring in greater depth. More concretely (to select just two helpful examples), it is worth considering how the beauty of dance is impossible without the constraints that both gravity and the human body supply, or how the way in which our love for another person, while it *binds* us in certain ways, can also constitute the most perfect form of human freedom.

Peirce once described the universe as a "great poem," as "a great symbol of God's purpose, working out its conclusions in living realities" (*CP* 5.119). Human beings are among these "living realities," their thoughts, feelings, and actions embodying a fragment of the meaning of this epic poem. What their lives mean will be decisively (although not exclusively) determined by what they choose to do, not just on any one occasion, but in the long run. These meanings will merge with and complement the meanings of other persons with whom they engage and interact in community. Traditional theologians have unpacked this semiotic insight in terms of their talk about prayer, about how all of life can be transformed into prayer, and about the necessity for individuals to be joined in communities of prayer. Theosemiotic is always already a theology of the spiritual life.

Prayer sometimes takes the form of meditative reading (*lectio divina*), and so theosemiotic will require a concept of reading as capacious as the closely related notion of interpretation that it presupposes. "Reading" is a word that designates not just one but rather a great variety of interpretive acts.[9] In the peculiarly religious sense most relevant to theosemiotic, it is the continuous act of reading and then rereading (*relegere*) that takes center stage, the kind of practice that typically constitutes one's mindful interaction with scriptural texts or love letters, and not to be conflated with the way in which one might scan the internet, the morning newspaper, or a soup can label for bits of information. From a theosemiotic perspective, such practices are at the very heart of the religious life. Properly understood, that life takes shape as a continuous act of reading, while itself constituting a text capable of being read, either by oneself or by others. The quality of attention is what is most important when one considers the practice of reading, also the way that one's attention might be captured by certain signs, or how one might choose in a self-controlled fashion to direct attention to this rather than to that. The significance of the element of repetition in any instance of rereading or reading again will need here to be investigated. The deliberate repetition of a specific action can be understood to support a variety of strategic purposes. These will range from intentional jading in order to soften the "noise" in any given environment that might act to distort perception to the development of some positive hermeneutical skill through practice—that is, through persistent exercise in reading.[10]

To the extent that the spiritual life can be taken to consist in acts of reading, one of the primary goals of theosemiotic will involve the attempt to render explicit those habits and tendencies that help to make such reading a religiously meaningful experience. This process of "making explicit" presupposes something like the distinction that Peirce drew between an "argument" and "argumentation"; while the former is any thought process that results in a certain belief, the latter proceeds "upon definitely formulated premisses" (*CP* 6.456). Unconscious habits can act as "silent" premises, continuously shaping the inferences and judgments that constitute our ongoing experience of the world. Theosemiotic exposes these habits, articulates them, as a kind of second-order interpretation of what already must be conceived as essentially interpretive. With respect to any experience construed as a religiously meaningful act of reading, then, it plays a role analogous to literary criticism. The latter should help us to understand better both the things that we read and the reasons we read in the way that we do.

If logic was dependent on ethics in Peirce's normative scheme, both were regarded as dependent on aesthetics, the science devoted to discovering that which is admirable in itself, apart from any extrinsic reason for its being so. A thing will be beautiful simply as it presents itself, because of the qualities of feeling that it embodies, and not as judged in comparison with other things or perceived as meeting certain objectives. The discernment of beauty requires a certain detachment, then, a playful vacation from those purposes that might otherwise give shape to our thought, and an attentive encounter with things just as they presently appear. The fulfillment of this requirement is realized in musement. It is the sheer beauty of the idea of God, Peirce claimed, that recommends it as an ideal to the one who contemplates it, prior to any affirmation of its truth and apart from any arguments that might be assembled in support of the claim that it is true. Theosemiotic is methodologically rooted in such contemplative activity, embodying at its core a distinctive type of theological aesthetic.

Anything that truly functions as a sign does so to the extent that it is self-effacing, the servant of meaning, transparent enough to direct attention beyond itself to what it signifies. Insofar as persons themselves can be conceived as signs, this sort of self-effacement will take on a distinctively religious quality, comparable to acts of asceticism. Moreover, the meaning to which any sign gestures is always, in some sense, a deferred meaning, something promised, partially realized now but more fully in the future (since every interpretant is itself a sign inviting further interpretation). Theosemiotic is always already a theology of hope.

It is not altogether clear or certain whether or not theosemioticians must remain committed to Peirce's anthropomorphism and vague theism or, metaphysically speaking, to his objective idealism. If persons are to be regarded as signs, to what extent must a world "perfused with signs" also be conceived as somewhat personal in nature? Is talk about love (for example, as Peirce talked about it in developing an evolutionary cosmology) in any way meaningful if the one who loves or the object of love are not properly to be regarded as "persons?" How vague is the concept of the "personal," and does that vagueness permit its application to anything not explicitly human? The search for answers to such questions would require at least some evaluation of the relationship between any philosophical theology conceived as theosemiotic and a variety of different forms—many historical but some contemporary—of philosophical *personalism*. (That process of evaluation can only be vaguely anticipated here.)

Regardless of how such questions are resolved, there is a tangible resonance between the general perspective of theosemiotic and that articulated in certain liberation theologies and theologies of praxis (most of which have been developed, of course, within an explicitly theistic framework, and many of which also tend to emphasize the intrinsic value and dignity of persons). This resonance consists, among other things, in a shared insistence on the primacy of practice; religious beliefs are theologically indispensable, but their meanings are best evidenced not in how we talk about them, but rather in what we are willing and able to do because of them, in our conduct and commitments. Sometimes that "doing" takes the form of operating directly on the self in order to dissolve old habits and form new ones. Sometimes it involves operating on those environments—natural, social, and political—that can so dramatically constrain human agency and to which selves must constantly adapt. In any given case, do we choose to change the self to fit the world or change the world to render it more hospitable to a diversity of selves, to empower or liberate those who might be oppressed or excluded by the presently existing state of affairs?[11] This is a question that every thoughtful theosemiotician will feel obliged to ask repeatedly. In searching for answers, both psychotherapy and political theory promise resources that can be invaluable to the philosophical theologian. (The former is treated here at greater length than the latter.)

Attending to liberation motifs and concerns will also help to ensure a necessary balance within theosemiotic between a commitment to traditional perspectives and the goal of consensus, on the one hand, to the importance of complementary heterogeneities and interpretation-as-critique, on the other. Theologically speaking, this can be a delicate balancing act. Some interpretations reinforce each other in the building up of a consensus, in the gradual coming to agreement. Others complement or supplement one another precisely in their difference, a harmonious rather than a chaotic heterogeneity. Some interpretations will need to be vigorously resisted as inappropriate or false, if not abandoned altogether then perhaps forcefully criticized and modified (so that the occasionally "martial" character of both our spiritual and our interpretive practices ought not to be ignored). Finally, all interpretations will be hedged around by the constant awareness that "we only wildly gabble about such things," that no symbol perfectly represents its object, no interpretation exhausts the meaning of a complex symbol, and meaning itself is often less of an achievement than a gift.

Recognition of the gift of meaning, wherever and whenever it appears, presupposes the cultivation of an exceptional capacity for attention, manifested as a distinctive kind of "reading skill." Spiritual practices across a variety of religious traditions are designed to develop just such a capacity, just such a habit of attention. Part of the task of theosemiotic, in continuity with the lived experience of religious practitioners, is to duplicate some of their results, moreover, as a theoretical extension of their project, once again, to pay careful attention to attention itself. The exercise of attention, to be sure, is a fully human pursuit, soaked in finitude, irremediably contingent, circumscribed by stubbornly hidden realities and buffeted by noisy forces and factors (some internal, others external to consciousness) never completely under one's control. Nevertheless, one can only properly interpret, respond to, love, or be grateful for that to which one also pays attention—and, indeed, in order to sustain all of the above, it must be a certain quality of attention. This deceptively simple pragmatic truth, I have long been convinced, lies at the very heart of any inquiry conceived as theosemiotic.

1 / A Brief History of Theosemiotic

I

One brief but rather prominent account of the tradition of American religious thought that stretches from Jonathan Edwards through Ralph Waldo Emerson to William James and beyond focuses on its distinctive character in promoting a form of "esthetic spirituality"—that is, in fostering a "consciousness of the beauty of living in harmony with divine things."[1] My own "history" borrows from but also expands the scope of this earlier account: first of all by moving outside of (while nevertheless still emphasizing) specifically American intellectual life; second, by recognizing that the religiously meaningful experience of beauty is only one, albeit rather a significant, kind of theosemiosis. Moreover, I want to begin with Peirce as central to my narrative, rather than starting with Edwards, moving both backward and forward in time in order to trace a lineage of individuals, the thought of each displaying features regarded as relevant for the purposes of this inquiry. Finally, consistent with a Peircean perspective on the unity of the normative sciences, any emphasis on the beautiful here is intended to expose rather than to obscure the peculiarly moral significance of that religious worldview held in common by these thinkers; "living in harmony" is to be conceived as *both* an aesthetic and an ethical desideratum.[2]

To contemplate the world as a great work of art, divine in origin, while also considering the idea of divinity itself to be compelling by virtue of its supreme beauty, is to frame religious experience as being aesthetic at its core. The encounter with evil and suffering in the world will challenge this picture, sometimes in ways that the classical American pragmatists were not always best equipped to understand. Theology in its apophatic mode will also delimit and counterbalance any line of reflection that focuses on the beauty of religiously meaningful representations (although to observe this is not simultaneously to deny that there is a certain dark beauty toward which only such a theology is equipped to gesture). Notwithstanding these qualifications, religious experience has an important aesthetic dimension, attending to which often marks the birthplace of theological insight.

Whatever its alleged imperfections, the status of its composition, or the limits of human interpretive ability to probe its meaning, Peirce did conceive of the universe as a vast, divinely inspired work of art. The "book of nature" metaphor has roots that run historically deep, extending at least as far back as the late medieval period.[3] Peirce seems to have tapped into these roots, his thought flowering into a worldview that displayed several distinctive emphases. Indeed, the metaphor shades toward the literal, given the power and scope of Peirce's semiotic theory, his central insight that ours is a world veritably perfused with signs. From this vantage point, the universe is less adequately perceived as something that could be treated *like* a text, than as an actual book, still incomplete, being written in a language so extraordinarily complex that in many instances it remains indecipherable.[4] Moreover, it is hardly just any kind of text in Peirce's view, but rather, a "great poem," so that the reading of it is not merely informative, but also provides the occasion for a powerful kind of aesthetic experience. This is what Peirce had in mind when he described and then prescribed for his own readers the activity of musement (*CP* 6.458–67 and 6.486). When later pressed by one reader, Victoria Lady Welby, to say a bit more about what he meant by musement, he immediately linked it to Friedrich Schiller's aesthetic theory—in particular, to the latter's talk about the *Spieltrieb*, with which Peirce confessed that his own notion was "thoroughly soaked."[5]

The idea of God, albeit vaguely conceived, arises naturally in the process of reading the book of nature. This result occurs, Peirce suggested, only if the reading is performed in a certain way, with an appropriate disinterestedness and quality of attention. The divinely authored text is sufficiently vast and complex that we can hope to catch but a "glimpse" of God's nature and purposes. Yet this negative moment in Peirce's religious thought is balanced by a more positive claim; if *what* God is and plans for creation cannot be readily discerned, *that* God is should appear obvious to anyone appropriately disposed to see the truth of the matter. For such a person, it will be as difficult to doubt the reality of God's "living personality" as it is to doubt one's own existence (*CP* 6.436). Moreover, among the more prominent features of the idea of God that make it "irresistible" to the person who contemplates it in genuine musement is the extraordinary *beauty* of that idea. The more carefully and consistently you consider such a notion, the more it "grows on you" or, more accurately, *in* you. Its meaning does not emerge all at once in a single reading, but is enhanced through rereading. Growing in power, it also manifests itself as an ideal so luminous that one will desire "to shape the whole conduct of life" in conformity with it (*CP* 6.467). The attractiveness of this idea is hardly limited, then, by the muser's inability clearly or completely to understand the nature of God or the divine plan for creation. Instead, its extraordinary vagueness actually contributes to the power and persuasiveness of the idea.

Ralph Waldo Emerson was an occasional guest of Charles Peirce's father, Benjamin, in their Cambridge, Massachusetts, home, when Charles was a very young boy.[6] Despite his midlife reservations concerning transcendentalism as a philosophy, it is important to consider Peirce's admission, in remarks appearing at the beginning of his 1892 essay on "The Law of Mind," that he was influenced by some of its doctrines. There he reported that "it is probable that some cultured bacilli, some benignant form of the disease was implanted in my soul, unawares, and that now, after long incubation, it comes to the surface, modified by mathematical conceptions and by training in physical investigations" (*CP* 6.102; *W*8: 135). Here, Peirce's characterization of transcendentalism as a "virus," along with his identification of thinkers who had been stricken by this "monstrous mysticism of the East," are comments that were probably made with his tongue pressing at least lightly against his cheek. In any event, toward the end of that same essay, Peirce concluded that "if there is a personal God, we must have a direct perception of that person and indeed be in personal communication with him" (*CP* 6.162; *W*8: 156). The transcendentalist germ of an idea that embedded itself in his mind and gradually developed there was obviously one not lacking in religious significance. Peirce's recognition of transcendentalism's influence on his own mature philosophy, albeit modified in form, establishes Emerson as an important precursor in the history of theosemiotic.

Even if Peirce had never made this admission, evidence for an affinity between these two thinkers could readily be gleaned without having to look much further than Emerson's early essay on *Nature*.[7] On the account that Emerson developed there, our human words are to be regarded as the "signs of natural facts," while nature itself is to be perceived as "the symbol of spirit."[8] Nature is able effectively to mediate between spiritual reality and human discourse precisely because natural facts are themselves a type of meaningful utterance, divinely inspired. Thus, "the world is emblematic"; moreover, "the whole of nature is a metaphor of the human mind."[9] This thoroughly semiotic character of nature is complemented by its great beauty; for Emerson, the language of nature was a language of art.[10] In most persons, the contemplation of natural beauty will produce delight. For some, the love of beauty is so great that "not content with admiring, they seek to embody it in new forms."[11] These latter are the artists and poets, each one of whose creative works can be understood as "an abstract or epitome of the world"—that is, as "the result or expression of nature, in miniature."

Emerson's theological aesthetic reserved a place of special prominence for the creative artists among us. Yet for any person who seriously and properly contemplates the beauty of nature, there will be significant and self-transformative consequences. This hardly means that everyone who is touched by nature is thus dramatically affected. On the contrary, early in his essay Emerson bemoaned the fact that "few adult persons can see nature."[12] What is required in order to see is a certain kind of "discipline" (the title of *Nature*'s fifth chapter)—not one pursued in the abstract, as preparation for reading the book of nature, but rather one developed in the actual process of reading and rereading, in the living encounter with nature itself. Here Emerson anticipated Peirce's suggestion in the Neglected Argument that musement is both an act of reading the signs embedded in God's great poem and a practice designed to sharpen the reading skills that effective interpretation presupposes. And Peirce echoed his distinguished precursor when he commented on a widespread blindness among human beings, their inability to perceive the divine personality displayed in nature. Rather than attributing this inability to the remoteness or hiddenness of God, Peirce simply asserted "that facts that stand before our face and eyes and stare us in the face are far from being, in all cases, the ones most easily discerned" (*CP* 6.162; *W*8: 156–57). Nor was Emerson's God, despite the difficulty that many people might experience in perceiving the Deity, in any sense a "hidden" God. Indeed, in 1869, Emerson confessed his "simple belief" that the "Author of Nature has not left himself without a witness in any sane mind."[13]

Wrestling with this problem of discernment—not only with the articulation of such a problem but also with the formulation of effective strategies for addressing it—constitutes a fundamental task for theosemiotic. This task is to be subtly distinguished from those philosophical projects—either atheistic or apologetic—that share certain basic assumptions about the problem of "divine hiddenness."[14] For Emerson and Peirce, the God whose presence and purposes are difficult to discern is always necessarily "hidden in plain view." (Indeed, in order for any discernment even to be possible, for the meaning of any sign to be interpretable, Peirce insisted that the interpreter must already have some "collateral" or "previous acquaintance with what the sign denotes" [CP 8.179].)

In certain utterances attributed to Jesus, he warned his disciples that they must become, in some relevant sense, like "little children" in order to be able to enter the kingdom of heaven.[15] *Both* Emerson and Peirce echoed these remarks when they suggested that the key to discernment is the ability to see the world as a child sees it, to become childlike in one's contemplation of nature. It was "adult" persons, in Emerson's judgment, who have a special difficulty with perceiving the natural world in any way other than superficially. Yet, while the sun is visible only to the eye of an adult, it "shines into the eye and heart of the child." Emerson alluded here to the cultivation of an "inward sense" that, when properly adjusted to the outward senses, permits a person to retain "the spirit of infancy even into the era of manhood."[16] This process of adjustment is not a casual task, not something quickly or easily accomplished, but is achieved only by someone for whom the regular "intercourse" with nature has become "part of his daily food."[17] Only a life lived "in harmony with nature will purge the eyes to understand her text." This process of purgation, of self-transformation, occurs gradually, "by degrees," with the eventual result that "the world shall be to us an open book, and every form significant of its hidden life and final cause."[18]

Peirce was equally convinced that, while the child possesses a certain "wonderful genius," regrettably, "as he grows up, he loses this faculty" (CP 1.349). The character of this lost capacity was not described by Peirce in any great detail, only sketched with broad strokes. At the very least, however, it incorporated an instinctive awareness of the ideality of nature, an appreciation of "the great truth of the immanent power of thought in the universe." Elsewhere, Peirce suggested that the adult recovery of such an awareness was most likely to be accomplished, exactly as Emerson had recommended, by someone whose prayerful communion with the divine personality revealed in nature was "incessant" rather than "sporadic" (CP 6.437). It is reasonable to conclude here that what Peirce had in mind was an ongoing practice very much like the one that he later described as musement. Understanding the effects of regular engagement in musement—or of any interpretive exercise that is both playfully disinterested and consistent—should be considered essential for the purposes of theosemiotic inquiry. Both Emerson and Peirce recommended this kind of practice to their readers, understood its gradual influence to be in some sense the recovery of a certain childlike attitude toward the world, and doubted that a religiously meaningful relationship to nature could be established in the absence of such an attitude.[19]

Returning to the insight that religious experience has an important aesthetic dimension, this observation captures a certain tension between the claim that the beauty of God's poem is something that human beings are naturally capable of appreciating and the warning that this natural capacity may easily atrophy over time or, even if it survives, that it may be difficult to utilize due to certain distractions. At the same time, the ideal of a child-like attitude toward the world, present in both Emerson's and Peirce's reflections, should not be misunderstood. It may be worthwhile asking precisely what it is about "little children" that enables their access to the kingdom of heaven, while still insisting that the qualities considered essential for perceiving the divine beauty in nature are those that a properly trained adult will be most likely to possess. That is to say, presumably Jesus (or whoever originated the biblical warning), as well as Emerson and Peirce, were not suggesting that one must be or become a child in order to be properly disposed for religiously meaningful experience, but rather that one must become *like* a child, once again, supposedly not in every way but only in some relevant sense. A childlike freedom from bias, from well-entrenched, habitual modes of thought and perception, a certain playfulness, and a capacity for wonder even in the encounter with seemingly ordinary things—these are the qualities that make possible an appreciation of nature's beauty. In the play of musement, these qualities are cultivated by the adult practitioner, exposing beneath those habitual tendencies that typically shape human experience whatever natural instincts may lie dormant and restoring them to life.

Recall that Peirce predicted how the muser would be moved by the beauty of the idea of God to the point of desiring to shape all of life in conformity with it; thus, the religious experience of beauty can be regarded as foundational for human morality. This theosemiotic insight was already in evidence more than a century earlier, displayed in the work of Jonathan Edwards. Edwards's thought is relevant to the present inquiry in a number of important respects. His detailed analysis of those "signs" that should be considered as the most reliable indicators of authentic religious experience deserves careful scrutiny here.[20] It is also important to gesture toward Edwards's own life-long reading of the "book of nature," fragmentary meditations published posthumously as *Images or Shadows of Divine Things*.[21] More immediately, consider his argument about how "true virtue" is grounded in the saint's innate sense of beauty.[22] That argument by no means limited the relationship between beauty and morality to the experience of Christian saints who have been dramatically transformed by God's grace. Indeed, there was for Edwards a "secondary and inferior kind of beauty," the taste for which is responsible for the naturally virtuous behavior of many persons. It "consists in a mutual consent and agreement of different things, in form, manner, quantity, and visible end or design."[23] This sort of harmony was deemed sufficient to account for a natural sense of justice, adequate for the purpose of reconciling persons one to another in conduct that would typically be judged as morally praiseworthy. Nevertheless, it is a "particular" as opposed to "general" beauty, characteristic of an object "when considered only with regard to its connection with, and tendency to, some particular things within a limited, and as it were a private sphere."[24] True virtue for Edwards cannot be inspired by such a limited beauty but rather must be grounded in a love for or *"benevolence to being in general."*[25]

Now, while it is important to register the difference between Edwards's explicitly theological agenda and Peirce's more properly philosophical concerns, the latter's talk about the *summum bonum* as the goal of inquiry in aesthetics almost perfectly mirrors Edwards's discussion of a general as opposed to a particular beauty. On Peirce's reasoning, the ideal or highest good, as that which is admirable in itself, will necessarily be general (*CP* 1.613). Moreover, its beauty will not be a function of its relationship to this or that particular thing, nor can it be considered beautiful because it serves this or that particular purpose. Rather, the *summum bonum* would have to be regarded as such under all conceivable circumstances. And one's ethical choice of the ends appropriate to guide a specific action would have to be made with such an ideal in mind. Consequently, aesthetic considerations were fundamental to Peirce's theory of morality in a manner similar to Edwards's grounding of true virtue in a sense of the highest form of beauty.

Here the relationship between aesthetics and morality is neither simple nor singular. In one respect, the latter presupposes the former, true virtue requiring a taste for the genuinely beautiful in Edwards's view, ethics being based on aesthetics in Peirce's scheme of the normative sciences. Yet there is an observable seamlessness in the argument that each thinker supplied, not an insistence on the rigid demarcation of these categories, but rather, a very real sense conveyed in which one becomes manifested in the other. Edwards considered the Christian saint, for example, as being extraordinary not just in her capacity to delight in and affirm that which is beautiful, but also in her actual embodiment of beauty. Virtuous principles and conduct are to be considered as a type of "spiritual beauty" precisely because "they imply consent and union with being in general. This is the primary and most essential beauty of every thing that can justly be called by the name of virtue, or is any moral excellency in the eye of one who has a perfect view of things."[26] In the exercise of love for being in general, the saint personally radiates a divine beauty.

From Edwards's theosemiotic perspective, the saint appeared to occupy a role much like that played by poets and artists in Emerson's ruminations. Moved by an awareness of the beauty of nature, the latter "seek to embody it in new forms." Similarly, having fallen in love with the highest beauty, having given their consent to being in general, saints will manifest such a beauty in virtuous dispositions and behavior. The difference between these perspectives would seem to consist in the fact that saints themselves were to be conceived as works of art in Edwards's view, while the Deity was the primary artist (since attributing too much agency to fallen human beings would smack of "works righteousness"). There is a contrast here, to be sure, between Edwards's Calvinism and Emerson's decidedly more liberal theology. Yet it is important not to draw that contrast too sharply; rather, one ought to recognize those salient resemblances that warrant the inclusion of both thinkers on any list of individuals who can be considered as significant precursors of Peirce's theosemiotic.

Crucial among these resemblances, of course, is the emphasis on beauty as a key to understanding religious experience. Such experience is both an *encounter with* beauty (the divine beauty visible in nature) and an impetus for the *creation of* beauty (embodied in works of art or in virtuous character and conduct). Peirce carefully developed such themes in his own thinking, so that his theosemiotic was also always already a theological aesthetic. The ongoing realization of certain ideas "in man's consciousness and works" was a process, on his account, "whereby man, with all his miserable littlenesses, becomes gradually more and more imbued with the Spirit of God." In the exercise of self-control over this process, "by action, through thought, he grows an esthetic ideal . . . as the share which God permits him to have in the work of creation" (*CP* 5.402, notes 2 and 3).

All of the tensions that emerge in a comparison of Edwards with Emerson are embodied and affirmed in these brief remarks. While hardly a Calvinist, Peirce nevertheless recorded humanity's "miserable littlenesses." The process that he reflected on here was described in passive rather than in active terms, as one in which a person "becomes gradually more and more imbued" with the divine spirit. The primary locus of the divine beauty manifested in this process was internal, a disposition embedded in human consciousness. All of this resonates with Edwards's thinking. At the same time, Peirce confirmed that the divine spirit could also be displayed in human "works." And an Emersonian emphasis on self-reliance was maintained in Peirce's talk about self-control. If one is careful to note that each of these three thinkers was an objective idealist, for whom all of reality was Mind, some of these tensions are considerably reduced.[27] As Peirce would have been inclined to express it, to talk about a person thinking or having an idea is a somewhat misleading way of indicating that the Idea has used that person as a "vehicle" to get itself thought. Since all three of them conceived of the divine as working frequently in and through the human, it is sometimes difficult to mark the nature and limits of human agency as delineated in their religious philosophies. In a revealing comment, Peirce once asserted "that the service of Christ is perfect freedom" (CP 5.340, note 1; W2: 261, note 6). Here his conflating of the notion of "freedom" with "service" indicates, at the very least, that the meaning of the former cannot be reduced to talk about individual autonomy, pure and simple.[28]

This is a general issue to which it will be important to return in a later discussion of religious practice, the primacy of which must be affirmed from any genuinely theosemiotic perspective. Edwards insisted on that primacy when he evaluated consistent Christian practice as chief among all the signs of God's grace being truly present and operative within the soul of a believer. Yet he granted no causal efficacy to such practice, no power actually to transform a person's heart and mind in ways that might facilitate genuine religious experience. For Peirce, too, practice was an important sign, but signs could also be causes on his account—if not efficient, then most certainly final causes; moreover, practice was an important element in deliberate habit formation: as he saw it, the key to self-control. A good pragmatist like Peirce, however, being allergic to many of the rigid dualisms that have troubled Western thinkers historically, would have likely been inclined to eschew any kind of sharp theological distinction between nature and grace. And despite Edwards's theological predispositions, which inclined him at all times to emphasize the effective presence of God's grace, he was a religious naturalist of sorts (since God's revelation is embodied in nature as well as in Scripture)—indeed, given the semiotic significance for him of "Christian practice," also a certain kind of pragmatist.

The recognition of beauty as a transcendental attribute of being in general, of creation as consisting of things each "related by an essential order" to every other being as well as to being in general; the grounding of moral goodness in the beauty of harmonious relations; the conception of God as an artist, the divine source of the world's beauty; and the understanding of human agents as "artists of human living" who participate in the divine creativity through their cultivation of virtuous conduct—all of these ideas, central to the development of theosemiotic, were embodied in the medieval philosophy of John Duns Scotus.[29] Yet it is not Duns Scotus's concept of beauty, but rather his treatment of signs and the sign-relation that presently requires attention here. That treatment, shown to be in clear continuity with Peirce's later deliberations, represents a key event in this brief history of theosemiotic.

II

The beauty experienced by the reader of the book of nature is a consequence of both what and how that book *signifies*. In fact, the experience of anything beautiful, as with all experience evaluated from the position being developed here, is a matter of interpretation, a mode of awareness that can be analyzed as a semiotic phenomenon. Now, while Peirce is often considered to be a foundational figure in the development of modern semiotic theory, there is considerable evidence to suggest that he may have been indebted to medieval predecessors for some of his ideas. The influence, most especially, of Duns Scotus on Peirce is documented by his own clear admission of it; and the relationship between these two thinkers is one that has been carefully and frequently, although by no means exhaustively, probed.[30] The story of that relationship is a complicated one, also multifaceted; but the relevant foci of concern, for present purposes, are those respects in which Peirce may have drawn upon medieval resources in the development of his theory of signification.

Before beginning to tell that story, it is important to locate on our intellectual map a much less obvious, somewhat indirect pathway between medieval scholastic and modern American approaches to theosemiotic. When Peirce worried out loud about catching the transcendentalist disease, it was an infection that he believed had spread to Emerson and others primarily from F. W. J. Schelling (albeit, in Emerson's case, with Coleridge as intermediary). Yet Peirce had his own independent perspective on Schelling's objective idealism—in fact, one favorable enough that it inspired the self-appraisal from Peirce that he himself was "a Schellingian, of some stripe" (*CP* 6.605). For Schelling, nature is "Mind made visible." His affirmation that the "world is simply the original, as yet unconscious, poetry of the spirit" or, again, that "nature is a poem lying pent in a mysterious and wonderful script," embodied an insight that was also central to the theosemiotic deliberations of both Emerson and Peirce.[31]

Moreover, Schelling's distinction between *natura naturans* and *natura naturata*, while most immediately borrowed from Spinoza, nevertheless originated in the deliberations of the medieval scholastics. That distinction was not only crucial for the development of Schelling's own religious metaphysics, but may have helped to shape Peirce's later contrast between the "germinal nothing" or "boundless freedom" (*CP* 6.217) from which everything that exists in nature is determined and that which is in fact determined, the whole of nature as God's signature, God's poem. Here the relation between *natura naturata* and *natura naturans* is a thoroughly semiotic one, the relation of sign to signified.[32]

In addition to providing a link between the medieval scholastics and Schelling, Spinoza's philosophy itself displays theosemiotic tendencies toward which this history can gesture but not thoroughly explore. Spinoza's subtly complex view of "Nature" is only one possible topic of relevance. Peirce's remarks about Spinoza are scattered throughout his corpus of writings and tend to be generally quite positive, apart from his critique of the latter's adaptation of Euclid's geometrical method for the purposes of doing philosophy. Not only did he judge Spinoza to be an authentic realist and enemy of nominalism, but Peirce also seems to have regarded him as an exemplary pragmatist. "Spinoza's ideas are eminently ideas to affect human conduct," he reported. "If, in accordance with the recommendation of Jesus, we are to judge of ethical doctrines and of philosophy in general by its practical fruits we cannot but consider Spinoza as a very weighty authority." Indeed, Peirce considered the "practical upshot" of Spinoza's thought to be "more Christian than that of any current system of theology" (*N*2: 86–87).[33]

As already indicated, the brief history of theosemiotic that these remarks are intended to supply is historical only in a vague sense, less preoccupied with establishing causal lines of influence than in noting the intellectual resonance among ideas articulated by thinkers often far removed from one another in time. Talk about one philosopher "drawing upon" or "borrowing" ideas from another could prove in any given case to be more the occasion or excuse for exploring this resonance than its logical presupposition. Nevertheless, it is interesting to note how, even in instances where there appears to be no *direct* historical indebtedness—for example, there is no evidence that Peirce ever read John Poinsot's important seventeenth-century *Treatise on Signs*—there are *common* historical sources that help to account for the similarity between thinkers and ideas. Both Poinsot and Peirce leaned heavily on Scotus, as well as on the writings of those Jesuit philosophers at Coimbra who developed some of

Scotus's ideas in the period shortly before Poinsot's arrival there.[34] In any event, both Duns Scotus and Poinsot need to be regarded as important figures in the early history of theosemiotic.

Scotus formulated the rule that "a sign of a sign is a sign of what is signified."[35] In doing so, he foreshadowed Peirce's later announcement that a sign is determined by its object but itself determines an "interpretant"; this interpretant can also be conceived as a sign referring to the same object (e.g., see *CP* 4.536, 6.347). For Peirce, a sign mediates between object and interpretant, bringing them into relation, an explicitly semiotic relation in which the latter comes to signify the former. Each interpretant is thus a sign with some previous sign as its immediate object while also referring in a mediated fashion to what that previous sign signifies. Signs determine interpretant-signs in a causal chain or series, then, and these causes, on the analysis that Duns Scotus provided, are to be understood as "essentially ordered."[36] Although the implications of this analysis will eventually need to be spelled out in greater detail, some preliminary observations might be useful here.

An accidentally ordered series of causes is one in which the causal activity of one item in the series is unrelated to the causal activity of others. And so A may be the mother of B, who is the father of C. But B's becoming the father of C is accidental to the causal action by means of which A, as his mother, engendered him. Only B's existence, but not his procreative agency (which he might have chosen never to exercise), depends on his mother's act of procreation; in fact, he may have fathered C long after his mother had died. In contrast, if my hand (A) swings a hammer (B) that strikes a nail (C), the causal influences exerted by A over B and by B over C are essentially ordered. The latter does not occur without the former's prior occurrence; moreover, the latter depends on the causal activity of the former for its own causal efficacy. If my hand does not swing the hammer, then the nail is not driven into the wood. Swinging, striking, and driving are all events that occur in an essentially ordered series of causes.

Consequently, as Duns Scotus himself explained it, "where an essential ordering or concatenation exists, all the causal factors must coexist both to produce and to conserve their effect."[37] This relationship among causes, it should be observed, is one that can exist *both* among efficient causes occurring in a chain or series *and* between a final and an efficient cause operating together to produce a specific effect. In the latter case, the efficient cause depends upon the final cause for its efficacy. Peirce devoted considerable attention to this type of dependency, concluding that "an efficient cause, detached from a final cause in the form of a law, would not even possess efficiency; . . . without law there is no regularity;

and without the influence of ideas there is no potentiality" (*CP* 1.213). Especially noteworthy here is Peirce's claim that this is the proper way to understand "the action of a sign," not as causation by "brute force," but rather "intelligent" and "triadic," as when "an event, A, produces a second event, B, *as a means* to the production of a third event, C" (*CP* 5.472–73; Peirce's emphasis).[38]

In the first place, then, Peirce's triadic concept of signs and the sign-function (object-sign-interpretant) is prefigured in the exceedingly subtle account that Duns Scotus developed centuries earlier. Second, and by implication from this first observation, what each thinker articulated in his philosophy was less properly a theory of signs than of *semiosis*, with signs never appearing in isolation but always as part of an often-complex system of relations, a living stream of meaningful events. Third, these relations were metaphysically *real* for both Peirce and Scotus.[39] Semiosis constitutes a real relation among things, so that Scotus, for example, understood the connection between spoken words and things to be metaphysically grounded. Words actually and directly signify the essences of things rather than merely our thoughts about them, albeit always doing so through the mediation of some sign. (For Scotus, this necessarily involved the mediation of some intelligible species as sign;[40] likewise, for Peirce, experience-as-semiosis, even if it appears to be direct and the inferences that shape it are unconscious, was never unmediated.) Finally, the relationship between signs in a series should be understood as one that is essentially ordered. In theosemiotic terms, it might be possible to argue that everything in creation is related to every other thing, by each also being linked to the divine source of all that exists in an essential order. This explains why anything that exists, at least potentially, is the sign of its ultimate source, a religiously meaningful sign. Such an essential order also accounts for the beauty of creation, so that one who is properly disposed not only is able to perceive but also to embody that beauty, to become a living symbol of it.

The Portuguese philosophers at Coimbra, in their early seventeenth-century treatise on signs (*De Signo*), borrowed extensively from Duns Scotus even as they labored to refine his ideas.[41] At the same time, their assertion that "there is nothing which leads to the cognition of anything else which cannot be reduced to some sort of sign" directly influenced Poinsot's thinking, and much later probably also helped to shape Peirce's nuanced understanding of human thought and experience as consisting in a "living metaboly" of symbols.[42] Centuries earlier, Augustine had already laid the groundwork for a truly general theory of signs, with language for him constituting only one particular domain within a much larger universe of signifiers. In his treatise *On Christian Doctrine*, Augustine explained that "a sign is a thing which, over and above the impression it makes on the senses, causes something else to come into the mind as a consequence of itself."[43] Rejecting the Augustinian suggestion that all signs must be sense-perceptible, these Iberian thinkers argued instead that *anything* that brings something else into awareness functions as a sign. Consequently, concepts can be regarded as "formal signs"; this is the case because, despite not being mind-independent objects of perception, they mediate the awareness of things other than themselves (so that when I think about my wife, I become aware of *her* and not just of my thoughts about her). This mediation is a relation that has "objective being" (*esse objectivum*), in the Scotistic sense of the kind of being that can be ascribed to a thing precisely insofar as it is known or exists as the object of awareness.[44]

With Poinsot, the refinement of this perspective achieved a special status. More so than his predecessors and much in anticipation of Peirce, Poinsot conceived of the objective being of the sign as constituting a dynamic process or relation—that is to say, as *semiosis*. Possessing a being that is (once again in the Scotistic sense) "indifferent" to the contrast between mind-dependent (*ens rationis*) and mind-independent (*ens reale*) realities, such a relation was to be understood in a metaphysical rather than in a purely epistemological fashion. (For an objective idealist, this contrast is already softened by the realization that the connection between mind and world is always one between mind and Mind, better modeled as an ongoing conversation than as a simple act of sense perception.) Here one encounters a version of the "extreme realism" that scholars have long observed to be a crucial part of Peirce's Scotistic legacy—articulated in specifically semiotic terms by Poinsot and rendered even more extreme in Peirce's later development of it. Such a theoretical stance on the reality of relations, I would propose as a hypothesis worth consideration, is one of the defining features of any theology conceived as theosemiotic.

Without moving very far in historical time or geographical space, one would appear to have moved a great distance indeed, conceptually speaking, in the consideration of another Iberian thinker's ideas, in this case, those of Ignatius of Loyola. Ignatius's highly pragmatic manual of meditations, designed to facilitate or renew the making of crucial decisions in the Christian devotee's spiritual life, displays none of the philosophical subtlety or detail that characterized either Scotus's deliberations or those of Poinsot and the Conimbricenses.[45] Yet the similarities become tangible enough once elucidated, as a variety of theosemiotic themes coalesce in Ignatius's succinct but nevertheless deeply insightful instructions.

Consider first that a good deal of Ignatius's attention was directed inward to the human psyche; while not philosophically preoccupied with understanding the nature of mental concepts as "formal signs," he was supremely interested in the role played by feelings of "consolation" and "desolation" as religiously meaningful signifiers.[46] In a manner that resonates with Poinsot's semiotic theory, this meaning is neither buried in the sign nor projected onto it, but emerges through the sign for an interpreter whose attention is properly disciplined and directed.[47] The essential triadicity of semiosis is tangibly represented by the invaluable, indeed necessary presence of a director for the spiritual exercises, whose role one might conceive as that of providing a vital source of "interpretants" for the person struggling in meditation to discern the will of God in his or her life.

The fact that these spiritual exercises are conducted over a period of time (traditionally for thirty days and often at several different but crucial junctures in one's life journey) reinforces the conclusion that interpretation is a process and suggests that the meaning of any given sign can change with time and varying context. Meaning is manifested as an ordered series of events, much as the significance of a particular utterance will be shaped by where and when it occurs in the flow of a conversation. The correct interpretation of what is happening in one's spiritual life is felicitous not only because it renders the meaning of certain signs accurately, but also because it produces additional signs pragmatically useful for knowing and doing the will of God in the future. These signs will be embodied in appropriate habits of thought, feeling, and conduct, the cultivation of which is one of the primary aims of Ignatius's exercises.

Wrestling with the problem of discernment has already been portrayed as central to the task of theosemiotic in the earlier discussion of Peirce and Emerson; but it was first Ignatius and then later Jonathan Edwards who developed the most ambitious strategies for addressing this problem, supplying careful semiotic rules for the "discernment of spirits." While ordered in a certain way, interpretation is not always "orderly." Voices sometimes compete for hegemony over the process of interpretation. The task of discernment is necessitated for Ignatius by the realization that there exist both "good" and "evil" spirits, with radically conflicting agendas. Any insightful Ignatian spiritual director will facilitate discernment not always by validating but sometimes by challenging an exercitant's reported judgments. Consequently, any future theosemiotic ought also to supply an appropriate framework and resources for occasional contestation and critique.

The discerning self may focus on what and how it feels, but always only in order to determine its relationship to spiritual forces and factors that altogether transcend the self as something private and isolated—that is to say, consolation and desolation are always to be regarded not merely as feelings but *as signs*. A certain attitude of detachment or *indiferencia* needs to be cultivated by anyone properly engaged in Ignatius's exercises, much as Peirce's reader was urged to strive for a kind of purposelessness in the practice of musement. In an interesting way, this ideal attitude can be shown to mirror the "indifference" of a concept of being that permits its application both to realities regarded as internal and those external to consciousness. This is the "objective being" of the sign, which, following Scotus, Poinsot, and Peirce, consists in its forming a relation not altogether reducible to the terms that it links together. Nominalism is banished on such an account, giving way to an extreme scholastic realism that is formulated in explicitly semiotic terms.

Finally, Ignatius was especially observant of patterns of behavior, both in the form of spiritual practices that might help to facilitate insight and those manifested as habits of conduct that could themselves serve as religiously meaningful signs. In this respect he was most assuredly a pragmaticist. On the Peircean account to which I am indebted here, habits have this double semiotic function. In the first place, habits of interpretation enable us to perceive something as a sign, to recognize some X as being a sign of Y. One of the ways in which such habits can best be formed and developed is through deliberate practice, through regular exercise. Once formed, these habits are themselves meaningful signs, embodied in persons who constitute their sign vehicles. The character of a person will be displayed in dispositional patterns of feeling and conduct, not in flashes of feeling or in random thoughts and actions. This is why it takes time to "read" a person's character, even as it does to read a poem or a novel.

Here, by contrast with the earlier turn to Ignatius, the leap back to Jonathan Edwards marks an abrupt movement across an ocean and several centuries forward in time, yet is relatively insignificant with regard to the conceptual distance traversed. Edwards was the same kind of pragmatist as Ignatius of Loyola, a theosemiotician for whom consistency in Christian practice was "chief among all the signs of grace."[48] It is useful to pause here in order to establish a link between Edwards's pragmatism and his theological aesthetic. Recall his insistence that the true saint, whose love for God takes the form of a disinterested benevolence, is by virtue of God's grace able both to perceive and to embody authentic beauty. This beauty radiates over and through creation in much the same way that an earthly landscape is illuminated by the sun. It is incarnated in multiple forms. Consider, then, the various ways in which the divine semiosis is manifested on Edwards's account. It is revealed first of all in the book of nature: for those who have eyes to see, God's great artwork. Human beings, despite their fallen status, are the peak of creation, so that God's grace is even more perfectly exemplified in the virtuous dispositions that form the heart and mind of a pious believer. These same dispositions are the foundation of Christian practice as they shape the saint's behavior in determinate ways.

It is important to notice both the variety and ordering of signs to which Edwards directs our attention. As for Emerson, nature is a sign. Words are signs; for theological purposes the words that constitute biblical texts have a special status, while those that one might utter in order to describe one's own sanctity have little value. (Edwards knew that talk was cheap and that the human capacity for self-deception was extraordinary.) Thoughts and feelings are also signifiers, although less religiously revelatory for Edwards to the extent that they are abrupt or ephemeral—so that suddenly having a verse from scripture leap into consciousness, for example, is hardly a reliable indication of God's grace at work. Finally, Edwards insisted that "there is a language in actions; and in some cases, much more clear and convincing than in words."[49] (This is not to deny, of course, that words themselves can sometimes constitute powerful verbal actions.) Behavior was "clear and convincing" only if it displayed a certain pattern. There should be consistency in behavior if it is to be regarded as religiously meaningful; moreover, it should be beautiful, radiating the disinterested love that motivates it. Barking like a dog or speaking in tongues, conduct frequently enough displayed during the eighteenth-century New England revivals, was dismissed by Edwards as failing to meet these criteria.

Behavior or Christian practice is "chief" among all the signs of God's grace because of where it stands in the order of signs, as the last and typically the most visible. Yet virtuous action is determined by a virtuous disposition, the "true virtue," that each saint possesses. The latter is a more immediate sign of God's grace at work, with the former serving as its interpretant, thus also signifying the divine presence in a way that is mediated and yet more readily accessible from a third-person perspective. Importantly here for Edwards, such a viewpoint was not only the one naturally occupied by members of the Christian community with respect to each other, but also one necessarily to be adopted by each Christian as the only effective means for achieving accurate self-interpretations and for avoiding self-deception. In insisting on its necessity, Edwards developed yet another pragmatic theme relevant to the purposes of theosemiotic. One's relationship to oneself may be somewhat different, but not fundamentally different *in kind*, from one's relations to other persons in a community. In strictly philosophical terms, as Peirce was inclined to express it, we have no "intuitive self-consciousness" or "power of introspection," but rather all knowledge about ourselves is the "result of inference," of carefully interpreting signs.[50] Just as others must make inferences about our true character based on observations of our behavior, we must make similar judgments about ourselves, distinguish reliable from unreliable signs displayed in our conduct, and struggle to discern meaningful patterns.

The saintly person is best equipped to interpret both the book of scripture and the book of nature. That person embodies a divine beauty in the form of true virtue and expresses it in holy deeds. A real disposition in the soul of the saint is a sign of God's grace being operative there. Her conduct is ordered to character and cosmos, signifying the divine presence in each. On the view being articulated here, semiosis takes the form of an ordered series of signifiers, each one determined by another. In and through each of them, the divine beauty radiates outward from its source like rain water from a storm cloud or beams of light from the sun.

Very many different types of things—nature, physical objects, words, concepts, feelings, dispositions, persons, actions—can all serve as religiously meaningful signifiers. Language represents only one form of semiosis, and to insist on its being the paradigmatic instance is potentially to obscure important details about how other signs function. Peirce's semiotic theory (following Augustine and the scholastics) was never restrictive in this fashion, and his elaborate classification of signs was enormously nuanced in its details. Different features of that classificatory account might (and will) be explored for various purposes, but the distinguishing of one kind of interpretant-sign from another deserves brief examination in this context.

As already indicated, an interpretant will have some sign as its immediate cause, with that sign's object serving as its remote or mediate cause. Being itself a sign, the interpretant will invite and so be subject to further interpretation. In Peirce's view, "the first proper significate effect of a sign is a feeling produced by it," what he called its "emotional interpretant" (*CP* 5.475). In addition, "through the mediation of the emotional interpretant," the sign may have the effect of producing some mental or physical effort, a determinate action that Peirce identified as its "energetic interpretant." But this can never be the full meaning of a sign, "since it is a single act," so that the "logical interpretant" must consist in a general disposition to act—that is to say, in some type of "habit" (*CP* 5.476–93).

In an essentially ordered series, signs produce a stream of interpretants that have their logical upshot in a discernible pattern (or habit) of action. This pattern embodies some ideal or purpose that stands to each sign in the series as its final cause. While looking through an explicitly theological lens, Edwards arrived at much the same conclusion as Peirce, culminating his analysis of religiously meaningful signs with a discussion of "practice" as the last of twelve (a discussion that by itself was more than twice as lengthy as his consideration of any of the previous eleven signs). The saint's virtuous disposition is the source of powerful emotions, producing a delight in the beautiful, as well as a love for being in general. Mediated by these feelings, true virtue enables and inspires holy deeds; and these deeds are not isolated or sporadic, but disciplined and habitual, thus, purposeful. This brief history of theosemiotic must turn finally, then, to a survey of those thinkers who have emphasized its pragmatic dimension, the teleological impulse for interpretations to become exemplified in praxis, and also for praxis to become embedded in community.[51]

III

The refusal to drive a deep wedge between theory and practice is of course one of the distinguishing features of pragmatism as a philosophical movement. Despite their appreciable differences on this issue, a sharp theory/practice dichotomy is one that Peirce, James, and Dewey were all eager to reject. Significantly, Duns Scotus was somewhat distinctive among the medieval schoolmen in conceiving of theology as a thoroughly "practical" science.[52] "The intellect perfected by the habit of theology apprehends God as one who should be loved," Scotus argued, "and according to rules from which praxis can be elicited. Therefore, the habit of theology is practical."[53] This should not be read as a complete denial of theology's theoretical character or as undermining its commitment to the discovery of truth; far from being anti-theoretical, Duns Scotus, like the American pragmatists centuries later, conceived of the relationship between theory and practice as being essentially continuous. Theology's final purpose is not the discovery of some truth abstractly conceived, but rather the apprehension of a living ideal worthy of devotion and capable of shaping behavior in distinctive patterns. Such a practical ideal was not the negation, for Scotus, but rather the "extension of theoretical truth and knowledge."[54]

Consider Duns Scotus's pragmatic characterization of the Deity as "*cognoscibile operabile*," the "doable knowable," that is, as a God who can best be understood by one who is engaged in deliberate actions, properly directed. Such action both facilitates and validates our understanding of God. Moreover, the ultimate purpose of theology conceived as a practical science, once again, is the ongoing development of appropriate habits of conduct. Theology was thus understood as a *"practica cognitio"* by Scotus—that is, as a theorizing that prepares the way for the love of God. Love was primarily a matter of volition rather than of intellection for the Subtle Doctor, so that theology as praxis must engage the human will as well as the intellect. In summary: theology is a kind of thinking that comes to completion in love, and this love is displayed in deliberate action, shaping and shaped by habits.

Six hundred years later, the pragmatists' treatment of religion in writings published at the very beginning of the twentieth century resonates deeply with this Scotistic position. William James, for example, organized his new "science of religions" around the description and analysis of the varieties of religious experience, the authenticity of which is best evaluated in terms of the demonstrable "fruits for life" that such experiences yield in the lives of those who report them.[55] Peirce was even more emphatic than James in his insistence that such fruits must be habitual rather than episodic if they are to have any evidential value. Recall that he portrayed musement as a type of meditative activity that predisposes one who is engaged in it eventually to consider the idea of God's reality; the more such a person contemplates this idea the more powerful will her/his love for God become, to the point of earnestly desiring to adapt all conduct in conformity with the idea. Much like Duns Scotus, then, Peirce conceived of God as "one who should be loved," while also understanding the love of God as a gentle but powerful force capable of generating "rules from which praxis can be elicited."

William James's nominalistic tendencies may have led him, at least at times, to think about "practical results" or the "fruits" of experience in a narrower way than his friend Charles Peirce would have been inclined to do. Nevertheless, his breadth of vision was sufficiently generous to embrace a great variety of human actions that might be regarded as pragmatically meaningful. Already on Jonathan Edwards's account, Christian "practice" could never be completely reduced to publicly observable forms of conduct, but should include certain "immanent acts" of the soul—for example, acts of volition or of contemplation.[56] Now on one reading of James's pragmatism, for him the most significant thing that we can "do" is to direct our attention to this rather than to that, to care about this rather than that, at least for present purposes. These volitional acts of attention dramatically shape the quality of our experiences as well as determining the character of our future conduct.

Since the "practice of paying attention" is one very simple but useful way of understanding what the word "meditation" means, James's pragmatism serves here to elide yet another traditional conceptual dichotomy, this time the theological one between "contemplation" and "action."[57] Such a dichotomy may be regarded, of course, as a more narrowly conceived version of the theory/praxis contrast already discussed. But it is important to recognize clearly that the pragmatic point being made here is not simply one about *continuity*—that is, not merely an insistence that action is appropriately shaped by contemplation, with healthy practice being informed by carefully articulated theories. An even more basic insight reveals that contemplation is always already a kind of activity, with theorizing itself a very important type of deliberate exercise.

Note the *deliberate* quality of practice as a mode of human behavior. Not just any kind of human action will be classified as a form of practice. Actions can be random, unreflective, either playing no role in habit formation or resulting in the development of accidental, unconscious (and so in some cases undesirable) habits. From a Peircean point of view, conduct becomes practice only when it is self-controlled. One of the necessary purposes of such deliberate behavior, no matter what else one intends to accomplish in the short or the long run, is some kind of meaningful self-transformation, the exercise and enhancement of some capacity. Whether one is engaged in exercising one's body, or in disciplined thinking, or in directing the attention purposefully through certain acts of will, the self is discernibly shaped by such activities in a way that justifies regarding them as practices.

For reasons that it will be important to explore further, however, it seems wise to resist the conclusion that *only* deliberate actions can be semiotically significant ones. There is nothing deliberate or self-controlled, for example, about the typical behavior of those individuals whom William James described (with some autobiographical poignancy) as "sick souls."[58] Far from being able to care about this or that, to attend with interest to this or that, in the case of such individuals the will has become almost completely paralyzed. The sick soul experiences neither beauty's delight nor love's purposes. Indeed, his paradigmatic experience will be of darkness, of a terrible emptiness, but to suggest that this dark emptiness is meaningless, that it fails altogether to function as a sign, would represent an important philosophical and theological mistake.

James most definitely thought otherwise, which is why he devoted considerable effort to developing the rich phenomenological account of the sick soul's experience that he presented in these pivotal lectures. Similarly, desolation was for Ignatius of Loyola no less of a religiously meaningful sign than were feelings of consolation, despite the fact that in the former condition the soul was entirely "slothful," with decisive action having become difficult and genuine purpose obscured. One relevant question for theosemioticians that emerges out of this historical survey is about whether it is more appropriate in such a case to talk about a "negative sign" *or* to speak instead about the "limits of semiosis." In a very real sense, the condition of the sick soul is that of a person who has become incapable of making certain religiously meaningful interpretations. Nevertheless—at least upon reflection or perhaps from someone else's point of view—this very incapacity, the feelings of emptiness and frustration that it engenders, might be regarded as significant.

Here again is an indication of the pragmatic importance of a third-person perspective (as well as of second-person perspectives emerging in various encounters and conversations), whether it happens to be mediated through an actual other—a spiritual director, for example, or a psychotherapist—or self-mediated. These cases can be surprisingly difficult to distinguish with absolute clarity. On theosemiotic premises, all thinking is a stream of semiosis that can take the form of a conversation. Since humans are essentially social beings, in most cases thoroughly enculturated at a very early stage in their psychological development, the voices of multiple others will be represented routinely in that conversation, even when those others are not somehow actually present. ("Somehow" seems appropriate here because in our high-technology, information age, "virtual" rather than actual physical presence is often a sufficient precondition for conversation to occur.) Moreover, since the vital energy of semiosis is displayed in the fact that any sign will tend naturally and continuously to produce additional interpretant-signs, the boundaries of "selfhood" must always remain somewhat permeable on theosemiotic analysis. But what, more precisely, does it mean to talk about a self without clear boundaries?[59]

Precision may not be the most reasonable goal to pursue in this instance, since the meaning attached to persons-as-symbols will necessarily be quite vague (although making that meaning just a bit more determinate is a challenge that must be embraced in the next chapter). Consider, first, the rather remarkable claim that persons *are indeed* symbols. Jonathan Edwards laid the groundwork for such a proposal by asserting that the virtuous disposition of a Christian saint signifies the active presence of God's grace. Such virtue becomes especially evident or visible as it displays itself in practice. Emerson was even more explicit in reporting that "we are symbols, and inhabit symbols."[60] And Peirce was no less emphatic when, very early in his philosophical career, he concluded that all persons are essentially signs (*CP* 5.310–17; *W*2: 238–42), an opinion that he continued to affirm decades later when he repeated that a "person is nothing but a symbol involving a general idea" (*CP* 6.270; *W*8: 182). On such a view, some general ideas become embodied concretely in habits, each of which lends unity, a definitive shape, to the continuous stream of semiosis that constitutes any person's thinking, feeling consciousness. At the same time, persons do not think or feel in isolation. They regularly converse with one another. They interact with one another in multiple ways. Through conversation and interaction they sometimes form communities.

His younger contemporary, Josiah Royce, was deeply influenced by Peirce's delineation of selves-as-signs, especially as it had been articulated in those early publications. Royce was also comfortably familiar with the German objective idealists, including Schelling, whose speculative inquiries have already been identified as an important strand woven into the fabric of modern theosemiotic. Peirce's scientific community of inquiry came to be conceived in Royce's later work more explicitly as a "community of interpretation," and this conception greatly informed his philosophical thinking about religious community.[61]

Nothing in the argument that Royce developed departed significantly from the perspective that Peirce had already labored to establish. Peirce had carefully blurred the boundaries that might be drawn on other accounts between individual selves and the communities in which they flourish. His reflections on the experience of "espirit de corps" had yielded the hypothesis that, in order to explain such a phenomenon, it made good sense to talk about "corporate personality," to describe communities as greater persons (*CP* 6.271; *W*8: 182–83). Royce's detailed investigation of what it means to understand interpretation as an essentially ordered "time-process" is the logical extension of what Peirce (indeed, following the scholastics) had already observed about semiosis as an event. The causal power of any action (or, in semiotic terms, its *significance*) will consist in its having been guided by some basic purpose, conducted at least in partial conformity to what Royce called a "life-plan."[62] It was also always true for Peirce, as Royce himself came to believe, that the community is a richer, a more complex and complete symbol than any of its members, in much the same way that the meaning of a person's life is deeper than the meaning of any particular thought that he or she happens to have. If what a person does deliberately in living a life conformed to a certain ideal—the habit or pattern displayed in that doing—is the logical interpretant of that ideal-as-symbol, then what we do *together* in community brings the process of interpretation to a whole new level of meaning and semiotic fullness.

Despite his indebtedness to Peirce, the originality and importance of

Royce's ideas should not be underestimated. In a remarkable way, semiotic became explicitly *theosemiotic* in Royce's mature writing (so that, in a very real sense, he launched the inquiry that is now being pursued in these pages).[63] Philosophical discoveries concerning the nature of signs and signification were applied directly to the basic problems of philosophical theology. Royce's recasting of traditional Christian perspectives (on faith, sin, atonement, the church, the Holy Spirit as third person of the Trinity, and so on) within an elaborate semiotic framework yielded fresh insights, some of which have never been adequately explored or evaluated. If Peirce's "A Neglected Argument for the Reality of God" was, as he himself admitted, little more than the "poor sketch" of an argument, a mere "table of contents" (albeit brilliantly conceived) for what might be regarded as a full-blown treatment of theosemiotic, Royce's *The Problem of Christianity*, appearing five years later (and gesturing in a footnote toward Peirce's important 1908 essay),[64] supplied much of the missing text. Peirce himself produced additional text, in disparate materials scattered throughout his published and unpublished writings. Identifying, developing, and then weaving together these various strands, along with the insights generated by the earlier figures in this history, is the basic task that confronts us.

Before turning fully to the constructive dimensions of that task, it is worth delaying just long enough to extend this brief history forward, closer to the present, in order to include the mention of three additional and potentially quite valuable historical resources. Consider first the deliberations of another American thinker, in this case, not primarily a philosopher interested in religion, as Peirce and Royce were, but himself a professional theologian. H. Richard Niebuhr carefully studied the work of both Edwards and Royce. He was also indirectly impacted, not only through his reading of Royce, but as a result of his engagement with the social psychology of George Herbert Mead, by a number of Peirce's ideas.[65] Much like his distinguished predecessors in the history of theosemiotic, Niebuhr understood God's creation or kingdom as "being like the pattern of a life, a poem or a New World symphony."[66] In a series of lectures delivered not long before his death and published posthumously, Niebuhr displayed the full fruits of his decades-long meditation on Edwards's theology, especially the latter's doctrine of religious affections. He also demonstrated how thoroughly saturated with Royce's semiotic ideas about experience and community his own mature thinking had become—for instance, as when he observed that "there seems to be no perception of anything that does not contain an interpretation, and there is no interpretation that is not a function of our social communication as well as our interaction with the objects."[67] (Even some of the echoes of Peirce's semiotic realism seem to reverberate here.)

Niebuhr also articulated a "radical monotheism" that needs to be carefully assessed for explicitly theosemiotic purposes. Here the influence of Edwards appears once again to be on display. The ultimate object of human devotion and fidelity cannot be someone or something that is limited in any respect. It cannot be a particular being or community, but must be the principle or source of being for everything else that exists. This insistence on a monotheism that is of such a "radical" kind raises questions that any future theosemiotic will struggle to answer. While the signs that permeate nature are determinate to some extent, the divine reality that they might be thought to signify cannot be any determinate thing. This primordial reality is the indeterminate source of everything else that exists, a divine "No-thing" that ought never to be confused with its signs or symbols. In what sense can such a reality be properly signified? How is a divine nothingness in its infinite plenitude to be distinguished from a blank nothingness, empty and so impotent as a giver of meaning? The emphasis here will not fall heavily on such metaphysical questions, but neither should they be completely ignored. From a theosemiotic perspective, there can be no path that circumnavigates the various signs and symbols that mediate to human interpreters the reality of something divine. Since it will be argued that our knowledge of anything at all must be mediated by signs, there can be no direct or separate access to such a reality. The *only* path to religious meaning is the path of interpretation. Moreover, all of the signs encountered in experience are necessarily vague, and our interpretations of them are inevitably fallible.

Now the question has already been raised here about the extent to which a theosemiotic perspective presupposes the commitment to theism of any kind. It may seem at first blush that Peirce, Royce, and Niebuhr—each now identified as representing such a perspective—were all also proponents of theism. Yet the extraordinary vagueness that Peirce insisted must attach to the idea of God (see Chapter 3) and the special emphasis that Royce placed, not on a divine Creator, but on the "Spirit" of the "Beloved Community," along with Niebuhr's insistence on a monotheism that must be conceived as truly "radical"—these are all strategies the logic of which complicates any simple or straightforward assertions about the existence and nature of a personal God. Emerson's "God talk" was idiosyncratic as well. Even as traditional a Christian thinker as Jonathan Edwards translated ordinary speech about the love of God, as just indicated, into philosophical talk about "benevolence to being in general," very likely serving as the inspiration for Niebuhr's own later tendency to identify God as "the principle of being." To what extent might such strategies resonate with those developed by certain contemporary "religious naturalists" or by thinkers within religious traditions (such as Buddhism) not typically classified as "theistic?" On the other hand, and by way of contrast, to what extent might these same strategies be taken to suggest that theosemiotic entails some form of metaphysical personalism, so that there is no better way of conceiving of the divine reality (to invoke Charles Peirce) than as being "vaguely like" a person?

Now surely one of the more original contributions that Royce made to the theosemiotic project was the philosophy of loyalty that he developed at roughly the same time that he was adapting Peirce's semiotic theory for quasi-theological purposes.[68] Love as loyalty became the volitional linchpin in Royce's arguments about community—about the relations among individuals in any given community as well as those that might develop between the members of one community and another. A community of interpretation is not just formed out of the ideas that people possess and then exchange, but rather is grounded in volition, a fundamental "will to interpret" displayed by each of its members. Niebuhr, in turn, adopted and adapted Royce's thinking about loyalty, so that it came to be the life blood of his own extended meditation on faith and fidelity.[69] Accordingly, a vital, authentic faith radiates the "beauty of living in harmony with divine things."

Perhaps this blood has flowed through many generations, and this meditation has roots that reach, once again, far beyond Royce and Niebuhr, deep into the medieval period. Yet however far removed in time, the conceptual distance from H. Richard Niebuhr on "fidelity" to Josiah Royce on "loyalty" and then to Duns Scotus on "firmitas" or steadfastness of will seems, on close inspection, not to be so very great at all.[70] In any event, the semiotic background for Niebuhr's deliberations must be kept clearly in view whenever his remarks about the kind of faithfulness exemplified by true believers are examined. That kind of believing, that type of loyalty or fidelity (it will be regularly affirmed here) involves a deliberate and repeated choosing, not always of new things, but often of things already chosen, things made new, or at least perceived anew, in the fresh appropriation of them through a living act of faith. Such an act, this quite ordinary but still remarkable form of appropriation, needs also to be understood as a semiotic phenomenon.

Standing a bit outside of the (predominantly American) current of thought that this historical survey has been tracing are several other key individuals whose relevance to theosemiotic inquiry will need to be further evaluated. The French philosopher, mystic, and activist Simone Weil may seem like an unlikely choice for inclusion here. Living and writing in the decades immediately following the deaths of James, Peirce, and Royce, she does not appear in any observable way to have been influenced by pragmatism. Yet her terse articulation of "an experimental ontological proof" displays a striking resemblance to the basic logic embedded in Peirce's Neglected Argument.[71] The concept of beauty was as central to her theological vision as it was for Edwards, Emerson, and Peirce. Moreover, the emphasis that she placed on the importance of cultivating a highly disciplined habit of attention provides a natural link to the reflections of both Peirce and James, while also making her insights crucial for the development of a contemporary theosemiotic perspective.

By contrast, the relationship between pragmatism and modern Latin American liberation theology is a bit easier to establish.[72] Despite the numerous and important differences between them, both intellectual movements underscore the importance for inquiry of an emphasis on praxis, as well as on vibrant communities of interpretation. Both pragmatists and liberation theologians tend to direct their gaze toward the future, not in a way that blinds them to the present and its problems, but in a fashion that animates inquiry and practice with a spirit of hopefulness. Both groups of thinkers are allergic to a number of sharp conceptual dualisms (most notably, the one that separates theory from practice, but also of talk about an ethereal "soul" as something completely different from the human body) that have historically proven to be quite troublesome for philosophers and theologians. Here it will be argued, further, that when philosophical pragmatism becomes adapted to the special purposes of theosemiotic, the liberationist commitment (shared by Simone Weil) to a "preferential option for the poor" can be readily illuminated and defended.

Numerous theologians have given voice to this commitment and to the general principles and methods of a liberation theology; toward the ends envisioned for this inquiry, the work of the movement's "founder," Gustavo Gutierrez, will receive special consideration.[73] In addition to the liberationist motifs already identified, Gutierrez's theology underscores the gratuitous quality of divine love in a manner that can be shown to resonate with a theosemiotic emphasis on the gift of meaning. A further resonance can be observed in his method of "rereading" canonical texts and basic doctrines in light of the concerns and agenda characteristic of a theology of liberation. The manner in which Gutierrez links perception to action has a pragmatic flavor. And his espousal of the need for adults to recover and sustain a "spiritual childhood" echoes Emerson and Peirce.[74]

Some of the threads of this "brief history" will need to be taken up and further unraveled in the deliberations that follow. But there is no need to postpone any longer the contemporary undertaking that a lively conversation with such historical figures is intended to expedite. How does one most effectively portray a philosophical theology conceived as a method of reading the universe of signs? What sort of discipline enables that reading? Is it the same kind of discipline or skill developed in the reading and rereading of scriptural texts? What sort of *self* is capable of engaging in such a practice? How do specific purposes and ideals emerge in and from the act of reading, and in what way is that act related to other forms of religiously meaningful behavior? Finally, what sort of distinctive agenda is the conception of such a philosophical theology most likely to yield?

2 / Signs, Selves, and Semiosis

I

All thinking is in signs. Moreover, every person is a living sign or symbol.[1] The move from this first claim to the second will prove to be theologically significant. To affirm that *homo symbolicus* designates an animal distinguished by its capacity for language, an ability to use and understand signs, to create and flourish in cultures, seems relatively uncontroversial (while the importance of such an affirmation for theosemiotic, nevertheless, cannot be overestimated).[2] To argue that human cognition is semiosis pretty much "all the way down" is a stronger claim. Yet to perceive the self *as* a symbol is to grasp what human beings essentially *are*, to define them, and not merely to contemplate their special capabilities. Here the multiple observations that signs do not exist in isolation but rather in a semiotic series, that persons are always already *embodied*, and that self-knowledge is continuous with what and how we come to know about other persons, should all be deemed crucial for the purposes of theosemiotic inquiry.

Signs in combination can form a complex symbol, much as a poem consists of words and phrases or a painting of blended images. In the case of persons as symbols, this is not a static phenomenon; rather, the self consists in what Peirce might portray metaphorically as a living, moving train or stream of thought-signs.[3] It seems rather obvious that this metaphor needs to be amended, our understanding of persons properly nuanced to involve the conception of multiple currents coexisting alongside each other within each stream, while also intersecting with one another in a complex network of relations.⁴ The source of these currents can often be subterranean, buried in the human unconscious; moreover, since the boundaries of the self are porous, streams can overflow and move between otherwise distinguishable selves, as in cases of empathy or when persons effectively engage each other in acts of communication. Each person navigates these streams of thought, also partially constituting or shaping them, shifting from one to another or linking one to another, by the exercise of *attention*. Nevertheless, the capacity for attention is not unlimited, with the factors that can determine or constrain it being numerous and often chaotic (recall James's "great blooming, buzzing confusion").⁵

When Kierkegaard argued that the "self is a relation which relates to itself," he affirmed a conception of selfhood similar to the one that is being defended here, albeit one not yet articulated in explicitly semiotic terms.⁶ The crucial similarity is that he portrayed the self as relational. Yet he also understood the achievement of selfhood as a project, a religiously challenging task, and in the absence of divine grace as one destined for failure, eventuating in despair. Since a person is not a static thing but a process, a motion picture of the self is required for proper understanding; no frozen-framed photograph will do. Semiosis is an essentially temporal phenomenon, as Peirce insisted, with meaning to be regarded as always in a state of "incipiency," the self-as-sign consistently capable of new developments, real growth. Conversely, meaning is fragile and can be eroded over time. For a variety of reasons, then, it might be more philosophically appropriate to talk about human "selving" than to conceive of persons as separate, stable "selves."⁷ And for the self to *mean* (anything at all) is for it always necessarily to-be-in-relation.

There is a passive, inert sense in which a person can be a sign, much as a human corpse can be a sign of the devastation caused by war, famine, or disease or human bodies can be used in advertising as signifiers for economic purposes, designating a vast array of marketable commodities. On some accounts, one might want to distinguish between this sense, in which the human *body* is a sign, and the idea seeming to be more relevant to theosemiotic inquiry that the cognitively active human *self* is what is truly significant. Yet theosemiotic is fueled by a pragmatic perspective that resists any simple distinction between self/person and body. If persons cannot be completely reduced to their observable bodies and bodily states (a hypothetical claim that merits further consideration), they are nonetheless inseparable from the latter. The human body is of crucial importance for establishing the unity of the self, its continuity as a single self, in *some* sense distinguishable from others even as it interacts with them and is linked to them in a complex variety of ways. All that we know about other selves, all that they can possibly signify for us, is achieved through our response to discernible facial expressions, postures, gestures, actions, speech, and so on. What we see or hear in our interactions with other selves, what we also taste, smell, and feel, constitutes the warp and woof of our semiotic relations with them while also supplying the basic building blocks for the creation of communities. These interactions can be mediated, of course, as when what we hear is the voice on a telephone of someone far removed from us in distance, or what we see is the writing produced by someone long dead, or our knowledge is based on the verbal report of another person's actual encounter. Nevertheless, the human body remains a fundamental symbol of the self, the primary token or sign vehicle at the heart of human semiosis.

It is not altogether clear that Peirce himself treated the human body seriously enough when he formulated his semiotic conception of the self. Some commentators, in fact, have worried that Peirce "ignored" the body with his emphasis on cognition-as-semiosis in both his early and later accounts of the self, much as Aristotle had conceived of rationality as constituting the essence of what is human.[8] But this potential imbalance in Peirce's thinking can be easily repaired. Moreover, the perception of any imbalance may very well represent a misinterpretation of Peirce's true position. One needs only to be reminded once again that he was an objective idealist who rejected the Cartesian dualism of mind and matter as vigorously as he eschewed the Cartesian strategy of methodological doubt.[9] Mind and matter are continuous. Ideas "get" persons to think them, and we think *with* our bodies (so that the body can serve as symbol in a highly active as well as in a somewhat passive sense).[10] This is a more properly Peircean way to describe our relationship to ideas than by saying that we think *in* our bodies or that our bodies contain our thoughts. Rather than deemphasizing the role of the body in his portrayal of human selfhood, it may be more accurate to conclude that Peirce decentered it. One's thoughts can be said to "reside" in the pen or the inkstand that one uses to write them down as readily as in one's brain (*CP* 7.366). On this view, the body and brain are not privileged as being the only possible locus of the mind's incarnation. (And for reasons that flow from this discussion, it will be important to argue that Peirce's defense of "anthropomorphism" can in no way be regarded as an example of anthropocentrism.)

In any event, since Peirce would have been comfortable embracing materialism if a satisfactory materialistic account of human feeling had been forthcoming, but then leaned toward idealism as a more attractive alternative, this is an issue about which he may not have always been perfectly clear. Here it will be argued that the self is a product and form of semiosis; human beings are living legisigns. Meaning is not embodied in some isolated or static thing, but rather emerges in a process. So the human body is an important sign of the self, yet only when a coherent story can be told about what that body reveals over time. To be sure, I may catch a momentary glimpse of someone and be able to infer something meaningful about that person (based on what I judge to be an expression of fear or of rage, for example, or what I might hear her say). But this is not the sort of meaning that Peirce was referring to when he announced that every "man has his own peculiar character," one that "enters into all that he does" (*CP* 7.595; *W*1: 501). And it is certainly not the kind of meaning with which theosemiotic is preoccupied. Undoubtedly, this line of argument will need to be unpacked a bit further in order to become fully intelligible.

The issuing of a crucial caveat is warranted at this juncture. To say that anything might potentially function as a sign is not to say that the being of anything is exhausted by those qualities that make it significant. To put this point in a slightly different way, calling something a sign should not be interpreted as insisting that it is *nothing but* a sign. Peirce himself made this distinction between the semiotic and the nonsemiotic features of a thing when he referred to the "material quality" of a sign (*W*3: 66–68). If a sign had no qualities apart from those that function to signify its object, then it would not be in any way distinguishable from its object; the sign-object contrast would evaporate, with the otherness of the sign to its object collapsing into identity. He also differentiated between "the mere body of the Sign" and the "Sign's soul," with the latter consisting in an "active power to establish connections" between things (*CP* 6.455).[11]

The relevance of such a distinction will need to be evaluated here for the purposes of theosemiotic inquiry. In characterizing the self as a sign, it may prove to be important not to reduce human selves to their semiotic function. It may be positively important not to do so insofar as a consideration of the material quality of selves, their "suchness" so to speak, can be shown to add real value to any theological account of what it means to be a self. Alternatively, this observation might be important for what it reveals about any given self's failure to be significant, its resistance to meaning, exposing the limits of semiosis as a negative rather than as a positive state of affairs. This opens the door to a line of inquiry that cannot be immediately pursued; but it is a door that surely must be left ajar.

It will be recalled that Peirce's was a truly general theory of signs, with human language constituting only one among many possible forms of semiosis. This is a feature of Peirce's perspective that needs to be properly understood and emphasized, one that distinguishes it from that of later neo-pragmatists who took "the linguistic turn" much more sharply and with a vengeance. As C. I. Lewis observed in his commentary on Peirce's position, words are "signs for other signs more immediately grasped and pertinent to the operations of intelligence. To identify meaning exclusively with the phenomena of verbal symbolization would be to put the cart before the horse and run the risk of trivializing the subject."[12] At the same time, Lewis admitted that "the development of language may operate retroactively to modify the meanings entertained." For the purposes of theosemiotic, language cannot be regarded as purely expressive of meanings already embodied in nonverbal form, but rather must be conceived as playing a constitutive role in the production of meaning. Nevertheless, semiosis cannot simply be reduced to language.[13]

In some of Peirce's early writings it is certainly the case that persons were conceived *as* signs primarily because they are users of language; we use words to communicate with one another, but any individual's thought is also a kind of ongoing conversation internal to the self. The leap in these early essays was from conceiving persons as employing language in communication to the conclusion that "the word or sign which man uses *is* the man himself" (*CP* 5.314; *W*2: 241). While the mature Peirce may have clarified the extent to which he conceived of human semiosis as more than a purely linguistic phenomenon, it is worth pausing over these early formulations of his perspective in order to glean insights that, even if they underwent further development, were never entirely abandoned.

A person uses words in order to signify something. Yet the distinction between "user" and "used" is not perfectly clear in this instance. On Peirce's account, it is entirely consistent to say *both* that persons make words mean this or that by using them in a certain fashion *and* that persons are complex signs whose meanings are determined by the words that form their stream of consciousness. In this regard, "men and words reciprocally educate each other; each increase of a man's information involves and is involved by, a corresponding increase of a word's information" (*CP* 5.313; *W*2: 241). Speech is never purely innocent on such an account, never merely expressive. One cannot consistently speak in a certain way (like a racist or a sexist, for example) and yet avoid being shaped or transformed by such patterns of speech. This insight is embodied in the Buddhist teaching about training in "right speech" as an important component of the Eightfold Path. Disciplined speech is regarded as a spiritually felicitous practice by Buddhists, but *not* because they regard the role of language here as exclusively communicative, expressive of who one is or what one is already thinking or feeling. Rather, words have an important creative function so that how one speaks habitually is a fundamental determinant of the sort of person that one is likely to become in the future. On such a view, right speech is a form of spiritual discipline. This is the power of any sign—that while it is partially determined by its object, it itself has the capacity to determine an interpretant.[14] As already observed, this power is by no means unlimited. Meaning is both created and discovered by human interpreters. It is both an achievement and a gift.

Any sign can have multiple interpretants. Some of these will be internal to the stream of consciousness, as when one thought-sign determines as its interpretant a subsequent thought-sign. Now every person considered at any given point in time is a symbol, analogous to a word, so that a "man denotes whatever is the object of his attention at the moment; he connotes whatever he knows or feels of this object, and is the incarnation of this form or intelligible species" (*CP* 7.591; *W*1: 498). That person's "interpretant" may be embodied in subsequent cognitions—that is to say, in his "future self"; but his interpretant could also be "another person he addresses." Indeed, the existence of a person is not "cut off from the external world, for feeling and attention are essential elements of the symbol itself" (*CP* 7.593; *W*1.500). Every self is a sign that can find its interpretant either in a future version of itself or in another person.

Notice the absolutely crucial role played by acts of attention in Peirce's description of how the self signifies. The person-as-symbol denotes whatever constitutes the object of that person's attention "at the moment." The meaning of the self will vary over time then and can be shaped by multiple forces and factors. A self-controlled individual acting in a purposeful manner will direct the attention to this or that particular object with discipline and skill. But there will be numerous occasions when the attention wanders a bit more aimlessly, first to one object then to another, with no specific purpose in view. (Such occasions can themselves be classified in different ways, as Peirce wanted to distinguish the practiced purposelessness of musement, for example, from any kind of idle daydreaming.) In addition, objects will attract our attention as they appear more or less lively to consciousness, their appearance being a function not only of the characteristics they display (a shout might attract attention more readily than a whisper, a bright color more readily than a dull one), but also of the particular habits of attention that any given individual may have developed. It is most meaningful to talk about one's attention being "captured" when *intention* is involved rather than accident—that is, when one's attention being directed to an object results from effective strategies designed by others for the purpose of achieving just such a result. To be sure, one may try to resist such strategies. In any event, the present analysis suggests that the project of human "selving" can sometimes take the form of a struggle, with real risks involved and much at stake, different outcomes determining what a human life will eventually come to mean.[15]

It follows from Peirce's account of the self as semiosis that "a person is not absolutely an individual" (*CP* 5.421). A person's thoughts are addressed to "that other self that is just coming into life in the flow of time." Moreover, one's "circle of society (however widely or narrowly this phrase may be understood) is a sort of loosely compacted person, in some respects of higher rank than the person of an individual organism." There is both an ethical and a theological twist to this story that Peirce told about the self. The moral lesson is that one should never be tempted to assert that "I am altogether myself, and not at all you," the perspective articulated in such a claim constituting for Peirce "the vulgarest delusion of vanity" (*CP* 7.571). "When I communicate my thought and my sentiments to a friend with whom I am in full sympathy, so that my feelings pass into him and I am conscious of what he feels," Peirce queried, "do I not live in his brain as well as in my own—most literally?" (*CP* 7.591; *W*1: 498)

At the same time, persons can be related to one another in multiple and complex ways—for example, linked insofar as they share a common purpose or engage each other in meaningful conversation. While these interactions can occur between individuals of the same "rank," they might also define the relationship between a person and some "greater self" within whom that person is somehow embedded. Both possibilities can have theological implications. Persons exist alongside one another and interact with each other in religious communities. But one person might also be related to another as "lesser" to "greater"—either in cases where personality is attributed to the community itself or when a personal deity is understood to enfold all of creation (as in pantheism or panentheism).

In any given instance, to talk about "persons" or "selves," on Peirce's account, is not to identify "anything more than vicinities"; indeed, from his perspective, "personal existence is an illusion and a practical joke" (*CP* 4.68).[16] Despite the hyperbole employed here, Peirce was not actually denying the reality of the self, but only its existence conceived as something determinate, fixed, and isolated, rather than understood more loosely as a neighborhood of semiotic activity. Moreover, and to rehearse a point already made, the self cannot be revealed in a snapshot of that vicinity but must be exposed over time. This narrative dimension of selfhood is theologically meaningful in a manner that will need to be carefully probed. In anticipation of that discussion, it might be useful to observe here that any portrayal of the self as a vicinity or neighborhood helps dramatically to reframe the question that launched Jesus's parable about the Good Samaritan: "Who is my neighbor?" (Peirce's own response to this question—that our neighbor is anyone "with whom we live near, not locally perhaps but in life and feeling" [*CP* 6.288; *W*8: 185]—also deserves careful theological scrutiny.)

To the extent that anything can be identified as a self at all, in the sense of what Peirce would conceive as "a single logical individual," it will form a continuum of signs, display a "continuity of reactions" (*CP* 3.613). While they might overlap and be in some sense continuous, notwithstanding, since no one current within a stream of consciousness is constitutive of the self, it would be problematic to identify the self as an "essentially ordered" series of signs. The signs in each series will be essentially ordered, and distinct currents will stand one to another in a variety of relationships. The ideals and purposes to which any individual is devoted will also act as final causes to which certain aspects of that person's life will be essentially ordered. A person's life as a whole will be more or less unified in this fashion to the extent that the selving process involves real growth in meaning. Yet the self can also experience significant fragmentation, be caught between competing ideals and purposes, or even fail for stretches of time to be guided by any purpose at all, so that in such cases meaning ebbs rather than grows, and the vitality of the self declines. Theologically speaking, it is important to remain aware that the achievement of selfhood involves struggle and that the meaning achieved is always at least partially a gift. (This awareness can be framed by talk about "sin" and "grace," or "suffering" and "freedom from desire," or in various other ways.)

Insofar as it *can* be accomplished, however, the unity of the self will be "the unity of symbolization—the unity of consistency." From his earliest reflections on this topic until the end of his career, such consistency for Peirce was embodied in a certain kind of habit. It is a habit of attention, to be sure, since the self-as-sign can signify only those things to which it attends. Yet since the self-sign "connotes" what it "thinks and feels" about the object that it signifies, it is also a habit of thought and feeling. Attention, thought, and feeling blended together in this fashion form a habit of love, giving unity to the self and constituting its deepest meaning. From this Peircean perspective, it is "sympathy, love" that "serves as evidence" of a person's "absolute worth" (*CP* 7.593; *W*1: 500). (The exploration of this claim as a fundamental hypothesis must be central to the agenda of a theology formulated as theosemiotic.)

Compare now Peirce's general approach to the topic of selfhood with that of his friend William James. James's early forays into psychology had also exposed the extent to which the self is defined by a process of selection that involves the continuous exercise of attention. There is a vast and constantly "fluctuating" set of possibilities to which any individual may choose to attend; consciousness was regarded as a flowing "stream" for James much as it was for Peirce. As a result, James developed an extraordinarily expansive notion of the self, again, much like Peirce's, albeit not cast in explicitly semiotic terms, but rather, one emphasizing the feeling-content of consciousness.[17] "*In its widest possible sense*," he explained, "*a man's SELF is the sum total of all that he CAN call his*, not only his body and his psychic powers, but his clothes and his house, his wife and children, his ancestors and friends, his reputation and works, his lands and horses, and yacht and bank account."[18] Here, once again, is the articulated notion of a self without clear boundaries, rather fuzzy at the borders, including but in no way restricted to an individual's body, thoughts, perceptions, memories, feelings, desires, and so on.

This is no merely metaphorical way of speaking. Surely there may be a variety of different things that one might intend to designate by calling it a "self." Yet for James the word must have this capacious sort of meaning if one intends to use it "in its widest possible sense." Such an observation exposes what should become a working assumption for any theosemiotic analysis of selfhood: the word "self" is necessarily vague, having no single, determinate meaning, but instead, being capable of interpretation in a variety of ways. Within the present context, as it was for James, the task is to discern what it might mean to be a self in the wider rather than in a narrow sense. In addition, as it was for Peirce, while also echoing Kierkegaard, on this account to be a self is necessarily and essentially (and so not accidentally, eventually, or occasionally) to-be-in-relation.

Peirce's account of thought as most typically taking the form of a dialogue, a continuous conversation internal to the self (albeit not always one conducted in words; see N3: 258–59), received its most elaborate early development in Josiah Royce's philosophy, then again somewhat later in the social psychology of George Herbert Mead.[19] Royce observed that "when a process of conscious reflection goes on, a man may be said to interpret himself to himself."[20] As such, "the self is no mere datum, but is in its essence a life which is interpreted, and which interprets itself, and which, apart from some sort of ideal interpretation, is a mere flight of ideas, or a meaningless flow of feelings."[21] Royce's sometimes imprecise but theologically productive employment of Peirce's semiotic merits thoughtful assessment.[22] At this juncture, it is especially important to note that the self is both a process and a product of interpretation, oriented toward the future because even in the present it is continuously interpreting itself to or for some future version of the self. This interpretive behavior is not blind but rather will be governed by certain ideals (albeit themselves vulnerable to change). To engage in such a deliberate process is what distinguishes a person *as a self* from some "meaningless flow of feelings." It is what differentiates a genuine conversation from a mere cacophony of voices. Once again, the self cannot be posited exclusively as something *given*, but must also somehow and to some extent be *achieved*.

George Herbert Mead's interests were more narrowly restricted to the picture of the self that this complex dialogical perspective might illuminate, without so much concern for its possible religious significance. "The self," he asserted, "has as its most fundamental character that of being an object to itself."[23] In this respect, it is to be distinguished carefully both from other kinds of objects and from the human body.[24] What Mead appeared to have learned from Peirce and like-minded pragmatists is that one's relationship to oneself is different, but not fundamentally different in kind, from one's relationship to other persons. Moreover, the self emerges into being only as a result of such relations with others. That is to say, "the self, as that which can be an object to itself, is essentially a social structure, and it arises in social experience."[25] Persons do not merely converse and interact; they come to be as persons only through conversation and interaction. The self is a story that one tells about oneself, then, both to oneself and to others. This story unfolds in conversation, again, both with oneself and with others. Its plot is not fixed in advance but develops gradually as the self-at-present continuously reinterprets its meaning to future versions of itself. This future is largely indeterminate, yet to some extent and in a certain crucial sense, it is self-controlled.

These last few remarks may be more typically Peircean than they are explicitly characteristic of Mead's philosophy. For Mead, the core of the conversation that constitutes the self is one that occurs between the "I" as present self and the "me" as its recollected past. By contrast, Peirce's self-as-dialogue is oriented toward the future, toward that "you" that is "just coming into life in the flow of time." The internal conversation is one best construed as a dialogue *between* one's present and one's future, emerging self *about* the past. Now, this contrast in emphasis hardly represents a fundamental contradiction. The flow of time as consciously experienced is such that the "I" of the present moment is continuously slipping into the past, also repeatedly being reconstituted by some future version of the self. Moreover, a keen awareness of time's perpetual flow is crucial to any account of the self as consisting essentially in semiosis. In the final analysis, conversation-as-interpretation is always a triadic and never merely a dyadic event. Royce was especially clear and emphatic in this regard, as he adapted Peirce's semiotic theory for the purpose of better understanding both persons and communities. The self in any given moment is a sign that mediates between the past and the future. The self is constantly engaged in interpreting its remembered past to future versions of itself.

Since selves are persons, of a greater or lesser generality, the nature of the self can be further illuminated by what Peirce had to say specifically about "personality." The latter will need to consist, he reported, in "some kind of coordination or connection of ideas" (*CP* 6.155; *W*8: 154). On this view, as already suggested, personality (much like selfhood) "is not a thing to be apprehended in an instant. It has to be lived in time." Moreover, this coordination of ideas will not be confused with just any type of connection among them; "it implies a teleological harmony in ideas" (*CP* 6.156; *W*8: 155). In the case of genuine personality, this teleology must be developmental, not the sort of purpose that consists in the "pursuit of a pre-determinate end," but rather, one "already determinative of acts in the future to an extent to which it is not now conscious." This gentle shaping of ends over time is the form of semiosis at the heart of selfhood, as signs are determined by their objects and subsequently determine their interpretants, but not in a way that any crude account of efficient causality could hope to describe. To make sense of this semiotic relation, some concept of final causality will have to be invoked. (Here, again, Peirce may have been indebted to the medieval scholastics; an ideal as final cause and the semiotic self in action will stand in a relationship that is essentially ordered.)

Royce developed such a concept when he argued that the achievement of a self is a matter of volition displayed in commitment to a life plan.[26] He concurred with Peirce that interpretation was a process distinguished both by its triadic structure and by the ordering of events in time. To the extent that this ordering is "essential" rather than "accidental," it could supply evidence of the self's adherence to a plan and to specific purposes. Peirce, Royce, and Mead were all in agreement that no such plan can be formulated in abstraction from some living social reality, an actual community shaped by its own purposes and so displaying its own peculiar personality.

For a great variety of reasons then, the picture of a "dialogical self" sketched by the philosophical pragmatists—of the self as a living stream of consciousness or of thought-signs—will need to be expanded here. Peirce's less commonly utilized picture of the self as a "vicinity" where various streams of semiosis both intersect and run together will prove to be a bit messier yet nonetheless quite useful for the purposes of this discussion in the long run. Even as the self is a relation that relates to itself, as Kierkegaard surmised, it is also always already existing in relationship to others, partially constituted by those others, fixed by their gaze, affirmed by their love, threatened by their contempt, not the mere product of these interactions, but nevertheless inextricable from them. The *continuity* of the self, supplied by body, memory, consistency of intentions, fidelity to purposes, and so on must be balanced in any accurate portrayal by a description of the self's porous nature. The sharp distinction between "inner" and "outer" with regard to personhood is yet another misleading dichotomy that the pragmatist will be wise to eschew. "Subjectivity" is at best an impure concept, needing to be carefully nuanced in order to be moderately useful. And the achievement of a robust intersubjectivity is the only form of "objectivity" to which the enlightened pragmatist is ever likely to admit.

Other sources can be tapped in order to fill in details of the sketch supplied by the American pragmatists. The Russian philosopher and literary theorist Mikhail Bakhtin, for example, understood the self not simply as one engaged in continuous dialogue; rather, the self *is* dialogue, constituted and configured by it, with the logic of that dialogue governing its relationship to other selves.[27] Observing the "polyphonic" character of works of literature, especially the novels of Dostoevsky, sparked insights that resonate deeply with Peirce's semiotic theory. For Bakhtin, every utterance is inherently responsive to something in the past, while also being open and oriented to the future, addressed to a listener and provoking an answer. Utterances cannot be isolated one from another, any more than a sign's function can be understood apart from the living process of semiosis. Every "concrete utterance is a link in the chain of speech communication," shaped by the conversation in which it emerges. The meaning of that conversation is always open and partially indeterminate on Bakhtin's account, its teleology most properly conceived as "developmental" in the sense that Peirce described. Even the meanings of past utterances are not fixed and stable, but remain labile, subject to change, renewable as the conversation unfolds.[28]

When an individual's train of thought is portrayed as semiosis, the relationship between particular thought-signs can be construed in different ways. In one sense every sign can be said to mediate between its object and some interpretant. Yet from another perspective, the interpretant plays a mediating role, establishing a genuinely semiotic relationship between some sign and its object. This is a complicated issue, because one might choose to argue in support of the claim that it is not the present existence of an actual interpretant that establishes something as a sign, but rather, its interpretability[29]—that is to say, the sign's interpretant may be potential rather than actual, having its being only *in futuro*. On this view, some of the most significant "others" to whom any self might become related may not yet exist. (Such is the relationship between Charles Peirce himself and the community of interpreters now engaged in trying to understand him.)[30]

It can also be argued that this normative importance of the future is a crucial and defining feature not only of Peirce's pragmaticism, but of philosophical pragmatism in general. For Peirce, meaning will be embodied in any given interpretant, partially realized there, but with its further determination always being deferred to the future. Self-control was less a matter for Peirce of the self acting *now* to constrain impulses to think, feel, or behave in a certain way just as those impulses arise, than it was an attempt by the present self gently, deliberately to shape future versions of itself. To be sure (and this is a process that John Dewey was at great pains to describe),[31] such an attempt will necessarily involve the human imagination. It will involve perceiving in some existing state of affairs a certain ideality, some real possibility that must remain invisible to one who is not prepared to see it—that is, to one lacking the imaginative capacity to do so. When Peirce described the self as a "bundle of habits" (*CP* 6.228), he did not intend to suggest that it was a bundle haphazardly assembled, but rather one displaying a certain consistency, guided by a developmental teleology, thus, to some degree purposeful and so oriented to an imagined future.

II

If the self is a sign, what sort of sign can it be? At this juncture, the concern is less with how Peirce or others might answer such a question than with using their insights to develop an account for the purposes of theosemiotic. Yet Peirce's elaborate classification of signs does suggest that there may be a great variety of plausible answers. Not all of them need to be explored here, but a few might be selected for further consideration on suspicion of their potential religious significance. To follow a well-beaten path, consider first Peirce's best-known categorization of signs in terms of their relationship to their objects, constituting them as icons, indices, or symbols. Briefly stated, icons represent their objects by resembling them, indices by being caused by them, and symbols are linked to their objects by virtue of some rule or convention. For reasons quite important to the present inquiry, it is helpful to observe the following: Icons draw attention most immediately to the sign itself, inviting the playful contemplation of its various connotations. Indices forcefully direct attention to whatever objects they denote. Symbols emphasize the role and importance of interpretants, signifying only by virtue of some established habit of attention.

If the self-as-sign is an icon, its relationship to what it signifies would have to be understood as consisting in some kind of resemblance. Here, too, there are a variety of possibilities. A woman may resemble her mother because they share a number of prominent physical features—hair color, facial characteristics, height, for example. But she may also have mannerisms that are similar to those her mother displays or have pursued the same activities or career as her mother. Here the resemblance will be of a different kind, so that to make sense of it requires a brief detour, back to an important distinction that Augustine made between natural signs (*signa naturalia*) and given signs (*signa data*).

Natural signs signify something other than themselves "apart from any intention or desire" that they should function as signs. Given or "conventional" signs, by contrast, involve just such an intention to communicate something.[32] Looking like one's mother by virtue of one's physical appearance represents one way, while pursuing the same career inspired by her another way, of representing her iconically. Of course, from a Peircean perspective, in order to exercise its function, any natural sign must be regarded as such by some interpreter. Meaning is not a property of the sign itself but emerges only in the interaction between sign, object, and interpreter. Even where the resemblances between a sign and its object are natural, rather than established by some purpose or intention, they will be more or less extensive, and they will need to be discerned *by* someone. In the case of a photograph, its iconic features will be prominent. Yet two things may resemble each other in only a very limited way, nevertheless enabling one to signify the other as an icon. The sense in which a human being might be taken to signify something iconically, whether by nature or intentionally, is likely often to be more subtle and complex than the resemblance displayed by a photograph to its object. In much theological talk—for example, about humans being created "in God's image"—the subtlety of how and what that image signifies will need to be dramatically underscored.[33]

The philosophical key to this distinction for Augustine, once again, is that *signa naturalia* are not intended to function as signs, while *signa data* signify purposefully. (Of course, with regard to the earlier example, a woman's behavior or career choice may in fact *not* represent on her part any conscious intention to be like her mother.) Many of the latter (*signa data*) can be classified as humanly constructed conventional signs (i.e., symbols), but not all, since Peirce perceived the operative presence of real purpose in nature apart from any human attempt to construe it as purposeful.[34] Here is another instance of how from a pragmatic perspective one must be careful not to draw too sharp a contrast between "nature" and "culture." Not only might purposes be sometimes discernible insofar as they shape certain natural processes, but also, our cultural practices are to some extent rooted in basic, natural human instincts.

To be sure, on Peirce's account, a "pure icon is independent of any purpose" (*EP2*: 306; *NEM4*: 242). Consequently, if human selves are to be regarded as the embodiment of semiosis they should not be conceived as icons pure and simple, but rather as complex signs possessing iconic features. It makes more sense to talk about their iconic function than to designate them simply as "icons." Peirce's extensive classification of signs, pursued late in his philosophical career, is somewhat misleading, then, insofar as it appears to supply clearly delineated categories of the various types of signs that might be apprehended and distinguished. In fact, it ought to be regarded as an exercise in "aspect seeing" (in the Wittgensteinian sense), as a way of understanding the subtle intricacy of semiotic phenomena. In any event, the primary concern here is not to offer a detailed account of Peirce's theory of signs; rather, it is to utilize aspects of that theory in order better to understand the claim of Peirce and others that the self can be portrayed as a form of living semiosis.

The words that I use in conversation might best be understood as symbols. Nevertheless, they will be framed in various ways, their meaning shaped by meta-communicative strategies of various kinds, so that the context in which I speak them, my tone of voice, whether I utter them loudly or softly, gestures and facial expressions accompanying my speech, etc., all must be taken into consideration. That is to say, any given speech act is likely to blend together various iconic, indexical, and symbolic features. If speech can be thus characterized, so too can the speaker.

How might the self be conceived as displaying indexical features? Persons signify indexically when one person causes another's attention to be directed in a determinate fashion, here rather than there. Now this may seem like a rather imprecise way of putting the matter. Technically, indices are determined to be as such by their relationship to their objects, not to their interpretants; an index is related to its object as effect to cause. (On a certain theistic worldview, for example, every human being is an indexical sign of some divine volition, the act of a Creator.) Nevertheless, Peirce also observed that quite typically the interpretant of an index will consist primarily in a sharpening or shifting of attention. Persons-as-indices display their semiotic potency often in terms of what they are able to get their interpreters to *do*. This is a complicated matter, not entirely separable from the purposes that shape human behavior, so that as with iconicity, it makes no real sense to talk in simple terms about the self-as-index. In light of the Augustinian distinction between *signa naturalia* and *signa data*, it would be an open question in any given case about whether or not one person's directing the attention of another occurred in conformity to some purpose. My falling off of a ladder with a loud crash might draw your attention immediately and forcefully apart from any plan on my part to make it so. On the other hand, I could invest considerable effort in the task of attracting and directing your attention, doing so for reasons that I may or may not be able to specify (since purposes can be either conscious and readily articulated or subterranean and largely inaccessible). If I *am* able to articulate my reasons and I am also able to shape your attention, then there may be a fairly straightforward sense in which *I myself* (in contrast to my accidental falling) can be understood as a sign having indexical features.

This sort of phenomenon is difficult but important for us to analyze, for both its political and its religious implications. Whenever one hears talk about the "power" or "force" of ideals, for example, their capacity to inspire and determine human conduct, a complete semiotic analysis of what is being claimed will certainly involve an account of the symbolic content of such ideals; but it might also refer to their indexical character. If these ideals are embodied in my speech and behavior in such a way that catches and shapes your attention, subsequently adopted by you as a result of our interaction, then I would argue (on Peircean grounds even if Peirce's thought might be interpreted differently by others) that such an interaction needs to be portrayed at least partially in indexical terms. Recall that every sign in a semiotic stream is itself an object for some subsequent sign that interprets it. If I model behavior for my friends or children that they subsequently embody in their own lives and practices, then my conduct is a sign that has somehow moved or caused them, as a result of their interpretation of that sign, to do one thing rather than another in certain relevant circumstances. Such conduct, consisting of both verbal and nonverbal behavior, is a symbol with indexical force; it is very likely iconic as well, to the extent that my behavior mimics or is patterned on that of others. Moreover, to the degree that what I do is deliberate and consistent, rather than accidental or episodic, there is no real gap between my "self" and my conduct regarded as signifiers.

Consider more carefully the claim that it makes less sense to talk about icons, indices, and symbols than about the iconic, indexical, and symbolic aspects of semiosis. Sometimes this insight is fairly simple to illustrate. I shout something at you to get you to listen. What you understand my words to mean may be communicated symbolically, while we might attribute to the volume of my speech a certain indexical quality. (I could instead have clapped my hands to get your attention.) Yet I want to suggest for theosemiotic purposes that the indexical force of a sign may have something to do with its content and not just with how it is presented or framed. And so, as instances vary, it becomes legitimate in each case to ask the question: What is it, more precisely, that makes this sign *compelling* for its interpreter?

When questioned about the consistently grotesque quality of both the characters and the events described in much of her fiction, Flannery O'Connor responded that when the people with whom one wishes to communicate are hard of hearing, it sometimes becomes necessary to shout.[35] Clearly, her attempt at communication with readers could not be described in any literal sense as "shouting." Rather, this was her way of saying that some of the typical effects of shouting—to be clear, effects on attention—can be achieved by a certain skillful use of language, also by the particular words that one chooses to employ and the images that they might convey. Now words are primarily symbols, their meaning established by well-entrenched linguistic conventions; images represent iconically. What is being suggested now is that words and images can be used in such a way that they also function indexically. This suggestion is not framed as a report about Peirce's ideas but rather as an attempt to extrapolate from and apply them. When Peirce himself described how words as conventional symbols can also be regarded as indices, he was typically referring to demonstrative pronouns, to how words like "this" or "that" can be said to signify by shaping the attention of listeners or readers (*CP* 2.287). Yet here the crucial point is not about any particular part of speech, but about a specific way in which many different kinds of words might be employed and said to function. Even if one were reluctant to classify such words as indices pure and simple (since, once again, an index really is defined in terms of a sign's relationship to its object), one might suggest that such a word has a certain indexical force, that it shapes or directs attention in a way that indices tend to do.

Clearly, there is also an important, explicitly symbolic aspect to selfhood, since it will not be achieved to even the slightest degree without the embodiment of ideals or purposes in concrete form—that is, as habits that "rule" behavior. Now the self should never be conflated with just any kind of sign that functions symbolically; rather, a person is best characterized (once again, not on Peirce's account, but now using his theory) as a "living legisign," a label already proposed. What is such a designation intended to convey? That is to say, what about the self-as-semiosis will this more determinate conception of persons as living legisigns be designed to reveal?

On Peirce's theory, the aspect of a sign that is emphasized when it is described as an icon, index, or symbol, is one specified by the relationship to its object. Signs can also be classified in terms of how one conceives of their relationship to various interpretants. Any sign considered in itself, however, rather than in terms of its relationship to its object or to its interpretant, will be one of three general kinds. If the sign is of the nature of a pure quality, an appearance or a "mere idea," then it is to be regarded as a "qualisign." If instead the sign is something individual, an actual, specific object or event, then Peirce labeled it as a "sinsign." In contrast to both qualisigns and sinsigns, if a sign is something general, of the nature of a law, it should classified as a "legisign." Such a sign "signifies through an instance of its application, which may be termed a *Replica* of it" (*EP2*: 291). Every word or conventional sign, on Peirce's account, is properly to be regarded as a legisign. To the extent that a person can be identified with the words that she or he uses, it seems apt also to classify persons as legisigns. This is just to insist that the self-as-sign cannot be reduced to some quality that it displays or to some individual regarded only here and now, but rather, it is "the entire thought-life of a person" that constitutes such a sign (*MS* 1476).

In labeling something as a legisign, as just explained, one is considering the nature of that thing regarded as a sign in itself, apart from any possible relationship that it might have to some object or interpretant. One is prescinding from these relationships in order to focus primarily on the very thing that is taken to be a sign. Yet one is hardly denying the reality of these relationships, which is why the self as living legisign can signify both iconically and indexically, as well as symbolically. The self-as-semiosis stands in relationship to objects that are highly variable, continuously shifting. But in focusing on the nature of persons themselves, the characterization of each as an organized "bundle of habits," the narrative quality of their experience, their commitment to ideals and principles, etc., it would be impossible to convey adequately what it means to be such a self on the perspective supplied by identifying them either as qualisigns or as sinsigns.

Another caveat may be appropriate here as a qualification of the proposal that selves can best be conceived as legisigns. Throughout the preceding discussion of Peirce's theory of signs, the emphasis has been placed on semiosis, rather than on the concept of a sign considered as a static or isolated thing. Indeed, a sign can never be either static or isolated on Peirce's account because it always already designates a dynamic relationship between sign, object, and interpretant. To avoid confusion on this point, Peirce sometimes specified that this relationship is one in which some sign *vehicle* links its object and interpretant, with "sign" being a label reserved for the resulting triadic relationship. In fact, the distinction between qualisign, sinsign, and legisign is essentially based on the observation and classification of different kinds of sign vehicles. Moreover, the goal moving forward in this discussion is to use Peirce's various classifications of signs as a stimulus for thought, rather than to be rigidly bound by them.

Peirce's earliest version of his semiotic theory appeared in 1867 in his seminal essay on a "A New List of Categories" (*CP* 1.545–59; *W* 2.49–59), took a quantum leap forward with articulations produced in 1903 and then developed almost continuously from that point until his death eleven years later. A good deal of scholarly energy has been devoted to the analysis of these developments and to the various classifications of signs that resulted, each more elaborate than the one preceding.[36] Yet the minute details of such classificatory schemes do not seem entirely relevant to the general task of reframing theological inquiry as theosemiotic. Interestingly, even Peirce himself, despite his extraordinary attention to these matters, did not think that it was important to be "very accurate" when trying to determine "to what class a given sign belongs" (*CP* 2.265). To call something an "icon" or a "sinsign" or anything else is hardly to insist that it is exclusively so. The hunch motivating these remarks is that Peirce's ongoing attempt to elaborate increasingly detailed classifications of signs represents an extended thought experiment intended primarily to illuminate semiosis in all of its multifarious forms and manifestations; as already suggested, it was an exercise in aspect-seeing.

The self as a sign—understood, more accurately, as semiosis—cannot be reduced to its object on the one hand (as in certain materialist conceptions of the self) or to its interpretant on the other (as with theories that understand the self to be socially constructed, a cultural product pure and simple). This is not to suggest that a self-sign is in no way shaped or determined by its object. (As Peirce argued, a sign is always in some fashion determined by its object.) Nor is it to insist that the various interpretants of such a sign fail to capture any part of its meaning. It is just to say that the self cannot be *reduced* to any of the factors that are indeed relevant to self-interpretation. Persons are bodies—physical, chemical stuff interacting continuously with other physical things. They also have personal histories, form relationships, live in communities, and participate in social and cultural practices. All of these observations are relevant, but none of them is adequate for the purpose of understanding what it means to be a self.

On the Peircean account being developed here, the self is constituted as a system of relationships. Each self is continuously relating itself to itself, but it is important to remember that this takes a distinctively semiotic form, as an ongoing process of self-interpretation, often in the pattern of a dialogue. Interpretation is not arbitrary, a free play of signifiers, one following another in an endless stream of semiosis. Rather, every person is also a "bundle of habits"—bodily habits, habits of movement and perception, habits of imagination, thought, feeling, and conduct—all exerting a gentle influence on the self-as-semiosis. Moreover, persons are to some degree constrained in their self-interpretations by all that they encounter in experience, everything to which they attend. Within the boundaries imposed by the world, by habits, and by others, the self is free to play any one of a variety of interpretive games. It is free, in the first place, to attend to this rather than to that element of experience (although at any given moment, many things will compete for its attention) and, in addition, to attach this meaning rather than another in the ongoing process of reading the signs encountered. Where habits are powerful and well-entrenched, and where the multivalence of signs is forcibly reduced by the stubborn quality of an experience that is rigidly determinate in form, this freedom to interpret will be limited. All of this changes over time.

The ability to change over time is how Peirce conceived of a freedom consisting in the exercise of self-control. In any given instant, the particular habits that shape a person will be more or less well established. At any isolated moment, that which a person encounters in experience will impose itself more or less forcefully, appearing vague enough to permit a number of possible interpretations or seeming adamantly to insist on one of them. Yet over time these factors can change dramatically, and the self can play a significant role in changing them. (On the first tasting, some food or beverage may be experienced as repugnant but over time and with retasting become valued as a delicacy.) For Peirce, this will primarily involve dispersing old habits and establishing new ones. On his account, self-control is a form of meta-cognition, of interpreting one's own habits of interpretation and of continuously imagining new possibilities for how they might be reformed. I can also work to alter or transform the objects that I encounter in experience, but in a much more limited fashion, for example, by gravitating toward or choosing to inhabit one kind of environment—supportive of a certain mode of self-interpretation and conducive for the cultivation of certain types of habits—rather than another one. This sort of freedom is limited only because much of what occurs in experience happens *willy nilly*, altogether independent of any choices that one makes. The sun rises and sets, the tide rolls in and out, lightning strikes, earthquakes rumble, that driver running a red light crashes his car into the passenger side of my own.

Extreme caution in analysis is required at this point. What occurs in experience may in some sense happen independently of my choosing, but the *meaning* of what occurs is not so rigidly fixed. To give just one theologically relevant example, that everyone dies is inevitable, but the meaning of one's death is a matter of interpretation, of the semiotic relationship that any given individual will have established to the event of dying. Consequently, to affirm that freedom consists in an ability to shape one's own habits over time is not to argue that one has some limited control over only the "subjective" factors determining human experience. Habits are not monadic qualities embedded in the self, but rather are dynamic relations established between self and world. Meaning, too, is a relationship, isolated neither within the self nor attached to objects in the world perceived as signs, but emerging continuously in the process of semiosis, occasionally degraded, but also typically growing over time.

Since the self must be portrayed not as existing here and now, once and for all, but best to be regarded as an emergent product of semiosis, to some degree it directs this process (especially by the way it pays attention and by means of a long-term project of habit formation) and yet is also the product of it. Thus, human "selving" is in some respects something achieved, a task for each individual, but in other respects selfhood appears as a gift, much as meaning in general is both created and discovered or received. Now to the degree that the self is something achieved, it will not be an accident, but rather a purposeful, or to use Peirce's preferred descriptor, a deliberate process. Habit formation occurs continually, to be sure, and often in ways about which one may be completely unaware. Yet insofar as it can be and is *self-controlled*, this process will involve a critical assessment of habits already established and the development of strategies for inculcating new ones that are deemed desirable. This "consciousness of taking a habit," a habit of habit change, is what Peirce referred to as "habituescence" (*MS* 930: 31). It is a form of meta-cognition that involves acting *on* one's habits rather than simply acting habitually.

None of this could ever occur minus the assumption that there are certain ideals, values, and purposes to which one can refer in order to facilitate habit formation. One has to have, consistent with such values and objectives, at least a vague picture of the sort of person that one hopes to become in the future. This is how self-control proceeds: with the present self, now reflecting critically on the past and exerting a gentle influence over future versions of itself according to some plan. Such a view of self-control is consistent with a Peircean portrayal of the self-as-semiosis, as the self at any moment is a sign mediating between past and future, determined by the past (and all of the habits already developed) but then determining a future self as its interpretant. Where ideals and purposes are operative, this process is not blind, and the "determination" is never a kind of brute efficient causality. Certain habits will be selected as being felicitous for given purposes. Their inculcation is typically a gradual process, and the influence that they exert over behavior is what Peirce often described as "gentle," a general tendency to behave in a certain sort of way under specific circumstances.

At the same time, no rigidly fixed picture of one's future self, no perfectly envisioned ideal, will bind the self to a single, narrow path of development. As the future becomes present, the perspective on one's ideals and purposes also inevitably shifts. Semiosis involves continuous growth in meaning. Every new interpretant is a sign that not only reshapes our understanding of the past but also gently determines new ways of envisioning the future. Purposes are continuously renewed, reconceived, become ever more nuanced, and take on new depth of meaning. My commitment to be a "good father" for my adult children is continuous with but nevertheless quite different in shape and substance from that commitment as it was first established when they were infants. This is what Peirce meant by a truly developmental teleology.

In the final stages of the evolution of his theory of signs, Peirce (as already indicated in Chapter 1's brief history) identified the "ultimate logical interpretant" of a sign with the specific habit or habit change in which any given stream of semiosis may eventuate. There is considerable scholarly disagreement about precisely how to interpret Peirce's mature theory. Nevertheless, for the theosemiotic project being sketched here, establishing a link between two different ways in which Peirce depicted the self—as a living symbol and as a cluster of habits—is especially crucial, and the implications of doing so will need to be explored. (A third Peircean ingredient that can be added to the mix is his characterization of "persons" and "personality" in terms of the special kind of teleology that he analyzed as developmental.)

The very word "legisign" already provides a link between these two conceptions of selfhood. It designates something that is at one and the same time a law *and* a sign, indeed, a sign whose very essence consists in its being a law. The self-as-legisign is a more or less well-coordinated system of habits, each of which has a law-like effect on how the self behaves, also on how it tends to think and feel, even on how and to whom it pays attention. What distinguishes the human self from other organisms that develop habits in response to environmental demands and changes is the purposefulness with which the former does so. Humans not only react to their environment, but also continuously reinterpret themselves.

That process of interpretation has been shown to take a narrative form, a story told about the self that requires constant editing in the light of various ideals and specific goals, also in response to new situations as they arise. In this respect, while the universe might very well be "perfused" with signs and semiosis, the human self-as-sign appears somewhat distinctive as an instance or example of *meta-semiosis*, a continuous relating of the self to itself in explicitly semiotic patterns. This selving process can be described, on Mead's account, as taking place within the context of an ongoing dialogue between the *I* and a *me*. Peirce, in addition to providing a similar account, also analyzed the self-as-meta-semiosis in terms of the "replication of self-control upon self-control" (*CP* 5.402, note 3), resulting in the ever more finely tuned coordination and development of a person's instincts and habits.

Interpretations and conversations may prove *not* to be purposeful, of course; they may *not* be governed by a person's ideals in a way that seems at odds with the observation that they ought to be self-controlled. Since selving is best understood as a project, it is most certainly one that can potentially fail, if not once and for all (that would be a rather drastic judgment!), certainly from time to time. Such an observation adds an implicit ethical dimension to any theory of the self while opening the door to an investigation of its possible religious significance, as well. Movement toward and through that doorway seems the appropriate direction in which any inquiry conceived as theosemiotic should now turn.

III

How is a portrayal of the self-as-semiosis pertinent to the task of understanding what Peirce regarded as the role that "God permits" human beings to have in the work of creation (*CP* 5.402)? Put less poetically, how would one begin to articulate a theological anthropology rooted in and so nourished by these particular semiotic resources? The discussion of theism in general and of Peirce's own brand of vague theism in particular are topics that I want to reserve for Chapter 3. Within that context, it will be pertinent to ask what it might mean to say that humans are created "in God's image" or (reversing the direction of this claim) to say with Peirce that God is best conceived as being somehow "vaguely like a man." Moreover, delineating the full significance of this idea of a semiotic self for understanding the nature and purpose of religious community is a topic that will also have to be postponed. Finally, this chapter began with the admission that even those less-radical claims about *homo symbolicus*—claims about how *natural* it is for humans to develop language, employ symbols, and create cultures, how all of human experience is interpreted experience—are clearly relevant to the goals of this inquiry and cannot be ignored.

Recognition of the possibility that any sign might come to embody religious meaning will require thinking about the sign's relationship both to some object that would render it religiously meaningful and to any interpretants that could be brought by the sign into a similar relationship with that object, and so further develop the meaning of the sign. In the case of a self-as-sign, it is also worth thinking about the peculiar nature of such a sign vehicle—its suitability for embodying a specifically religious meaning. That is to say, the self will not convey or communicate meaning in precisely the same way that many other signs regarded as religiously significant—statues, temples, ritual acts, historical events, scriptures, etc.—might tend to do. How does one "read" such a sign? To be sure, "religious meaning" is a vague enough concept that any discussion of how it could most effectively be embodied, conveyed, or interpreted will need to be suggestive rather than exhaustive.

Consider, first, Peirce's observation that "religion is a life, and can be identified with a belief only provided that belief be a living belief" (*CP* 6.439). Here it immediately becomes important to distinguish a "living" belief from a "dead" one. Peirce completed his observation with the gloss that such a belief is "a thing to be lived rather than said or thought." This was not an attempt to deny that speech can be a form of verbal behavior or to insist that there is no such thing as a "mental act." (Clearly we can *do* things with words—make a promise or hurl an insult, for example—just as there are ways of deliberately thinking that, following Edwards, we might be inclined to regard as "immanent acts of the soul.") It was an attempt, rather, to underscore the significance of those beliefs that actively and regularly shape human behavior, in all of its forms. One can articulate a certain belief and assent to it with genuine conviction, yet still be hard-pressed to explain how that belief has or could have a discernible impact on the way in which one conducts one's life. Peirce was well aware that there are a great number of religious beliefs that seem to be of this type. (Although I think his choice of the example was problematic, Peirce characterized the Roman Catholic doctrine of transubstantiation as such a belief. See *CP* 5.401; *W*3: 265–66.) Thus, in all respects that would make a difference to a pragmatist, they are essentially "dead." Consequently, the deadness of a belief might consist in the nature of the belief itself; in this case, whether such a belief was true or not could have no bearing, make no claim on the way that one lives one's life.

Yet it is also the case that a belief might be something that I affirm in speech or thought without giving any vital assent to it. In this latter case, it is not entirely clear that such an affirmation represents any kind of belief at all, since for Peirce, following Alexander Bain, the essence of a belief was its functioning like a habit, as being something upon which one would be prepared to act (*CP* 5.12). It might seem curious to put it this way, but one could attempt to save the notion of "dead belief" by simply observing that it is possible for me to be convinced that I believe something, but without *really* believing it. In this way it could very well function as a habit shaping how I might think or speak about myself, while at some deeper level having no real effect on my behavior; indeed, I may hold a quite contrary belief and be unaware of doing so. This is essentially a claim about the human capacity for self-deception, a pragmatic claim about how the inferences that we make about ourselves can be as mistaken as those that we make about others. My judgment about whether or not I am a racist,[37] or have a healthy sense of humor, or am jealous of a certain acquaintance may differ from your perspective on such matters; moreover, I may be wrong and you may be correct with regard to any of these judgments. The same could be true of many different kinds of belief. I may say that "I believe X" and you could reply, "No, you really do not believe it." The debate between us would not be one about what I *think* I believe, but more accurately (in Peirce's terms) about whether or not my belief is "dead" or "living."[38]

If "religion is a life," then it stands to reason that one's being religious cannot manifest itself all at once or in an instant but must display itself over time. Recall that a self is not just any kind of sign, but a complex one, and not any kind of static symbol, but one typically narrative in form. The self is a story that one tells, both to oneself and to others, about oneself and always in relation to those others. This is not to suggest that everything embodied in the stream of semiosis that constitutes a given person's life fits neatly or rigidly into the plot of some well-defined narrative. Many of the thoughts and feelings, even the observable actions, that are woven into the fabric of a human life may display themselves as utterly random. Their causes or motivations may be partially or entirely unconscious. In any story, furthermore, the plot can get twisted or unravel altogether. There are plots and subplots, some of which can seem to be disconnected from each other, some reaching a conclusion and others left altogether unresolved. Certain novelists are remarkably skillful at linking together, sometimes in a highly imaginative and creative fashion, the various threads of a narrative. All of this is to say that there can be good or bad stories, more or less coherent and purposeful. There can also be stories that are never played out in reality. The self is to some extent virtual, its meaning more than whatever can be actualized, so that "all his life long no son of Adam has ever manifested what there was in him" (*CP* 1.615).

What is the relevance of such observations for the development of a theosemiotic perspective? What is it that might give some human life, some self-as-story, a particularly *religious* meaning? In an important sense that should not require much explanation at this point, no such meaning will be found by focusing narrowly on the individual—on her thoughts, beliefs, actions, and experiences. The self as a complex symbol will signify multiple objects beyond itself. While taking the form of a manifold relation with itself, its meaning will also be dramatically shaped by its relationships with others. Consider Peirce's observation that the meaning of a self-sign is determined by whatever it attends to at a given moment in time. Over the course of time, meaning will grow as the result of a continuous series of acts of attention. This growth, its pace and direction, will be dramatically affected by the objects of one's attention. We can assume for theosemiotic purposes that the religious meaning of a life likewise will grow in a way proportionate to how one chooses—in each moment and gradually over time—to pay attention, both in terms of the object and the quality of attention. But I want to suggest here that this is only half of the picture that needs to be sketched for present theological purposes.

A great deal has been already said about how the meaning of a self is determined by that to which the self attends. It is important also to explore the ways in which meaning is shaped and communicated by one's having become the object of another person's attention. This is an argument for mutuality, analyzed here in explicitly semiotic terms. As a result of attention paid to parents, lovers, friends, teachers, mentors, role models, strangers, enemies, and so on, the meaning of my life is continuously and dramatically transformed. In turn, its meaning will be affected by all of the ways in which these others attend to me. This is an observation important for theosemiotic purposes and one that justifies more extended consideration (some here, but also in Chapter 3). In being interpreted by others, I am changed in fundamental ways; the meaning of my life is developed and extended, even apart from any sort of response that I might then make to the other who is "reading" me.

Thoreau once remarked that he had never met a man who was "quite awake"; otherwise, how could he have "looked him in the face?"[39] This remark hints at the great power that one can possess by exercising complete attention, but in this case the suggestion is that such a power can seem overwhelming to others. I might become quite uneasy as a result of the unwanted attention that someone else pays to me or by my becoming suddenly aware that I am the object of attention. Warriors squared off in combat will often try to intimidate each other by the way in which, without blinking or flinching, they fix their gaze. Yet even lovers will discover that looking deeply into each other's eyes can be sustained for only so long before it begins to seem just a bit uncomfortable. My inability to look someone in the face may signal something about how threatening their presence and attention have become, or it could be explained differently. No organism flourishes without the gentle love the sun shows to all things that live and grow, but who would not be blinded by its brilliance if they turned to confront it directly? This seems to be what Thoreau intended by his remark. How to explain it in semiotic terms?

On Peirce's account, adopted and adapted here, the meaning of a self-sign is shaped by whatever that person is attending to at any given point in time. The "denotation" of such a sign is constituted by the object of attention, but its "connotation" consists in everything that the self knows or feels about this object. Moreover, included among the many possible interpretants that a self-sign might determine is "another person he addresses." Note that the role played by attention in shaping semiosis is subtly complex. It is both a matter of direction, of *where* attention is focused, and of the *quality* of one's attention—in Peirce's terms, what one knows and feels about the object of one's attention. I would want, further, to blend Thoreau's insight with this analysis in order to propose that the quality of one's attention can also be measured in terms of whether or not it is more or less full ("quite awake"). It is a matter of the intensity as well as of the nature of what one feels in attending so that, for example, I might feel more or less attracted to or repulsed by the thing that I am contemplating.

Full intensity dramatically augments the meaning of a self-sign, a meaning that can easily be read by the one to whom such attention is directed. In my contemplation of another person, that person constitutes the object but can also become an interpretant of myself-as-sign; here the object of my attention is also a subject, the text also a reader. This is why the steadily loving gaze of a parent can help a child to flourish, while a lack of mindfulness can cause considerable anguish or pain. It is also why we can become offended by people who stare at us or listen in on our private conversations. In each case, the experience of being interpreted is itself discerned and evaluated, as the one interpreted now becomes the interpreter.

This account will have to be much more carefully developed and refined, but enough has been said already to suggest that, at least from the perspective of theosemiotic, the locus of human agency (as well as the rationale for imputing responsibility) will consist in just such a capacity for attention, both for directing attention and for shaping the quality of attention. This sort of freedom is circumscribed, never absolute, but it is a form of freedom nonetheless. In the discussion of theological inquiry that will follow here (primarily in Chapter 4), it will be shown how such agency is operative and decisive in the making of various kinds of inferences. Yet even before or apart from any engagement in theological inquiry proper, the self-as-semiosis is already immersed in a continuous stream of ongoing interpretive activity. Inference is ubiquitous (and often unconscious) in human experience. The self can by no means be reduced to those volitional acts over which it has some control. If the whole is a rushing stream of semiosis, Peirce knew that the conscious and controlling aspect of it, which he sometimes called the "ego," is but a "mere wave" in the vast ocean of the self (*CP* 1.112). To play with this metaphor just a bit, on such a view, the exercise of freedom is a bit like surfing. Whatever control the surfer has when she rides a wave is displayed as a form of highly skilled responsiveness to powerful forces that are largely unpredictable. Mastery involves a blending with rather than the manipulation of these forces. It is an achievement that occurs only after the long and careful development of certain habits, habits of attention to be sure, but also those that are inculcated as both fine and gross motor skills.

While continuing to embrace William James's insight that the essence of volition is attention, it might be useful to describe in more detail the vast ocean of forces that confront it—that is to say, all of the ways in which the exercise of will is circumscribed, limited . . . and thus empowered. This paradoxical way of speaking about the self's freedom is altogether necessary. After all, it is as impossible to surf without the ocean waves swelling beneath you as it is to dance unless somewhat constrained by the pull of gravity. But while the limits to freedom can give it shape, enabling and empowering human agency, they can also be stifling, sometimes crushing. The judgment about how to evaluate the effect of such limiting factors in any given situation will often be a religiously meaningful one, requiring a certain skill at discernment. (Of course, sometimes the difference between oppression and empowerment is just blatantly obvious.) In order for any such evaluation to be possible, however, the various types of forces that compete for and channel the self's attention need first to be identified.

Without insisting on too rigid a delineation of the self's boundaries, I suggest that some of these potencies appear clearly to be external. The possible meaning of any self-as-sign is delimited by its object, by whatever "determines" it at any given moment, so that the self cannot mean just whatever it chooses without bumping into the resisting presence of such objects (Peirce's "secondness").⁴⁰ Some of the environing factors that shape the meaning of the self—indeed a great many of the most important ones—will appear in the form of other selves, persons with whom one enters into dialogue, attending to them even while one is in various ways "fixed" by their attention. Everyone who participates in such an ongoing conversation plays the role of a reader; religious meaning, if there is any to discern, will emerge in this process of reading. If the "other" with whom such a dialogue occurs is perceived as being divine in nature or as mediating something sacred, then this reading becomes a *lectio divina* and can take the form of prayer.

In addition to all of the external objects that constrain interpretation, the interpretive self will need to wrestle with a variety of forces that operate internally. Even those objects in an environment that seem most to warrant one's attention—indeed, they may even compete quite vigorously for it—tend to be ignored if there are powerful habits directing the self's attention elsewhere. (This observation should help to explain how the gorilla on an elevator can go undetected.⁴¹ It is also the key to understanding Peirce's insight that those facts that "stare us in the face" are sometimes not readily discerned.) These habits typically operate below the level of consciousness, although by acts of reflection they can to some extent be made conscious and become explicit. In addition, a vast array of thoughts and feelings typically or presently hidden from awareness may bubble into consciousness and suddenly become the objects of contemplation. Here too (as William James suspected) there may be an avenue of access to what is religiously meaningful.

Among all of these factors, both external and internal to the semiotic self, the most important to discuss for the argument being developed here are those habits of attention that can either prevent or facilitate the recognition of religious meaning. If Peirce was correct, then that self just *is* a bundle of habits, on my account, a complex legisign that purposefully weaves a narrative about itself in conversation with both itself and others. This storytelling is guided by a plan (albeit one that continuously develops) that conforms to certain ideals (perhaps only vaguely understood). All of the habits that constitute the self are to some extent malleable, capable of being modified, eliminated, or replaced. Even those tendencies that Peirce regarded as instinctive are to some extent capable of development (by a process that he described as "slow percolation"; see *RLT*: 121–22). Yet the present argument will underscore the special significance of habits of attention. Self-control as meta-semiosis consists primarily in the development and regulation of such habits. The suggestion here is that they often function as *meta-habits,* influencing the formation, dissolution, and adaptation of more determinate habits of thought, feeling, and behavior. The discipline required for such a purpose can be understood in certain contexts as an explicitly religious discipline, embodied and enacted in a variety of spiritual exercises of the kind in which religious practitioners frequently engage. The goal here is to portray such exercises in multiple ways: on the one hand, as the "replication of self-control upon self-control," a deliberate process that Peirce regarded as being constitutive of the self's gradual development; on the other hand, as exercises relevant to the task of interpretation, acts of reading again or rereading (*relegere*).

If agency is located primarily in the acts of attention that guide the continuous rereading of the self's story, the *identity* of the self consists in the unity of that narrative as it unfolds. As with agency, identity is shaped by a complex variety of factors, many of them the same ones that both circumscribe and enable a person's freedom. When Tennyson's Ulysses announced, "I am a part of all that I have met," he articulated from one angle of vision the Peircean insight that lies at the heart of theosemiotic. From another angle, all those others who are "met" become part of the self who encounters them, the story about these interactions gradually revealing the self's identity. The plot of this story is sometimes messy, sometimes neat. The memory of these others can be painful or can bring joy. Some encounters will be more prominent in consciousness, with others only dimly remembered or perhaps even forgotten. Yet "even memory is not necessary for love."[42] The shaping influence of someone else's love upon the self can have an effective history within the self's narrative, even in those cases where it is not consciously remembered.

The relationship between love, attention, and volition will form part of the subject matter of Chapter 3. At present, the primary topic of concern is the semiotic nature of the self. A careful reading of Peirce has suggested that his characterization of the self as a bundle of habits, combined with his identifying of personality with a certain kind of purposefulness, both complement his remarkable analysis of the self-as-semiosis. One final characterization, mentioned earlier, but needing to be recovered now, is of the self-as-vicinity, not as a single, determinate entity but as a "cluster." To underscore this picture of the self is to continue to insist on its porous nature, on its reality as an elaborate system of relations, not reducible to any of the many things thus related. None of this is to suggest, however, that the idea of the self as a legisign is problematic or that it needs drastically to be amended. As a legisign, the self is a law—actually a complex body of legislation. It enacts itself through the inculcation, development, and coordination of specific habits working together in order gently to rule the way that the self attends, feels, thinks, and acts. As a living, personal legisign, the self frames its laws and shapes its character in a manner that is purposeful, albeit not in any rigid or mechanical sense. From the angle of vision supplied by certain religious conceptions, among the most important purposes that guide the self are love's purposes, among the enduring habits that form its essence, a certain habit of love (perhaps conceived as *caritas*, perhaps as *karuna*, perhaps otherwise). Finally, a legisign, like any sign, is related to a myriad of objects that it signifies and to a plethora of interpretants (including some that may exist only *in futuro*), none of which are purely external to it, but all of which partially constitute its meaning as a being-in-relation. That meaning is emergent, always in process, partially realized in the present, while also being constantly deferred.

In noting once again this deferral of meaning to some future time, do we lay the proper foundations for a theology of hope while following Peirce's lead in conceiving of the self's immortality explicitly in semiotic terms (*W* 1.500–1)? What of the possibility that some stream of semiosis might be broken off, end abruptly, with no meaning deferred, no possibility of determining any additional interpretants, either immediate or ultimate? Moreover, what of the further possibility, invoked earlier, that the semiotic sign is always more than just a sign, much like the particular book lying before us to be read is also leather binding and paper and ink marks on a page, a vehicle for meaning whose reality is not exhausted by what we read. What book lover has ever failed to appreciate the size and heft of books, their wonderful smell either old and faded or fresh and new, from a distance as they sit within a row full of others on a shelf, the distinctive color or pattern displayed on their binding . . . in short, their radiant suchness? Is our relationship to these particular aspects of a thing in any way a semiotic relationship, or even possibly one, or rather is it a decisive marking of the limits of semiosis?[43] We will keep revisiting this question until we feel at last that we may be stumbling toward some kind of answer, however dimly perceived.

Remaining within the more limited but nevertheless capacious field of phenomena that semiotic theory describes, the attempt here has been to show how the reality of the self can be illuminated by following Peirce in conceiving of it as a sign. It is distinctive among other signs in the way that it also plays the role of an active reader, not just of a world perfused with signs, but also of itself as the embodiment of an intricate and evolving narrative. The self, moreover, presents itself to others as something/someone to be read. Its meaning cannot be exhausted by what it consciously hopes and remembers, because that meaning is to some extent constituted by the hopes and memories of others. Likewise, its meaning will be shaped not only by how the self attends but by all of the ways in which *it itself* becomes the object of attention. Relationship to others will often consist in such mutuality of attention. In addition, it can consist in the "joint attention" that persons direct to a shared interest or cause, to a particular belief or ideal, to some common object of devotion.[44] These modes of relationship should not be sharply contrasted. It is possible to move easily and frequently back and forth between the encounter with other persons and the consideration of what those persons are contemplating, so that there can be a dialectical relationship between mutual and joint attention. A fully adequate theosemiotic analysis will need to balance an emphasis on each person's agency in establishing both the unity and the identity of the self through the exercise of attention and devotion to certain purposes, with an insistence that each person's character is *essentially* social and relational. If Peirce, Royce, and Mead were correct, I learn what it means to be *this* self only through my interactions with others. I am constituted by them, individuated by their attending to me, before I can even really begin to tell a story about myself.[45]

This lengthy and (for reasons that I hope are justified) sometimes torturous analysis of selfhood was intended to unpack some of the implications and to evaluate the significance of a semiotic portrayal of the self—most specifically, as a living legisign. What it means to be a "legisign" has to some extent been explained. The importance of its being "living" has received less consideration. So perhaps a very brief remark about that topic can serve to mark a proper transition between this discussion and what is to follow. Recall Peirce's assertion that "religion is a life." The self-as-semiosis functions as a legisign, and any given sign will be capable of some growth in meaning. To underscore its status as living, however, is to emphasize the self's capacity for meta-semiosis, the role that it performs as a continuous reader of itself in relation to a world of signs. Lacking the capacity to play this role, the self would be largely habit-bound, its meaning more or less static or fixed (much like the meaning of a word might change with time and context, but is relatively stable). It is in such acts of reading/rereading that the religious significance of the self will be shown primarily to consist, with the unique blending of creativity, receptivity, and repetition in such acts being the key to understanding more clearly why this is so.

3 / Love in a Universe of Chance

I

Contingency, competition, and indifference are all prominent features of the Darwinian worldview that dramatically transformed Western thought in the second half of the nineteenth century. What is the chance that love could ever arise in a world thus conceived? Love is something experienced by human beings as a way that humans and (insofar as we are aware) only humans respond and relate to others perceived as beloved. Must all of these others be subjects, other persons or selves, in order for talk about love in such instances to make any real sense? Is the love that might be reported in various alternative instances (such as love for a particular place or possession or the love of art or music) to be understood in a strictly metaphorical sense? Does the human experience of love display a teleology that underscores its potentially religious significance? Following upon the consideration of such questions, one might then be inclined to ask: Is some conception of *theos*, of a personal deity, necessarily central to our understanding of theosemiotic as a meaningful form of inquiry?

A negative answer to this last question may seem to be ruled out etymologically and in advance of any serious consideration of its merits. When Augustine famously asked, "What do I love when I love my God?," only the precise identity of his beloved and not the fact of its existence seemed shrouded in mystery.[1] Nevertheless, Augustine did formulate the question with a "What" rather than a "Who"; moreover, the *telos* of his love might be judged as fictional or illusory rather than real. In any event, here it will be argued that the possibility of genuine theological reflection being pursued without a presupposition of the truth of theism ought to be considered as a real one. Such a possibility extends to include not only the sort of reflection that occurs within the context of atheistic traditions typically classified as religious (e.g., Jainism and certain forms of Buddhism), but also to certain strands of thought that, while rooted in classical theism, have eventuated in modern and postmodern announcements of the "death of God." Moreover, the emergence and development of various forms of religious naturalism as viable alternatives to theism in contemporary philosophy and theology suggest that a concern about deity may not be essential to the task of theosemiotic. So while the religious significance of our experience of love will need to be evaluated here,[2] its nature probed and clarified by utilizing semiotic resources that seem useful for that purpose, the necessity of God-talk as a way of making sense out of why and what we love will be left open to question. That question will by no means be ignored, but such a necessity will have to be argued for rather than simply presupposed.

Charles Peirce, for his own part, was convinced that a vague idea of the reality of God would arise naturally for anyone who engaged (in a proper manner and for a sufficient period of time) in the practice of musing on the origin and nature of the universe. After extended consideration of that idea, Peirce suggested, the muser would almost inevitably be inclined to fall in love with "his strictly hypothetical God" (*CP* 6.467). Josiah Royce followed Peirce rather closely here, announcing that "love, when it comes, comes as from above," declaring the necessity that one should have first "fallen in love with the universe" in order then to be bound in genuine relationships of love to other members of a human community.[3] The vagueness of their conceptions of the Deity may be considered relevant for understanding such assertions and will need to be carefully measured here. But note immediately how such thinking about God was perfectly continuous for them with the contemplation of nature, focusing most especially on its beauty, ideality, and purposefulness (as growth). Indeed, there is good reason to suspect that many of the individuals already identified in this study's brief history were religious naturalists—at least in the broad sense of regarding the "book of nature" as a primary locus of religious meaning—whose naturalism took the form of an objective idealism, with this idealism in turn providing some of the rationale for the vague theism to which they were also committed.[4]

Peirce acknowledged the prestige of Charles Darwin's theory of evolution, and his own philosophy of nature clearly registered its significance. Yet he hardly endorsed that theory without critique, accepting the importance for evolution of chance variations in nature by developing his doctrine of "tychism," but seriously delimiting the role played by natural selection in these same evolutionary processes.⁵ Instead, the Darwinian principle that leaves nature "red in tooth and claw" is replaced on Peirce's account by the gentle law of love. The claim that fierce competition is the motor driving evolution is supplanted by the belief in a spiritual force drawing all things into harmony with itself.⁶ Nowhere else do religious insights and scientific ideas seem to merge so seamlessly as they do within the context of Peirce's theory of agapism, or evolutionary love.

Peirce's 1893 *Monist* essay on this topic begins with a meditation on the opening verses of the Gospel of John. The meaning of John's claim that "God is love" is best exposed on Peirce's view by reading it against the Swedenborgian backdrop supplied by Henry James Sr. in his *Substance and Shadow: An Essay on the Physics of Creation*.⁷ In passages that Peirce is all too eager to announce as having disclosed "for the problem of evil its everlasting solution," James concluded that the creative love of God "must be reserved for that which is most bitterly hostile and negative to itself" (*CP* 6.287; *W*8: 185). Consideration of such passages prompted Peirce's own conclusion that "the movement of love is circular, at one and the same impulse projecting creations into independency and drawing them into harmony" (*CP* 6.288; *W*8: 185). Both phases of this movement, the affirming of the beloved in its otherness and the drawing of what is perceived as separate or independent "into harmony," merit careful theo-semiotic scrutiny.

It is also important to underscore the observation that almost immediately follows Peirce's poetic tracing of the circle of love when he reports that "love is not directed to abstractions but to persons"—indeed, not just to any persons, but to "our family and neighbors," with the latter being identified as those most "near" to us, not necessarily in space, "but in life and feeling." Such persons will form the group of individuals, as Peirce suggested elsewhere, with whom one feels most to be in "sympathetic communion" (*CP* 6.271; *W*8: 182). This observation potentially sheds some light, not only on the complex rationale for Peirce's theism, but also on how he understood the basic relationships that constitute human communities. Consider the latter first.

If there is anything like a "logic" of community, it could be delineated by emphasizing those commitments that the individuals in any given community might be supposed to share—commitments to certain beliefs, goals, interests, practices, values, ideals, and so forth. Individuals would then be defined as members of a community in terms of what they share in common, much like a logical *class* is defined by a character that is possessed by all of the members of that class. (All men are mortal. All of the marbles in this bag are white. All planets in the solar system revolve around the sun.) *Sameness* would thus be the salient criterion allowing one to identify those individuals who belong to a specific community; homogeneity and a solidarity best manifested in the form of consensus would be the features one might expect a community to display.

Now, one of the key insights articulated by Peirce in his development of the logic of relations—an insight that will be exploited at numerous points in the inquiry being pursued here—is that this relationship of sameness or similarity is only one of many possible types of relation that ought to interest the philosopher—that is to say, logical *systems* deserve as much or more scrutiny than that typically given to various classes of things (see *CP* 4.5; *RLT*: 156). Such a system is constituted by relationships very different from the one identified when we say that "X is the same kind of thing as Y and Z." Two examples that Peirce often referred to are the systems identified when we observe that "X is a lover of Y" or "X gives Y to Z." Here Peirce's primary logical interest was not in the similarity between various lovers or givers or gifts, nor in the act of comparing multiple instances of each of them in order properly to place them in some general class of things. Instead, he sought to analyze the system that defines two persons as lover and beloved, or the one that encompasses givers, gifts, and recipients—thus, in the purposes and habits of behavior that shape and determine their interactions. Preoccupation with the monadic predicate that designates the various members of a class is now superseded by a concern with the dyadic and triadic predicates that define systems. The relationship of generality (in the scholastic sense of a character or quality that is shared by many) is exposed as only one very limited form in which real *continuity* can be conceived.[8]

All relations are both continuous and real on Peirce's view, their reality by no means exhausted by or reducible to the specific things brought into relationship. In a world permeated with signs, semiosis is one especially important, virtually ubiquitous mode of relationship. Meaning emerges in the interaction between sign, object, and interpretant. To insist that meaning is the property or the character of a particular sign or sign vehicle would be to regard such meaning as a monadic predicate. Moreover, while it might allow one to compare that sign vehicle with others that resemble it, such a restricted view of meaning would be most unhelpful for understanding the specifically semiotic relation that exists between a sign and either its object or its interpretant; nor would it illuminate the relationship between object and interpretant that every sign helps to establish. Insofar as selves are signs, the selves that make up any given community could be analyzed, once again, in terms of those respects in which they are homogeneous, signifying the same things, or bound to one another by the power of some consensus. For theosemiotic purposes, this would be a dangerously impoverished way of understanding human community, not least of all making it difficult to understand how the very fabric of such a community might consist in some kind of mutual loyalty or love. While such a loyalty or love will also help to create solidarity among the members of a community, it will not be as a result of an enforced consensus or a demand for homogeneity.

In perhaps an even more pronounced fashion than on Peirce's view, for Royce love-as-loyalty was a golden thread woven throughout the universe; indeed, the universe is coextensive with an unlimited community of interpretation, formed and sustained by a love that manifests itself as the "will to interpret."[9] Both philosophers were semiotic realists; they envisioned the world as abundant with signs and conceived of the relationship between different signs as having a reality independent of what any given interpreter or collection of interpreters might posit as such, while also being irreducible to the reality of the things related. Both philosophers gave to love a primordial status among all other relationships, with agapism providing for Peirce the only satisfactory account of how the cosmos has evolved, and with love's teleology for Royce pointing inexorably to the eventual establishment of a Beloved Community. These were religiously significant ideas, carefully wed to certain metaphysical convictions on both accounts, with the added support in at least Peirce's case of evidence drawn from what he called the "special sciences." How idiosyncratic, yet also how plausible, should one regard such a way of thinking about the world?

The plausibility of any hypothesis affirming the primordial status of relationships of love in the universe, it should not be surprising, is difficult to assess. To begin with, one must recognize the extraordinary vagueness of such a hypothesis. One should also anticipate the challenge that will come from those who insist, in neo-Darwinian fashion, that we live in a universe of chance, the reality of love having emerged (insofar as we can judge) in only a tiny pocket of interhuman relationships within that universe. The cause of that emergence, moreover, is not some divine agent with benevolent intentions, but only the serendipity of a cosmic history, utterly indifferent, unfolding without plot or meaning.[10] To propose, furthermore, that the universe is populated with signs, that human selves are best conceived as living legisigns, and that the proper object of human love must consist in something that can be characterized as "personal"—all of these must be evaluated as highly speculative proposals that ought clearly to be regarded as contentious.

The clear recognition that these *are* proposals, it seems to me, is the best way to save them for further consideration, as *hypotheses*, much like the hypothesis about God's reality that Peirce sketched in his Neglected Argument. The burden for theosemiotic lies not in the need to demonstrate their truth (a burden that no pragmatist should rush to embrace), but instead, in making a convincing case for their being *live* rather than dead hypotheses. Assuming any progress could be made in accomplishing the latter, then simply to reject them as unworthy of attention would be nothing more than to block the road of inquiry.

Agapism was clearly not a theory the application of which was intended by Peirce to be restricted to human communities or interhuman relationships. It was designed, rather, to explain the evolution of the cosmos, as indicated earlier, to do the same kind of intellectual work that the principle of natural selection was expected to perform within Darwin's theory. In the essay on "Evolutionary Love," agape is sharply contrasted with that Darwinian principle, the latter being portrayed as a theoretical embodiment of the "gospel of greed" (*CP* 6.294; *W*8: 189). That growth might occur instead because of the gentle force exerted by a loving sympathy, that the power of love in a universe of chance, rather than the stimulus of vigorous competition for essential but limited resources, might best explain the fact and course of evolution—these are the hypotheses that Peirce defended in his *Monist* essay. Three observations are noteworthy here.

In the first place, despite both the primordial and enduring reality of contingency and chance in the universe, Peirce does not portray the evolving cosmos in its earliest stages simply as "random stuff," but rather as "slumbering" mind or consciousness (*CP* 6.198, 221). The argument for love as a key evolutionary principle will be perceived as making considerably more sense than otherwise within the metaphysical context of an objective idealism like that defended by Edwards, Emerson, Peirce, and Royce. Of course, one might choose to reject this argument as implausible on the grounds that such a metaphysics is quaint and outdated, of interest only to historians curious about exploring intellectual trends in the nineteenth century. But that would also involve a choice to ignore the fact that various forms of idealism, panpsychism, and dipolar monism have continued to be defended as plausible options by philosophers in both the twentieth and twenty-first centuries.[11] It is important, in any event, to recognize that Peirce understood love to consist in a certain kind of *reasonableness* working itself out in the world. This is why the world can be perceived not only as a "great poem," but also as a kind of "argument" (*CP* 5.119). Reasonableness rules over "all other powers . . . with its scepter, knowledge, and its globe, love" (*CP* 5.520). Love is the way that mind develops (*CP* 6.289; *W*8: 185–86) and also the way that meaning grows. Whether one refers to this perspective as objective idealism or semiotic realism (my preference), ultimately, both love and mind need to be conceived as forms of semiosis.

A second observation redirects our attention to Peirce's claim that love must have a "person" as its proper object, a claim already briefly explored in order to evaluate its significance for our understanding of community, but also mentioned as relevant for assessing the plausibility of theism. This assessment will be ongoing, but the mere fact that love occurs at all in a universe of chance—moreover, that it might constitute a natural response for human beings to such a universe—suggested to both Peirce and Royce that something at least vaguely personal was to be discerned at the very heart of nature.[12] (The "rules" that might be thought to govern and discipline such a process of discernment will need to be delineated with some care.)[13]

Third, and perhaps most crucially, natural selection supplies a hypothetical explanation for how particular organisms might evolve through adaptation to the exigencies that arise in a specific environmental niche. Yet the universe as a whole has no environment. There is nothing beyond itself to which it needs to adapt or within which it might be said to evolve.[14] The principle of its development must be somehow internal to the process of evolution, a creative connection between ideas, as Peirce described it in this series of essays, the law of mind now also conceived as the gentle law of love. It is the continuous connection of one idea with another, the gradual spreading of ideas thus connected, that best accounts for the real growth of meaning in the universe. As Peirce's summary statement of this "law" stipulates, any given idea will lose intensity during such a process of growth while nevertheless becoming more general and so capable of affecting other ideas (*CP* 6.104; *W*8:136). Both of these results, loss of intensity and increase in generality, invite further consideration and analysis.

One way to proceed with such a task, however odd it might seem at first blush, would be to think about how this gentle law of love could help to explain one's experience of reading and then rereading a specific text. Suppose that I "fall in love" with a book that I have just read. (In order to pursue this thought-experiment, I am simply assuming that even if it were decided that such a love must be understood metaphorically, the result of the experiment could still be illuminating.) For any number of reasons, some explicable and others not completely apparent, if someone were to ask me for my list of "favorite books," this one would now be ensconced firmly at the top of the list. Given its favored status, I am motivated to reread it, not just once but on several occasions. After a number of encounters, the reading experience may lose a little bit of its flavor, but in each instance I would probably notice something new about the book, make connections—intratextual, intertextual, or between the text and my experience of the world—that had not been made previously. It might be possible—perhaps because of a long gap between readings, or because of having read something else, or because of an experience that I had in the interim—that when I reread the book on one particular occasion, I have an especially powerful experience, falling in love with it all over again. That a certain level of jading is inevitable as a result of frequent rereading certainly does not preclude the possibility of such a renewal of interest and enthusiasm at some future point in time. This is no mere recovery or repetition of an experience that has already occurred. The growth that results with the spread of ideas, their increase in generality, facilitates new insight, novel connections, fresh ideas. At least some of the *habits* of interpretation developed in the practice of reading may function as interpretive *skills* that make possible the discovery of some meaning that was previously inaccessible.

Now suppose we repeat this thought-experiment with a number of different variations in order to test the plausibility of my prediction. Substitute for a lengthy book one's favorite film or a poem where, in either case, the likelihood of "rereading" might be greater. Spacing will be important in terms of the perceived loss or growth in meaning (how much time has elapsed between one reading and the next) and the manner in which the experience is framed (under which conditions or in what particular context does each reading occur).[15] Invoking an explicitly religious context, suppose one were to perform the same experiment with a scriptural text. That "love is as strong as death"[16] is a biblical declaration that may be deeply moving on first reading, maybe less so on subsequent rereadings, but then can take on a whole new level of significance when it becomes incorporated into the funeral liturgy for one's deceased beloved.

Such observations suggest that this law of mind, one that correlates the loss of intensity with a concomitant increase in generality as ideas spread, needs to be reformulated for our purposes, albeit in a way that Peirce would very likely find unobjectionable. Growth in meaning includes the possibility of fresh insight, renewed intensity—not merely the accumulation of additional bits of information, but movement to an entirely different level or depth of meaning. Habits formed in rereading can dull sensibilities in the short run but might also in the long run generate reading skills that yield new, different, or more nuanced interpretations. The law of mind is clearly a principle governing semiosis. And where growth of meaning takes place, Peirce also wanted to discern the gentle influence of love, whether at the level of individuals conceived as living symbols, of communities embracing many individuals, or of the cosmos itself as a great "argument" gradually unfolding in time, working itself out in living realities (*CP* 5.119).

If we turn our attention to other forms of reading, not the reading of poems or novels, but rather of other persons as living legisigns, the thought-experiment sketched might take a dramatically different form. In the first place, there are persons (family, friends, colleagues) with whom we almost continuously interact, so that the "gap" between our various readings of who they are and what they mean is not very great at all. This suggests that the possibility of boredom or jading in such relationships is significantly greater than in the type of case explored earlier. It also suggests that the potential for achieving greater depth of insight or meaning is proportionately greater; that is to say, "falling in love all over again" with a person of long acquaintance is likely to be a more compelling experience than discovering some new depth of meaning in a book that I am now reading for the fourth or fifth time.

Growth in meaning is a process of both habit formation and habit dissolution, thus, as Peirce indicated in identifying the ultimate logical interpretant of any sign, essentially a matter of *habit change*. From the theological perspective being developed here, I want to suggest that the development of a well-established habit of love is what any person conceived as a sign should ultimately come to *mean*, in relation not only to other persons but to the entire universe of signs. Since I am also arguing that love is volitional in nature, a certain kind and quality of attention, it will necessarily follow that the love being described here manifests itself as a certain *habit of attention*. The person who truly embodies the sort of *agape* that Peirce portrayed—not only as the exemplification of an ethical ideal but more broadly as the manifestation of a fundamental evolutionary principle—will be disposed in a certain distinctive fashion, "fully awake," not just on this or that occasion, but as a consistent way of being toward others and in the world.

Such a disposition, its mode of formation, and the sort of behavior that might supply evidence of its operative presence will need to be scrutinized with considerable care. At this point, it must suffice to observe the relationship between discrete acts of loving attention and the cultivation of such a habit. Peirce talked about "falling in love" with the God revealed as author of the book of nature, but having an experience of this sort does not occur as a completely serendipitous event. The argument to be made here is that it takes time and considerable practice, the development of a certain skillfulness, the path to its occurrence perhaps consisting just a bit less in solitary exercise than Peirce's description of musement may have tended to suggest. To be sure, love is a phenomenon that can be described in terms of Peirce's category of firstness, as one might tend to do precisely in the case of trying to make sense out of the initial experience of falling in love; such an experience manifests itself as the sudden awareness of some quality or qualities in one's beloved. Moreover, love displays its secondness insofar as it is directed to some "other," and also insofar as it is perceived to involve discrete acts of volition. Nevertheless, in its fullest sense love must be recognized as a matter of thirdness: a drawing of what was once separate into living harmony, the achievement of real mutuality, so that love is never reducible to a single feeling or action, but rather best displays itself as an enduring habit of love.

That love is also a form of semiosis is a conclusion strongly indicated by the analysis as it has unfolded up until this point. In order to press that analysis a bit further, it now becomes important to supplement Peirce's logic of relations with a brief account of his logic of vagueness. In the first place, "love" is a word that is itself notoriously vague. Moreover, to the extent that persons can be conceived as signs, it will have to be admitted that their "meaning" must also be quite vague. Finally, it is only against the background of his logic of vagueness that both Peirce's defense of anthropomorphism and his commitment to theism will come into fuller relief and begin to make sense.

II

The belief that all signs and symbols are to some extent necessarily vague is linked in Peirce's thought to his synechism, his metaphysical conviction that all of reality is continuous. Indeed, both fallibilism and the logic of vagueness can be regarded as the flip side of a philosophical coin that bears on its surface the imprint of Peirce's elaborate metaphysics and mathematics of the continuum. This logic of vagueness is also in certain important respects a "logic of dialogue."[17] Conversation, whether it unfolds between two persons or within one person in the form of an inner dialogue—as Peirce, Royce, and Mead all understood the essential nature of thinking—involves the ongoing process of rendering vague signs ever more determinate. (At least this is the case if the conversation under scrutiny displays some kind of purpose or teleology, rather than being idle chatter or, in the case of a solitary person, deliberate thought rather than foggy daydreaming.) The limits of this process also constitute the limits of semiosis. No sign can be perfectly determinate in every respect. And some signs are so vague and powerful that even to delineate their meaning in great detail and with considerable nuance would still leave a great mass of significance completely unexposed. Important religious symbols, it will be suggested here, are of this latter type.

Such symbols represent a special interpretive challenge for anyone engaged in theosemiotic inquiry. To ignore this challenge is to risk a long list of theological dangers, framed by fundamentalism or idolatry on one end of the spectrum, with the collapse into either fideism or vacuous nonsense at the other. Vulnerability to the first type of risk stems directly from a failure to appreciate—or perhaps a refusal to admit—the vagueness of religious signs and symbols, rendering their meaning more precise and so more limited than what is warranted by careful interpretation. At the opposite extreme, a sign considered to be completely vague and so indeterminate in every respect would have no meaning at all—in effect, would be a sign of nothing.

This last claim needs to be carefully qualified. There *is* a peculiar sense in which one could indeed conceive of "nothing" as being the proper object of some religious symbol. Such a way of thinking about the ultimate reality is typical of the perspective articulated in certain schools of mystical theology, not only the mysticism of nontheistic traditions like Daoism or Zen Buddhism, but also in Judaism, Christianity, and Sufi Islam. Yet this admission presupposes that not all concepts of "nothing" can have the same meaning, so that symbols with such a reference may be vague but nevertheless will be partially determinate in meaning. These religious symbols, one might argue, are intended to direct attention to a divine reality improperly conceived as *simply* nothing, but rather, best understood as a mysterious something, a reality that, in its infinite plenitude, cannot be conflated with this or that particular thing. "God," "Brahman," "the Dao," or any reality conceived as ultimate in this fashion should be regarded as nothing in the sense of being "no-determinate-thing." This is a concept of divine nothingness potentially loaded with meaning, precisely because it is so extraordinarily vague.

Theosemiotic will be genuinely apophatic to the extent that it marks the limits of semiosis and recognizes the extreme vagueness of certain powerful religious symbols. Such an apophaticism, however, must be securely grounded in the Scotistic doctrine of the univocity of being, properly understood, and embraced for precisely the reasons that Duns Scotus formulated and defended that doctrine in the first place. The incomprehensibility of something ultimate or divine (assuming, hypothetically, that there is such a reality) is by no means compromised by the claim that there must be some sense in which both it and all other realities can be said to "be." For Duns Scotus, this was the very barest of senses, revealing nothing about how one might then further conceive of a truly infinite reality, "intensively infinite," because possessing all of its properties to a maximal degree. Scotus clearly did not deny that much of our religious discourse is analogical. Yet without the affirmation of this one univocal sense in which all realities, infinite or finite, are claimed to "be," no knowledge or meaningful talk about God would be possible whatsoever.[18] As a result, and following Scotus's lead, any theosemiotic perspective conceived as apophatic will underscore the vagueness of signs and symbols, while nevertheless affirming this doctrine of univocity, thus avoiding a collapse into meaninglessness. (Peirce himself, despite his keen interest in scholastic philosophy, was not preoccupied with medieval debates about analogy, but his synechistic insistence on the *continuity* of all things, combined with his logic of vagueness, suggests that he would find merit in something like Scotus's position.)

Now it is important to observe here that Peirce's understanding of vagueness rubs against certain philosophical discussions of the same subject matter. The vagueness of specific terms, as they are used in the discourse associated with particular pursuits and purposes, can be regarded as troublesome, even as a serious obstacle to be overcome. I suspect that one of the most frequent critical comments that college instructors supply as feedback to student essays is that the argument or analysis in this or that instance is simply "too vague." In our ordinary, everyday conversations the vagueness of what someone communicates to us can be the source of great misunderstanding. We quickly become suspicious or irritated, when pressing someone for his opinion about a significant issue, if his replies are consistently and stubbornly vague.

As a philosopher and logician, Peirce was committed to the goal of achieving the greatest clarity and precision possible in one's discourse, even displaying a penchant for inventing new terms so as to avoid the vagueness attached to old words that carry multiple meanings. Yet he agreed with Aristotle that one ought not to be more precise than any subject matter allows—that to do so arbitrarily can in fact result in a serious distortion of meaning.[19] To take as just one example the principal subject matter of the present chapter, "love" is a notoriously vague term with a great breadth and depth of meaning. That meaning varies with varying contexts and relationships; what one means when one talks about loving dark chocolate may be loosely related but also will be quite different from what one means when one talks about the love that defines a marriage or friendship or about the love of God. One can simply stipulate, of course, that "love" means something quite determinate, ruling out all other possible shades of meaning, just like one might decide that a "tall person" is anyone six feet tall or greater as determined by the most advanced technology for measurement. Yet in doing so, the greater precision that one would be insisting on for terms like "love" or "tall" would add nothing to our knowledge of the phenomena that we use them to describe. Indeed, this arbitrarily enforced precision would actually make these words far less useful for a great variety of purposes. Here, once again, an attentiveness to the vagueness of terms or symbols actually saves rather than sacrifices meaning.

The observed notoriety of the word "love" as a vague term will be matched or exceeded by the use of the word "God" (or any word that could be plausibly translated as such) within multiple cultures and contexts, spanning across various traditions and historical time periods. Hardly a cause of consternation, this is a conclusion that Peirce recognized and in fact chose to celebrate (while at the same time scolding Josiah Royce for failing to do so properly). His logic of vagueness, along with his endorsement of a certain species of "anthropomorphism," supplies the background against which one might best begin to understand his claim that there cannot be "a more adequate way" of understanding the cause or creator of the universe "than as vaguely like a man" (CP 5.536).

Now, for contemporary philosophical naturalists, even for those who would identify themselves as "religious naturalists," Peirce's anthropomorphism will most likely represent a peculiar and troubling doctrine, a serious stumbling block for anyone who otherwise would be inclined to embrace his philosophy. Yet I want to argue forcefully that anthropomorphism *just is* the form in which Peirce's naturalism most comfortably presents itself, concomitant with both his objective idealism and his evolutionary theory.[20] And so while it has been frequently ignored or misunderstood by Peirce scholars—also at the risk of causing anyone committed to philosophical naturalism to become a bit uncomfortable—it is important to make some sense out of Peirce's anthropomorphism.

On Peirce's view, the claim "that a conception is one natural to man" can readily be translated into the judgment "that it is anthropomorphic" (CP 5.47). Indeed, "anthropomorphic is what pretty much all conceptions are at bottom." Moreover, to label an idea as anthropomorphic is "as high a recommendation as one could give to it in the eyes of an Exact Logician." As Peirce indicated in his correspondence with William James, while others might be inclined to categorize pragmatism as a form of "humanism" (and here he had the British pragmatist F. C. S. Schiller clearly in mind), he preferred the word "anthropomorphism," the latter being far more "expressive of the *scientific opinion*" (*CP* 8.262). It is a philosophy thus conceived as anthropomorphic, in Peirce's estimation, that most fully qualifies as a "good sound solid strong pragmatism."

What is it, more precisely, about the "scientific opinion" that recommends such a label for pragmatism? Anyone who rejects this recommendation should be advised "to remember that every single truth of science is due to the affinity of the human soul to the soul of the universe, imperfect as that affinity no doubt is" (*CP* 5.47). That such an "imperfect" affinity exists is a conjectured presupposition that Peirce embraced as the best way to account for the otherwise inexplicable success with which scientists have so rapidly and efficiently discovered truths about nature. While they err with regularity, their success is vastly disproportionate to the infinite number of candidate hypotheses available for the explanation of any given phenomenon. It is not a mysterious presupposition, but one buttressed by an evolutionary theory explaining how our capacity for reasoning must have developed in continuous adaptation to the natural world in which human beings live and move and have their being. Human reasoning, especially in its initial phase as abductive or hypothetical inference, is rooted in instinct and shaped by practical concerns. Peirce's defense of anthropomorphism thus embodies a claim about the role that instinct plays in abduction, a claim presupposed by his philosophy of science and explicated in terms of his understanding of human evolution.[21] Once again following Duns Scotus, Peirce believed that ideas can exist in the mind either *actualiter* or *habitualiter*; instinctive ideas are of the latter sort: even when they are not "actually conceived," nevertheless, they are able to "directly produce a conception" (*CP* 8.18; *W*2: 472).[22]

Far from idiosyncratic or peculiar, the idea of God as being "vaguely like a man" is a perfectly "natural" one in the sense of being an idea prompted by instinct. In the very same letter to William James in which he defended anthropomorphism as "strong pragmatism," Peirce also quickly observed how it implies theism, not belief in James's finite God, but the affirmation of a supreme "Ideal" conceived as "a living power." Echoing the declaration made two years earlier about our human "affinity" to the universe, Peirce now gives it an interesting theological twist: "Moreover, the human mind and the human heart have a filiation to God." Not only then is it natural and instinctive to believe in the reality of a personal God, but pressing the point even further, in a review published in 1903, Peirce warns that "if we cannot in some measure understand God's mind, all science . . . must be a delusion and a snare" (*CP* 8.168).

Recall that for many of the historically prominent proponents of what is here being called "theosemiotic," the whole of nature is a vast text that can be read as religiously meaningful. Yet such a reading is possible at all only given the premises supplied by Peirce's semiotic realism; and it is against this same background that his anthropomorphism should be conceived and understood. While "the nominalists are fond of insisting on the distinction between words and things, between signs and realities," for a realist and an objective idealist (like Peirce) "the very entelechy of reality is of the nature of a sign."[23] To be sure, "we ought not to think that what are signs to us are the only signs; but we have to judge signs in general by these" (*NEM* 4: 297). Note carefully that such a perspective cannot be directly conflated with anthropocentrism (ours are not the "only signs"), even while it does represent an articulation of anthropomorphism in semiotic terms (we can only judge "signs in general" by "what are signs to us"). This "judging of signs" is the task of interpretation. In a world filled with signs, that task is ongoing, but such a world is potentially knowable, at least in the long run, for a vast community of inquiry operating with sound scientific principles.

For the purposes of a contemporary theosemiotic, Peirce's claims will have to be carefully interpreted, understood precisely in the way in which he intended them, his anthropomorphism regarded not as a logically *necessary* presupposition of all inquiry but rather as a plausible hypothesis about why inquiry succeeds. Open to question from a contemporary perspective, however, might be the level of confidence with which Peirce affirmed his anthropomorphism; a belief in the affinity of the human mind to Nature's Mind is not one that he ever subjected to vigorous critical scrutiny. Nevertheless, to reject such a hypothesis without any further evaluation would represent an egregious case of short-circuiting the process of inquiry. Why should we think that a human mind would *not* be adapted to the purpose of understanding the natural world, that human reasoning is *not* productively guided by instinct?

It is important to observe here that iconoclasm (manifested, for example, in the rejection of any kind of anthropomorphism) can take many forms and can have a religious as well as a nonreligious rationale or motivation. The line that separates atheism pure and simple from a theology organized around arguments about the "death of God" can be a bit blurred. Moreover, there are species of otherwise quite traditional apophatic or negative theologies, theologies of mystery, that embody a powerful iconoclastic impulse. Now any theology conceived as theosemiotic could be "atheistic" only in some qualified sense—for example, in the sense that a religion like Jainism or certain forms of religious naturalism might be classified in that way. That is to say, *something* in such a theology would have to play the role that talk about God does within classical theism. In certain instances, the word "God" might even be employed to designate that something, as in the case of theologies that refer to God, not as a divine person, but as the "ultimate reality" or the "ground of being."[24] Such a "reality" or "ground" would be regarded as being (in some significant way) unlike anything else that is real or exists, and yet also as the source of meaning and being for everything else; but it would not possess consciousness, have purposes, or display agency.

To be sure, this would raise questions about how vague one can be in describing the reality so designated and still make sense out of the claim that one is articulating a "religious" rather than a nonreligious perspective, or that one is in any sense doing "theology." All of this is to say that, just as with "God" or "love," words like "religion" and "theology" must also be understood as quite vague. As the term is frequently used, a "religion" certainly need not be theistic, and the suggestion being made here is that the same is true for theology as theosemiotic. At the very end of the day, however, even if one were to follow Peirce and to defend some form of personal theism, the best path forward may be to try and balance anthropomorphism with apophaticism. That is the path being proposed here for exploration, and Peirce's logic of vagueness is crucial for our purposes.

Consider more explicitly some of the reasons for rejecting such an approach. One might begin with the assumption that anthropomorphism is as natural a human inclination as Peirce insisted that it was, but for reasons different from the one that Peirce posited. Evolutionary psychologists have suggested that a hyperactive tendency to detect "unseen presences" in natural environments would have had great adaptive utility for some of our early hominid ancestors. The "skittish" behavior developed in conjunction with such a tendency may have been irrelevant in the vast majority of cases, where such presences were imagined rather than real. But in the few cases where what was unseen posed a real threat, both the tendency and behavior could have resulted in survival for those ancestors. Here, then, is a simple evolutionary account that might explain the anthropomorphic propensity displayed by humans to believe in the existence of invisible agents who can affect their lives and destiny.

Note that this account is quite different from Peirce's hypothesis about human instinct, about the human mind being naturally attuned to the ideality of nature, mind to Mind. Indeed, the contrast between these explanations is quite pronounced. The tendency among members of our species to generate anthropomorphic hypotheses is reckoned on one explanation of it (Peirce's) as the sign of a highly fallible but nevertheless invaluable instinct for reasoning correctly. From another perspective, it is a natural source of false inferences, its survival value for our ancient ancestors more than overshadowed now by its negative effect on human beliefs and practices. Yet note also how in the Neglected Argument Peirce at least supplied the rubrics for an experimental test of his hypothesis about instinct, however difficult it might be in practice to conduct such a test or to evaluate its results. One might ask then what sort of experiment or evidence would be relevant to an assessment of the certainly plausible but nevertheless highly speculative proposal of the evolutionary psychologists. What might recommend or count against it? Why should one regard it as more "scientific" and so prefer it to Peirce's hypothesis?

The same is true of Sigmund Freud's famous critique of religion-as-theism.[25] Freud's explanation of the widespread tendency toward anthropomorphism among religious believers is rooted in his claim that such beliefs are illusions, not demonstrably false but with no evidence for their truth, constituting wish-fulfillments and fueled by powerful feelings of helplessness. Such an explanation is surely reasonable yet faces the same challenge as the one already posed to proponents of evolutionary psychology. What sort of data would be considered salient insofar as it counts for or against Freud's hypothetical explanation? Moreover, does one want to rush to the conclusion with Freud that there is absolutely *no* evidence that supports belief in God? That there is *some* evidence, both for and against such a belief, is a state of affairs that recommends fallibilism and invites a program of testing and experimentation. If there is absolutely *no* evidence worth considering, then any kind of theistic belief should surely be regarded as foolish—indeed, just as foolish as Freud's imaginary young peasant woman who spurns all of her suitors in the belief that a prince will come to ask her for her hand in marriage. On what grounds does she believe this to be true?[26] Is all religious belief clearly groundless in just the same way as such illusory longing?

Freud and the evolutionary psychologists focus on the "roots" of belief in a personal deity. Pragmatists like Peirce and James emphasized the observable "fruits" of such belief, not as isolated facts, but as forming a pattern and so as signifying something meaningful about the possible source and object of belief. For Peirce, the teleology traced by his agapism suggested that love's fulfillment, its greatest fruit, must consist in the continuously developing relationship with something personal, a certain reasonableness or ideality permeating the cosmos. Part of the task of theosemiotic is to assess what is at stake here, not only to examine our "cognitive defaults," those instincts and habits that affect our reading of the book of nature, but also to evaluate competing explanations of our tendency to read in the way that we do.

Even if one were inclined to honor theosemiotic's pragmaticistic legacy and to embrace or defend some version of Peirce's doctrine of anthropomorphism, it would seem wise at least to try and avoid the charge of anthropocentrism. Certain "posthumanist" lines of argumentation tend to indicate that the two are quite regularly conflated and that the former is problematic precisely because it entails the latter.[27] But is this necessarily the case? To the contrary, it has already been reported that Peirce's anthropomorphism was *not* anthropocentric. To observe that human thinking will typically take a certain distinctive form—as Peirce did in insisting that anthropomorphic conceptions are natural to the point of being virtually inevitable—does not entail the judgment that such a form should necessarily be preferred to other ways of thinking. These "other ways of thinking" might prove to be superior in any given instance, although on Peirce's view their being less "natural" would actually tend to count against them, at least initially and prior to further evaluation of the case at hand.

It is also worth noting that, from a metaphysical perspective portraying all of reality as mind, it is by no means necessary to regard the *human* mind as an especially paradigmatic instance of mental phenomena. (Is this perhaps why Peirce shied away from any description of pragmatism as a type of "humanism?") Indeed, Peirce regarded the presence of *purpose* rather than any indication of *consciousness* as being the most "essential attribute of mind" (*CP* 7.366). Moreover, Peirce's objective idealism was linked to a robust realism, far removed from any kind of subjective or epistemological idealism.[28] The universe, its nature and cause, is not in reality *precisely* as humans conceive it to be, but rather only *vaguely* as they do; moreover, it is not as conceived in the understanding of any isolated individual, but rather from the perspective developed by a vast community of individuals over a considerable period of time. This is why the widespread occurrence of different forms of theism, throughout human history and crossing many cultural divides, is a fact that must be taken with a great deal of seriousness in the evaluation of such a system of belief. That is to say, the ubiquity of this type of belief is a "surprising fact" for which any hypothesis about an anthropomorphizing tendency in humans could be considered as a candidate in the search for a plausible explanation.

The conclusion that God must be "vaguely like a man" is one that can be brought under critical scrutiny of various kinds. Not only might it appear from a posthumanist perspective to privilege the human over other species and forms of life, but the sexist implications of such language must also be taken quite seriously; in addition, depending on any further determination of "what sort of man" God can be said to resemble, real questions about racism might arise. The task of generating a critique of sexism, racism, or any other type of systematic bias or bigotry that infects our discursive practices is an appropriate task for theology; this seems beyond any reasonable doubt. Yet here the specific focus is on such bias as it contaminates theological discourse itself, the way in which one conceives and speaks about the Deity. As already indicated, any kind of God-talk whatsoever will be problematic from certain points of view. Some of these perspectives will embody a concern about the characterization of ultimate reality in anthropomorphic terms. Different ones will be vexed by any conception of a reality that is distinguished from all others by its "ultimacy." Once such talk eventuates, however, and even if it is actively embraced rather than abjured, an extended critique would need to be concerned about the slippage into various sexist and racist modes of discourse; indeed, under the social, political, and cultural circumstances shaping the development of modern Western religious thought, such slippage will seem virtually inevitable. Here perhaps a theology conceived as theosemiotic would be especially well positioned to generate such a critique, given the pragmatic emphasis entailed by such a conception on exploring how *habits* continuously shape human thought, speech, and behavior and, in addition, its insistence on explaining how such habits are created and dissolved.

Those who reject the idea of a personal Creator can press beyond specific complaints about how the Deity might be typically described (i.e., in sexist, racist, or other terms) by raising the problem of evil in general as a potential foil to any possible description. The presence of evil and suffering in the world significantly challenges the tendency to affirm such an idea as true. To save belief simply by admitting that God is capable of doing evil hardly seems felicitous as a strategy. The alternative strategy, employed by some process theologians, to limit God's ability to prevent or resist evil could be perceived as a kind of "halting atheism"; what is the motivation for believing in a smaller, weaker deity rather than in no deity at all? Finally, a contemporary theosemiotic will need to avoid the tendency, visible among some earlier representatives of this tradition (certainly Peirce) to salvage divine personhood by aestheticizing evil. The notion that evil "in the long run" will be perceived as something beautiful or glorious is a proposal that, for reasons to be sketched in Chapter 4, ought to be treated with critical suspicion.

Any defense of a contemporary theology as theosemiotic against such warnings and protestations must be firmly grounded both in Peirce's fallibilism and in his logic of vagueness. Insofar as the idea arises out of musement, Peirce's God is and remains a *hypothesis*. In point of fact, not only the idea of God that originates in musement but the various perceptual judgments that make up our everyday experience of the world are hypothetical in nature; on Peirce's view, they are to be regarded as a product of semiosis and so subject to correction. The oddness of Peirce's talk about the muser "falling in love" with his strictly hypothetical God underscores rather than belies the claim about vulnerability to correction. That a belief or judgment might *seem* indubitable (for example, my thinking that I see a friend approaching me from a distance) is a condition that does not by any means negate its hypothetical status (I could suddenly realize when the distance shortens that I was mistaken and it was only someone who resembles her). And so the practice of musement will be conceived here as a deliberate and recurring attempt "to have all beliefs as though one did not have them."[29] This attempt will not immediately involve the simple refusal of any belief that one suspects to be infected by sexism, racism, or some other problematic form of ideology; rather, it will require the development of a distinctive meta-habit exercised in musement for framing all religious beliefs. Such a frame marks the boundaries of an intellectual playground. Commitment to the playful contemplation of even those religious beliefs that seem most sacred and secure will supply for theosemiotic inquiry both a leading principle and its basic methodology.

This strategy will also be sketched with greater detail in Chapter 4. In announcing it here, it must be added that successful inquiry will eventually progress beyond such a playful stage to the point where beliefs of a certain kind or those embodied in a certain symbolic form most certainly can and should be "refused." The permission to contemplate an idea does not mean that it should necessarily be allowed to shape one's practices. Nothing about the methodology being prescribed for theosemiotic precludes critique—indeed, even the most vigilant and vigorous type of self-critique.

On the contrary, an insistence on and adherence to fallibilism makes such critique inevitable. If fallibilism is the epistemological consequence of Peirce's synechism, his logic of vagueness represents its semiotic upshot—the understanding of semiosis as a continuous, ongoing process and so the meaning of every sign as being partially indeterminate. Every interpretant will both reveal the meaning of some sign and simultaneously determine a future interpretant as standing in a mediated relationship to that sign. Whatever is revealed by any single interpretant, then, is a meaning that is always partial; what a sign can mean, furthermore, is something that changes over time. The twenty-first-century possibilities of meaning for religious symbols like the Gospel of Luke or an icon of the Buddha overlap with but differ dramatically from those available to medieval interpreters. To the extent that any given sign is perceived to be vague, the greater will be its potential depth of meaning. Here vagueness is not a license for semiotic chaos. As previously asserted, the fact that a sign can have an infinite number of meanings does not reduce to the claim that it can mean anything at all, much as the set of positive integers is infinite but excludes negative integers, many fractions, irrational numbers, and so on.

Peirce considered the word "God" to be an extraordinarily vague symbol for a knowable but deeply mysterious and vastly indeterminate reality. The extreme vagueness of this term, however, does not rule out the critique of various ways in which it might be interpreted, nor does it suggest that in the matter of such interpretation "anything goes." What sort of self-critical perspective, then, would preclude (for example) sexist, gendered talk about God but still permit, albeit at a very high level of vagueness, an anthropomorphic interpretation? Why might it be important to conceive of the ultimate reality as "personal" in some vague fashion, given the severe restrictions on what that might entail, in any determinate sense, for the way in which one then talks about God? (Here it is assumed but not argued that talk about an "ultimate reality" actually makes sense, that it is reasonable, without perfect comprehension, to designate something as being both radically different from anything else that exists and yet somehow in continuity with every other reality as the source of its meaning/being.)

Consider again how Peirce defined the concepts of "person" and "personality" (as coordinated ideas displaying purpose) and how he understood the cosmic and evolutionary significance of love. Extrapolating from Peirce's account, it becomes possible to argue that love's teleology presupposes the existence of a relationship between persons, albeit not necessarily human beings. The experience of falling or being in love with the universe (as Royce expressed it) makes sense only if something personal can be discerned at the heart of the cosmos, only if (as Peirce articulated it) a hypothetical God emerges into view as the author of the book of nature. This is precisely why, as it should become gradually more and more clear, both Peirce and Simone Weil endorsed an experimental, a posteriori version of the *ontological* argument. That the perfect object of one's love is anything other than *real, personal,* and *living* is a state of affairs that both thinkers regarded as inconceivable. That is to say, the reality of God as personal is something that love requires, so long as that love has been purified by continuous and appropriately calibrated acts of attention.[30]

At least for Peirce, if not for Weil, this requirement falls short of constituting a "proof" of God's existence even if, on Peirce's account, the muser will be so deeply moved and pragmatically mobilized by the object of her devotion that no such proof will be deemed necessary.[31] Here and in the pages that follow it will continue to be argued that musement is an experiment, that the idea of God is quite vague, that any belief in God is fallible and subject to correction or refutation, and finally, that alternative explanations for the origin and ubiquity among humans of belief in God need to be evaluated carefully. Even to ask the question in precisely the form that Augustine posed it—"What do I love when I love my God?"—is no guarantee that every reasonable answer will be consistent with theism in any of its forms. Nevertheless, Peirce, James, and Royce all seemed convinced that theism in at least one of its forms represented the best answer available given the present state of inquiry.

This rules out for theosemiotic the simple embrace of an apophatic theology without serious qualifications. To affirm our ability to know *that* God exists, without knowing anything at all about *who* or *what* God is, would be a problematic result of the sort of experimentation that Peirce described. While the divine reality may remain deeply mysterious from the perspective of theosemiotic, almost completely shrouded in vagueness, some limited knowledge about that reality is a genuine possibility. If the reality that one then comes to know was in some sense "hidden," for Emerson as well as for Peirce, it will have been hidden in plain view, this epistemological state of affairs having more to do with certain human incapacities, the atrophy of what they regarded as quite natural habits of perception, than with any characteristics that make the divine reality inaccessible.

When Peirce portrayed the act of "contemplation" as an attempt to discern "what may lie hidden in the icon" (*CP* 7.555), he was clearly anticipating the strategy later articulated in his Neglected Argument. Admittedly, God's "great poem" will have to be regarded as a sign of extraordinary complexity, with indexical and symbolic as well as purely iconic features. And whatever serves as an index within the book of nature will forcefully draw and direct the attention of the muser. Concerning the ultimate source or "author" of such a text, this index might signal *that* but could hardly communicate *who* or *what* it might be. Any philosophical theologian wishing to preserve humility, avoid idolatry, and ensure that theological inquiry remains decisively "apophatic" in character will tend to emphasize the indexical function of signs insofar as they constitute a source of religious knowledge.[32] Indices may put us in contact with a divine reality, but the precise nature of such a reality will not be exposed by what they signify.

Nevertheless, if a contemporary theology conceived as theosemiotic is to follow Peirce's lead, this cannot be the point where inquiry both begins and ends. If indices were the only reliable signs of a divine reality, how could one even judge it to be ultimate or divine? Rather than a singular emphasis on the primacy of indices, an insistence on the extraordinary vagueness of all religiously meaningful signs will be crucial for defending a theology of mystery. Moreover, discerning elements of what may lie hidden in the icon through acts of disciplined contemplation should only serve to deepen this sense of mystery. To promote the value of such contemplation as a practice, while continuing to insist on the significance of iconicity, properly measured and qualified, is hardly a recipe for promoting idolatry. Peirce conceived of the universe as an extraordinarily complex symbol with *both* iconic and indexical features. That the best interpretation of such a symbol may be embodied in some disciplined practice, first the vague thoughts and feelings that it engenders but then the conduct that it inspires, is a theosemiotic insight of the greatest significance.

III

Love is very much a matter of attention, of both the quality of one's attention and the choices made in directing it, thus also a matter of volition.[33] One cannot pretend to love that to which one never pays attention, and, indeed, it must be attention of a very special kind. Acts of attention are a necessary but hardly a sufficient condition for love's appearance. On the sort of pragmatic account being developed here, love consists in a certain habit that will display itself as a pattern of conduct rather than in a more or less random choosing to attend now to this, now to that, without being steadfast in purpose. As such, love establishes relations between things, or, to put it more accurately, it is within those very relations that love abides. One's self and one's world are at least partially a product of the choices that one has made in loving. They are also a result of the choices made by others with whom one stands in relations of love.

These choices are ongoing, even when they involve the renewal or reaffirmation of decisions already made, so that (as Peirce saw so clearly) love is evolutionary, admits of growth. If the plot of this story begins to sound familiar to the reader, that is only because love is being portrayed here as a particular form of semiosis, one in which the growth of meaning displays love's teleology, while the shape of meaning reveals the peculiar effect of love's attentiveness. "Love, recognizing germs of loveliness in the hateful, gradually warms it into life and makes it lovely" (*CP* 6.289; *W*8:

186). At the heart of Peirce's agapism is this extraordinary insight concerning the transformative power of a love conceived as being rooted in attention. In the mutuality of relations established between selves, each serves as both a sign and an interpretant for the other, as both text and reader, as both the object of attention and the one who attends. In the exchange between individuals bound to one another in relationships of love, one of the primary gifts that is given and received is the gift of meaning.

Consider more carefully the nature of love (agape) as semiosis. In his articulation of the logic of relations, Peirce argued that triadic relationships were irreducible, while those involving more than three elements could be analyzed as a combination of simpler ones with three or less. To return to one of Peirce's favorite examples, "X gives Y to Z" is not a phenomenon that can be adequately explained in terms of X laying something (Y) down and then Z picking it up (*CP* 8.331; *SS*: 29–30). It is by no means simply equivalent to these two dyadic relationships but rather fundamentally different, as different as thirdness is from secondness in Peirce's categorical scheme. Now consider how on Peirce's basic understanding of semiosis it occurs anywhere but only where something signifies something else to or for someone—that is, "X signifies Y for Z." My present interest is in how the necessarily triadic structure of gift giving maps so neatly onto this account of semiosis. Beyond mere similarity, it is possible to conceive of the former as itself constituting a semiotic event. Perhaps the reverse is also true, so that one can claim about every instance of semiosis that it results in a gift being both extended and received, once again, the precious gift of meaning.

What does this reveal about the special nature of love? On Peirce's standard list of illustrations provided in discussions of the logic of relations, "___ loves ___" or "___ is a lover of ___" would often be used as examples of a dyadic predicate, to be distinguished both from "___ is hard" and "___ gives ___ to___" as monadic and triadic predicates, respectively. Yet I want to suggest that such examples are potentially misleading, that Peirce's agapism follows naturally on the heels of his synechism, and that neither philosophical doctrine can be understood apart from the conviction that there is real thirdness or "reasonableness energizing in the world" (EP2: 72). Even the "hardness" of a thing is a dispositional property, a way in which something *would* tend to react if pressed upon, thus, a continuity of reactions. If we assume that love, like meaning, is something given, then relationships of love can also be readily analyzed in semiotic, essentially triadic terms (lover/love/beloved). Moreover, in those cases where love is mutual, it is not simply given but exchanged. The real distinction between lover and beloved, their otherness, does not completely negate their continuity; in the circular movement of love, as Peirce described it, the final impulse is toward harmony.

While love has the power to form relationships, and the experience of these relationships is typically associated with particular feeling states, love itself ought not to be identified with such feelings. Once again, following a certain line of analysis that can be traced back to medieval scholasticism and culminates not only in Peirce's agapism, but subsequently in various twentieth-century versions of philosophical personalism,[34] love here is being understood as essentially (while not exhaustively) volitional in nature. This line of analysis has now been extended to include the insight that love also involves the exercise of attention. Before pursuing it even further, this link between volition and attention itself might need to be more firmly established.

As already indicated, these two concepts were perhaps most closely associated in the philosophical psychology of William James, both in his earliest work on this topic and upon his later exploration of its relevance for understanding the varieties of religious experience. For James, quite simply and explicitly, the essence of volition was attention. Even when other forms of freedom may be lost, he suggested in the *Varieties* that one's freedom to direct one's attention might still be preserved. In cases where those freedoms have not been lost, the exercise of volition in human action presupposes that one's attention has been directed to the matter at hand. If I do something automatically without paying any attention to what I am doing, it would hardly seem appropriate to label my action as one involving volition. In James's discussion of the "will to believe," to consider only one well-known example, my choosing to believe that something is true even without the conclusive evidence that would compel my belief in its truth is a volitional act that requires careful attention. In those special cases where my believing contributes to the truth of my belief, attention will play an especially vital role. If my willing to believe that I can safely leap across a certain chasm has a positive effect on the outcome of my jumping, it is only because I paid proper attention before making the attempt; here either a failure to keep the mind fixed on such an imagined outcome or excessive attention to the possibility of failure could result in my stumbling into the ravine to my death.[35] Poor attention in the form of a lack of vigilance as I attempt the leap, of course, might also prove fatal.

In seemingly sharp contrast to this Jamesian perspective, Simone Weil carefully distinguished between the will and attention. "Attention is something quite different" from willing, she asserted, and it is the former, not the latter, that she regarded as being religiously significant.[36] Most of the nuances of Weil's argument will be examined in this book's final chapter on prayer, but it will be useful to identify at least some of them here. At the heart of the matter is Weil's conception of attention as being passive in a way that volition is not and so as involving a *waiting* either *for* or *on* the thing or person attended to.[37] Willing is "muscular" and aggressive on Weil's view, a choosing rather than a waiting, while attending is far less active and robust.

From the perspective of a contemporary theosemiotic, it will be most useful to endorse James's general claim linking attention to volition, but in a way properly chastened by the sort of account that Weil provided.[38] One can avoid a straightforward contradiction here simply by noting that "attention" is itself a somewhat vague term that supplies the label for a variety of different but related cognitive acts. Returning to the narrower environment provided by Peirce's philosophy, it becomes a relatively straightforward matter to delineate some of these differences. Consider first the kind of attention exercised in the form of abstraction that Peirce described as "precission." Such an abstraction involves focusing narrowly on one aspect of some thing or perception, a form of mental separation that "arises from *attention* to one element and *neglect* of the other" (*CP* 1.549; *W*2: 50). This forceful narrowing of attention requires a certain kind of effort and, in order to be achieved with regularity, even a type of skill. For Peirce, this was the skill of a *sommelier*, able to discriminate in a taste of wine even the most subtle flavor or aroma by carefully isolating it from the rest.

Contrast this kind of attention with the sort that Peirce described in his Neglected Argument as being essential for success in musement. This mode of attention is difficult to accomplish without practice and also requires the development of a particular type of skill. But rather than involving a muscular narrowing of attention, musement seems to begin only when the muser is alert to whatever might appear, manifesting itself as something either external or internal to consciousness ("about or within you"; see *CP* 6.461). This is achieved by a "softening" of attention, resulting in a widening rather than narrowing of awareness.[39] Focusing neither on this or that exclusively, "neglecting" nothing in a predetermined fashion, the muser is in an attentive state of readiness. Indeed, Peirce's word choice seems entirely appropriate here. This is a kind of attention that constitutes the state of being fully "awake" (similar to what Thoreau recommended and to what Buddhists advocate as "mindfulness").

One important precondition for being awake in the fashion that Peirce prescribed is the cultivation of an attitude of detachment, or what he called "purposelessness." Actually, Peirce's word selection in *this* instance is potentially misleading. It is not that the muser is altogether without purpose, but rather, in a way consistent with Peirce's understanding of developmental teleology, attention will not be fixed on any predetermined purpose, on any goal set in advance of entering into musement. Recall too that the activity itself takes the form of "pure play." This element of playfulness is one of the key features distinguishing such a state of mind from other species of attention.

To be sure, there may be some games or play activities that require intense concentration of the sort that involves focusing on something in particular while ignoring everything else as irrelevant. But in most cases this will be a recipe for losing a game or playing poorly. In the game of American football, a middle linebacker who is focused on a running back will be vulnerable to a "play fake" and a pass thrown down the field to a wide receiver. A basketball player on defense, focused on blocking a three-point shot, can also be faked out of position and easily circumnavigated on a path to the basket. A tennis player intent on covering the baseline is most likely to become the victim of a drop shot. And a chess player should be able to see the whole board and not be fixated on a single perceived threat. In each case, it is the defender prepared for everything because not in anticipation of anything in particular who is likely to be most successful in responding to whatever occurs—once again, to be "ready" for whatever occurs. This is true also of aesthetic play. I do not enjoy the performance of a symphony orchestra by focusing all of my attention on one instrument or musician and trying *not* to hear the rest. At the ballet, it would be ludicrous to rivet my attention on the movement of the dancers' feet, completely ignoring the rest of what they do.

Now there is a significant body of traditional religious literature that identifies this same quality of detachment or disinterestedness as a necessary feature of the sort of love that a devotee ought to cultivate in her relationship with God and, secondarily and derivatively, in relationships with other human beings. Since love is being characterized here as involving a form of attention, this type of prescriptive discourse can be translated accordingly. "Disinterested love" will thus not be easily confused with an "uninterested love" emptied of emotional content, detached from everything and so completely dispassionate. Rather than lacking any interest at all, such a love will have no determinate or predetermined interest, no specific motivation for loving. Attention will not be focused on some specific quality of the beloved selected in advance as being of particular significance. The truly disinterested lover will attend not to what she chooses or prefers, but to whatever she happens to find, just as it manifests itself.[40]

How does one look in order thus to find? It is inconceivable that one's loving gaze could be purified of all intention and interpretation. On the pragmatic perspective established by philosophers like Peirce, Royce, and Mead, even the way in which one comes to know oneself involves interpretation and is to a great extent parasitic on one's social relationships and the knowledge obtained about others. Now being properly awake certainly does require the avoidance of any way of looking or thinking that might blunt the "secondness" of experience, its insistence that things are one way rather than another. But being open to secondness, and so vulnerable to whatever correction it might bring, is quite different from prescinding altogether from any act of interpretation; rather, such openness characterizes a distinctive kind of interpretation, one that here has been variously labeled as "disinterested," "detached," "purposeless," even "playful."

Theosemiotic displays its roots in pragmatism by emphasizing the need for and importance of an appeal to third-person perspectives, either as adopted in order to facilitate self-knowledge or in the form of an emphasis on intersubjectivity as the key to acquiring reliable knowledge about anything whatsoever. Yet it seems crucial at this point to tease out some of the subtle differences that distinguish a third-person from a second-person perspective. If musement as Peirce described it is intended to evolve into a lively "communion" of self with self, then perhaps it is the latter perspective that best characterizes what it means to be thoroughly awake in the sense that musement requires. If the meaning of love is only fully realized, as Ignatius of Loyola suggested, in the mutuality of what is shared in the relationship *between* lovers, then we must speak in such an instance of "I" and "you," and not of a "him" or a "her."[41]

This is not to deny that I might lovingly observe someone who is unaware of my presence—a sleeping lover, for example, or a newborn infant. There might even be something noble or heroic about a love that is given anonymously, without any hope of recognition or return (as in the case of an act of charity directed to someone living in a place far removed, with whom one will never have the opportunity to interact). Moreover, it is important to consider the phenomenon of a love shared by two persons who stand side by side rather than face to face, their attention directed to a common object of concern, as with parents devoted to a child or with friends committed to the same activity or cause. Nevertheless, it is being suggested here that love's teleology extends beyond such instances in anticipation of the kind of communion that Peirce referred to in his Neglected Argument, but that he had already described more thoroughly in the opening pages of his essay on "Evolutionary Love." There he sketched the portrait of a cherishing love that combines an act of recognition, a being awake to what is present in the beloved, with a creative act that elicits from the other some form of response. In this sense, although I must truly love what I find and not what I project or prefer, I might nevertheless communicate to another my preferences as a possibility, perhaps for his own growth or transformation, or perhaps as the offer of a new way of conceiving our relationship.

The offering of a possibility, the tendering of a suggestion, must at all times be distinguished from a love that makes demands. But then a question presents itself: Is there nothing that authentic love has the *right* to demand, if the relationship of love is to be fully mutual, nothing that it can legitimately require? If it is a truly disinterested love, a cherishing attentiveness that seeks the good of the other, it is hard to know how to make room for the language of requirement or demand. To use an example that Peirce found especially instructive, if I am a devoted gardener who cherishes the flowers in my garden, attends to them with great care, and wishes to do everything that I can to help them grow and flourish, is there any sense in which I can demand this outcome? The immediate response, of course, is that there can be no mutuality of love with a flower in a way that there can be with another person, no expectations about what the beloved should do (even if, assuming the cooperation of sun and soil, there might be an expectation about what the flower can be or can become). The seeds or "germs" of loveliness that one perceives in the hateful can only be gradually "warmed" into life on Peirce's account and so made lovely. Here the gentleness of Peirce's own imagery may be misleading to the extent that it belies or obscures the potential violence of love, not so much resulting from aggressive demands made by the lover upon the beloved, but because of the very real suffering for the lover that even a truly disinterested love may bring in its wake.[42]

"Tending," "nurturing," "cherishing" may all work well to describe the form of attention that love brings in relationships that are fundamentally asymmetrical, between gardeners and their flowers, parents and infants, or (hypothetically) God and God's creatures. This is not to deny that some kind of mutuality might exist in such relationships; it is only to note their special character and to suggest that not all other instances of loving may be perfectly captured by such descriptions. For a more general account, one more broadly useful for the analytic goals of theosemiotic inquiry, it might be wise to return once again to the example that Peirce used in the development of his logic of relatives to illustrate thirdness. This is the paradigmatic case of someone *giving* something to someone. Even if genuinely triadic, however, we do not yet have an example of the full mutuality in which love consists, at least in its most perfectly developed form. Such a love must also involve *reciprocity*, the mutual giving and receiving of gifts. It must involve, on the part of the one who receives a gift, some meaningful type of response, something shared or given in return.

Love's reciprocity ought not to be understood in crudely economic terms. This would run the risk of judging any exchange of goods or services as constituting a loving relationship. In the simplest and yet most profoundly important instance, *gratitude* may be conceived as the "something given in return," always the most appropriate response to any act of love and all that is required for the achievement of some kind of reciprocity or mutuality. Gratitude is one of the ways that a habit of love will manifest itself, expressions as well as feelings of gratitude in response to another person's gift of love. In fact, from the theosemiotic perspective being developed here, one plausible hypothesis is that such gratitude is an essential aspect of what we mean by love.[43]

Reconsider the "cherishing" love that Peirce described in his meditation on agape, for example, in the form displayed by the gardener toward the flowers that she is tending or the nurturing father toward his child. Now suppose that this is not an asymmetrical relationship in exactly the way just portrayed. Suppose instead that one perceives the flowers or the child as a gift and therefore as "the sign of a giver."[44] On that "reading" of the situation, cherishing is itself always already a form of gratitude, a perceiving of the other as something precious *and* given. This sort of love is not something to be regarded as *sui generis*, generated in the heart of the lover and then directed toward some other. It is itself always first a response. Here the self as legisign is the embodiment of meaning precisely insofar as it functions as an interpretant, denoting whatever is the object of its loving attention "at the moment."

This semiotic analysis of love solves some of the puzzles presented earlier in the discussion. The formulation "X loves Y" is misleading because it encourages the perception that X is a subject, Y a direct object, with "love" as an active verb, something that someone *does to* someone else. Reformulated in triadic terms, however, love describes a relationship between two persons. Since persons are living legisigns, this relationship between them can be construed as a form of semiosis, each serving as a sign for the other, each an interpretive response to what the other signifies. To the extent that this response embodies an element of gratitude, it is being suggested here that the beloved other *must* be a sign, if not only a sign then at least a sign, a gift, and so the sign of a giver.

This last suggestion is a hypothesis that will need to be further interrogated and tested. Why could one not be grateful simply for the fact of the other, signifying nothing, grateful for her *being as such* and not as *being toward* another, not as something given? Does this constitute a difference between the way in which Zen Buddhists or certain religious naturalists might portray gratitude as a religiously meaningful disposition and the way in which it would tend to be interpreted by a Jewish, Christian, or Muslim theist? Moreover, does this difference, if measured as significant, actually *make a difference* with regard to any decision about whether or not the human experience of love as grateful leans in the direction of theism? It would seem a bit reckless to insist that such experience provides strong evidence in support of theism. Nevertheless, might it not constitute a religiously meaningful sign?

It could facilitate progress toward answering these questions by turning to the consideration of what sense it makes to talk about the "love of enemies" and of how such a love could possibly be characterized as grateful. While Peirce did not speak directly about the love of enemies, he portrayed God's love for creation as being directed toward that which is radically other than the divine, since God *is* love as John proclaimed, toward that which is most "defect of love" or hateful (*CP* 6.287; *W*8: 185). Insofar as human love is to be modeled on the divine agape, this would make it necessary for Peirce to take quite seriously any talk about the love of enemies. William James, for his part, *did* take it quite seriously. He speculated in one of his famous Gifford lectures that the widespread achievement of such a love would result in a dramatic "breach" between the universe as we now know it and what it might possibly come to be under such circumstances.[45] Yet neither pragmatist described this kind of love in concrete terms or indicated how it could also be regarded as an expression of gratitude.

This lacuna in their thinking about love is filled by an appeal to the philosophy of *aikido*, articulated by Morihei Ueshiba, aikido's founder, in a series of aphorisms. Some of these aphoristic utterances are a bit obscure, but his teaching about the love of enemies was relatively clear and straightforward. For the appropriately trained and skillful martial artist, for one properly disposed, even an act of violence can be *interpreted* as a gift, the gift of vital energy or *ki*, to be adapted and used by the martial artist for creative purposes. By blending with and redirecting an attack, the moving body of the martial artist supplies an alternative interpretation of the situation, signifying possibilities beyond violent encounter, including peaceful reconciliation. In this fashion, Ueshiba came to conceive of the performance of aikido as consisting in acts of love and of aikido itself as an "art of peace."[46]

In addition to martial skill then, the aikidoka must also work to cultivate a distinctive habit of love, one gently determining her response to a variety of persons and situations encountered. Such a person is a living legisign capable of embodying alternative interpretations to the ones proposed by others, in the case of enemies offering dramatic reinterpretations of what might appear as a toxic situation or a hateful relationship. If an enemy reads such a sign and embraces its meaning, the result can be a new and harmonious relationship rather than a simple clash or conflict of interpretations. In the development of his martial arts philosophy (one shaped both by his experiences in Japan during the Second World War and by certain religious influences), Ueshiba offered an account that is both perfectly consistent with and illustrative of Peirce's agapism.

This excursus on the love of enemies may seem like a digression, even a distraction from the questions raised immediately before it began. The point that needs to be emphasized here is that those questions have not been abandoned but merely recast in this discussion. Does the "love of enemies" yield a possibly productive *misreading* of some person and situation (surely the enemy does not intend to be offering me what I may choose to perceive as a gift), or does it produce an alternative but perfectly valid interpretation? The latter possibility presupposes that there really are "seeds of loveliness" even in what presents itself as most hateful, but that one must be able to see with the eyes of love in order to recognize them. From such a perspective, true love is never blind. It transforms the awareness of a world of things into the vision of a world perfused with signs, with love's essence consisting in a fundamental gratitude for the gift of meaning that each sign presents to one who is ready to discern and prepared to receive it.

Even if gratitude is identified as a disposition of basic religious significance, it is still not perfectly clear that this would require the acceptance of theism in one form or another. Gratitude may prove to be an appropriate response to the encounter with things *not* perceived as gifts (although it would need to be explained how this could be the case). In addition, it is not perfectly obvious that gratitude even for something recognized as a gift presupposes belief in the reality of a divine giver. (That too would require some explanation, although, once again, many Buddhists and religious naturalists would regard it as plausible.) Peirce's conjecture, however, was that in the course of musement there would be a natural tendency to contemplate the possibility of a giver of meaning for the universe filled with signs, something vaguely personal and purposeful. Such an idea is itself a seed that might become embedded and take root in the heart and mind of the one who contemplates it without bias, an idea eventually bearing fruit in the conduct shaped by it.

4 / Theology as Inquiry, Therapy, Praxis

I

Peirce told two quite different stories about the roots of inquiry: one that identified the irritation of doubt as inquiry's primary stimulus, a second that traced its gradual emergence as rigorous science from out of the womb of playful thinking. Of the two stories, the first is far better known than the second. The kind of reasoning more likely to produce religious belief, however, Peirce portrayed in the latter narrative. It will be important, eventually, to blend these two narratives into one, to understand theosemiotic as a complex form of inquiry shaped by multiple factors. On the way to achieving such a goal, it will be necessary to paint a clearer picture of this playful, "sporting" consciousness. Some of the features of that portrait have a source that can be located in what Peirce wrote elsewhere about cosmology, about aesthetics as a normative science, and about phenomenology.[1] Here a more relevant concern is to capture the relationship between musement as a way of thinking and Peirce's logic of abduction. Once that relationship is understood, how does it inform one's conception of the muser as a "semiotic self," or, more narrowly, a "living legisign?" In what respect, on a Peircean account, can musement be regarded as preparatory *either* for prayer (the topic of Chapter 7) *or* for rigorous scientific inquiry?

The origins of classical pragmatism have frequently been traced to several essays that Peirce published in the 1870s as "Illustrations in the Logic of Science," in *Popular Science Monthly*—most especially, the first two of these on "The Fixation of Belief" and "How to Make our Ideas Clear." In an 1898 lecture presented at Berkeley on "Philosophical Conceptions and Practical Results,"[2] when James famously anointed Peirce as the founder of pragmatism, these two essays are the place that he marked as the special point of origin—despite the fact that the word "pragmatism" does not ever appear, even once, in the whole series of essays. The subsequent impact of these essays, it can be argued, tells us more about the effective history of James's Berkeley lecture than it does about the substance or the development of Peirce's philosophy. Among his best-known and most influential publications, nevertheless, one could argue, ironically, that they ought to be evaluated as being among his weakest. While his perspective certainly evolved and matured in the decades following the appearance of these essays, it is demonstrably the case that they did not clearly and accurately represent the nuances of his basic philosophical position *even at the time that he wrote them*.[3]

By the time Peirce turned to writing the second essay in the series, for example, he was already worried about distortions and exaggerations in the first, his discussion of the "irritation of doubt" as the primary stimulus to inquiry being "too strong" for his purpose, almost as if he had "described the phenomena as they appear under a mental microscope" (*CP* 5.394; *W*3: 261). Later in his life, Peirce would return to these essays quite frequently—making further corrections and qualifications—in large measure because the spotlight that James had shone on them made it necessary for him to continue to try to make the best sense out of what he had written there. Nevertheless, upon any careful examination of them, it is hard to ignore the disconnect between the philosophical perspective that they articulate and the ones embodied either in Peirce's writings of the 1860s (where he first presented his semiotic theory) or in his twentieth-century discussions of pragmaticism. Focusing on this series and ignoring much of the rest of what he wrote makes it easy to understand how Peirce came to be celebrated as an early representative of logical positivism or more closely linked to some later pragmatists than a careful and balanced reading of his corpus would encourage or license. Moreover, focusing on these essays as normative for understanding Peirce leads to a very harsh judgment of many of the other things that he wrote, even motivating the attempt to explain them away, in some instances, as evidence of a temporary insanity.[4]

Theosemiotic is inspired by but not rigidly bound to Peirce's theory of inquiry.[5] At the same time, that theory deserves the most thoughtful consideration, including his formulations of it that might be judged as incomplete or that involve hyperbole. Even if one were to concur with Augustine and Anselm that theology is a matter of "faith seeking understanding," it would not be possible to ignore altogether the vital role that doubt can play as a catalyst in this process.[6] The experience of doubt suggests that there is a problem with the way that one's beliefs are presently formulated. Moreover, there are a great variety of problematic issues—philosophical, existential, ethical, social, and political—from which it would be irresponsible for the theologian to shrink. One obviously meaningful response to such problems is to identify and articulate reasonable solutions.

Yet it will be argued here that "problem-solving" is neither the sole nor even the primary task of theosemiotic. On the contrary, interpretive behavior might be judged quite successful when it renders as problematic some idea, action, or situation that hitherto had not been recognized as such. In this respect, the theosemiotician may be engaged, on any given occasion, in generating more problems than she actually solves. Moreover, "finding a solution" may be only one among a variety of religiously meaningful responses to some problem. Consequently, it will be necessary to evaluate carefully the role that doubt can and does play as a valuable stimulus to inquiry, to identify the sort of pragmatism that an emphasis on the effects of doubt inspires, as well as the limits to any inquiry thus conceived.

The claim that human inquiry does indeed sometimes occur as a meaningful response to the irritation of doubt hardly seems worth refuting; that it occurs only in such instances and given such a motivation is demonstrably false. Peirce's worries about "paper doubt" in the Fixation essay need to be both contrasted with and balanced by his advocacy of a certain form of "feigned hesitancy" in other writings. Indeed, he argued, one can generate a certain "dissatisfaction with one's present state of opinion," apart from any surprising occurrence that casts a shadow of doubt, simply by exercising the "Will to Learn" (*RLT*: 170–71). It needs also to be observed that for Peirce the mild "irritation" of boredom could be as effective a motivation for inquiry as that of doubt (*CP* 5.394; *W*3: 262). This is an especially important observation for present purposes, given the dialectical relationship that exists between boredom and play. Boredom is antithetical to the spirit of play so that when it occurs during a game it can actually cause us to cease playing. Yet it might also in many other circumstances motivate the search for a game or some other activity that will alleviate the boredom, thus acting as an impetus to inquiry in the form of play behavior.[7]

Peirce's emphasis on doubt as a starting point is not the only difficulty with the theory sketched in 1877. Even if there are "milder" forms of irritant, it should not be assumed as necessary that inquiry must originate with the experience of any irritation at all. Notice that the Neglected Argument begins as an exercise in the philosophy of religion but soon evolves into a rather extended analysis of Peirce's mature pragmaticism, a detailed account both of the various stages of inquiry and of the role that instinct plays in such a process. Thirty years after the publication of "Fixation," this process is no longer being portrayed as one arising out of some kind of problematic situation that undermines belief and so generates doubt; by contrast, in the latter essay the type of inquiry under consideration is described as a process initiated simply by the decision to take a walk.

For the sake of accuracy, one ought probably to characterize the ideal occasion for musement as a "stroll" (this is the word that Peirce himself uses) rather than as just any kind of walk. Some walks are purposeful (intended as exercise or to reach a particular destination) in ways that would disqualify them for the activity that Peirce had in mind.[8] Moreover, even the act of strolling, while it might be considered as exemplary, hardly constitutes a necessary concomitant for the launching of some new inquiry. Sitting in the doorway of one's home, as Thoreau reports having done for the better part of a day, carefully attending to what immediately presents itself for observation, might work just as well for musement—so long as what it facilitates is a "lively exercise of one's powers" rather than any state of mind that might be characterized as "vacancy" or "dreaminess" (*CP* 6.458).[9] In any event, while Peirce worried that prolonging this kind of playful meditation runs the risk of seeing it "be converted into scientific study" (*CP* 6.459), he left no doubt that such cognitive play does indeed constitute "the first stage of a scientific inquiry" (*CP* 6.485). Note carefully that the strolling muser need not encounter any unexpected difficulties along the way—need not experience some disturbing situation that threatens or undermines a particular belief previously held with confidence. The experience that Peirce relates has a distinctly aesthetic rather than a practical character. Unless aesthetic pleasure can be completely explained in terms of the relief that one feels when some nagging irritation has been assuaged, the doubt-belief theory of inquiry is not at all what Peirce is describing here.

Any theology conceived as theosemiotic will be fueled by Peirce's rich and discriminating pragmaticism, to be contrasted sharply with a crude or narrow instrumentalism. Such a theology will display an intellectual trajectory the teleology of which must be truly developmental, thus not bound by goals or problems rigidly designated in advance. Nevertheless, to insist that theological reflection cannot be reduced to problem-solving or portrayed as a series of episodic responses to the irritation of doubts as they arise, once again, is *not* to deny that a part of the theological task involves addressing specific questions and predicaments. One of the most fundamental questions linked to the traditional theologies produced by classical theists (but hardly ignored by others, such as Buddhists) concerns the problem raised by the existence of evil and suffering in the world. Here it will be argued that the legitimacy of any response to this problem that takes the explicit form of a "solution" can be seriously challenged, and often for strictly theological reasons. But this is hardly to suggest that one must remain mute in such instances. The alleviation of suffering, for example, is a pragmatic issue that need not be conflated with the project of supplying some reasonable *explanation* of why suffering occurs (or is "permitted" to occur). In fact, an excessive attention to one project (explanation) can be a source of distraction from the challenge represented by the other (alleviation). If the reality of suffering and evil can be comfortably reconciled with a theological narrative about God's power and goodness, then the "problem" itself has been dissolved and is no longer compelling. Some of the traditional "explanations" provided by classical theists—for example, that suffering persons are being righteously punished for transgressions and deserve what they are experiencing—not only distract from but actively undermine the practical task of alleviation. At the same time, this latter task should not be confused with what might sometimes be regarded as an excessively optimistic and so naïve intention to *eliminate* altogether or perfectly to *heal* suffering. In certain instances, it might rapidly become reimagined as the challenge of developing resources that would simply enable someone more effectively to *endure* suffering.[10]

Now, to imagine meaningful interpretive responses to the problem of evil that involve neither explanation nor solution is to conceive of a "theology without theodicy." In any given instance, it may not be the problem of evil but rather the paradox of love that summons us to inquiry—a love that simultaneously celebrates the presence and mourns the absence of its beloved, one directed toward a divine reality that is experienced both as supremely real and as no-thing. This is the path that theosemiotic ought to pursue, properly understood as a theology of mystery, yet one deeply sensitive to the reality of human suffering and so also to the need, in certain instances, of a firm commitment to liberatory praxis. Such praxis is also the work of love, this time directed toward the one who suffers. In addition to the features of love already described in Chapter 3—a recognition of loveliness (this is the first semiotic moment) and cherishing of the other combined with a deep gratitude for the beloved's presence/ existence—a further element now needs to be identified: that is, a compassion that moves the one who loves to action.

A similarly nuanced perspective needs to be formulated with respect to the pragmatic ideal promoting the vulnerability of hypotheses. As it is most typically articulated, this ideal affirms the need to submit any hypothesis to rigorous testing, thus making it vulnerable to correction. Indeed, its status as vulnerable is one of the features of a hypothesis that might recommend it for adoption. For the inquirer, the ease with which it can be evaluated and refuted may make it a more salient choice than some competitor—for reasons suggested by the economy of research— not the perceived likelihood of its being true.[11] Within the context of theosemiotic inquiry, however, such an ideal can be fully embraced only if reformulated. Here "vulnerability" will take on a richer meaning, implying more than a simple openness to correction or refutation. The precariousness of one's perspective, indeed, the poverty of one's understanding of any particular issue or phenomenon, once exposed, might in some instances be a condition that one embraces rather than chooses to flee. This could occur for multiple reasons. Once the vulnerability of my position has been illuminated by some countervailing argument or experience, it nevertheless remains the case that I need someplace to stand. Unless some plausible alternative is immediately offered for my consideration, seeing the world as I see it, from here and in this fashion, may not be a state of affairs that I should readily abandon. Abandon for what? Seeing through a glass darkly is all that we can hope for at the present time, in any event. Why would I choose simply not to see at all?

This is a tricky business, a complicated judgment, in every case when I choose to remain committed to the principles of a pragmatic fallibilism, to cultivate an epistemological humility that underscores the poverty of all human knowing, without thereby falling victim to a very dangerous form of self-deception (i.e., allowing what is actually my stubborn resistance to correction to masquerade as a virtue). Yet this is hardly the entire story that one needs to tell, for the purposes of any theosemiotic project worth pursuing, about being in just such a position. For any theology of the spiritual life worth its salt, the "embracing of poverty" can be as much a celebration of as it is a capitulation to the existing state of affairs. There is a "weariness of the flesh" that follows in the wake of our recognition of the futility of certain forms of inquiry, a conscious turning away from the hubris that can afflict and then poison our epistemologies. This is a recognition that lies at the heart of every apophatic theology. But it can also take a less dramatic form, as it does when I affirm the limited truth and value of what I know and see, a truth made vulnerable by the encounter with alternative perspectives, but then also defined and renewed by such an encounter. To the extent that I recognize these alternatives as complementary, my vulnerability will simply be the precondition for any kind of meaningful dialogue, my embrace of poverty a natural, essential prerequisite for semiosis as the real growth of meaning.

Against the background supplied by these initial considerations, the present challenge is threefold. In the first place, following Peirce's lead, it will be important to give an account of the general form that inquiry takes, not this or that specific inquiry, but at a certain level of abstraction the formal properties that anything describable as inquiry can be expected to display. This will involve exploring the stages of inquiry that Peirce carefully identified; it will also involve portraying inquiry as semiosis, exposing the fundamental sense in which all thinking is analogous to a form of reading. Next, the type of thinking that can be classified as theological will be shown to have a therapeutic function, resulting in habit-change, with the purposes of "therapy" in this context being multiple and diverse, but almost always including the cultivation of an attitude of "mindful acceptance." Third, and finally, a nuanced explanation of how the relationship between theory and practice can best be understood will be crucial for framing the theosemiotic project. Here, again, there is more than a single line of analysis that will need to be pursued. That theorizing is itself a form of praxis, contemplation itself always already a type of meaningful action, is an insight the truth of which must be defended. In the long run, and more generally speaking, inquiry can be expected to yield a great variety of potentially practical results. This discussion will need to expose how deeply committed to pragmaticism a theology conceived as theosemiotic must be, most especially if it is to be classified in any meaningful sense as either a species of or the prolegomenon to a theology of liberation.

Take as a working presupposition Peirce's claim that all thinking is in signs. This claim has already been examined at some length, and its implications for much of what will be argued here are wide-ranging and of considerable significance. On the Peircean view being adopted, while thought can be conflated with semiosis, the latter cannot be reduced to language. Despite the importance of linguistic signs, not all thinking can be represented in verbal form. Mathematical reasoning provides an obvious case in point. One can talk about the "language of mathematics" in order to describe the medium in which such reasoning occurs, but such talk seems clearly to be metaphorical. It may also have been an instance of metaphor when Jonathan Edwards alluded in his writings to "the language in actions; in some cases much more convincing than words." And it is commonplace enough to encounter references to the "language of music" or to some person's effective use of "body language."[12] Rather than demonstrating that all human thinking can be reduced to language, such ways of talking link these phenomena one to another as forms of semiosis. However broadly or narrowly we decide that it means to refer to some expression or communication as "linguistic," as a form of "language," from a theosemiotic perspective, acts of reading and rereading will need to be understood in the widest possible sense as involving a great many different types of nonverbal interpretation. To use an example already often repeated here, my reading of another person's character will require paying attention to a good deal more than what she communicates in words. Habitual modes of conduct, including but not limited to the habits that typically shape her speech acts, will be of the greatest relevance for this particular purpose.

Similar to the case reported in such an example, one ought to regard many of the instances of semiosis most relevant for theological inquiry as forms of semiotic *behavior*. In any event, this is the best way to express oneself if one intends to speak in a distinctively pragmatic tone of voice. The clichéd wisdom that "actions speak louder than words" is rendered somewhat problematic by the observation that words very often *are* actions, at least insofar as they form utterances and constitute observable linguistic behavior with real effects. Moreover, all instances of deliberate behavior represent modes of thinking. The use of language in scholarly activity or in debate is a prominent and readily identifiable example of reasoning. So, too, is the concentrated search for a solution to some mathematical problem. An athlete or martial artist thinks with her body when engaged in training or in competition. A different kind of artist is thinking in a very intense and highly creative fashion whenever he carefully applies oil to canvas or gives distinctive shape to metal or clay. Surely I am thinking also when I stir ingredients together in a skillet and carefully adjust the intensity of the stovetop flame as I prepare dinner for the evening. There may be a conversation unfolding in consciousness that involves words in each of these cases; but what one is actually *doing* in each case can hardly be reduced to verbal behavior.

All thinking is in signs. Feelings are vague thoughts. Emotions can be analyzed as judgments. And deliberate human conduct can display a logic as vividly as an argument consisting of propositions and appearing in the form of *modus ponens*. All of these conclusions follow from or are illuminated by Peirce's important assertion that the primary relationship between signs is one of *illation* (CP 2.444, note 1). This assertion has been described as expressing a pragmatic belief in the "ubiquity of inference,"[13] at least insofar as human consciousness and behavior are the primary object of concern. Does it also entail commitment to a further belief in the "ubiquity of inquiry"?[14] While understanding the logic of a positive response, my inclination is to answer such a question with extreme caution, leaning toward the negative. While the word "inquiry" is not perfectly precise—clearly vague enough to be applied to a range of human behaviors that are comparable but not identical—it is certainly precise enough to rule out some phenomena that do not appear to display a requisite pattern. (What pattern? That is the relevant question at hand.)

In 1877 Peirce himself described those conditions under which inquiry arises and those causing it to cease. Yet I have already argued here that this well-known account is inadequate as a general theory, too limited in scope to do justice to the full range of human inquiry—an argument motivated by my reluctance to identify human thinking with problem-solving. Even if inquiry is conceived as taking other forms, however, it is not clear that these exhaust the possibilities for human thought and semiosis. In 1908, when Peirce proposed that inquiry might begin with musement, he described such a state of mind as being "antipodal" to day-dreaming. This observation would seem also to undermine the claim that inquiry (like semiosis) is virtually ubiquitous in human experience, so that all thinking must take this form. (What about daydreaming, after all?)

Now, whether or not every form of *scientific* inquiry can be understood to originate as a form of cognitive play in Peirce's view, the sort of theological reasoning that eventuates in a consideration of the God-hypothesis does appear to be rooted in such ludic meditation. Peirce's terse description of musement, limited to a few remarks appearing in the Neglected Argument and then in his subsequent correspondence with Victoria Lady Welby about that essay, needs to be amplified and extended here for the purposes of contemporary theosemiotic.[15] In the first place, consider more carefully a topic already introduced in Chapter 3—that is, the precise sort of attention that the practice of musement is said to require. Peirce explicitly identified musement as a form of meditation, if pursued properly, as beginning in pure play and then gradually evolving into religious meditation (*CP* 6.458, 483, 487). Recall that one very simple and general definition of meditation, appropriate for its manifestation in a wide variety of contexts, is that it is the practice of paying attention. This seems accurate for the sort of cognitive activity that Peirce understood as musement, which he bemoaned is "not as commonly practiced as it ought to be" (*CP* 6.458). In addition to regular practice, we have seen that his instructions for the prospective muser suggest that one should be "awake to what is about or within" (*CP* 6.461), with the more passive absorption of impressions soon giving way to "attentive observation" (*CP* 6.459). These instructions provide the rubrics for a careful experiment that Peirce invited his reader to perform, one that involves the exercise of attention, but not just any kind of exercise—rather, one peculiar to his understanding of abduction or hypothetical reasoning.

Insofar as any type of reasoning is a deliberate form of behavior, it will involve certain acts of attention, since the essence of volition *is* attention, both as James argued and now also from a theosemiotic perspective as I am attempting to articulate it.[16] These acts will vary for each one of the basic modes of inference that Peirce designated as the three stages of inquiry in his Neglected Argument. The last of these is the inductive stage. After generating some hypothesis and explicating deductively all of the consequences that such a hypothesis would entail if true, the inquirer must then test to see if these consequences obtain in fact. Here the sort of attention that such testing requires can be easily described. Bear in mind the discussion of precission presented earlier. Induction involves "prescinding" from most of the features of some experience or phenomenon in order to focus attention on those aspects considered salient for the purpose of evaluating a particular hypothesis. The determination of what actually is to be regarded as salient in any given case will be established deductively, but the careful "looking" in order to detect how often such characteristics are actually manifested in some thing or situation is a matter of observation and experiment, an essentially inductive process.[17]

To be sure, deduction also involves specific acts of attention, although not directed to a broad sample of objects or experiences, but instead focused on a particular idea, one entertained hypothetically in the imagination so that its various entailments can be carefully traced. Rather than attending to what is the case in fact, the inquirer engaged in deduction focuses on what would have to be true given some imagined state of affairs. The results of induction are as unpredictable and uncertain as the deliverances of our ongoing human experience can often prove to be, rendered gradually more predictable only when, after the frequent repetition of some observation or experiment, they have accumulated over time. By contrast, the results of a deductive inference are necessarily true and certain, although only on the assumption that the hypothesis under consideration is also true, and only in those instances where the person making the inference has paid proper attention to the relationship between ideas and has thus reasoned correctly.

The way in which attention is exercised in abduction, the form of hypothetical reasoning that Peirce identified as the first stage of inquiry, is a bit more difficult to describe. On the one hand, it seems to resemble induction, because both can involve a process of careful observation, a heightened attention to phenomena as they actually manifest themselves. Yet in the case of induction, such observation is a focused "looking for" this or that, much as in a simple litmus test it is the color of the litmus paper that draws my attention, prescinding from whatever else might also be observable as irrelevant to the objective of determining if some substance is acidic. In abduction, there is no such narrowing or focusing of attention. Abduction involves a kind of "looking pure and simple" rather than any type of purposeful "looking for." Once again, it involves, as Peirce himself prescribed, being awake to phenomena as they appear either internal or external to consciousness.

This softer gaze, this awakening to the significance of anything that happens to appear because no one sign has been preselected and isolated for interpretation, is a state of mind that can certainly be portrayed as playful. It is a playing with signs and their potential meanings, the signs appearing to an attentive observer, but meanings arising from "within," so that as in deduction, the process of abductive reasoning also engages the imagination. Quite unlike deduction, however, there is absolutely no necessity to the conclusions reached in this process; to insist on such a necessity in the assignment of meanings to signs would totally undermine the spirit of play. Beliefs, as habits of thought that constrain us to think in certain ways, cannot simply be evacuated from consciousness; the attempt to achieve such a state of mind would amount to what Peirce called "paper doubt." One can "feign" a certain "hesitancy" to embrace such beliefs, however, in the form of a playful make-believe, so that the muser at play will have all beliefs as though she did not have them. This sort of pure play is fertile ground for the experimentation with ideas in the imagination, the "trying out" and "trying on" of fresh interpretations even for signs that may appear already to have established meanings. It might begin to occur, in fact, simply because one has become bored with old habits of interpretation and with meanings now grown stale.

Note that even in this first, abductive phase of inquiry, the inquirer will be performing some rapid deductions to explicate hypotheses as they arise and will begin imaginatively testing them against an array of remembered experiences—although not in the sustained or systematic way that would "convert" musement into "scientific study." The key difference between how deduction and induction occur in this playful mode and how they might be pursued in the later stages of inquiry is that only the "law of liberty" remains held in place for the muser (*CP* 6.458). Other constraints on the process of inquiry, typical in those later stages, have been importantly removed. In a world perfused with signs, the muser is both relaxed and alert, fully *ready*, her perusing of the world taking the form of a drinking in of impressions rather than as looking with a definite purpose or for anything in particular. Moreover, in the consciousness of the muser, there will be no sharp delimiting of the way in which signs can be linked to meanings or of how ideas might be developed, combined, or configured in this playful process of interpretation.

All of these deliberations about the role that attention plays in human inquiry—more narrowly, the role (or roles) that it plays in shaping each mode of inference as a distinctive way of thinking—this entire discussion is rooted in Peirce's phenomenology, what he labeled as "phaneroscopy," even now a poorly understood yet crucially important element of his thought. Within Peirce's architectonic, his classification of the various sciences into something of a hierarchy, phaneroscopy occupies a foundational position. While mathematics is even more foundational, both metaphysics and the normative sciences draw on Peirce's phenomenology for inspiration and resources. My immediate interest here is in the classification of phenomenology by Peirce as a "cenoscopic" discipline. Such a mode of inquiry is strictly and rigorously empirical, but the type of experience to which it refers is accessible to anyone, anywhere, without special apparatus or expertise; that is to say, the subject matter for cenoscopy is the world of experience that is available to anyone who is willing and able to pay proper attention.

All of philosophy, as distinguished from the "special" (physical and social) sciences, is cenoscopic in this sense, dealing with the commonly accessible fabric of human experience, not as it is revealed in a particular location only, but as it is manifested always and everywhere.[18] As a result of his phenomenological inquiries, Peirce was able to conclude that there are three basic features of all human experience: firstness or pure qualities; secondness or a sense of otherness and opposition; and thirdness, best displayed as a kind of energizing reasonableness that manifests itself as semiosis. Now, while phenomenological inquiry is somewhat preliminary to theological thinking proper, the special methodology developed for phenomenological purposes as well as the nature and scope of its subject matter ought to be considered relevant to the task of theosemiotic. Peirce worked for many years to refine that methodology. For present purposes, it must suffice to observe how the three "faculties" that he prescribed as essential for students of phenomenology—first, the "faculty of seeing what stares us in the face, just as it presents itself," second, the capacity for "resolute discrimination," and third, a certain "generalizing power" (*PPM*: 152)—correspond loosely to the three ways of paying attention earlier identified as distinguishing the various modes of inference. As with phenomenology, any theology conceived as theosemiotic must cultivate the most lively but rigorous exercise of attention directed to the features of our shared, everyday human experiences (not only of things external to the self, but including those constituted primarily by thoughts and feelings internal to consciousness).[19]

With regard to subject matter, the theosemiotician, once again much like the phenomenologist, will be preoccupied *not* primarily with what can be revealed in experience under only the most extraordinary of circumstances, appealing to special revelation or using special aids and instruments, but rather with its common and everyday deliverances. It was because of the accessibility of its subject matter and because virtually anyone should be capable of arriving at its conclusions that Peirce identified at the core of his discussion of God's reality a line of reasoning that he classified as a "Humble Argument." Here I want also to propose or predict that cenoscopic inquiry, under the discipline of a habit of love, will tend to expose poverty as a pervasive feature of human experience. The achievement of such an insight is an outcome that requires a certain training or exercise rather than happening immediately or automatically; it takes some practice. Yet it is an insight, in principle, that is accessible to anyone.[20]

Used as a verb, the word "exercise" means quite literally "to bring into play." On Peirce's view, the pure play of musement was to be regarded as a "lively exercise of one's powers" (*CP* 6.458). Here the "powers" being brought into play are primarily cognitive, constituting our human capability for reasoning about the nature of things; given the preceding analysis such capacities must certainly include our powers of attention and imagination. Now, these latter are not neatly separable or perfectly distinguishable from each other. Indeed, at least in a conscious state of mind, acts of attention will occur in a continuous stream. The manner in which we attend will significantly determine the nature and quality both of our sense perceptions and of our playful imaginings (and subsequently of our memories). Moreover, although I will not elaborate the claim here, it can certainly be argued that the imagination itself is also involved in virtually every act of perception.[21]

Here the relationship between three concepts—experience, experiment, and exercise—is worth carefully probing. The first two terms are in fact linked etymologically. For the goals of this discussion, it is important simply to observe that experimentation is one of the many forms that experience can take, different from other forms perhaps most decisively in the way that it is deliberate and self-controlled. Experiments also tend to be repetitive, this redundant quality distinguishing them from experiences that would be regarded as occasional, perhaps even as "once in a lifetime." Here the element of redundancy forges a connection between experiments and exercises. In order to be effective, each must be repeated. Running a single trial in the laboratory will be just about as valueless as doing a single push-up or trying to learn how to play the piano in one lesson. Both experimentation and exercise are essentially inductive processes, the end result of which is habit formation. Indeed, on one very simple but quite accurate way of looking at the matter, the exercises in which one engages are nothing other than experiments performed with one's self. Musement, it seems to me, is just such a form of self-experimentation. So, too, are almost all religious ritual and meditative practices in which devotees regularly and repeatedly participate.

If musement is to evolve into some form of sustained theological reasoning, more light needs to be shed on the deductive and inductive phases of inquiry. As already indicated, some initial deductive clarification of hypothetical ideas intended to facilitate the contemplation of their significance will already have occurred in musement. Yet for any properly theological investigation to take place the attention will have to be focused at some point in time on a single hypothesis, much as it was on the God-hypothesis that emerged from Peirce's Humble Argument. Not much more needs to be said in the present context about precisely how such attention will be exercised for specifically deductive purposes. It is worth remembering, however, that for a philosophical theology conceived as theosemiotic, the role of deductive reasoning will be essentially explicative rather than strictly demonstrative. There is no purely a priori path to the conclusions (always tentative and highly fallible) of any theosemiotic inquiry. Theology thus conceived cannot and does not ride on the back of deductive proofs, in contrast to how it was understood in its traditional medieval/scholastic manifestations. Rather, deduction mediates between the playful semiosis that marks a starting point for inquiry and the disciplined experimental praxis in which inquiry eventuates. Indeed, while Peirce embraced a version of the ontological argument, it was not Anselm's, but rather one that he understood to be experimental and a posteriori; it can thus be classified as belonging to the extended family of "ontological arguments" only to the extent that all such reasoning proposes how a careful contemplation of the *idea* of God will tend eventually to produce a powerful belief in the reality of such a being.

Such a belief will be regarded as vague but instinctive from the perspective supplied by the sort of religious naturalism that informs theosemiotic inquiry. This remark introduces the consideration of theology's final inductive stage. What sort of experimental praxis is best suited for the purpose of evaluating the hypothesis that "God," however vaguely conceived, is real and really effective in the universe? (A fuller response to such a question is the goal of this chapter's final section.) For Peirce, so too for James when he wrote about evaluating the "fruits for life" of such an idea, and most certainly for any future theosemiotic, the primary laboratory for testing such a religious hypothesis will be the ongoing experience of individuals who deliberately shape their conduct in conformity with it as an ideal for human living (*CP* 6.467, 486–91). Test results will be more valuable if they involve scrutiny of the character of such individuals developed over a lifetime rather than only during a brief period. Likewise, it will be more profitable to compare the characters and behavior of many individuals rather than a few while also exploring the effects of religious ideals on various communities of individuals that share a common devotion to them, not just in the present, but over many generations. Such is the nature of all induction that it is specifically designed for discerning patterns rather than for marking episodes, its conclusions growing in confidence with the gradual accumulation of cases and samples.

As a pragmatic enterprise, theosemiotic will regard such praxis as both the upshot of inquiry and its perpetually new beginning—that is, as both experiment and preparatory exercise. It presupposes a religious naturalism that honors as plausible the hypothesis that human minds have evolved in such a way that they have become vaguely but instinctively attuned to whatever religious meaning is conveyed by a world populated with signs. If this hypothesis is to be properly tested, the conditions for such an experiment must be carefully put in place. That is what Peirce was suggesting when he prescribed the rubrics for musement. The book of nature can only be read by someone who waits on its meanings, allows them to emerge freely in contemplation, resisting any "temporary urgency" (*CP* 5.339, note 1; *W2*: 261, note 6) or practical purpose that might otherwise obscure or occlude such meaning. For Peirce, the spirit perfected by such a practice is a spirit of aesthetic playfulness. Beginning as a *petite bouchee* (*CP* 6.458), a "little kiss" with the universe of signs, musement will tend if unimpeded naturally to result in the muser's falling in love with "his strictly hypothetical God" (*CP* 6.467). This practice not only tests for the naturalness or instinctiveness of the idea of God, then, but also serves as an exercise useful for developing the *habitus*-as-skill that is crucial for effectively performing such an experiment.

Every scientist knows that the skill needed for success in the laboratory is only honed by repeated experimentation, by actual engagement in inquiry. This is the sense in which the praxis that is the goal of inquiry is also its necessary presupposition. One becomes good at playing anything only by playing often and attentively. This is as true for the play of musement as it is for tennis or for chess. Yet the inculcation of a habit of play in such an ongoing process is intended typically for ends that transcend mere skill development; playing well is also a matter of playing to win. What does this mean for the person engaged in theological inquiry?

When Peirce portrayed the pragmaticist muser as someone destined to fall in love with the idea of God, he echoed his medieval mentor John Duns Scotus. Recall how the latter classified theology as a "practical science" because "the intellect perfected by the habit of theology apprehends God as one who should be loved and according to rules from which praxis can be elicited."[22] Here the connection between means and ends seems subtly different from the one that links the development of tennis skills to winning tennis matches; theology is not a game with winners and losers. Nevertheless, just as with any game, the primary goal of theology will be conceived as a "good internal to the practice."[23] The play of musement, from first kiss to falling in love, is always already internal to love's teleology. Once the habit of love is established it facilitates ever more skillful, sophisticated forms of play, a falling in love again and again with one already well beloved. This is the recipe for a theology as theosemiotic, one that moves from sign to meaning to habit of interpretation, and then repeatedly back to a fresh encounter with the world of signs and toward the continuous renewal of meaning.

II

Despite what some contemporary scholars would suggest, philosophical pragmatism is most distinctive not for the theory of meaning or truth that it embodies, but as a robust and carefully nuanced theory of inquiry. Consequently, to report that theosemiotic has deep roots in pragmatism is to underscore the significance for theology of how these philosophers understood the nature and purpose of inquiry. Moving on now to the possible ways in which theology might also be construed as a form of therapy is not simultaneously a turning away from this earlier conception. Despite the differences between them, most of the classical pragmatists followed Peirce in regarding habit formation or habit change as the primary goal of inquiry. Such, too, is the basic goal of psychotherapy, the effecting of a treatment for some disorder or maladjustment resulting in newly developed habits of thought, feeling, and behavior. That the word "therapeutic" is linked etymologically in the Greek to a word best translated as "attention" or "attentiveness" is intriguing and further establishes the continuity between theology considered as a mode of inquiry and as a form of therapy. Since therapy is to be regarded as a kind of disciplined practice, the discussion here will also flow easily into the one that follows. Much like distinguishing between different classes of signs against the background of a moving picture of semiosis or between the stages of inquiry when each stage actually presupposes and incorporates elements of the others, this division of theosemiotic into various modes—as inquiry, therapy, praxis—is an exercise in aspect seeing, of freezing in place what is always already in motion, for purposes of emphasis and understanding.

To observe such a continuity is not to argue for identity. Not every inquiry will be comfortably classified as having a therapeutic function, except perhaps in some fairly trivial sense, as might be the case if one were to diagnose every case of ignorance as a "disorder" and then to prescribe inquiry as the treatment or "cure." On the other hand, it is difficult to imagine any practice of therapy that did not presuppose deliberate inquiry, involving the making of careful observations, followed by the formulation, explication, and testing of hypotheses. That therapy—at least of the sort being considered here—typically occurs within the context of an actual conversation between persons resonates with pragmatic insights concerning the dialogical nature of all human thought, as well as its virtually inescapable social dimension. All of these connections notwithstanding, what does therapy have to do with specifically theological forms of deliberation and reflection?

The project of human "selving" was announced as being crucial for theosemiotic very early on in the analysis here, with its potentially religious significance already briefly exposed. Traditional Christian and Buddhist discourse, not uniquely among world religions but with special emphasis, registers in almost medical terms the spiritually unhealthy condition of persons as typically observed and the need for radical self-transformation on the part of religious devotees. Whether the disease is identified as human sinfulness or as suffering (*dukkha*) caused by craving (*tanha*), and however the treatment or cure is envisioned, the devout individual will eventually need to undergo some kind of dramatic change. "Conversion," "*metanoia*," "salvation," "liberation," "enlightenment," "awakening," "*moksha*," "*nirvana*,"—these are all ways of labeling such a change.

Now there are strategies that individuals can pursue on their own and for themselves in order to facilitate self-transformation. Yet therapy is typically understood to involve a relationship between some person and a therapist, the latter offering a third-person perspective on those factors both preventing and enabling real and positive change for the former. The emphasis on such a perspective as vitally important for the achievement of authentic selfhood is another classical pragmatic theme that, as noted previously, can be traced from Peirce through Royce to Mead and beyond. Moreover, the adjustment that one seeks in therapy is not something episodic or occasional, but rather enduring in the form of a habit; such a habit will tend to persist to the extent that it results in an individual's flourishing—that is, for so long as environing circumstances are stable enough to render a certain pattern of thinking, feeling, or behavior felicitous.

For purposes of analysis here, "therapy" will be taken to designate an emphasis on this type of personal adjustment or adaptation, especially insofar as it is facilitated by third- and second-person perspectives and results from some kind of dialogue—including dialogue with oneself. (This may seem like a confusing way to put the matter, but what unfolds internally can take the form of either thinking *about oneself* or talking *to oneself*.) That persons can also change as a result of dramatically altered environmental circumstances is a commonsense conclusion too obvious to need defending. Sometimes the movement from one environment to another is sufficient for human flourishing, without any significant adaptation on the part of those individuals presently in distress. If what I am suffering, for example, is caused by exposure to the incredible heat while sitting under the noontime sun, a rest in the shade or a dip in the lake may be all that is really needed.

Whether it involves individual self-transformation or not, the serious work that needs to be done in order to modify social structures or environments that are deemed oppressive, dangerous, or unhealthy for the persons that occupy them is also an important part of the work of theology—again, for purposes of analysis and emphasis, to be labeled here as "praxis." Among the pragmatists, Dewey was especially sensitive to the need for this kind of social, political, and institutional change; as such his work and insights are crucial for theosemiotic. The continuity between a theology conceived as therapy and one conceived as praxis flows in both directions. As just observed, therapy is itself a form of praxis. Moreover, one might choose to regard the sort of political and social action that constitutes praxis as itself being therapeutic in a sense, as following logically upon the heels of a type of therapy conducted not with individuals, but with institutions or communities that are judged in one way or another to be unhealthy, sometimes even poisoned and dying. To return now to a well-worn theme, in the case either of suffering individuals or communities in need of repair, the first step toward any successful outcome will require paying the proper kind of attention. Indeed, the very problem needing to be addressed might be said to consist in a peculiar kind of inattentiveness.

To better understand how a theology conceived as theosemiotic can function therapeutically, it will be useful to invest considerable energy first in exploring the links, both historical and conceptual, between philosophical pragmatism and modern psychology. This relationship is hardly one that has been ignored. After all, William James, Josiah Royce, John Dewey, and George Herbert Mead, in addition to their more explicitly philosophical deliberations, all published significant and influential work in psychology proper. James and Mead, most especially, have had an enduring impact on the field of psychology, both as it first emerged in the late nineteenth and early twentieth centuries and as it has subsequently evolved. Here my primary interest is more narrowly focused on specific psychotherapeutic practices than on the field of psychology in general.

Even more narrowly, I want to emphasize certain contemporary "mindfulness-based" psychotherapies that have appeared within the wider context of modern cognitive behavioral therapy. These include, perhaps most prominently, acceptance and commitment therapy (ACT), mindfulness-based cognitive therapy (MBCT), and dialectical behavior therapy (DBT). Even here the relationship to pragmatism has not been completely neglected. The development of ACT, for example, has been explicitly linked to its roots in a certain type of American pragmatism that is most typically called "functional contextualism." Nevertheless, within such accounts, the term "pragmatism" is very broadly and vaguely construed; moreover, functional contextualism, as a theoretical perspective, seems more immediately indebted to B. F. Skinner's behaviorism and Stephen Pepper's metaphysics than it does to the pragmatism of Peirce, James, Dewey, or Mead.

My suspicion, however, is that the classical American pragmatists supply important and hitherto unexamined theoretical resources that could be useful for psychologists engaged in these mindfulness-based therapeutic practices. Indeed, even the turn to mindfulness meditation itself as an effective strategy for dealing with various forms of mental disorder can be articulated and defended in terms supplied by philosophical pragmatism. While both traditional and contemporary Buddhist sources and materials are typically cited for this purpose, I would argue that the pragmatic insights of Charles Peirce and William James, in particular, might be just as useful or even more productive. Here, once again, I am thinking most directly about the special significance that both philosophers attached to the concept of *attention*.

Functional contextualism is a philosophical perspective that has been linked to pragmatism and identified as supplying the theoretical background for the development of these so-called third-wave behavioral psychotherapies.[24] The challenge posed by an empirically based behavior analysis to classical psychoanalysis earlier in the twentieth century formed the first wave; the emphasis on cognition associated with the emergence of cognitive therapy beginning in the 1970s constituted the second; more recently, these new-wave therapies are being distinguished by the commitment of their practitioners to understanding "the context and functions of psychological phenomena, not just their form."[25] If the second generation emerged because the first had failed to pay sufficient attention to cognition in the diagnosis and treatment of various psychopathologies, this third generation was launched by the insight that context and function were not being adequately dealt with. Identifying a particular thought or emotion as negative in form does not entail that it has a negative function in every context. Mindfulness techniques, for example, might allow one to observe anxious feelings without judgment, thus creating a situation in which they have no deleterious effect. In a different context, these same feelings might very well prove to be harmful. But third-wave practitioners are not narrowly focused on bringing about first-order change in the form of psychological events; rather, their "contextualist assumptions" and the employment of new therapeutic strategies allow them significantly to "broaden the focus of change."[26] Working directly to change the content of one's thoughts and feelings through therapy moves backstage as the meta-cognitive attempt to transform one's relationship to those thoughts and feelings becomes the central object of concern. From the Peircean perspective being developed here, if the self is a living stream of semiosis, successful therapy will consist in effecting a certain strategy of meta-semiosis, a fresh reading or interpretation of the way that one habitually interprets the meaning and value of specific thoughts and feelings.

Contextualism was one of the four basic "root metaphors" that the philosopher Stephen Pepper explored in his widely influential book *World Hypotheses: A Study in Evidence*, first published in 1942. In the Preface to that work, Pepper recalls how he was first awakened from his "dogmatic materialist" slumber when he began "to feel the impact of Gestalt psychology and pragmatic doctrines,"[27] with the latter in particular clearly shaping his understanding of contextualism. In the account that follows, Peirce and James are identified by Pepper as "early contextualists."[28] John Dewey's philosophy is portrayed as a later development of this same perspective, and C. I. Lewis is also invoked in the discussion. Pepper locates the point of origin for contextualism in what he calls the "historic act" or "event." His concern is not with history in the abstract, as some later re-presentation of past events, but rather, with "the event in its actuality," as something that "is going on now, the dynamic dramatic active event." Such an act or event can never be properly conceived in isolation from environing conditions; always, it is to be regarded as "an act in and with its setting, an act in its context."[29] (This is also why therapy can never effectively be separated from praxis.) Moreover, "these acts or events are all intrinsically complex, composed of interconnected activities with continuously changing patterns. They are like incidents in the plot of a novel or a drama. They are literally the incidents of life."[30] Such a theory resonates with, even at times intersects with, the dialogical account of the self articulated by Bhaktin and his successors, despite their being widely disparate both in point of origin and with respect to the concerns that motivated their development.

In his 1988 review of Pepper's book, Steven C. Hayes, generally regarded as the leading figure in the contemporary development of Acceptance and Commitment Therapy, was even more succinct in his summary of this perspective: "The root metaphor of contextualism," he reports there, "is the ongoing act in context."[31] Moreover, inquiry conducted in this vein operates with what he perceived to be a thoroughly pragmatic concept of truth. The truth criterion of contextualism is quite simply whether or not the results of inquiry can be shown to work successfully, whether or not they can be used to accomplish particular goals. While Pepper did not write his book primarily for the purposes of psychologists and therapists, Hayes observes obvious parallels between this account of contextualism and B. F. Skinner's mid-twentieth-century development of what he called "radical behaviorism." Skinner's insistence that we cannot understand the behavior of any system until we "turn to forces operating on the system from without" is most readily articulated and defended in explicitly contextualist terms.[32] Skinner's pragmatic, contextualistic assumptions allowed him to admit that private cognitions are real and open to examination, while simultaneously warning that attending exclusively to such phenomena has often "stood in the way of the inspection of more important things"—in particular, blocking examination of "the environmental conditions which would have led to a much more effective analysis."[33]

From such a psychotherapeutic point of view, analysis will be effective precisely to the extent that it results in predicting and influencing behavior.[34] Moreover, on Hayes's account, prediction and control represent one goal, not two. Successful prediction, he argues, should involve the identification of variables that "would, if they could be manipulated, affect the probability of the event."[35] Now no action or event can even be conceived as such apart from some set of enveloping circumstances. Yet any given act can be analyzed for a great variety of purposes and in varying contexts. In fact, the analysis of such an event will require "an ever-widening examination of context." To use one of Hayes's examples, a movement of the legs will be perceived as walking in one context, kicking in another. Once identified as ambulation, "walking to the store" presents a different context for analysis than "walking for exercise."[36] The appropriate choice of context will be fixed by the particular goal of any analysis and then evaluated in terms of the pragmatic criterion of "successful working."

This is a very crude sketch of both Pepper's articulation of contextualism as a root metaphor and Hayes's application of it to the practice of psychotherapy. Moreover, details left out of this sketch might easily be considered relevant to any thorough assessment of the relationship between contextualism and philosophical pragmatism. In analyzing events under the category of "fusion," for example, Pepper observed that "contextualism is the only theory that takes fusion seriously," conferring on it a "cosmic dignity," in stark contrast to other theories that interpret it away "as vagueness, confusion, failure to discriminate, muddledness."[37] In the process of fusion, the details of any given event "are completely merged in the quality of the whole." Pepper used William James's example of how the taste of lemon, sugar, and water are fused in the drinking and tasting of lemonade. But, of course, the concept of vagueness was as central to Charles Peirce's synechism as it was to James's radical empiricism. This insistence on taking vagueness seriously is one of the distinctive features of classical American pragmatism, well noted by Pepper, but otherwise largely ignored. It is also a distinguishing feature of theosemiotic inquiry.

Against the background of functional contextualism, Steven Hayes and others have developed the Relational Frame Theory (RFT) of human language.[38] By virtue of a phenomenon that Hayes calls "cognitive fusion," our reaction to certain things and events can become conflated with the language that we use to talk about them. This extraordinary human capacity for creating links between things, best exemplified in our verbal behavior, has proven to have enormous adaptive utility for our species, while also being the source of considerable psychic pain.

With its emphasis on exposing infelicitous belief-habits and correcting false interpretations that result in distressful emotional and behavioral consequences, cognitive therapy appears to be a practice solidly grounded in fertile pragmatic soil.[39] Yet, when queried about the philosophical roots of cognitive theory, its lead architect, Aaron Beck, has most typically gestured toward the importance of ancient Greek philosophy, especially Stoicism, in the development of his thought.[40] Now, from a certain point of view, Stoicism may seem as far removed from pragmatism on the philosophical spectrum as one might be able to imagine. A perspective that advocates a radical acceptance of the limits of human powers and capacities would seem to be at odds with one that seeks to harness the resources of human intelligence and creativity for melioristic purposes. But this contrast ought not to be drawn too sharply. Neither Stoicism nor pragmatism is an abstract philosophy unconcerned with the actual complexities of human life and behavior. Both are committed to the project of identifying and cultivating what for various reasons might be judged as salient habits of thought, feeling, and conduct. Stoicism can never be reduced to pessimism pure and simple. And the confident optimism of the pragmatist, ideally, should be that of one who knows the inevitability of suffering, one who appreciates the depth of suffering that can afflict a "sick soul," thus one who has been "twice-born," rather than simply being "healthy-minded" by natural disposition (to borrow William James's categories).[41]

Finally, dialectical behavioral therapists have identified Hegel as an important philosophical precursor. A systems approach to behavior, emphasizing the ubiquity of change and the primacy of a whole that is greater than its parts (along with the insignificance of parts that are isolated from relationship to the whole) are all Hegelian insights that DBT proponents regard as crucial to their practice.[42] But here again the pragmatists might just as readily have been invoked for inspiration. This observation is hardly intended to astonish anyone. Recall that Peirce (and also Royce) wrestled with the philosophy of the German idealists, especially Hegel and Schelling, throughout much of his career. The young Dewey was also steeped in Hegel and Hegelianism, with his own pragmatic systems approach to philosophizing being further shaped by elements of Darwinism. In any event, whether described as a commitment to "holism" by specialists in DBT or an advocacy of "contextualism" as in ACT, the philosophical background for these new-wave psychotherapies seems sufficiently pragmatic in flavor to warrant further exploration and comparison.

To be sure, labels like "pragmatism" and "behaviorism," as they are typically employed, are a bit fuzzy at the borders. It has already been noted that even Skinner's "radical behaviorism" is capacious enough to accommodate talk about private cognitions. The turn toward the cognitive during the second-wave development of CBT probably ought best to be conceived less as a direct rebuttal of earlier forms of behavioral analysis than as a plea for the recognition that cognition itself is a form of behavior. This is a conclusion, of course, that Peirce had arrived at more than a century earlier. Moreover, as Peirce, Royce, and Mead were so emphatic in insisting, there is no special power of intuition or introspection that supplies direct access to one's private cognitions. We learn about ourselves in very much the same way that we come to know others, by virtue of observation and inference. Thus, it is this privileging of the third-person perspective in pragmatism, also an underscoring of the logic embedded in our practices (and not limited to what is articulated in our discourse), that might render it quite congenial as a theoretical background for behavioral analysis.

Sometimes these observations and inferences are ones that we make ourselves, while sometimes we lean heavily on others to help us make them, as when engaged in a session with a psychotherapist or in a conversation with a friend. Whatever strategy is employed in order to achieve it, meta-cognition is the realm in which the third-wave mindfulness-based therapies are designed to operate successfully. "Distancing" or "decentering" is considered a crucial precondition of mindful awareness.[43] The distance one needs to create is that which opens up between present awareness and some well-entrenched habit of thinking and behaving that has become identified as the source of psychic pain. This distancing is always also, in terms of context, a kind of broadening—for purposes of therapy, a "broadening of the focus of change."

Arthur Lovejoy reported more than a century ago that it was already possible to identify at least "thirteen pragmatisms."[44] Since the emergence, post-Rorty, of various forms of neo-pragmatism, that number has surely grown. Some pragmatists, especially of the decisively "neo" variety, will be more comfortable with "successful working" as a truth criterion than others will. Peirce, for example, could embrace such a criterion only if it refers to what might prove itself to work for many rather than for any single individual, and only in the long run, never just the short term. So different pragmatisms will be more or less friendly to behaviorism, judging it as intellectually congenial to a greater or lesser extent. In addition, the more expansive and sophisticated third-wave perspectives on human behavioral analysis will be most likely to find in Peirce's pragmaticism some helpful source of insight.

Toward such an end, consider yet again not Peirce, but in this instance the importance of the concept of attention in William James's philosophy and psychology. "My experience is what I agree to attend to," he announced. "Only those items which I notice shape my mind—without selective interest, experience is an utter chaos."[45] Yet the phenomenon of attention is remarkably complex, manifesting itself in a variety of ways, each of which is delineated in James's account. Attention may be directed either to sense objects or to inner thoughts and feelings, for example; it may be passive and reflexive or active and voluntary.[46] James makes other distinctions and subdistinctions within each category. The analysis of attention with regard to volition seems especially significant for present purposes. Recall that for James, "volition is nothing but attention" so that on his account "the turnings of our attention form the nucleus of our inner self."[47] My will is finite in scope and power just to the degree that my attention can be diverted or captured. To the extent that I *am* free, however, my attention will have real causal power. It is by "voluntary acts of attention" that one is able temporarily to arrest the stream of thoughts and feelings that constitutes the self, causing it to pause here or there, perhaps even to flow in a new direction. Without this capacity, the self must be regarded as a "pure effect" of material causes, the feeling of choice being nothing more than the "inert accompaniment" of one brain cell acting on another.[48] It will lack altogether the kind of freedom that Peirce identified as self-control.

James admitted even as early as his writing of *The Principles of Psychology* that the question about whether we possess such a capacity is as deeply metaphysical as it is psychological; but there is no doubt about how he chose to answer this question. A dozen years after the publication of the *Principles*, in his Gifford Lectures on *The Varieties of Religious Experience*, James portrayed the moral hero as one who, even if sick and unable to act outwardly, nevertheless "can willfully turn his attention away from his own future, whether in this world or the next. He can train himself to indifference to his present drawbacks."[49] This training is complicated and multifaceted. One can train the will to attend to this sort of thing rather than to that, also to choose the amount of effort with which to attend to various things that attract one's interest. Even the choice not to exert the will at all, somewhat paradoxically, is an act of volition. James described a religious state of mind, different from that of the moral hero because, for the former, "no exertion of volition is required." But here I would argue that the emphasis should fall on the concept of "exertion" rather than "volition," since James immediately proceeds to characterize such a state of mind as resulting from "a willingness to close our mouths and be as nothing in the floods and waterspouts of God."[50] Here is a kind of willing not to exert the will, of choosing not to choose, better understood as the cultivation of a certain habit of volition rather than the performance of a series of determinate volitional acts. (Such a reading of James further softens the potential contrast between his view and that of Simone Weil, already briefly sketched.)

At the risk of stretching metaphors to the breaking point, this surrender to divine "floods and waterspouts" can readily be conceived as involving a stepping outside of the narrow stream of thoughts and feelings that enacts the self in its everydayness. Even the moral hero's "training to indifference" already signals a movement into meta-cognitive space, a certain "distancing" or "decentering" of the self. But "the mystic or ascetic saint" moves much further into this territory by cultivating a state of mind that reduces the self to "nothing"—while in such a state, to silence. Since the third-wave psychotherapies have been directly influenced by Buddhist meditative practices, it does not seem far-fetched to link the religious mindset that James depicted here to the meta-cognitive training that they prescribe. Interestingly enough, James compares this religious attitude to the sort of resignation advocated by ancient Stoicism, but then also contrasts it as being "much more active and positive."[51] Here is further evidence that, on some level and in some fashion, the will is actively involved in the process of attaining this ideal state of mind and being to which the religious devotee aspires.

The theological label for such a process is "conversion," but James delineates it in explicitly psychological terms. The self is comprised of what James refers to as "waves of consciousness," each of which embraces "the field of objects present to the thought at any time."[52] Each wave or field is succeeded by another; each has a certain center, as well as margins that are more or less indeterminate. To be converted involves replacing what now constitutes the "habitual center" of one's interests and energy with ideas or aims that presently lie at the periphery of consciousness. There is a voluntary or "volitional type" of conversion, one that involves the gradual building up, piece by piece, of new habits and then the "type by self-surrender" that results from an exhaustion with this process, a relaxation and then the sudden flooding in of transformative impulses from just beyond the margins of consciousness.[53] Here several observations seem in order.

In the first place, one should note that conversion always involves a shift in attention. The center of any field of consciousness draws the bulk of one's attention; beliefs and ideas at the center of attention, in James's view, are "hot and live."[54] This is what, at least for the present duration of time, one cares about the most. One can only really love that to which one pays a rather deep and ongoing attention. Conversion (which in this respect is a bit like falling in love) is a decentering, a distancing of oneself from what had occupied the center of attention previously and a focusing on what was at or perhaps beyond the margins of consciousness.

Even traditional cognitive behavioral therapy involves such a process (albeit understood in secular terms), as the therapist helps the client to expose and identify certain "automatic thoughts" that are typically preconscious or at the fringe of consciousness. CBT strategies best fit James's model of voluntary conversion as an emphasis is placed on the gradual building up, through "homework" exercises and repeated exposures, of new habits of attention and interpretation. Mindfulness-based psychotherapy resonates with the second type of conversion that James scrutinized, where self-surrender eventuates in "a feeling of being in a wider life," a powerful and liberating "sense of enlargement."[55] The resonance here is with the "radical acceptance" strategies typically proposed by mindfulness-based therapists and with the constant broadening of the context of analysis emphasized by third-wave practitioners. James refused to drive a deep wedge between the two types of conversion, arguing that "even in the most voluntarily built-up sort of regeneration there are passages of self-surrender interposed."[56] Similarly, mindfulness-based therapists understand their practice as the fruitful enhancement rather than a repudiation of traditional CBT. The complementarity of these practices, it seems to me, might best be illuminated against a Peircean background.

When Peirce instructed the prospective muser to be awake and to open conversation with herself, he added the descriptive judgment "for such is all meditation" (*CP* 6.461). Now whether or not Peirce is correct that this is an accurate portrayal of all forms of meditation, it does seem to capture the spirit of Buddhist mindfulness meditation, with its emphasis on the open and nonjudgmental awareness of whatever one encounters in the present moment. For both Peirce and the Buddhists (and, I might add, for William James in his discussion of how attention can dispel a state of distraction), this practice stimulates the awakening from a more typical state of consciousness that, by comparison, resembles sleep.

According to Peirce's most well-known account, inquiry is all about replacing a problematic habit of thought with another that is more felicitous, much as the CBT practitioner directs attention to those automatic thoughts at the fringe of consciousness that have been identified for a client as the source of anxiety, depression, or undesirable behavior. What is being suggested here is that Peirce's most mature theory also makes room for a practice like musement, which he clearly identified as constituting the proper first stage of inquiry. While it may become more specialized and thus "converted into scientific study" (*CP* 6.459), musement itself is open, never avoiding but always ready for what experience might reveal, playful and not purpose-driven or directed toward the solution of some problem. Its immediate goal is a kind of *exposure* to reality, a state of nonjudgmental readiness for whatever is revealed in experience, that forms the background for and then blossoms into a lively conversation with oneself.[57]

The self is a complex semiotic relation, a process of interpretation shaped by attention, with meaning not attached to individual thought-signs but only emerging over time as semiosis unfolds. It can and often does slumber along, attention easily captured by this or that distraction, or even diminished as the self sinks into a state of semi-awareness. Nevertheless, by the careful exercise of attention, it is possible, Peirce argued, to achieve a certain self-control, often in the imagination and within the context of a lively conversation with oneself. In this meta-cognitive space, one can imagine future versions of oneself; guided by certain ideals and by attending properly in the imagination, one can gradually shape the self into new forms over time. As portrayed earlier, the human self is an emergent property of complex semiotic relations. It is only by "indefinite replication of self-control upon self-control that the *vir* is begotten" (*CP* 5.403, note 3). (This assertion was Peirce's own colorful way of describing what we now tend to refer to as meta-cognitive behavior.)

Now, given the standard account of the history of pragmatism, one might be tempted to reduce self-control to a process of dissolving old and forming new habits in response to what could be perceived as problematic states of affairs. A good deal of psychotherapy in the cognitive-behavioral tradition, of course, takes precisely this form. Yet, by unraveling the logic of musement we discover a practice that does not focus on changing the form or content of any particular habit of thought, feeling, or behavior. In this playful practice, one can have all thoughts and feelings as though one did not have them. Distanced from them, one can contemplate them without being victimized by their hegemony. As both the Buddhist and the mindfulness-based therapist would agree, "I am not my thoughts."

Despite appearing to have clearly stated otherwise (since very early on he argued that a self essentially *is* a living stream of thought-signs), I suspect that Peirce would agree as well, but only with careful qualification. "I" cannot be reduced to any particular thoughts or feelings that make up the stream of semiosis from which my self emerges. Consequently, I cannot be reduced to my feelings of anxiety or sadness or to my negative thoughts about myself . . . but they are a part of who I am nevertheless. The livelier and broader my conversation with myself becomes—the more nuanced and well-developed the habit of attention that shapes this conversation—the more generous and balanced is the self that eventuates. This habit is really a kind of meta-habit, supplying an important perspective on all of the habits of thought, feeling, and conduct that constitute the self. When Peirce, Royce, and Mead insisted that we can only come to know ourselves in much the same way that we learn about and know other persons, they were simply reporting that the self always already is a self-in-relation—for Peirce and Royce especially, a semiotic relation. The self always already is a conversation in context, so that it is shaped by everything that one has ever experienced and includes the voices of every person that one has ever known. The goal of therapy is to succeed in restructuring this internal dialogue so that certain voices now silenced might be empowered to speak, with others gradually muted.

It would be unwise to conclude that Peirce was a behaviorist pure and simple or that pragmatism entails a commitment to behaviorism, especially when the latter is narrowly conceived. Interestingly, a standard exercise recommended by ACT therapists to clients is also one that was prescribed to his readers by the late philosopher-novelist Walker Percy in an essay that constitutes, at least in part, a Peircean critique of behaviorism.[58] That exercise involves repeating a word over and over again until it becomes gradually drained of meaning. The ACT strategy is to convince clients that they need not avoid or react to the words and symbols for things as they might to the things themselves. It is an attempt to sever the link (or "cognitive fusion") between symbol and thing so that words and thoughts do not continue to cause us so much psychic pain. By contrast, Percy's Peircean emphasis is on the irreducibility of the triadic relationship between thing, sign, and the sign's interpretation. The self just is a continuous series of such relationships, unfolding over time. On this view, the link between sign and object is not dissolved; instead, that link becomes a thread woven into a complex process of interpretation, its meaning transformed by becoming part of a story always still to be told, just one thread of a great conversation.

Having established at considerable length these multifold points of contact between pragmatism and psychotherapy of a certain type and orientation, how can we then further evaluate theology's therapeutic function? The seeds of an answer to this question have already been sown in the preceding discussion; there is no need at this point to strike out in an entirely new direction. In the first place, faithful to pragmaticism and eschewing pragmatisms that assume a more rigid and narrow form, theology conceived as therapy will take up the task of guiding habit formation and facilitating a more capacious kind of self-transformation for religious devotees rather than looking to "fix" some particular problem or to address a specific issue that might confront them. Nevertheless—and somewhat distinct from the kind of habit formation associated with other forms of inquiry—theology as therapy *will* focus on those dispositions and tendencies that are deemed to be generally problematic in some discernible way—as moral vices or sources of sinful behavior, for example, or as the cause of suffering and psychic pain. Contemporary theology performs such a task, to identify just one type of example, when it critically examines beliefs that can be identified as racist or sexist or homophobic or classist or elitist or as forms of religious bigotry. Such beliefs, on any pragmatic account, are properly to be regarded as habits, yet often escaping our attention even as they dramatically affect our behavior. The work of theology here involves the proper focusing of attention, a task that can be identified as meta-cognitive, also as an example of meta-semiosis. The ideal result is a reshaping of the self conceived as semiosis—in James's terms, a moving of what may have been at the margins of self-consciousness closer to its vital center.

The potential scope of theosemiotic inquiry is vast, but when it takes the form of therapy its primary subject matter will be the self as living legisign, what it means, and how its meaning might best be enabled to grow in positive and fruitful ways. As with all theology, this is an exercise in interpretation, but here of the sort most typically identified as discernment, some rules and strategies for which will be further explored in a subsequent chapter. Such rules, to be sure, will almost always be supplied by some religious community of interpretation, directly linked to how the members of that community conceive ideally of what it means to be a self, of how the process of "selving" can fail, of how the damage resulting from some failure might be repaired, and so on. Even for communities of Buddhists who conceive of the very concept of an individual "self" as illusory and problematic, there are rules for how attention can be beneficially directed, strategies for eliminating the suffering that clinging to such a conception might engender. Pragmatically speaking, then, certain habitual tendencies remain a primary object of concern, a key focus of theosemiotic inquiry, with the goal of undermining the hegemony of some while increasing the potency of others (or establishing altogether new ones) continuing to be basic for theology as therapy.

Pragmatists have traditionally refused to drive a wedge between theory and practice, between thoughts and actions. It seems obvious that cognitive therapy operates within the same general framework. Cognitions are tangibly linked to emotions and actions; meanings really do influence what we feel and do. Theologians have explored a variety of meditative disciplines designed to enable a practitioner to achieve some measure of control over what they feel and do, primarily by shaping the process of how they interpret the meaning of certain feelings and behavior. Musement is a playful form of self-inquiry that, as Peirce himself acknowledged, resembles such meditation (with further parallels, one might observe, in the psychotherapeutic practices of free association and role-playing).[59] Here there is an implicit acknowledgment of what Peirce designated as the more "deeply shaded" regions of the human psyche. In the process of such cognitive play, thoughts and feelings that may lie well below the surface of consciousness are permitted to bubble to the surface and become available for contemplation. On the premises articulated both by Peirce and by the cognitive therapists, however, much of this subterranean material is nevertheless to be perceived as cognition (indeed, feelings were vague thoughts in Peirce's view). Even when unconscious it can dramatically shape the human project of making meaning. Once exposed, its own meaning can be interrogated and explored, even submitted to critique.

Musement, while it can be conceived as an introspective exercise, is by no means exclusively so. Playful but disciplined attention to what lies "about" or beyond the self can result in fresh insight concerning how certain institutions, environments, or relationships are functioning to produce or support specific habits of thought, feeling, and conduct. Equally important, it can take the form of a "deep listening" to those others (human and nonhuman) who for any variety of reasons have been confined to the edges of consciousness, often with deleterious moral effect.[60] The fact that listening to and learning about the experiences of such others can be transformative for the listener is morally secondary to the fact that these others ought to be heard. That is to say, this kind of listening is morally obligated and not merely felicitous as a catalyst for deepened self-awareness. (Here is an instance of where therapy merges with praxis.)

Meanings are born, have a lifespan, and then die. Sometimes they compete with one another, one sign series intersecting with and trumping another. Sometimes they drown and disappear in the "powerful waves of an unconscious sea" from which they first emerged.[61] Anything that functions as a sign is clearly always already something other than a sign. One does not have to be a Lacanian in any straightforward sense in order to affirm that semiosis reaches beneath the level of consciousness, that at least a part of the human unconscious is semiotically structured. But it would be presumptuous to insist without argument that the unconscious is semiosis "all the way down." Since it seems impossible in principle to reach all the way down, any claim about where semiosis begins and ends must be and remain a conjecture.

Perhaps, then, there is no single answer to the question raised and repeated earlier about the limits of semiosis. What Peirce regarded as the "dynamic object" of a sign, determining and constraining the path of semiosis, but not in the exact same way that a sign determines its interpretant, represents one such limit. We cannot be directly conscious of such an object—our awareness of it is always mediated—but it gives shape to what we can know or conceive. As just indicated, the fact that signs can "bubble up" from the unconscious mind into consciousness is no proof that such a sea is bottomless, consisting only of signs. The extraordinary vagueness of some signs, an inexhaustible source of meanings, always also leaves a vast space of meaning dark and inaccessible. A sign can lose its meaning, just as any living thing that grows can die. Everything that serves as a sign is also a thing. Something that once spoke to us with clarity and eloquence can now just stare at us, in dumb silence. Some things may never speak at all. This silence could be judged as problematic or as edifying. What was once famously asserted about a poem could be adapted and applied to anything at all: it should not simply mean, but also be.[62] All of these factors taken together mark the limits of semiosis.

Boredom, I have argued at some length elsewhere, can be conceived as a form of "semiotic breakdown."[63] The irony of such a theory of boredom is that, when semiosis breaks down and meaning evaporates, the experience that results is an experience of something that is nothing in particular, so that deep boredom can come to be recognized as a sign of no-thing. Ecstasy plays a similar role for anyone engaged in the task of evaluating fundamental moods and their meaning, anxiety and melancholy also. The theosemiotician needs then to fix careful, sophisticated attention on these deep, pervasive moods. If I am bored with this or that (like I might be in reading a book that fails to hold my interest), philosophically speaking, my situation may not be noteworthy. In contrast, if it is the case, as Heidegger best expressed it, that *I myself am bored*, this boredom might prove to signify something meaningful. Boredom marks the death of meaning, but can also serve as midwife in its rebirth.

In deep boredom or melancholy or ecstasy, there is a space created for the self to be "opened," the possibility of awakening—but an awakening to what? what therein is revealed? Is it a primordial nothingness, or "being itself," or "nature naturing," or a divine reality both vaguely personal and profoundly mysterious? It is certainly nothing that can be perfectly captured in signs, but rather something that often "muffles our speech."[64] Yet we do continue to speak, both theologically and in other ways, sometimes in poetry and song, continuously producing signs. Here, then, is a hypothesis worthy of theosemiotic scrutiny. These signs can never capture, but are themselves occasionally seized by, a power so infinite in potency that it can be manifested through them as no-thing in particular. It crucifies, crushes our symbols, and then brings new ones to life amidst the semiotic debris. As Peirce might express the point, we do not think it, but it uses us as a vehicle to get itself thought. This is part of the raison d'etre of any theosemiotic inquiry: we struggle to interpret what lies most deeply "hidden in the icon," and so to signify the mystery encountered therein, always mostly failing, but sometimes being grasped by it, graced by it, becoming its sign, and so embodying (at best, I think, in conduct shaped by love and in communities rather than alone) a tiny fragment of its meaning.

III

Praxis is a sign. If Jonathan Edwards was correct, it is in fact the most religiously meaningful of all the signs that are woven into the fabric of human experience and behavior. Theology can be conceived as a form of praxis, in the first place, because theory is continuous with disciplined human conduct from the pragmatic point of view endorsed in these pages. This is true, not in any crude sense that would make them utterly indistinguishable, but rather, only in the precise way defined by Peirce's pragmaticism, so that the relationship between them is typically mediated by habit. Since the therapeutic function of theology has just been identified with the role it plays in promoting habit formation and habit change, there is also a clear link connecting therapy with praxis; indeed, therapy can be portrayed as a special kind of praxis. The same is true for inquiry, even of the most seemingly abstract and theoretical kind; not only might its results eventually help to shape our other practices, but inquiry can itself be understood as a quite deliberate, rule-governed form of human behavior. Since inquiry can be conceived in this fashion—either as a means to facilitate habit formation, thus shaping conduct in the long run, or as itself a form of praxis with its own intrinsic meaning and purposes—one should be careful to resist the sort of cliched pragmatism that depicts inquiry as taking place, anywhere and always, for the sole purpose of scratching some sudden practical itch.

To underscore the nature of theology as praxis, moreover, is to insist on its thoroughly experimental character, among the stages of inquiry, to focus especially although not exclusively on the importance of induction. Finally, and as already suggested in earlier remarks, the crucial significance of praxis in theology will attach preeminently to its role in transforming communities and institutions, to its political, economic, and social effects. The work of theology in this vein is somewhat distinct from, but also clearly related to, its role in effecting religiously meaningful self-transformation; one focuses on the context while the other emphasizes what is contextualized, but these are clearly two aspects of the same phenomenon, separable only at the risk of distortion.

The tracing of theosemiotic's roots as they run deep in the tradition of philosophical pragmatism is not meant to blind us to possible links with other schools of thought. Marxism and existentialism are both philosophical perspectives that evaluate the meaning and purpose of thought as best being displayed in its tangible effects on human life and conduct, the former conceiving of such conduct in ways more typically sociopolitical, economic, and public, with the latter tending to emphasize individual volition and behavior. The "value added" by pragmatism to these other ways of thinking about the relationship between theory and praxis, at least for the argument being sketched here, is twofold: first, a bringing together of what otherwise might be separated, so that political and institutional change on the one hand, self-transformation on the other, can be conceived as different aspects of a unified process (here Dewey is crucial); and second, a clear emphasis on the nature of the continuity between theory and praxis as one consisting in *semiosis*. (In framing the latter argument, it is Peirce's pragmaticism that moves to the center of our deliberations.)

John Dewey commented that the "formation of habits of belief, desire, and judgment is going on at every instant under the influence of the conditions set by men's contact, intercourse and associations with one another. This is the fundamental fact in social life and in personal character."[65] As for the other classical pragmatists, but with a singular clarity on his account, it is the process of habit formation for Dewey that undermines any sharp distinction between inner and outer, self and society, personal and political, thus also, in the terms supplied here, therapy and praxis. Once again, while attention or action may at any given point in time be directed to one or another of these aspects of the process of habit formation, nevertheless, achieving the aims of morality, improving the quality of education, and insuring the health of democracy are all results that depend ultimately on the extent to which we grasp the meaning and significance of this "fundamental fact." It is a fact, moreover, that one obviously cannot ignore in doing philosophical theology. Here the Darwinian roots of pragmatism are once again exposed. Genetic forces exert their influence from within, while environmental factors supply an external constraint. What the classical pragmatists added to this picture is an account of how human *inquiry* represents a meaningful response to both, so that human evolution is no mere vector analysis of those various lines of force impinging on the species, but involves the creative response of *homo symbolicus* to past and present exigencies in the light of an imagined future.

For the purposes of theology, what is the advantage of a pragmatism informed by semiotic theory when compared with other philosophical styles and systems? Although it might seem like a peculiar way to approach such a question, consider very briefly how best to understand the meaning of "meaning." On the standard account provided by analytic philosophy, meaning is to be construed exclusively as a property of sentences, of the words that populate them and the grammatical rules that shape them. For an existentialist philosopher, however, "meaning" is something that attaches potentially to a human life; the discussion of life's meaning or meaninglessness will unfold in an entirely different intellectual space from the one carved out by analytic philosophy. Now it might seem that the pragmatist is closer to the existentialist here, far removed from the philosopher focused narrowly on language. Yet if the pragmatist in question is a pragmaticist, then she will at least faintly echo the analytic philosopher by arguing that meaning is a property and product of semiosis. The salient difference between the two perspectives is that semiosis can hardly be reduced to language or meaning to linguistic meaning. Nevertheless, there is a certain continuity between these ways of understanding the meaning of "meaning," a continuity best exposed by a clear insight concerning the nature of all human experience as semiosis. When that experience is also judged to be experimental, a deliberate doing rather than a purely passive perceiving, its character as praxis is highlighted, and a conversation with various forms of existentialist, neo-pragmatist, and Marxist philosophizing can be readily established as well.

My intention here is not to wave the concept of semiosis like a magic wand over a complex variety of distinct philosophical perspectives in order to obliterate the differences among them. Any two things might be continuous in *some* important or relevant respect and still be quite different in innumerable other ways. Once again, an emphasis on continuity is not an argument for sameness, the logic of systems not to be confused with a logic that traffics only in class concepts. Any theology framed as theosemiotic will be vastly more indebted to philosophical pragmatism than it will be to other schools of thought. Moreover, as the analysis here will attempt to show, theologically speaking, it will be more akin to the position developed by certain liberation theologians than to various other religious perspectives (although the fact that such theologians have themselves been typically indebted to Marxist thought should be duly noted). Since the challenges confronting philosophical theology are formidable, however, one would be wise to take intellectual help and utilize conceptual resources wherever one might happen to find them.

If praxis is best conceived as a sign, then *what*, more precisely, might it be said to signify? This question is related to a second one about *how* such signification occurs. Consider the latter question first. From a Peircean perspective, feelings and actions as well as thoughts can be construed as signs—on any given occasion, as interpretant-signs that embody and develop the meaning of something encountered in experience. A single action can be meaningful, as when a person turns away in anger or disgust from something that is encountered. Yet a solitary action cannot be said to constitute a practice. In the first place, practices are deliberate in a way that might contrast with actions that are perceived to be random or episodic. Moreover, they will tend to display a certain consistency, not necessarily a rigid sameness, but a discernible pattern that enables one to identify their meaning. Your isolated observation of my emptying the contents of a watering can in my backyard forms a fragile basis for any interpretation of what I may be up to. Perhaps I am just getting rid of water that has been sitting in the can for weeks, now grown rancid and stale and becoming a haven for mosquitos. Perhaps I am emptying it before lending it to a neighbor. Reading my action will be like reading one sentence of a novel—hardly meaningless, but nevertheless inadequate for a reliable interpretation.

If the observation is repeated on every morning when you emerge from your own home to collect your newspaper, enough of a pattern in my behavior might be displayed to make you confident in concluding that I am tending some form of plant life in my yard, maybe watering the grass, or if the action is quite localized, moistening a patch of soil where seeds have been planted to grow. This pattern, the consistency of my behavior, is what allows you to interpret my actions as a practice, to read my behavior in the way that you would a meaningful text. It licenses your judgment that deliberate intentions motivate my actions, even if those intentions, formed some time ago, have now become thoroughly embodied in habit. This habit also is significant, as Jonathan Edwards explained in his treatise on true virtue, a sign that serves as fountain and source of the observable behavior that both articulates and perfects it. Such a habit, made visible in the consistency of our practices, is what Peirce identified as the ultimate logical interpretant of a sign.

Consistency implies sameness only for the dullest of habits, those that result in a deadening of human sensibilities and the routinization of behavior. To the extent that habit represents some kind of skill, as both Peirce and the medieval scholastics understood the concept, it will be manifested in quite different forms of behavior. The well-engrained habits that must be developed by professional musicians or athletes can yield virtuoso performances, enabling extraordinary creativity. The very same habit, under different conditions or with varying circumstances, will elicit contrasting forms of behavior. For present theological purposes, it has been suggested that the cultivation of a certain habit of love can be conceived in ideal terms as the ultimate logical interpretant of the self-as-legisign. This is what the self should gradually come to mean in the lifelong process of interpreting and responding to a great variety of religiously relevant signs and symbols (as different, for example, as the "great poem" embedded in nature on the one hand, and some person encountered as a stranger displaying signs of distress on the other). Yet surely love will move a person to act in disparate ways depending on the type of situation in which such action unfolds. My love may require me either to speak or to remain silent. On one occasion it may impel me to intervene actively, on another to wait patiently. It could cause me to leave or to remain. I may be moved to contemplate or to celebrate, to bemoan the suffering that love brings or to praise its delights. The decision about which action is appropriate must be rooted in a process of careful interpretation, of skilled discernment. Virtuosity in loving presupposes a practice of continuous reading and rereading.[66]

Some of Peirce's own scholarly readers conceive of the ultimate logical interpretant in any sign series as constituting the termination of that particular stream of semiosis.[67] On Peirce's theory, they remind us, every interpretant of a sign is itself also a sign, available for further interpretation and related in a mediated fashion to the first sign's object. This is how meaning develops or "grows." Notwithstanding, if such a process was interminable, the result would be an infinite, endless stream of signifiers. Now, this may suffice as an accurate interpretation of some of Peirce's early writings, they suggest—it is the reading that Jacques Derrida preferred when he appropriated Peirce's semiotic for his own purposes—but it was not Peirce's final opinion about this issue. Peirce came to recognize that a stream of signs must eventually bear fruit in human conduct, terminating in some habit of behavior that serves as an interpretant but is *not* itself another sign. (Not every habit will have this interpretive function, but only those that are "deliberately formed" and "self-analyzing"; see CP 5.491.) It is in precisely this fashion, such a reading suggests, that Peirce's semiotic theory eventually hooks up with his pragmaticism.

That the ultimate logical interpretant is not just another thought-sign like the ones that may have preceded it in a stream of semiosis is a claim that I would be willing to affirm. I would refrain, however, from arguing that such a habit is not a sign in any sense at all.[68] What we are reading when we interpret another person's behavior consists largely of the meanings embodied in a cluster or bundle of habits. To the extent that such an individual has achieved any kind of unified self, these habits will be connected in distinctive ways, display a certain purposefulness, indicate the shaping presence of certain desires and ideals, and so on.[69] That is why it makes sense to think of the human self as a living legisign. To embrace such a conception is by no means to suggest that everything that the self does, every act or instance of behavior, is rigidly governed by some law, regulated by a fixed pattern to which it must adhere. In the first place, habits of the sort being considered here do not influence behavior in such a narrowly determinate way, instead acting as general tendencies so that a certain type of conduct will be elicited under appropriate circumstances. Moreover, habits are continuously evolving, being modified, some dissolved either through conscious effort or because of dramatically changed circumstances, with new habits also being cultivated. On occasion, the reasons for doing something altogether different from how one has generally been disposed to act in the past can be readily identified; it may require no further explanation than that one had grown bored with the way one did things previously. But sometimes the motivations for action are buried in the unconscious, their source an unruly one, potentially accessible for partial inspection to the extent that one can with effort expose the territory just beyond the edges of consciousness, but otherwise and often inscrutable.

While the question already repeatedly raised about the limits of semiosis does not point to a single, obvious answer, how that question is framed will play a major role in predetermining the way in which any given answer is to be evaluated. Once again, if linguistic meaning is the only kind of meaning there is, then semiosis will be confined altogether to the realm of verbal behavior. Such a narrow view of meaning and signification has been emphatically rejected here. That a nonverbal gesture can be profoundly meaningful is a claim that seems easily defensible. (The truth of this claim, moreover, does not rest on the condition that the meaning of a gesture must be readily translatable into language.) Pressing beyond this point, it is now also being suggested that a gesture linked to some developed habit will be more meaningful than one that is random, indeed that such a habit is itself a sign that can be evaluated and interpreted. The habit is quite inaccessible, to be sure, apart from the conduct that gives evidence of or displays it. At the same time, this is very different from proposing that the habit is completely *reducible* to some set of actions, a position defended by certain behaviorists but one that Peirce was more than blithe to repudiate. Even a great many actions, performed over a long period of time, could not exhaust the meaning of a habit that shapes and informs them. On any given occasion, the same habit might inspire an act that seems quite different from any that has hitherto been observed.

To summarize and also emphasize: habits are not permanently fixed but are somewhat labile and capable of being modified. Not only is human behavior rather gently determined by the habits that any given individual will possess, but such behavior itself, especially if it is either strikingly novel or faithfully consistent, is a key strategy for bringing about habit change. A habit of love, for example, is never fully developed as a fixed or static thing, but admits of continuous growth (so that it might even be more appropriate to talk about love as habituescence).

Theology as praxis is directly focused on the project of habit formation and habit change. This is a challenging project because the proper designation of a habit is not a monadic predicate describing some character or quality possessed by an individual; it is a complex relational concept indicating the tendency of that individual to behave in a certain manner under certain conditions. Traditionally, the spiritual practices developed and fostered by various religious communities have also been conceived as focused on habits, but almost always in a way that emphasizes, in a therapeutic fashion, the work and effort needed in order to achieve some kind of self-transformation. This is the way that Peirce himself understood self-control, as rehearsal in the imagination of how one might best respond to certain circumstances in order to inculcate habits appropriate for flourishing in precisely those circumstances. Not limited to Peirce, the concept of habit was crucial for all of the classical American pragmatists. As philosophers profoundly influenced by Darwin and Darwinism, they were each concerned with how organisms develop by adapting to changing environmental conditions, and furthermore, how human organisms utilize distinctive intellectual capacities for precisely this purpose.

Here the narrative needs to be complicated quite a bit. That task has already been initiated in the examination supplied earlier of Peirce's complex theory of inquiry. What is the significance for theology of a form of inquiry that is more akin to growing an aesthetic ideal than to fixing beliefs that have suddenly become problematic because of shifting circumstances? This narrative will be even further complicated by adding the voices of John Dewey and the liberation theologians in the telling of our story. For Dewey, the exercise of critical intelligence is often a matter less of acting directly to transform the organism struggling to cope with the exigencies of a particular situation than it is a matter of working strategically to alter that situation; this is a project that needs illumination from both the social sciences and political philosophy. Its goals are not at odds with psychotherapy but clearly and necessarily complementary, as already indicated, part of the same complex process (evaluating the "ongoing act in context"). In doing the work of theology, whether one or the other—therapy or praxis—or perhaps both are required in any given situation in order to bring about an optimal state of affairs is a judgment that requires a certain "wisdom to know the difference."

Theological praxis will tend to display certain characteristic features, crucial among them an emphasis on community rather than on individuals engaged in solitary inquiry or isolated conduct. In addition, such a theology will underscore the crucial role that human *bodies* play in the actual doing of theology. For a theology of praxis, liberation is never about a release of the ghost from the machine. It is always, rather, about the real habits that shape identity and supply purpose for embodied selves; additionally, it is about the kinds of communities and institutional arrangements that either promote or discourage the cultivation of such habits. I can only do theology *as* an embodied self, and the primary focus of my concern will be *other* embodied selves, their beliefs and experiences, the environments in which they live and the relationships that they are able to sustain. Such a theology may be judged anthropomorphic in a Peircean sense, but it certainly need not be regarded as anthropocentric. If theosemiotic is a form of inquiry grounded in the ongoing practice of reading the book of nature, its praxis must extend in some tangible and meaningful way to all that nature embraces. A certain kind of religious naturalism, capacious rather than narrow in its scope and methods, seems readily compatible with such a theology.[70] A keen attentiveness to the suffering, needs, and habits of species *other* than the human would appear to be required.

From a theosemiotic perspective, following Duns Scotus and much in the spirit of pragmatism, theology (even a philosophical theology of the sort being explored in this book) is to be classified as a practical science, a mode of reflection the ultimate purpose of which is the guiding of human actions. Some of these actions will be therapeutic, some liberating in a more broadly political and social sense, once again, with no sharp line to be drawn in order to distinguish between them. In either case, the concern is to enhance human agency even if, in a certain religious context, the ultimate rationale for doing so is to facilitate a certain kind of self-sacrifice or self-surrender (as William James suggested). From this same perspective, the constraints on human agency consist primarily in constraints on attention, resulting from the fact that we are embodied creatures, occupying a certain temporal and spatial location, enmeshed in diverse relationships, governed by laws, living in communities, affiliated with various institutions, and so on. It has already been suggested that many of these constraining forces are rather continuously operative (we cannot take a vacation from our bodies), while others occur episodically, either because what confronts us does so in a serendipitous fashion or because it represents a concerted attempt on the part of others presently to capture and control our attention. In instances where such attempts at control are purposeful, liberation appears as an inevitable goal and task for theology, while in the other cases (where the constraints are inevitable or serendipitous) a different type of analysis is required, since the very same forces that compel attention can also be ones that give it a distinctive shape, in a sense enabling rather than altogether undermining the exercise of freedom in action.

A theosemiotic analysis of those more insidious forms of coercion calls both for a theology of liberation and for the kind of martial spirituality that represents its natural concomitant. The latter is rooted in a pragmatic insight clearly articulated by William James—that there is real evil in the world and that we have a duty to resist it.[71] The basic strategy of resistance that such a spirituality will seek to develop for practitioners is one that will be organized (quite obviously at this point) around the conviction that persons can only act in freedom to the extent that they can control their own acts of attention; moreover, that doing so is prerequisite for being able to choose the habits that they wish to cultivate and embody. It will also be organized around the recognition that forces threatening such a freedom have multiplied exponentially in late modernity, taking a variety of technological forms and representing a complex array of competing political and economic interests.

Much like a pragmatically inspired theosemiotic, liberation theology emphasizes the continuity of theory with praxis, the insight that inquiry is itself a form of praxis—moreover, that all inquiry must be devoted primarily to the task of understanding our most entrenched practices, the meanings that they embody, and their role in shaping our dispositional attitudes . . . finally, to the task of submitting them to critique. Like any other genuinely pragmatic enterprise, such a theology identifies some community of interpretation as crucial to the proper execution of these tasks. The creative work and insights of dedicated individuals are never precluded from analysis, but they are always properly understood as at least implicitly involving a specific community as their enabling background and condition. Critique is possible at all only to the extent that certain values can be recognized as shared property. The demonstration of at least a measure of consensus about ideals is what distinguishes serious and healthy critique from a meaningless squabble.

Not only are embodied human selves both the potential agents and victims of oppression, but they also can be conceived as living legisigns, the reading of which supplies a crucial narrative about both the history of freedom and of whatever threatens or limits its enactment. Not content merely with tracing the plot of such a story, a theosemiotic rooted in pragmatism and inspired by liberationist models and motifs will look steadily to the future, calling for a renewed praxis, one guided by theology but extending its range to include the goal of real transformation (targeting communities and institutions as well as individuals). Among the pragmatists, Peirce and Dewey were especially emphatic about how inquiry must always be oriented toward the future—not just the immediate, but often a distant future. And liberation theology, throughout its development in the latter stages of the twentieth century and now early in the twenty-first, has always been preeminently a theology of hope.

Additional observations suggest that the fruitfulness of this comparison can be extended even further. Not all but certain forms of liberation thought have been articulated in such a way that they are grounded—much like the theosemiotic of Edwards, Emerson, and Peirce—in a powerful theological aesthetic.[72] The beauty that inspires theological reflection is also one that acts as an ideal to shape and motivate praxis. This praxis is both the upshot of inquiry and an experimental test of its presuppositions, thus also a potential starting point for new modes of inquiry. In this respect, both pragmatists and liberation theologians recognize any inquiry as being incomplete prior to the execution of its inductive phase.[73] The logic of inquiry for liberationists suggests a pattern that moves from "seeing" to "judging" and then to "acting."[74] This logic clearly resonates with Peirce's own, as he formulated it in numerous ways—for example, in moving from abduction through deduction to induction as stages of inquiry, as well as in his insistence that the logical pedigree of any idea will be determined by its having both passed into consciousness through the "gate of perception" and then exited through the "gate of purposive action."

Finally, both pragmatism and liberation thought share an allergy to sharp conceptual dualisms, as well as a commitment to overcoming them. A deep chasm placed between the natural and the supernatural would be among the most prominent of these, a clear separation between theory and practice constituting another, and as a third example, the isolating of human spirit or "soul" over against bodily existence. Such conceptual dualisms, moreover, can often be linked through careful analysis to tangible "gaps" in human life and experience that typically signal some social injustice, like the one that separates the oppressed from the oppressor or the very rich from the very poor.

To explore further the compatibility of a pragmatically inspired theosemiotic with classical liberation thought would involve some creative extrapolation from the ideas associated with each of them; but the prospect for doing so seems bright rather than dim. Consider first how Gustavo Gutierrez's portrayal of all human thought and praxis as being empowered by a mysterious and thoroughly gratuitous divine love clearly echoes Peirce's defense of agapism[75]—his startling claim that the laws governing both nature and logic display (even if at present only dimly) love's teleology. Human love and creativity are at best only a faded and fragmented image of this gentle but powerful divine agape. On the other hand, the proposal that liberation theology's emphasis on *poverty*—as a spiritual and material condition that must both be acknowledged and then addressed in praxis—can be interpreted in light of Peirce's semiotic and his fallibilistic theory of inquiry may seem like an extrapolation stretched too far, an attempt to bridge these two thought-worlds that appears forced and artificial. Nevertheless, the development of just such a proposal will prove central to the task of articulating and defending a robust theosemiotic of the spiritual life. Whether one stretches to make the connections or focuses instead on those that seem readily apparent, the agenda here is not just to show how theosemiotic is compatible with the sort of inquiry already being pursued by liberation thinkers; rather, it is to suggest how a liberation theology imagined as theosemiotic might genuinely manifest itself as "a theology in a new key."[76]

First and foremost, such a theology would operate self-consciously within a world clearly recognized as being perfused with signs, a theology now equipped with a thoroughly pragmaticistic understanding of how signs function and what it means for anything to be a sign. We began this discussion with the very important example of the concept of praxis itself. A liberation perspective certainly has no need for a theory of semiotic simply in order to understand both that theology is itself a form of praxis and that the final fruits of inquiry must be established inductively, experimentally, by the testing of ideas in the crucible of lived human experience and interaction. Once again, the value added by such a theory is the insight that such praxis is itself an important sign, that "fruits" and "roots" stand in a relationship of sign to object. Moreover, praxis is not just any kind of sign, but for the pragmaticist it will be the most complete and reliable interpretant-sign of its object. That object itself will invariably be mediated by other signs—for theologians, quite typically a concept, like the idea of "love" or "liberation" or "community" . . . or "God." For any liberation theology formulated as theosemiotic, the best *interpretation* of what these concepts might possibly mean is one that will be embodied in deliberate and disciplined human conduct.

This account is a bit asymmetrical and so should be further developed and balanced. What might it mean, on the other hand, to conceive of theosemiotic primarily as a theology of liberation? Pragmatism is a philosophical perspective, an invaluable resource for theologians but not itself ever designed or intended specifically to do the work of theology. Now Peirce *did* insist that the clearest explication of the meaning of the idea of God, as well as the surest evidence for God's reality, would be displayed in the human conduct conforming to it as an ideal. Nevertheless, in his Neglected Argument, the account that binds ideal to practice was left a bit vague. This is the great strength of liberation theology. It enlists a broad but also a nuanced and thickly described concept of praxis so that always and everywhere the articulation of even a primarily philosophical theology will be directly related to a specific set of historical, social, political, economic, and moral concerns. The task of learning to "see" poverty and injustice, their causes and conditions, ought to be one that falls squarely within the domain of any theological mode of inquiry conceived as cenoscopic. To ignore this task is to turn a blind eye to what is demonstrably embedded in the common fabric of human experience; if it *seems* otherwise, here is another case of something being "hidden in plain view."

To be sure, a sound philosophy is not irrelevant to performing such a task, and the thought of philosophers like Marx and Dewey has nourished generations of liberation thinkers—Marx from the very beginning. Some, but much less, attention has been paid to Peirce and to Royce. While their portrayal of communities of inquiry/interpretation is not linked in their writings so directly to specific political and social issues, it has served as a prolegomenon to the development of contemporary theories of democracy grounded in a fully "communicative rationality."[77] All such theories are potentially valuable resources for theosemiotic. Here, in a more limited way, the discussion has been confined to exploring the nature of praxis as a sign, in addition to developing a conception of the human beings who engage in such activity as legisigns, the living embodiment of meaning.

From such a point of view, it is insufficient to observe that theology is continuous with various forms of political, social, and economic behavior. It must further be noted that no perfectly sharp line of distinction can be drawn between theosemiotic inquiry and specifically *religious* practices. The repetitive, ongoing examination of Peirce's concept of musement in these pages is intended, at least in part, to underscore this fact. Musement is an exercise that is one of the wellsprings *both* of rigorous inquiry—including diverse forms of theological inquiry—and of prayerful meditation. The medieval thinkers whom Peirce so greatly admired would hardly have been surprised by such an observation, as many of the most complex and subtle intellectual analyses produced by the thinkers of this period began with acts of prayer.[78] If there is any contrast between prayer and inquiry to be made here, unsurprisingly, it would be neither sharp nor absolute. It would involve the careful distinguishing of theology from spirituality as a specialized form of rereading, a meta-semiotic exercise, like literary criticism, designed to illuminate our everyday (in this case religiously meaningful) reading experiences. (I attempt to trace the outline of a theosemiotic of the spiritual life in Chapter 7, this book's final chapter.)

Poverty is a sign, also—for theology a multivalent and potentially powerful sign, and one that has received far more attention from Simone Weil and the liberationists than it has from pragmatic philosophers. This does not belie the fact, however, that Peirce's semiotic offers an important tool for understanding how poverty functions as a sign and for helping theologians to read its many layers of meaning. On one level, material poverty of an extreme sort represents an oppressive condition, the enormous gap between the rich and poor signifying a morally problematic state of affairs and raising questions about injustice that have been the primary motivation for the deliberations of generations of liberation theologians. Indeed, the actual and organized work of liberation is the most appropriate and fully adequate interpretant of what poverty and oppression signify, one that a habit of love will urge, if not require us, to recognize and affirm.

The embracing of a voluntary material poverty can be construed as meaningful in different senses, from the perspective of liberation thought as one way of achieving solidarity with the poor or, for someone like William James, as a potent kind of spiritual exercise and the sign of having achieved a certain level of spiritual perfection. In the latter case one must be careful at all costs to avoid "romanticizing" poverty—never to allow one's talk about spiritual exercise to obscure the very real suffering caused by certain material conditions, including the crushing oppression of extreme poverty. Even in its involuntary forms, however, poverty can register as a religiously positive signifier, the poor being those whom God has "preferred" and whom we ought also to prefer in our policies and practices. It is a strong sign that demands our attention.

More generally, poverty can be read as a fundamental sign of human finitude and radical dependence, one not to be interpreted exclusively in terms of economic or social class relations. Human memory is a record of continuous loss. Human self-awareness involves the recognition that all things must run their course and pass away in time, with the poverty of everything now alive and flourishing suddenly exposed by the anticipation of disease, aging, and death. (Consider those visions to which the legendary accounts point as crucial preconditions for Siddhartha Gautama's liberating insight.)

There is an explicitly spiritual form of poverty that may or may not be linked to the condition of being poor in some tangible material sense. This is a cultivated attitude whereby one has all things as though one did not have them, a certain attitude of indifference that would persist in equanimity even if one should lose the things that one presently owns. More radically still, it is a way of coming to understand all forms of "having" as illusory.[79] Throughout this discussion, and for specifically theosemiotic reasons, it has been suggested that such an insight is important for understanding the nature of inquiry; one ought to treat even one's well-entrenched beliefs as though one did not "have" or possess them, not by embracing a corrosive skepticism, but rather by adopting a spirit of playfulness. This is also the spirit of fallibilism. Moreover, from a Peircean semiotic perspective, it makes less sense to say that a sign "has" meaning than that meaning emerges only gradually in semiosis, a process involving the continuous deferral of meaning.

The raison d'etre of liberation theology is its preoccupation with poverty, with the oppression and suffering of those who are poor, and with the kind of liberation that such a state of affairs demands. On first inspection, by contrast, the connection between philosophical pragmatism and poverty as its potential subject matter seems to be much looser, perhaps accidental. Yet the thought of Simone Weil, who was neither a pragmatist nor a liberation thinker, may help us to establish this connection as a necessary one. On her account, for anyone paying proper attention, the brutal fact of poverty will become obvious and elicit an immediate response. Translated into the terms supplied by theosemiotic, this means once again that any form of theological inquiry conceived as cenoscopy—and so dealing not with special revelations or equipment, but only with what confronts us in our everyday experience—also properly disciplined by a cultivated habit of love (recall Scotus here), will register the ubiquitous (in one form or another) and frequently crushing reality of poverty as central to its purview, with a pragmatic response to this reality being perceived as crucial to its praxis.

Theosemiotic can be regarded as a scientific discipline only insofar as it is committed to fallibilism, as well as to a kind of empiricism and to a broad understanding of the experimental method. To opt for fallibilism is not suddenly to lose confidence in all of one's beliefs but rather properly to understand their origin, as well as the nature of all experience, as semiosis. Even the most secure of perceptions, for Peirce, can be analyzed as perceptual judgments, abductive in form. The accumulation of experience, through induction, will make some of our judgments practically indubitable, but since the results of induction are probabilistic rather than deductively certain, they still must be evaluated as fallible in principle. Moreover, in the case of very vague ideas (like the God-hypothesis), the possibility of achieving deductive clarification of the idea in order to facilitate testing the consequences of adopting it as a hypothesis is quite limited. This also need not preclude a kind of practical indubitability; for Peirce, many vague beliefs are powerfully instinctive and highly resistant to the corrosive effects of doubt.

Theosemiotic is grounded in a new kind of religious empiricism, one that does not look to experience primarily as evidence for the truth of religious claims. Nothing is purely given in experience, but whatever is revealed empirically is always the product of some interpreter interacting with forces both external and internal to the self. It is appropriate to speak of "forces" here because what Peirce called the "secondness" of experience is being emphasized in doing so. On such a view, experience acts as an editor, correcting or admonishing us when our thinking about the world has gone astray, validating our judgments in other instances. The secondness in experience is not a portrait of reality, but rather a command to "pay attention!" It is felt as a kind of resistance—once again, one typically experienced externally over against the self (as when I bang my head trying to stand up straight in parts of my attic), but also often experienced internally (as instincts, drives, impulses, or habits that resist how I intended to act *or* as acts of volition themselves running against the grain of how I would normally have acted previously).

It states the obvious to point out for my reader that this element of volition is crucial to the account being developed here. Originating in how I first choose to pay attention, it then extends to everything that I deliberately do. This is the very broad sense in which experience is always also experimental, not confined merely to what appears at the gate of perception but reaching all the way to the gate of purposeful action. That Peirce developed a robust theory of human experience not limited (as he claimed it was by the nominalists) to sense perception is clear from what he wrote about it—for example, when he characterized experience as "the entire mental product," including hallucinations and imaginings (*CP* 6.492), or when he identified it with a "*personal history*, life" (*CP* 4.91; Peirce's emphasis). Experience like semiosis, indeed, *as* semiosis cannot be exhaustively captured in an episode or an encounter. But this is true (indeed, the recitation of its truth has become a philosophical *mantram* here) precisely because experience is given its determinate shape and meaning both by our repeated encounters with things in the world and then by what we *do* in those encounters and in response to such things. In this latter sense, experience is intrinsically experimental (except on those rare if even possible occasions where what we do is utterly devoid of self-control) and is perfectly continuous with praxis.

Consider the difference between a general awareness that all experience is semiosis and the recognition of some particular thing experienced *as* a sign. In the latter case, what is added to experience by the recognition of something as functioning semiotically? One might suggest that to see something as a sign is to see the "more" in experience.[80] It is to identify what is presented to me not just as a being but as a being-in-relation, so that what is absent also becomes a presence. This experience can be the source of great joy (as when Ignatius perceived everything in creation as a gift signifying a divine giver) or of deep melancholy (as when the Portuguese describe *saudade* as the powerful feeling of an absence that has become a constant presence).[81] Both types of experience can be religiously meaningful, as Ignatius himself suggested and as the forthcoming examination of discernment will hope to illuminate.

If it is truly a practical science, in the way that Duns Scotus envisaged it, theology should enable us to see more, to pay better attention, ultimately, to love better by helping to perfect in us a habit of love. Scotus seemed clear, and Peirce would agree in his own terms, that to judge a belief by its "fruits" is to evaluate how it enhances our capacity to love. For his part, Josiah Royce conceived of love in the theological terms supplied by St. Paul and as manifesting itself in loyalty; toward the end of perfecting such a love he advocated a kind of "training for loyalty."[82] The vagueness of theology's agenda, thus described, might be reduced to some extent upon further description and analysis, but it will be rendered even more determinate in practice.

Now, on pragmatic analysis, it is important to appreciate the enormous complexity of those practices that are religiously meaningful and so most relevant to the project of doing philosophical theology. Determinations of fruitfulness, of success and failure, accordingly, will also be complex. However one might evaluate pragmatic outcomes in other domains, it is safe to say that our religious practices do not bear very much of a resemblance to the practice of "hitting a nail with a hammer," nor can they be reduced to a pattern of "giving and asking for reasons."[83] To understand them properly will require appealing to only the most generous and sophisticated brand of philosophical pragmatism. In the case of some religious practices, questions about what one is doing and why one is doing it may have no immediately straightforward answers, at least not of the sort that can readily be formulated with words.

5 / Communities of Interpretation

I

What conditions must obtain in order for any collection of persons to be recognized as a community? Is there a maximal size beyond which such conditions cannot be maintained? What are the boundaries that distinguish one community from another? The modes of relationship that join members of a community one to another? Is it in any sense legitimate to describe communities as "greater persons" or as having "personalities"? How are the identities, characters, purposes, and practices of individuals shaped by their membership in certain communities? And what is it about a community that qualifies it, in Roycean terms, as something that demands our loyalty? That is to say, what makes a community something worth caring about?[1]

Without pretending to supply exhaustive answers to these questions, nevertheless, each of them deserves at least minimal treatment here. Since that treatment will involve attempting to articulate answers in explicitly semiotic terms, it will be a reasonably straightforward matter later on to adapt it for particular theosemiotic purposes. This strategy is not one chosen, however, simply to facilitate such an end. The key argument here is not that *some* communities (i.e., religious ones) can be properly regarded as communities of interpretation, but that *all* genuine communities must be conceived as such. This makes perfect sense against the background of an account that has already portrayed human selves as living streams of semiosis, continuously engaged in reading themselves, interpreting other persons, and struggling to create or find meaning in a world so thoroughly pervaded by signs.

It might be useful to begin with the elaboration of an argument already partially articulated here. One very natural way to think about community is in terms of relationships of similarity. Fraternities, clubs, athletic teams, families, corporations, cities, neighborhoods, schools, and churches are all comprised of persons who are typically considered to be similar in some relevant respect. They may share the same interests or goals or beliefs or language or geographical location or ancestors and so on. Because they are linked by this criterion of sameness, they can also be distinguished from the members of other communities by means of the identification of certain salient differences. Republicans are different from Democrats. Roman Catholics are different from Theravada Buddhists. And no one will be likely to confuse a Yankee supporter with a Red Sox fan.

Sameness and difference can be either extraordinarily useful or highly problematic when employed for the purpose of identifying the members of a certain community. To be useful there must be a clear demonstration of relevance. Choose any two things whatsoever and they will be similar to each other in *some* respect. But the way in which they resemble each other may contribute nothing to their membership in a community. That two individuals are very tall or that both enjoy playing chess would have no bearing on their relationship as members of the same political party or church. This is not to suggest that an investigation of what binds persons together in community would be in any way likely to yield *no* relevant similarities. Such a result, in fact, would seem highly improbable. Rather, the analysis here indicates *both* that the sorting out of salient from uninformative similarities will be crucial to the success of such an investigation *and* that no complete or adequate understanding of community will be achievable if it is limited to the scrutiny of relationships of sameness.

Class concepts and the relationship of sameness might be regarded as both useful and problematic ways of thinking about community in yet another respect—in this instance, one framed by primarily political or ethical concerns. Shared ancestors, interests, traditions, and beliefs can be the joints and sinews of communal life, linking persons together in powerful bonds of solidarity. At the very same time, these connecting factors can be viciously exclusionary, reinforcing sharp insider/outsider distinctions, building solidarity at the cost of stimulating more lively imaginings of who constitutes the "other" or "enemy." That is to say, the very same factors crucial for the definition and development of an *identity*, both individual and communal, fuel the temptation to caricature or evaluate in all sorts of troublesome ways anyone who cannot be so identified. Moreover, one's own sudden or gradual discomfort with any of those elements deemed crucial for this purpose can result in *identity crisis*, sometimes with truly terrifying impact; one suddenly feels alien, no longer recognizing this community as a home. (I would characterize such a crisis as a kind of semiotic breakdown, quite different from but related to the experience of boredom, in both cases involving the evacuation of meaning from a place where it once thrived.)

Whether viewed positively or negatively, one of the things that members of any genuine community must share will be a certain set of *ideals*. This is an appropriately vague term, but it is useful nonetheless for the purposes of a discussion such as this one. Given the pragmatic emphasis on fruitfulness that theosemioticians maintain, one must recognize the futility of trying to evaluate the outcome of believing or acting in any particular way without some set of ideals to provide a measuring stick. It might be possible, even if highly improbable, for some person to formulate and embrace an ideal that was completely personal, not shared with anyone, but entirely his own. Judgments of success in conforming to such an ideal would matter to no one else, however, and such success would contribute nothing to the building up of community. This is not the sort of ideal that is of interest here. Belief in an ideal, like any other belief, ought to be fixed and then tested pragmatically through some process of inquiry. Such a process presupposes intersubjective communication, sometimes even contestation.

Communities on a grand scale rather than an intimate one—religious and scientific communities as opposed to families, for example, or democracies in contrast to fraternities and clubs—tend to be more heavily invested in ideals that can and should be *broadly* shared. For the philosophical theologian, religious community constitutes the primary object of concern, although for Peirce and Royce one could not hope properly to understand such an entity apart from comparison with the ideals that inform and enliven scholarly or scientific communities; for Dewey, in addition, neither religious nor scientific communities could be healthy if segregated from the life-giving power associated with the ideals of democracy. All three thinkers had a good deal to say about ideals: what they are and how they function.

Now, while the word "ideal" still occupies a prominent enough place in our twenty-first-century vocabulary and still proves useful in our everyday communications with one another, it has for some time ceased to designate a concept that receives very much philosophical scrutiny. Idealism, in whatever one of the many forms it might happen to take, does not at present constitute a popular item on the philosophical menu. For the purposes of theosemiotic inquiry, nevertheless, it will be important to think hard both about the nature of ideals and about the plausibility of a certain type of philosophical idealism. Toward that end, Peirce, Royce, and Dewey will each prove to be reliable guides.

Recall how Peirce's logic of relatives fueled his insight that sameness is only one and hardly the most important of the relationships that might obtain between the members of a certain group. By extension of this insight, for communities of interpretation, the reaching of some consensus will be only one and possibly not the most significant of objectives that they might pursue in their inquiries and conversations. Accordingly, the narrow focus on sameness and consensus in order to understand what defines a certain collection of people as the members of a community can be as problematic and dangerous as ignoring it in instances where it is clearly relevant.

What sorts of other relationships might one expect to qualify as community-building? For Royce the answer to this question was both clear and compelling. Communities will be constituted by the loyalty of their members. From a certain point a view, such loyalty will have a homogenizing effect, insofar as it binds everyone in the community to a particular ideal or cause. Yet Royce clearly understood that loyalties could compete and collide without necessarily or altogether undermining community. Diversity is preserved as an important feature of community on his account through the articulation of a principle that demands of each member a certain "loyalty to loyalty" itself.[2] One's adherence to such a principle would require one to defend the right of others to be loyal—even more, positively to enable other persons to remain devoted to ideals or purposes that are quite different from those shared by oneself or by most members of the community. Red Sox and Yankee fans can indeed both flourish living in the very same neighborhood. To be sure, there are challenges to maintaining such a state of affairs. But are there absolute limits to the amount of tension between competing values that any community could endure?

Dewey ought not to be ignored here, either. The ideals of democracy are directly related to the optimum conditions under which scientific inquiry can be said to proceed. Peirce wrote very little about topics in political philosophy, but what he recorded about the logic of science and about communities of inquiry has been subsequently used as a resource by others for the development of a theory of democracy.[3] In contrast, Dewey had much more to say about political philosophy, most especially about the importance of democratic ideals, not only for the purposes of government, but also, in relationship to education, as a guide in solving social problems, and even (although not quite as explicitly) as a resource for imagining the future of religion. With the thought of Peirce, Royce, and Dewey as a springboard, later pragmatists have formulated theories of communicative rationality that have been identified here as relevant to the goals of theosemiotic. Like Peirce in his earliest essays, such theories underscore the thoroughly semiotic nature of rationality itself ("all thinking is in signs"), its essentially intersubjective character and vital communicative function. They also describe in great detail the rigorous conditions that must obtain in order to achieve an authentic intersubjectivity and for genuine communication to occur without distortion.

Royce, Peirce, and Dewey each wanted to formulate ideals broad enough that the consensus achieved in affirming them would not result in an oppressive sameness or exclusion. This is the one exception to the argument being made here about the necessary limitations of any appeal to consensus. Only if the ideal conceived is sufficiently broad, and also sufficiently vague in the sense that Peirce regarded as salutary, should it be identified as one that all responsible inquirers would eventually affirm. This, once again, is what Royce was after with his talk about the loyalty to loyalty; despite differences between particular loyalties, this is the one loyalty that could be universally shared. For Peirce, the agreement among religious believers—as when gathered together they affirm the articles of some creed—is potentially dangerous, since religious creeds are intended to be exclusionary and to divide one community from another. Nevertheless, if a creed could be formulated that enshrines as central for its believers a commitment to the kind of nurturing love that he celebrated in his philosophy of agapism, then it ought to be affirmed by everyone (*CP* 6.3). Such mutual affirmation would represent a healthy kind of consensus. (Compare, also, Peirce's reflections on the "summum bonum," as that which would have to be judged as supremely good, not just in this or that situation, but under all conceivable circumstances; *CP* 1.573, 575ff., 2.118.) Finally, Dewey was convinced that the ideals of a genuine democracy, properly understood, are ones that all reasonable persons should embrace and promote. Any ideal thus conceived, the love and loyalty that it inspires, defines a community as a living system rather than as a rigidly uniform class of individuals. All of the members of a community being committed to the *same* ideal—when that ideal is loyalty to loyalty, or agape, or a commitment to genuine democracy—is quite different from all of the members *being the same*, in the sense of shared race or ethnicity, common language, or similar customs.

Although it is perhaps less useful to think about Dewey in this way, for Royce and Peirce it is belief in the possibility of adhering to just such an ideal that renders intelligible any kind of talk about a truly universal or unlimited community. Moreover, anything thus conceived would also have to be regarded as being a community of inquiry or interpretation. Now, I have previously suggested that every authentic community is always already a community of interpretation. But this is true in the more limited sense that any group of persons interacting in community with each other will inevitably (and for many different reasons) need to be interpreting each other, as well as themselves in relation to others, and both in an ongoing fashion. In the case of a universal community, the ideal in which it is grounded is one that prescribes the optimal conditions under which interpretation in general can best proceed and succeed. Here the ultimate goals, both of the community and of interpretation or inquiry, are identical. This community is unlimited because the scope of inquiry is itself unlimited. Indeed, for Peirce, the commitment to an "indefinite community," as well as a "hope in the unlimited continuance of intellectual activity," were both necessary presuppositions of meaningful inquiry, regulative principles for logic as he conceived of it (*CP* 2.652–55; *W*3: 281–85). Nor did Peirce or Royce think it was necessary to imagine such a community as consisting only of human beings (any form of intelligence capable of inquiry could qualify as a member) or as being confined to a specific historical location (it reaches deep into the past and anticipates the future as a vast community both of memory and of hope).

Needless to say, this is not the way that we normally think about a community. The limitless nature of it, to begin with the most glaring difficulty, would seem to disqualify it from belonging in that category. Whatever constitutes something as a community is the very same thing that distinguishes it from others, its finitude, the fact that it is determinate in some respect and identifiable in an appropriately specific way. This is also the source of the strength of those bonds that link one person to another as members of the community. To be the member of an infinite community would mean belonging to a group of persons, the vast majority of whom are utterly anonymous—mostly strangers with whom one would find it impossible to develop such a bond. And so, as the hypothetical argument being sketched here might conclude, it makes no real sense to talk about a genuinely universal or unlimited community.

Is such an argument valid? Assume first that the word "community" is vague in pretty much the same way as many of the other words with which theosemiotic is preoccupied ("God," "ultimate," "religion," "person," "self," "love," and so on). Consequently, while it might make perfect sense for me to consider my nuclear family, my academic department at the university where I teach, and the Roman Catholic Church all as communities of which I am a member, there would certainly be a variety of ways in which these are different one from another. I do not mean "different" here just in the sense that they involve different loyalties, interests, memories, goals, etc., that distinguish one from the others. I am also proposing that they are communities in a very different sense of what *that word* might be taken to mean, so that while the word is not being used merely equivocally to cover all instances, neither is the usage perfectly univocal; rather, its meaning in any one instance is analogous to its use in the others.

How far then does the concept stretch without breaking? Later in this chapter I will explore the issue of whether or not it makes sense to talk about "virtual" communities, examining the meaning and limitations of such a way of speaking. But consider first the idea of an international community—for example, the one consisting of all "Peirce scholars" on the planet, or all of those people who are affiliated with Amnesty International. There are shared goals and interests defining such groups of people, but nothing like physical proximity or direct acquaintance with all of the other members of the group. Still, it seems that there is enough continuity of meaning with the way that the word is employed in other contexts legitimately to label such groups as communities.

Notice that the emotional bond that is often deemed necessary for relationships to be understood as constitutive of community does not itself always require direct acquaintance or face-to-face interaction. Large numbers of people can mourn with genuine and intense grief the death of an individual whom they have never met but with whom they closely identify. Such identification is symbolic—that is to say, it constitutes a relationship that is essentially semiotic in nature. No genuine relationship in community could exist, of course, without involving semiosis in some fashion and to a certain degree. Nevertheless, there are certain relationships that are formed as the direct result of some interpretation. Although it has been argued here that meaning is both discovered and created, such relationships will have meaning less because of what is given than what is constructed; the interpretation does much of the work to constitute the bond rather than being primarily a reflection on one already existing. (Contrast the members of a professional society with biological siblings, to consider one relatively simple example.)

Against this background of deliberations, I propose to explore exactly what kind of communal bond it might be possible to establish grounded in the sort of loyalty to loyalty that Royce advocated or the kind of agapism that Peirce described. I think that these notions are much more closely related than they might appear to be on first inspection.[4] As he developed the idea, Royce came increasingly to identify loyalty with what he understood to be the Pauline theology of love articulated in some of the Christian biblical literature. Consideration of such an idea will push the discussion in a more decisively theological direction. In anticipation of going there, I want also to wander briefly into a related but more secular territory. It is a terrain that emerges into view to the extent that one pursues some suggestions made by these thinkers, but never developed in quite the way that I will propose: Royce's suggestion was about the importance for any vibrant community of a certain "will to interpret." Peirce's not identical but quite comparable hypothesis was about the essential role played in all productive inquiry by a certain "will to learn." The potential philosophical projects that might be linked to such suggestions are very different from the one that William James inaugurated with his celebration of the "will to believe." Yet in all three of these cases (only the first two will be considered here), it is important to register the significance of a type of voluntarism that seems closely tied to the development of certain pragmatic perspectives.

Here, in the form of a bare sketch, all of the elements needed for a fuller theosemiotic account of the nature of community have been presented: the importance of sameness juxtaposed to an awareness of other types of relations, most especially, the crucial role played by a loyalty that in its higher forms is manifested as love; the defining power of ideals; a tension between determinacy and indeterminacy as factors either giving shape to community or making it more generous and inclusive; the equally important sustaining power of a certain kind of volition; and a clear recognition that the most useful context within which community (its rationale and its rationality) can best be understood is one supplied by a theory of semiotic. The next order of business is to put just a little more meat on these bones. In doing so, I will once again be "thinking with" Royce, Peirce, Dewey, and others rather than focusing narrowly on the exegesis of their writings or an explication of their ideas.

The logic of relations distinguishes dyadic and triadic from monadic predicates in a manner already illustrated. The simplest and most typical characterization of communities involves the use of a proposition employing a monadic predicate, focused on affirming that respect in which the members of each community are similar, in which they share something in "common." These are the bones. Now, I want to link any worry about the limitations of such an understanding of community to the Roycean and Peircean emphasis on agape. I begin by reminding the reader that love can be analyzed in triadic terms insofar as, like semiosis, it is portrayed essentially as an act of giving. This giving of gifts already implies a nascent mutuality to the extent that something more must happen (as

Peirce put it) over and above my putting something down and you taking it up in order for genuine "giving" to have occurred.

Even before blossoming and bearing full fruit, this primitive element of mutuality adds something vital to the static, rather lifeless picture of community that any excessive emphasis on sameness might yield. A group of individuals may appear to be like each other in any number of respects, even classified from someone else's perspective as belonging to the same community because of the way in which some of those resemblances are considered salient. Yet such a judgment would be problematic unless the relationship of sameness really works to bind these individuals together in solidarity; otherwise, they might constitute an identifiable "group" that could be meaningfully classified as such, but it would hardly make sense to think of them as forming a community. For the latter to be true, they cannot simply be existing alongside one another, recognizable from some external perspective as displaying features that make them similar to each other. In addition to being what they are, there must be manifested a tangible *being toward* the other that constitutes the communal relation. Note that this does not mean that one has to be actively aware of the identity of all of those others with whom one exists in community. One only needs to be disposed in a certain positive way toward anyone who might share the same heritage or interest or goal or whatever. It is not merely sameness but also consciousness of that sameness, combined with an evaluation of how being the same in this respect really matters, that results in the formation of community. This is a matter of interpretation. Just as with selfhood, community is an emergent property of semiosis.

Essential for establishing shared concerns or similarities as sources of solidarity, this being toward the other, a dispositional attentiveness to the other, is necessary also for establishing relations among persons in their difference. Such a disposition is always present in every example of one person's giving loyalty or love to another; moreover, it always also contains the seed of much deeper and richer forms of love, marked by a gratitude that mingles with delight, but then also displays itself as compassion, as nurturing and care. In the highest manifestations of love there is something approaching the circular movement that Peirce described or the full mutuality that St. Ignatius tersely but effectively celebrated at the culmination of his exercises. Here there is no characteristic or quality that must be held in common, no standard of sameness, with shared attention being sufficient to establish the bond.[5] This was the great insight of Royce and Peirce with respect to community: that it was necessary for such a love to take root and grow in order for community to exist in anything other than the most primitive of forms.

From a theosemiotic perspective, whatever else the persons in community may happen to be—members of a certain family, Boston Celtic fans, Moravians, or whatever—they must also be recognized (if this perspective has any validity) as living legisigns. In this fashion, they can be perceived both as active readers and as meaningful texts to be read. Since they are *not* to be caricatured as static selves but always as engaged in a dynamic selving process, the nature of that process will have significant bearing on the character of those communities that they form. Moreover, it would be impossible even to conceive of this process apart from some consideration of those communities to which these persons already belong or have belonged.

Personal development or selving is semiotic in nature, a continuous unfolding in which the self perpetually rereads itself. Communities of interpretation will be engaged in very much the same kind of evolution—albeit a bit more complex and potentially chaotic—with the collective understanding of what provides for the community its special rationale, its ideals and objectives, being vulnerable to continuous reinterpretation. It is only in those cases where the teleology of such a process is truly developmental in this fashion that it becomes possible to talk about any community as itself being "personal" or having a "personality." The sense in which a community is in fact a person will be more vague but not therefore less meaningful for theosemiotic inquiry than the manner in which any particular human being may be designated as such.

This last assertion amounts to a defense of anthropomorphism that cannot simultaneously be taken as a claim for anthropocentrism. To discern something vaguely personal at the heart of the universe (as Peirce and Royce both did) or to recognize that communities vast and small also display a personal character—these observations are not necessarily the distorted product of a frivolous projection of human qualities on something clearly impersonal. On an alternative reading, such observations might be judged crucial to the achievement of any genuine self-understanding for human interpreters. They show how the very character of such interpreters *as* personal is grounded in a broader and more fundamental reality than the one that emerges into view when human beings are treated as utterly distinctive and as the only authentic candidates for the status of personhood.

II

It was late in the nineteenth and then early in the twentieth century when Peirce and Royce both wrote prescriptively about the ideal of an unlimited community of interpretation.⁶ Now, in the twenty-first-century Internet Age, the emergence of virtual communities has greatly extended the power and range of what the word "community" can mean in ways that Peirce and Royce would surely encourage us to assess. Is the increasingly complex web of semiotic relations made possible by new computer technologies the realization of a Peircean/Roycean dream, or is it a nightmare from which they might help us to awaken? The rapidly expanding opportunity for conversation in virtual space must be balanced against the recognition that, in such mediated exchanges, the nature and quality of one's attention to others is inevitably transformed. Since love always requires the paying of proper attention, it is worth considering whether technological developments might enable or preclude the realization of what Royce called the "Beloved Community."

Some of the related issues that need to be raised in taking up this task of assessment are quite demanding philosophical and psychological questions, including but not limited to the following: What does it mean for one person to be genuinely present to another? How important is the real presence of the human body as a sign-vehicle in acts of communication and, thus, in the creation or emergence of community? Does the emphasis on virtual forms of community risk the reduction of semiosis to verbal behavior in these instances, occluding a great variety of metacommunicative strategies that persons typically and quite heavily rely upon in order to convey meaning one to another? How do the particular factors that give shape to conversations conducted in virtual space sustain or undermine our capacity properly to pay attention, both to the subject matter and to our interlocutors? Are virtual communities ontologically parasitic on actual communities—either in the foundational sense that the former will always be rooted in the latter or in the teleological sense that any virtual community, in order to be considered authentic, must prefigure something actual?

Recall that for both Peirce and Royce the idea of an unlimited community was necessarily prescriptive, an ideal rather than the reference to any actually existing state of affairs; whatever reality such a community might possess only had a being *in futuro*. At the same time, the contemporary technological reality of the internet is not something that was dreamt of in either of their philosophies. Moreover, there is a question on this list that neither of them appears ever to have asked, certainly not in the explicit form that it is being raised here. It is a question that both existentialist and contemporary Buddhist philosophers have sometimes asked, and it has to do with the minimal conditions under which one person can be regarded as being truly present to another. Leaving the terms of this question intentionally vague, one might simply wonder about the extent to which we should insist that someone must be actually and so physically present in order for such conditions to be satisfied.

Sometimes we seem to experience the powerful presence of a person in his absence. Perhaps in such instances it is less paradoxical and so more appropriate to refer to the experience of his absence as a presence, something that Portuguese poets, singers, and songwriters traditionally seemed to be doing when they wrote or spoke or sang about being haunted by feelings of *saudade*.[7] I can also feel intimately connected to a person thousands of miles away with whom I am having a lively telephone conversation, while simultaneously ignoring another person who is sitting in the room right next to me. These examples suggest that this question is not a purely metaphysical one—in the way that it was for theologians arguing about transubstantiation and the possibility of Christ being really present in the Eucharist—but rather, one about the nature, object, and quality of our attention insofar as it shapes our experience of a particular relationship.[8] It is a question about what Buddhists refer to as "mindfulness," one that can be framed in such a way as also to extend to Peirce's portrayal of musement.

As it has already been repeatedly affirmed, on the view maintained by both Peirce and Royce, what distinguishes a community from any mere collection of individuals is that the former will necessarily be guided by certain ideals; its members will have a definite purpose. Of the two philosophers, Royce by far wrote at greater length about this topic. He understood a "Community of Interpretation" as consisting of "many selves with a common ideal." These selves will be bound both to one another and to the community's purposes by a powerful loyalty; and that loyalty is best to be understood, not simply as some feeling or emotion, but rather, as a form of loving devotion, essentially, a habit of volition.[9] Indeed, for Royce, it is the "will to interpret" that has the capacity to transform three or more separate selves into a genuine community.[10] For both thinkers, the ideal community of inquiry or interpretation was imagined to be of a distinctively religious character. Echoes of Peirce's prescription for a religion of science, with the church being modeled on a scientific community (*CP* 6.428–51), reverberate in Royce's talk two decades later about the Beloved Community, consisting of individuals who have "somehow fallen in love with the universe."[11]

This territory has already been surveyed. Here I want to underscore for emphasis the extent to which any genuine community must be grounded in the volitional acts of its members, what Royce referred to as a basic will to interpret, and what Peirce called the will to learn.[12] In each case, volition will be shaped and motivated by shared ideals or purposes. This observation should lead us to focus on those virtual communities that are forged specifically around the exchange of ideas and opinions about interests and objectives held in common by their membership. One certainly would not feel compelled to label as a "virtual community" just any group of individuals whose communication with one another is technologically mediated. Many online conversations are episodic and random. Their purposes are momentary, thus easily and quickly achieved, or even abandoned. Such conversations are not fueled by a commitment to anything ideal. Nevertheless, there surely are virtual groups whose members display a shared loyalty to the loftiest kinds of ideals. And so the question once again resurfaces about whether or not there is anything problematic in referring to such individuals as constituting a "community."

The fact that the interaction among these individuals is technologically mediated does not automatically preclude their claim to being a community—at least not without further argument and analysis. On the semiotic account developed by Peirce and then later embraced and extended by Royce, there is no such thing as an unmediated experience. My encounter with another person is always already an interpreted experience, whether I am now reading his email sent from a thousand miles away or sitting directly across a table from him, engrossed in conversation. That is to say, there is no meaningful experience that does not take the form of a judgment, even in those instances where such judgments are unconscious, automatic, and—at least for the time being—indubitable. Consequently, technological mediation would have to be shown to make a specific difference, one that can be analyzed and thus evaluated as counterproductive for the purpose of community formation.

Consider, first, the nature of a typical representamen or sign-vehicle that the members of a virtual community will be likely to encounter when they engage in acts of communication. Conversations conducted over the internet usually take the form of written communications made visible on a computer screen, tablet, or cell phone. As computer technologies have evolved, to be sure, the capacity to supplement the written word with pictures and images has become rapidly enhanced. The time-gap between writing and reading has also shrunk to the vanishing point compared with the manner in which communication occurs when facilitated by other kinds of written media (such as books, periodicals, or letters delivered by "snail mail"). Indeed, a good deal of online communication now occurs in real time. Moreover, it is misleading to suggest that all interactions by computer rely exclusively on the written word. Candidates for employment are now interviewed by potential employers at a great distance, using computer technology to bridge the gap; once employed, they sometimes work "remotely," a possibility enabled by the same technology. International meetings involving visual contact and live conversation now regularly occur with their participants never leaving their offices or homes. "Distance learning" practices have also become commonplace; when it comes to the assigning of academic credit, it would appear that university registrars no longer make any significant distinction between the "actual" and the "virtual" in their treatment of classes as intellectual communities. In ever greater numbers, marriages occur only after persons have first met, learned about each other, and shared interests online. (Perhaps the salient question is whether the experience of "falling in love" in these instances occurs in virtual space or only after actual encounter.) With increasing frequency, romantic relationships are ending in this fashion as well, as "breakups" are announced in remarks exchanged by email or text message.

The rapidly increasing ability to more closely approximate with technology those encounters that occur between persons in the flesh should not obscure the empirical truth that many persons choose to have mediated encounters online precisely because of what they conceal, because of the level of anonymity that they preserve. The student who emails his professor a thoughtful question thirty minutes after class, even though there was dead silence when the instructor called for questions during the class period itself, may have needed a few extra minutes to digest his teacher's brilliant utterances before formulating something meaningful in response. But the frequency with which this happens lends inductive support to the hypothesis that many students are now simply more comfortable asking questions that way, that the mediated space is a "safer" one for them, with much less risk attached to their inquiry. Now if there is far less that is risked or ventured in such an exchange, is it also the case that there is far less to be gained? What, more precisely, is missing in such an encounter?

The instructor's professorial flesh-and-blood body is missing, to begin with, along with the bodies of all of the other students in that particular class. This observation is intended to be read also as a suggestion that, for explicitly semiotic purposes, human bodies matter. This suggestion is not a casual one. It would be tempting to promote it to the level of an argument, except that it is impossible to anticipate with perfect accuracy what types of technological advancements we may witness during the coming decades and what sort of skill and self-discipline future generations may develop and display in their technological practices. Not being in the actual presence of someone else's body may matter far less in the future than it does now for purposes of communication. But perhaps it will always matter to some extent. And certain key insights articulated by both Peirce and the anthropologist Gregory Bateson constitute the primary reasons for thinking so.

Bateson wrote with great subtlety about the meta-communicative signals that typically accompany, frame, and facilitate first-order communication events.[13] These signals are most typically nonverbal ones, such as body posture, gestures, facial expressions, and tone of voice. They provide a means of communicating about our communication, and they can make all the difference in the world with regard to how our verbal behavior is interpreted. Depending on both facial expression and tone of voice when someone addresses you with the four simple words "get out of here," for example, you will immediately infer either that the speaker is responding to what he thinks is a joke or that he is urging you to leave the room. In such a case, the "body language" makes a great deal of difference in terms of what ultimately will be communicated.

The human body is the primary sign-vehicle for human beings engaged in acts of communication. Sign-vehicles matter because they help to determine (in whatever peculiar sense of "determine" Peirce intended to convey) their interpretants. Either to abstract from the human body or to render it invisible is to risk the reduction of semiosis to some limited form or aspect of what Peirce conceived it to be in its richness. Even Wittgenstein understood how "language games" involve much more than just the words and grammar that we use to play them. And Peirce's semiotic theory, there can be no doubt, presupposes a generously expanded sense of what it means "to give an interpretation," for creatures living in a universe of signs, a capacious account of where and how semiosis can occur. Royce followed Peirce closely here, which is why his investigation of the "will to interpret" could finally bear fruit only against the background supplied by an elaborate "metaphysics of interpretation."[14]

What, then, is the possibility of our will to interpret becoming anesthetized—our attention scattered and our minds numbed with boredom—by the high information state of our postmodern existence, by the overload of information that assaults us continuously in technologically mediated forms? This anxiety is less one about the possible inauthenticity of virtual communities than it is about how our contemporary technological practices may threaten our ability to flourish in any kind of community at all. Now, perhaps this sounds excessively Luddite, so that there is a need to indicate in a slightly more detailed fashion what motivates such a statement of concern.

Consider again the type of voluntarism that has been linked to theosemiotic in this discussion. To the extent that we possess it at all, human agency is primarily embodied in our capacity to direct our attention to this rather than to that and, moreover, to choose the quality and intensity of attention that we will direct to any particular thing, on any given occasion. Even the decision not to attend narrowly to any single, determinate thing, but rather to be mindfully receptive to whatever might present itself in experience, involves volition. In this last case, it is a habit of volition that is required, not something in the moment that I turn on or off like a flashlight, but an acquired skill, which is why Peirce thought that musement, in order to be effective, must take practice. Any fully satisfactory account of human agency, of course, would have to be much more expansive and complicated than this. Surely one does many things other than simply paying attention. The hypothesis being explored here is that paying attention is foundational for anything else that one does, at least insofar as one does it deliberately. Love is impossible without attention. And Royce argued that loyalty as love is the force that binds persons one to another and to a shared purpose in some community. I shape myself, my experience, and my participation in various communities by directing my attention in specific instances as well as, in the long run, by developing salient habits of attention. This ability to attend is not the whole of our freedom but may very well constitute its essence.

Nevertheless, human agency is clearly limited and finite in this regard, as the account being developed here has also insisted. My attention can be distracted or even captured by forces beyond the conscious, deliberate self, whether they be ominous, indifferent, or benign. These forces can be external to the self but are often internal, operating at the fringe of consciousness or deep within the unconscious. I may be forcefully constrained from doing a great many things yet still able to choose how I can direct my attention. Yet there are circumstances under which such freedom is also attenuated, when I am unable to focus my attention as I wish to do (being distracted from study or from prayer, for example), or I am unable to withdraw my attention from where it has become riveted (if captured by an explosive event that occurs right in front of me or by some obsessive feeling or thought that haunts me).

It is hardly a profound insight to observe that modern technology multiplies exponentially the number of ways and instances in which our attention might be captured and controlled. It also tends to suppress the role of bodies in human communication, with all of the meta-communicative impoverishment that such suppression entails. Correspondingly, it often reduces semiosis to language, or at least affords verbal behavior a certain primacy that it might not have had in actual encounters.[15] (Our experiences at bedside in hospital rooms and in the midst or immediate aftermath of any kind of tragic event have taught us a hard semiotic lesson about the eloquence of silence, the importance of presence and attention, without any need or space in such moments for the intrusion of language.) Taken together, these comments represent the gist of a cautionary tale.

Yet it is also true that technology can enable us to attend to that which, if lacking these modern resources, we might otherwise remain oblivious. It is now possible, to a greater degree than ever before, to share interests and purposes with persons whom you have never actually encountered in the flesh. An American scholar at a conference in Paris, for example, might meet for the first time a number of European philosophical pragmatists with whom he had previously exchanged papers and ideas using the internet and email. As a consequence of their meeting, perhaps they discover that they were already members of a close-knit intellectual community even before the cups of coffee and glasses of Bordeaux shared over conversation on Parisian sidewalks. Yet they might also discover that, in some ways, there was a depth and level of understanding resulting from their actual encounter that had never been achieved in earlier email correspondence. This would reinforce the suggestion previously articulated that the actual presence of human bodies really does matter. Extending the thought-experiment, these scholars could proceed to send copies of their papers to each other as email attachments in order to facilitate even deeper insight into what they were hearing at their presentations and learning from the discussion. Is this to be regarded as an enhancement now, in virtual space, of a sense of community that somehow had first to be actualized in the flesh? Or was the community always already there, from the moment when this group of philosophers began to share interests and purposes, albeit across an ocean?

To be sure, one can decide to use a word like "community" as one sees fit, applying it loosely or strictly, speaking literally or in metaphor, as the context seems to make appropriate. There is no obvious reason to treat communities as a "natural kind" or to try and stipulate their "essence." There is no advantage to policing strictly the way that we talk or write about such things and perhaps real advantage in maintaining a certain level of vagueness. The question being raised here is about the logic of our practices. Peirce understood the practices foundational to community as being governed by the gentle law of love, an insight that Royce unpacked in his talk about loyalty. The concept of community that most interested both thinkers was not of something narrow, intimate, and exclusive—like a nuclear family, club, or fraternity—but of something capacious, infinite, and unlimited. The global reach of modern technology embodies a promise for the future of human community, then, that one can only assume Peirce and Royce (if they were alive today) would find compelling. Moreover, the ideal community that they envisioned was never intended to be restricted to the human. If we ever achieve community of any kind with intelligent extraterrestrial beings it will be most likely to occur in virtual space long before, if ever, it should result in a "close encounter."

Notwithstanding, the promise and possibility of actual encounter seems salient, too, and for good Peircean reasons. The spread of reasonableness that he posited as the ideal for all genuine communities of inquiry was always to be understood as a fully "concrete reasonableness"; this was the nature of Peirce's summum bonum.[16] It was an ideal not simply to be shared abstractly but one actually to be embodied, not just or even primarily in individuals but most especially in communities. This paves the way for another suggestion—again, one that falls short of an argument—that Peirce would regard the idea of a fully virtual community as an instance of thirdness without secondness. The love and loyalty that shape a community transcend all of the instances where they might be concretely embodied in actual persons and relationships. But without such embodiment there can be no community, at least not in a fullblooded sense. The idea of an *exclusively* virtual community would be, to stretch one of Peirce's own examples a bit, something like "a court without a sheriff" (*CP* 5.48).

Of course, one might argue that the person sitting at a computer screen exchanging ideas with an unmet colleague or friend across the ocean just *is* the embodiment that makes concrete the reasonableness of their conversation. This raises the question of whether love or loyalty can be embodied in any individual or if it must be embodied in the relationship between individuals and whether or not they can achieve such a relationship "online." This is not an easy question. Questions about love rarely are easy ones, as Chapter 3 in this book, devoted to that topic, should have amply illustrated. So once again, let us lean on Peirce for some help.

Common sense (hardly infallible but as we know greatly valued by Peirce) tells us that you can meet persons online, learn about them, become intrigued by them, and so on, but you can only actually fall in love or (if you prefer) learn or grow to love a person whom you have actually encountered. This may be the case because we do not simply or even primarily love *what* someone is (we can learn a great deal about that through technologically mediated communications), but rather, we love that he or she is *this* particular one, what Peirce following Scotus referred to as each person's *haecceity*.[17] Here we are exposing once again the kind of philosophical voluntarism that seems most congenial for inquiry in theo-semiotic. Love must begin with volition, a decision to direct my attention to this particular one that is present to me. Even in the absence of my beloved, the real object of my love is not that absence as a presence (this is why *saudade* is so deeply melancholic), nor is it the mere idea of my beloved (even with all of its rich details). It is that one, my actual beloved, now absent, whom I love.

This is not to suggest that the qualities that a person might possess play no role in motivating or sustaining our love for that person; perfect attention to the other will include the awareness of *what* she is as well as *that* she is *this* one.[18] Yet a strong love can survive the erosion or even the disappearance of such qualities. A healthy sense of humor, for example, may have been one of the things that one most admired about one's beloved. But this does not mean that love vanishes when one's beloved now lies, humorless, in a coma. Nor is this an argument that "love is blind," arguably the least illuminating cliché ever to have been formulated about the nature of love. With regard to qualities perceived as negative, love is not so much blind as it is stubborn. Infatuation may induce blindness, but authentic love facilitates a deeper awareness of the beloved, enduring *despite* some of the qualities thus perceived. This awareness deepens and grows precisely because love involves paying proper attention.

Now, information inebriation is a widespread contemporary phenomenon. This makes it difficult for someone in such a condition to pay proper attention, with all of the potentially negative consequences that such a failure could entail. Here the analytical spotlight has been turned to shine on the concept of community. It is probably misleading to talk about "actual" and "virtual" ones. There are just the ones that we happen to belong to. Sometimes we interact with members of our community in the flesh. At other times those interactions are technologically mediated. Sometimes my wife will text or email instructions about what to pick up at the grocery store. But then we will eat dinner together later that evening at home. The virtual is in such instances rooted in and an extension of the actual. (We woke up that morning in bed together.) It is also teleologically oriented toward the actual. (Shopping instructions bear fruit in a shared evening meal.) This example lays the groundwork for yet another hypothesis or suggestion: I want to propose that the virtual is indeed ontologically parasitic on the actual most of the time and in precisely this way.

A purely virtual community would be one to which I have loyalty, sharing interests and purposes with its members, without ever actually encountering any of them. It is hard to imagine what this would be like.

A person may regard herself as a citizen of Pittsburgh "Steeler Nation," for example, watch their games on television, visit and contribute to blog sites, and so on. The vast majority of Steeler fans are people whom she would never meet. Nevertheless, it would be somewhat odd if she had never met *any* of them. It would be equally odd if her "citizenship" did not actively dispose her to pursue interactions (in the flesh) with other Steeler fans whenever the opportunity presented itself.

All of these observations collaborate to suggest that someone who really cares about a community need not eschew its technological enhancements and extensions or avoid its virtual spaces. At the same time, it will take skill to navigate between the actual and the virtual and back again. There will be more complicated decisions than hitherto imaginable about how best to "spend" one's attention (on one's lunch partner or on the text that just popped up on one's cell phone now lying on the restaurant table, for example), and consistently making the right ones will take skill as well. It will take practice. It will require developing self-control in the way that Peirce conceived of it: as rehearsing various scenarios in the imagination in order to anticipate how one should respond to them—that is to say, how one should attend to them in the future should they occur.

Our decision-making regarding attention does not always involve our standing precisely at the intersection between the actual and the virtual. Nor are the skills that we need to develop unique to one realm or the other. Just imagine a mindful form of internet "web surfing" that somewhat resembles the practice of musement. Undoubtedly, it would be a very difficult thing to do well. The near-omnipotence of the computer mouse as a device that permits us to click virtual reality on and off at will does not facilitate or encourage the passive drinking in of impressions with which Peirce thought all real musement should begin. In fact, it is that ability so easily to control the stream of semiosis online, also to conceal significant aspects of our bodies and ourselves—the display of which might make us feel vulnerable—that gives the computer its seductiveness. Yet once immersed in an actual situation, there is no magical mouse that allows us to edit experience and so direct our attention. Sooner or later, the timid student who likes to submit questions by email will get called upon in the classroom. As a result, it may make the most sense to develop mindful habits of attention with the computer first turned off and then later see how they might be adapted for the purposes of communication and interpretation in virtual space. Successful—that is to say, *mindful*—web surfing may best be rooted in the type of musement that we engage in while taking a walk in the woods.

This discussion could be read by someone as a prophetic warning about the illusory, indeed, the idolatrous character of a "virtual community" and about the risk of danger that participation in such communities represents. That risk is certainly real enough, just as it is with riding in cars and airplanes or with using steak knives. (There is no technological practice that does not involve some risk.) The danger in this case is with a narrowing of the stream of semiosis and exposure to the threat of distraction, resulting in the gradual atrophy of our powers of attention. As a result, this discussion may also seem at times to have morphed into a homily about the need for better, more disciplined technological practices, for better awareness of how they can shape us, and so for the need in pursuing them to be properly self-controlled. The dream of an ever more expansive, diverse, and inclusive community is a Peircean/Roycean dream, whatever role technology and the global internet might happen to play in its realization. It is not a nightmare that we need to be awakened from, but its reality is something that we will need to be fully awake and attentive to if our collective efforts are ever to result in movement closer to its becoming an actual state of affairs.

Against the background supplied by this rather lengthy exploration of the idea of a virtual community, it becomes useful to raise again the question of "who is my neighbor?" Jesus's own parabolic answer to that question involved the story of a vivid encounter between two persons, the presence of their actual bodies seeming to be quite crucial to the encounter, since it is the physically bruised and battered condition of one of those persons that elicits a response in the form of bodily care on the part of the other. That the battered victim and his Samaritan rescuer were strangers before the encounter, indeed, classified as being members of very separate communities, seems like an important detail for discerning the meaning of the parable. This separateness was not sufficient to preclude their becoming neighbors when they encounter each other along the road, just as the common identification as being members of the same community was insufficient to elicit neighborly love from the other persons who in the story simply passed the victim by. Here it is just such a love that seems crucial for establishing a real relation as neighbors, and on this issue Peirce and Royce seem very close to Jesus (whose parable, after all, they would have had in mind even as they were raising the question).

While it may have originated in earlier actual encounters, from a certain perspective neighborly love exists only virtually, as a habit of love. It becomes *embodied* in practice when it is elicited on some actual occasion as a tendency to behave in a certain way under the determinate circumstances that the occasion presents. On any sort of pragmatic analysis this "embodiment in practice" is going to be of the utmost importance, and in this respect theosemiotic should honor its pragmatic legacy. Yet for many of the classical American pragmatists, the habit first formed and then elicited will also be of considerable philosophical interest and importance. For Peirce and Royce, in particular, even apart from its manifestation in actual conduct, such a habit will be regarded as metaphysically real. The reality of relations formed by a habit of love supports talk about virtual communities, even as Peirce's warnings about the impotence of a court without a sheriff and his insistence on the achievement of a *concrete* reasonableness as the highest of imaginable goods indicate some of the limitations of such talk.

Peirce's own response to the neighbor question seems neutral on the issue of physical presence. Neighbors may or may not be located near one another. "Nearness" is required, but not in space—rather, in "life and feeling." This criterion, as Peirce articulated it, remains somewhat vague, but the feeling he seemed to regard as necessary for neighbor relations is one that we would associate with love (recall that these remarks appear in his essay on evolutionary love). It could not be a feeling elicited accidentally or arbitrarily on the occasion in question. The nature of the occasion would itself summon precisely *that* feeling-response, as any other occasion appearing to be just like it would similarly tend to do. This tendency, displayed in the consistency of behavior inspired by such a feeling, is already virtually real before any feeling or conduct occurs, in the form of a powerful habit of love.

The issue of "before" and "after" is a complicated one, as previously observed and noted. For Edwards, since genuine religious affections are infused in the heart and mind of the saint by the power of divine volition as grace, the practice shaped by them is always only a sign and not the cause of their presence. For Peirce, it may also be the case that love, at least in its germinal state, is some kind of innate habit, since the love for God that he predicts will spring up in musement appears to be instinctive, the consequence of human selves having evolved within a cosmic neighborhood where the presence of the divine is ubiquitous. Yet habits are strengthened and perfected in practice, even in a somewhat odd way on Edwards's careful Calvinist account, decisively so within Peirce's theosemiotic. Signs appear in series, manifested as semiosis, so that while any sign will be determined by its object, it also has a causal, determining influence on some interpretant sign. To say that meaning grows in semiosis is just a different way of saying that habits grow—in strength, in scope, and in complexity.

For his own part, Royce was philosophically intrigued both by global neighborhoods and by the neighbors that greet us when we walk out of our front doors. His writings constitute a hymn of praise to the universal and Beloved Community, one embracing even rival loyalties because it is most deeply rooted in the loyalty to loyalty itself. At the same time, he wrote in celebration of a certain kind of provincialism,[19] his unique brand of cosmopolitanism taking the curious form not of precluding but actually of requiring such a positive evaluation. Both the Beloved Community and loyalty to loyalty must be regarded as ideals. The former cannot be identified with any actually existing community. The latter is not just one more form of loyalty, to be regarded alongside and in comparison to all of the other causes and communities to which one might already be committed. It is the form that such commitments take when they represent genuine loyalties. One does not establish the ideal community or achieve the highest loyalty by abstracting from every relationship to which one is presently devoted. The ideal must be achieved through and embodied in the actual; a healthy provincialism is the gateway to the universal, with global citizenship earned by behavior enacted on local streets and in neighborhoods; the love of God and devotion to an unlimited community are in a certain sense contingent on the love of neighbor. Indeed, they supervene upon the latter, much as an interpretant develops the meaning of a particular sign.

III

These meditations on the nature, purpose, and varieties of community set the stage for a concluding reflection on how such a concept might be most effectively extended and developed for theological purposes. There are two separate but related issues that constitute the twin foci around which this theological discussion can be organized. Each issue can be framed as a series of questions, to be raised and briefly explored here, with no pretense to supplying fully adequate responses. In the first place, how does an explicitly semiotic context enable one more clearly to delineate and to analyze the relationship between different religious communities? How might invoking that context help to facilitate interreligious dialogue, to address the challenge of religious conflict and religiously motivated violence? Are there continuities between the practices of certain religious communities that might be obscured from view by an excessive emphasis on the opposition between their teachings or doctrines? How from the pragmatic perspective defended here can such doctrines best be understood, the connection between doctrine and practice best defined? In more general terms, how would one begin to sketch the outline of a twenty-first-century theosemiotic of world religions?

A second series of questions, beginning in this instance at the more general level and moving to the particular, is worth considering: What would be entailed by a commitment to developing a liberation theosemiotic—that is, a theosemiotic of social justice? The link between liberation thought and theosemiotic inquiry has already been established in the earlier discussion noting their common emphasis on the primacy of praxis. Now the relevant connection will be supplied by their shared interest in the importance of community, not exclusively but most especially religious communities, more narrowly still (and contained within the latter), communities of theological inquiry. What is it that makes specific communities worth caring about? How might they be constituted as open, inclusive, democratic, and friendly to diversity? Who really *is* my neighbor, and if I discover that my neighbor is suffering and oppressed, what then must I do?

In pursuing the answers to any of these questions, it will be important to evaluate the conviction shared by pragmatists and liberationists alike that human beings are always already embodied persons, that there can be no human self-as-sign without the body serving as its sign-vehicle. The extent to which one person must be physically present to another in order for their relationship to be one that binds them in community is a topic that was discussed at some length in the preceding section of this chapter. Here the issues are a bit different in nature, but all are tied to the same general concern about how attention must be directed in order for the goals of a liberation theology to be achieved. Even if liberation means something more than emancipation from the physical suffering caused by extreme poverty and political oppression, it must certainly include *at least* such a result.[20] There can be no praxis devoted to social justice without attention being directed to suffering human bodies.[21] Moreover, how our bodies are disposed with respect to one another can either enable or delimit our capacity to pay attention.

The first set of questions centered on the task of developing a theosemiotic of world religions points us back in the direction of Peirce's logic of relations. From all that has been said thus far about logical systems, it should be easy to agree that any comparative theology will move rapidly beyond the most natural sort of comparison focused on similarities and differences (for example: In what way is Hinduism's conception of the ultimate reality as *Brahman* like or unlike the Muslim belief in *Allah* as a supreme, personal deity? Does the Buddhist description of *Nirvana* as a state of bliss in any way resemble Christian teachings about the afterlife? etc.) in order to explore examples of continuity and discontinuity among disparate theologies. Even beliefs that are quite different from each other in form and content can display a certain kind of *semiotic complementarity*. Moreover, the task of comparison can by no means be limited to the various *beliefs* affirmed by different religious communities. Following the precedent established by William James when he formulated his proposal for a "science of religions," it would also be important to compare and contrast the detailed descriptions of various religious *experiences* provided by representatives of a diversity of traditions and perspectives.[22] Finally, there may be similarities—also continuities—between the *practices* endorsed by these communities that, from the distinctively pragmatic perspective being maintained throughout this discussion, are of the greatest significance for theosemiotic purposes. In the final analysis, the pragmatic meaning of what religious persons claim to believe or experience will be most fully illuminated only by means of a careful examination of the patterns displayed in the conduct of their lives.

Most relevant to the discussion in this chapter is the added insight that the behavior of persons living together in community forms a more significant part of the "data set" for theosemiotic inquiry than the narrative description of any single person's life. Two different religious communities may appear to enshrine contrasting beliefs in their official creeds and doctrines and yet display in their behavior a significant number of overlapping practices. It may also prove to be the case that these two communities would find it difficult to negotiate the differences between their articulated doctrines while yet discovering that it is altogether possible for them to come together in practice. Coalition building, in either a religious or secular context—sometimes embracing both—is always a matter of bringing persons and communities with otherwise divergent beliefs and interests together within the context of a shared activity, perhaps but not necessarily one devoted to a common cause (however vaguely such a cause may be conceived).

Semiotic complementarity, therefore, is a phenomenon that is best displayed in praxis. A Roman Catholic devotee, for example, might come to the conclusion that the regular discipline of sitting *zazen* with Zen Buddhists adds something of real value to a spirituality organized around the kind of private, liturgical, and sacramental rituals associated with traditional Catholic piety. This would not require that Buddhist and Roman Catholic beliefs must be perfectly reconciled, so that a determination could be made that Buddhist and Catholics, on some theoretical level and in some essential fashion, believe the *same* things. It would be enough to show that, at a certain level of vagueness, there are no direct contradictions between their beliefs; moreover, *despite* any differences, both Buddhist and Christian beliefs could be exhibited as supporting the same practices, as providing a rationale for them, even if one rationale differs from the other. That is to say, the demonstration of some similarity-in-difference may not be necessary in order for some continuity-in-difference to be observed.

This keen theosemiotic attentiveness to the real presence of some continuity-in-difference—and to certain nonobvious similarities—is a safeguard, a way of avoiding the kind of community building that is achieved only at the cost of a stifling homogeneity and the insistence on near-perfect consensus among members. This cost will be judged too high even in the case of a single, specific religious community if its good health and positive growth are to be maintained for any duration of time. With regard to the broader ecumenical conversations that spring up *between* diverse communities, that cost can be prohibitive, a stumbling block to any sort of constructive dialogue. In order to function as a safeguard, the attentiveness alluded to here must be of a very special kind, like the open and capacious awareness more characteristic of musement than of precisive abstraction. It must also be skillful and discerning. While continuous relations of many different kinds may prove to be of vital importance for theosemiotic, it must be recognized once again that between any two things there will always be similarity of some type and in some respect. Not every similarity or continuity will prove to matter. The suggestion being made here with regard to religious communities is that the realm of praxis is an ideal place to look for possibly relevant similarities or continuities between them. Another place to look might be the biological legacies, in contrast to the widely divergent cultural ones, that the members of these communities could be expected to share. This explains the commitment of theosemiotic to a type of religious naturalism that affirms a subtly nuanced distinction between nature and culture while always refusing simply to contrast them.

Take as an illustration of the salutary import both of praxis and of biology for theosemiotic inquiry the example of breathing meditation. Upon careful consideration, breathing is an intriguing phenomenon, utterly basic yet quite complex in terms of the range of what it signifies. Breathing marks the difference between *life* and *death*. One can "hold" one's breath for a short period of time and remain alive, but its total cessation announces publicly (and typically before other biological indicators have been monitored) that one has died. The breath itself is a *physical* phenomenon, inhaled and exhaled through nose and mouth in a way that can be tangibly felt, filling the lungs, which act like a biological pump supplying oxygen to the rest of the human body. Yet it is also ethereal, circulating as something invisible (except when exhaling in a cold environment), and so readily *spiritualized*. The steady rhythm of inhalation followed by exhalation represents a continuous interaction between what is *internal* and what is *external* to the self. And breathing is both *passive* and *active*, involuntary and voluntary, occurring unconsciously and continuously as something that just happens to the body, even when one is asleep, yet to some extent also under one's control (ranging from complex forms of breathing meditation to the simple act of taking a deep breath in order to induce calmness or holding one's breath to "cure" hiccups). Breath and breathing are at the cusp of all of these pairs of opposites: life/death, spiritual/physical, internal/external, passive/active. At least the first two are ordered pairs, so that it is no surprise that the breath has become a prominent symbol of life and spirit in a great variety of religious traditions.

Breathing is also ubiquitous among human beings; it is something that all human beings do, for the most part, naturally and continuously. This observation brings us back to the initial contrast between the biological and the cultural. On the account that theosemiotic endorses, using symbols and creating cultures is natural for human beings in much the same way that breathing is natural. Nevertheless, nature and culture cannot simply be collapsed one into the other as if there were no distinction to be made; rather, culture is what we do with our biologically natural equipment, capacities, and dispositions. One among the many things that we do is to use breathing, to control or to regulate it, for a variety of purposes. Among these purposes, the use of the breath to reduce distraction and increase our capacity for paying attention is of special religious significance.

Here are two reasons that breathing meditation is a useful example for the task at hand. As a biological phenomenon, breathing is something that all human beings do. As a disciplined human practice, the control of breathing to facilitate paying better attention in meditation is widespread across an otherwise disparate array of religious traditions and communities. Daoists practice breathing meditation, Hindus and Buddhists as well, each of them having developed the discipline in astonishingly intricate ways. Sufi Muslims also engage in such a practice, as do Jesuit priests when they utilize Ignatius of Loyola's "third method" of prayer or Eastern Orthodox Christians when they repeat the Jesus Prayer as a mantram. In fact, these two reasons blend together and are continuous. Though breathing meditation is a cultural practice, something that human beings do with their biological natures, the fact that regulated breathing can increase relaxation, reduce distraction, and enhance attention is itself a biological fact, thoroughly natural. A sound religious naturalism will carefully note this fact, looking both to human biology and to human practices as a way to establish important connections between diverse religious communities.

This is not to suggest that cultural differences are illusory or that culture itself does not make or mark any kind of difference. In addition to being thoroughly naturalistic, the philosophical theology being recommended here is also deeply indebted to semiotic theory. There is no contradiction, as C. I. Lewis suggested with special reference to our verbal behavior, between admitting the enormous role played by culture and language in shaping human meaning and insisting that these are not the *only* sources of meaning in human experience. A theosemiotic of world religions will have to acknowledge multiple sources of meaning, a great many different forms of semiosis. A preoccupation with verbally articulated doctrines will tend to underscore with special emphasis the opposition between religious beliefs of different religious communities. Theosemiotic recognizes such oppositional differences, but also brings within the range of its inquiry both biosemiosis in all of its richness and religious praxis in all of its detailed complexity. The picture that emerges of the relationship among communities as a result of such inquiry is markedly different in character. All sorts of continuities will now be exposed, only some of them appearing in the form of similarities.

Consequently, two strategic maneuvers are vital to the success of such inquiry, both of them in resistance to a certain kind of reductionism. The first is to resist any temptation to reduce all of semiosis to language; biosemiosis and deliberate human conduct both matter as modes and makers of meaning. The second is to recognize that not all relations are of sameness, to prevent the collapsing of systems into classes of things. Much has been said already about both intellectual maneuvers, but the latter deserves a bit more extended consideration.

Semiotic complementarity is a somewhat vague concept that might be unpacked in a variety of ways. Every sign represents its object "in some respect." Consequently, every interpretant sign constitutes a form of aspect seeing or of "seeing as." My interpretation of X may contrast quite a bit with your own, yet nevertheless complement yours by regarding the same thing under a different aspect. In such a case, our sharing of interpretations will serve primarily neither to make one or the other more vulnerable nor to produce a consensus. It will result, rather, in the creation of a new kind of symbol. But this account is still a bit vague. Consider a simple example that illustrates the concept insofar as it is relevant to our understanding of community.

In the intimate community formed by a nuclear family, brothers are related to one another in a way rather different from how the relationship between a mother and her son might be defined. Brothers will tend to be compared and contrasted in a way that mothers and sons will not. If we want to emphasize the element of sameness, let us suppose even further that the brothers are identical twins; moreover, assume that they were adopted by their parents. The latter assumption notwithstanding, nevertheless, mother and son are also similar in certain respects, both being *homo sapiens*, for example, possibly both having the same color hair or eyes. In addition, each twin brother may display a nurturing love and loyalty toward the other that closely resembles the loyalty and love of mother toward children. Nothing at all is being insisted about the need to classify any two things rigidly, under a single aspect or with respect to only one criterion. Once again, the attempt to classify anything at all will represent a form of aspect seeing. One reading will accentuate certain features of a relationship, but in the process of continuous rereading, new meanings and different features will emerge more clearly into view. Readings that focus on the way that individuals affirm each other in their difference (one brother celebrates rather than merely tolerates his twin's decision to become a Muslim or the announcement that he is gay) rather than on their resemblances (they both look alike, went to the same schools, and support the same athletic teams) will create communal bonds between selves-as-signs grounded in complementarity.

Within communities, both the things that are shared (interests, beliefs, purposes, histories, identifying characteristics) and all of the various other modes or ways in which one person can be perceived as *being toward* others need to be taken into account. In loving one's twin brother, one forms a relationship that is simultaneously governed both by the logic of classes and the logic of systems. As one moves to a level of greater generality, a global perspective of the sort that one hopes to occupy in developing a theosemiotic of world religions, systems analysis will tend to become more important than class concepts. In asking questions about how people from communities quite separate and distinct—with very different histories, beliefs, and practices—can be conceived as being in relationship, it would only take us so far to assert that the members of both communities are *homo sapiens* or even that individuals from both of them engage in the practice of breathing meditation. This is not to suggest that either of these observations would be irrelevant to the theosemiotic task. To repeat, neither would take us very far.

To go further, one would have to explore territory in which both Peirce and Royce were early pioneers, the relevant issue being one about determining what would be needed for individuals ensconced in very distinct traditional communities in order to enable them to bond together in a larger community—one unlimited in time and scope, shaped by reading practices and so necessarily a community of interpretation, grounded in mutual love and loyalty and so also a Beloved Community. (Indeed, Royce insisted that the Beloved Community, if it is to be achieved, must always already be a community of interpretation.)[23] Peirce is pretty explicit that some commitment to agapism as a leading principle would fill this prescription, recommending the formulation of a revolutionary new creed organized around the law of love as its central article of belief. Toward the same end, Royce posits the loyalty to loyalty itself as a supreme ideal, placing it above every other loyalty. While empowering the members of such an unlimited community to remain faithful to their separate causes and commitments, it rules out any vicious loyalty of the sort that can be maintained only at the cost of undermining the ability of others to sustain devotion to their own ideals. In this instance, rather than having a homogenizing effect, the love of one individual for another affirms their differences, celebrates distinctiveness. Agape is a love directed not primarily to what one chooses or desires; it is a matter of loving what one finds.

In summary, a comparative theosemiotic will endorse the sort of naturalism that attends to those features of persons that they possess by virtue of being human, members of a species, biological features that help to explain why human beings experience the world in the way that they do. With regard to cultural behavior, such a theology will emphasize the significance of practices over doctrines while tending to interpret the meaning of doctrines in terms of the practices to which they are linked. Beyond the observation of similarities that might be exposed by focusing on biology and praxis, religious communities will be analyzed as complex systems, the ability of one community to interact with another quite different from itself being a matter of the extent to which that community, both as a whole and as represented by each of its members, has succeeded in cultivating a powerful habit of love. This habit also will best reveal itself in practice—in this case, an ecumenical sort of practice that involves careful reading and rereading.

Return for a moment to the example of breathing meditation. At the mundane level of human biology it is easy enough to identify breathing as something that all human beings do in an ongoing fashion. Moving to a consideration of religiously conceived cultural practices, it will also be fairly straightforward to compare the Buddhist practice of *zazen* with Ignatius's third method of prayer. But then extend the example more concretely to consider a Jesuit priest who now finds himself for a long period of time associated with a Zen Buddhist community and participating in its practices.[24] One might suppose that, in a reasonably short period of time, he would move beyond the point of observing the similarities between *zazen* and his own Jesuit form of meditation to the point where he would begin to appreciate their differences. If he learns to love what he finds, his own practice will even begin to incorporate these differences. To the extent that he is genuinely transformed by such a love, he will come to embody a meaning richer and more subtly complex than any that would be displayed in the simple juxtaposition of two similar but separate practices. This is how the law of mind is manifested as agape, as two things brought into relation come to embody a semiotic complementarity at a higher level of generality than the one on which their first encounter took place. This process, which theosemiotic is uniquely poised both to observe and to facilitate in its study of interacting religious communities, is very much what Peirce meant by the growth of concrete reasonableness.

Every self is a legisign. Communities are also complex living symbols, greater persons constituted by their members, but only insofar as the latter attend to each other, insofar as they share an attention and commitment to certain ideals and purposes. Without such attention, a community is reduced to a collection of individuals, patterns of resemblance between them perhaps observable from some analytical perspective but not in any way that brings them to unity or establishes solidarity among them. In order to achieve the latter, something more will be required: a deep loyalty both to the cause that unites them and to each other. This, at least, is the account that Peirce and Royce sketched more than a century ago and left as legacy for any future theosemiotic.

The emphasis on relations as a mode of being *toward* the other is not intended to obscure the significance, value, or integrity of the individual members of a community. The worry that it might or must do so is one that has haunted Peirce's theory of community for decades, Royce's to a lesser extent. To assert that an individual is a complex sign, a unified bundle of habits, *just is* to conceive of individuality in terms of a system of relations. Individuals are not simple monads with their identity established, their singularity affirmed, only to the extent that they are considered in isolation. Each individual is constituted as such by all of the relations that define her, by all of the objects of her loving attention, also by all of those others whose love is like a bright sun in which she basks. We are formed as selves by everyone to whom we have extended or from whom we have received this gift of love. To the extent that such relations multiply and grow, a person's individuality is enhanced, not mitigated or undermined. Intensity may be sacrificed to some extent; a self thus evolved is more like a "vicinity" than like a determinate location on the map. Yet neighborhoods have a quality or a flavor that can render them utterly distinctive and unique. Every person who has advanced beyond the most primitive stages of infancy is just such a semiotic "neighborhood."

By now it should be clear that "neighbor" and "neighborhood" are concepts not to be defined in the narrowest or strictest of geographical terms. To be sure, a certain kind of contact between neighbors does seem to be required. Yet it may be a continuity in "feeling" rather than in space that gives shape to a particular neighborhood, that establishes it as such. This was Peirce's suggestion, with the possibilities for creating such neighborhoods now in our century having been greatly enhanced by the development of new information technologies. Physical proximity was necessary in order for the Samaritan to perform an act of charity in Jesus's parable. But it would be relatively easy to create a twenty-first-century version of this story in which no such proximity was required. Teleologically speaking, the act of charity would still need to eventuate with *something* occurring in the physical presence of the one who suffers, yet the feelings of love and empathy, the relation of neighborliness, could be developed virtually. This relation is what makes any community worth caring about. Lacking this fundamentally dispositional way of being with and toward each other, persons can assemble, share interests, and pursue projects; but no genuine community will exist (at least not in a religiously meaningful sense).

The test case for determining true "neighborliness" in Jesus's parable was the practical response displayed by one person to the suffering of another. Now to extend an important Roycean insight, whatever afflicts us as human beings, whatever form of suffering such affliction takes, can only be healed *in* community. The romantic image of a solitary sage absorbed in private contemplation rubs against the basic Buddhist teaching that it is the community (*Sangha*) that constitutes one of the three great "refuges" for Buddhist practitioners. Liberation theologians have always affirmed such an insight, but no healing is possible, no refuge to be found, if communities are narrow and exclusive, one set off against another as oppressor to those oppressed, the privileged against the poor. What can a theosemiotic grounded in pragmatism contribute to the development of this insight?

First of all, the desideratum of a truly unlimited or universal community, emphasized in the philosophies of both Peirce and Royce, should be translatable in a liberationist context. That no community of this kind presently exists, or even looms on the horizon, underscores the reason why a liberation theosemiotic must take the form of a theology of hope. This is no mere utopianism, but that risk is avoided only to the extent that philosophical pragmatism supplies actual resources useful for the purpose of constructing such a community. One important resource is an emphasis on voluntarism, not pure and simple, but of the very special kind that can be utilized to develop a robust and carefully articulated ethics of attention. Another is a set of ideas—including James on the "moral equivalent of war," Peirce on self-control, and Royce on loyalty—all useful for the purpose of cultivating the sort of "martial spirituality" to which any liberation theology should be firmly committed.[25] Such a spirituality involves the developing of both habits and strategies of resistance to whatever might be judged as evil or oppressive, especially insofar as it manifests as an attempt to undermine our self-control with respect to acts of attention. A third is the strategic emphasis on a form of rationality that is essentially "communicative," understanding persons as living legisigns, with their interactions rooted in attentive acts of reading and rereading. When rationality is conceived in this fashion, the only factor that might legitimately exclude an individual from participation in the life of a community would be his own stubborn resistance to the openness and discipline that such a rationality requires. No other conditions—social, political, economic, or whatever—preventing full participation should be permitted to endure. Finally, theosemiotic adds depth and nuance to a liberationist insight that the human body is potentially an important sign and source of solidarity among persons.

"Inclusion" and "diversity" have become sacred terms dominating contemporary discourse about what it means to build or to be a healthy community. Yet the meaning of these words, insofar as they are in fact meaningful in such a discourse, is hardly transparent. Somewhat stringent requirements would have to be met in order for any person to feel actually *included* in a community. One can be nominally included in a conversation, for example, yet never be allowed to speak, or perhaps be allowed to speak but not listened to. Genuine inclusion requires that one become the object of a careful and respectful attention on the part of other members of the community, an attention that manifests itself, literally or metaphorically, as an act of *listening*. This is a minimal requirement to be established by any coherent ethics of attention. Similarly, not every form of diversity will be regarded as healthy for the life of a community, nor should diversity be valued simply because of how it might enrich the experience of more privileged members of the community.[26] The importance of diversity is to be established first and foremost as a requirement of social justice, with its cultivation and promotion to be defended by an appeal to talk about semiotic complementarity, the law of mind, and the gift and growth of meaning.

Now, to suggest, as I have done repeatedly throughout this discussion, that semiosis cannot be reduced to language is not necessarily to deny that words and humanly constructed texts might have a special significance. A pragmatic refusal to drive a deep wedge between nature and culture should not be interpreted as a refusal to recognize any distinction between them at all. It need not result in the swallowing of textual hermeneutics by a "totalitarian" biosemiotics that pretends to offer an exhaustive account of how human meaning is generated.[27]

My modest hope is that theosemiotic may represent an alternative *both* to a perspective that focuses exclusively on the crucial difference that belonging to a specific religious community might make in determining religious meaning *and* a crude form of natural theology that ignores the importance of such community as a source of meaning. Thinking about how meaning might be "modified" by language, as Lewis suggested, represents an important task if such an alternative is to become viable. Further considering the implications of Peirce's anthropomorphism represents another. And observing how Jonathan Edwards developed a theological method operating in the intertextual space created by placing the book of nature in conversation with biblical texts might open up a third line of analysis.[28] Turn then to the brief consideration of each of these topics.

Consider first the contrast that has become commonplace in recent postliberal theology between "experiential-expressivist" and "cultural-linguistic" theories of religious doctrine.[29] From a theosemiotic perspective, the truth lies somewhere in between. It will not do *either* to suggest that human experience is prelinguistic and only subsequently expressed or thematized in verbal form *or* to insist that any experience that we might be capable of having is completely shaped and conditioned by the language that we speak and the manner in which we have become enculturated in some community. Experiential-expressivists are naïve to assume that we can come to experience the world in some way not always already informed by a great variety of cultural, social, and linguistic habits of interpretation. On the other hand, the cultural-linguistic perspective takes social constructivism too far. The fact that language and culture clearly do shape our experiences does not mitigate the extent to which those very same experiences are also conditioned both by human biological factors (the structure of our bodies, our sense organs, the chemistry of our brains, natural instincts and capacities, etc.) and by the nature of the thing experienced. Peirce's semiotic theory carefully evaluates the significance of all of these factors, and so must any contemporary theology conceived as theosemiotic. Symbols can be either linguistic or nonlinguistic. Experience-as-semiosis is a process in which meaning is both discovered and created, as the result of the interaction between human interpreters—who are culture-creating biological organisms—with the environment that they inhabit (itself a complex blend of natural and cultural elements, with no clear line that can be drawn to mark their boundaries).

All of this having been said, the significance for human experience of language and of specifically linguistic signs is enormous. It can hardly be reduced to the function of "expressing" the meaning of some experience already established otherwise. Once again, the use of language modifies the very meaning of human experience. While a great variety of verbal and nonverbal signs are involved in human cognition—thus forming a stream of semiosis that constitutes the self as a living, feeling, thinking, acting human being—it is primarily our capacity for language that enables us to occupy a meta-cognitive space, thus to further constitute the self as a being always in relationship to itself. Language allows us to step outside of a particular semiotic stream in order to reflect upon it, not simply to use signs for various purposes, but to recognize a sign *as such*. This puts the meaning-making game on steroids, pushes meaning to a whole new level, modifying in a profound way what the sophisticated human animal might otherwise have taken an experience to mean. (Just think about Anne Sullivan's dramatic account of what happened to Hellen Keller when Helen—already capable of responding to certain signals—first learned that there was a word that could be used as a symbol for water.)[30]

As should already be evident, Peirce's anthropomorphism is a curious thing. It is as far removed as possible from any kind of anthropocentrism. The world and its hypothetical Creator do not display personal features because our experience forces them uncomfortably and embarrassingly into humanly contrived categories; rather, as humans we have evolved within the womb and at the bosom of the universe as it really is. We are subtly but decisively attuned to it as a result of this natural evolutionary process. It is precisely when we contemplate the natural world without human artifice or analysis that, as Martin Buber argued nearly a century ago, we experience it as "you," there being at the heart of the universe something deeply personal. We do not contrive it; our love for it is always only a response to a love already given. Peirce and Buber were on the same page here, as Peirce predicted that the muser's contemplation of the natural universe, if conducted without any practical or strategic purpose, would eventually result in her falling in love with what it reveals.[31]

For anyone who embraces theosemiotic, the entire universe is a text, not so much a library, where two separate volumes might be pulled off the shelves and juxtaposed, but a single grand narrative, with an infinite variety of subplots. If there is any way for us to read the book of nature, to be sure, the reading produced will be one at least partially articulated in human words, in language. But this cannot be taken to mean that *nothing* in nature itself contributes to such a reading. It cannot mean that the significance of *everything* that we feel or that we do in response to nature is a function of how we use language or that such significance can be perfectly captured in words. For the theologian, it cannot mean that, in the mind of the reader, the whole of the universe has been absorbed into the world of the biblical text.[32] Such a theological point of view seems as problematic as one that permits biblical hermeneutics to be swallowed by biosemiotics.

We need a new theory of intertextuality, but not a crude one. For theosemiotic, there can be no deep chasm between nature and culture; once again, the "book of nature" is not a text on the library shelf, sitting alongside the Hebrew and Christian bibles, the *Qu'ran, Bhagavad Gita,* and *Dao de jing.* When Jonathan Edwards spent hours walking through the woods and fields of New England doing a close reading of the book of nature, his interpretations were clearly shaped and informed by the scriptural texts that had become a part of his lifeblood. Yet rather than one text "absorbing" or "swallowing" the other, his intertextual musings drew both on his scripturally formed Christian identity and on his continuously fresh encounters with the natural world. This kind of intertextuality does not involve making one text the interpretive key for understanding the other. It does involve creating a semiotic space in which a lively conversation between *different reading experiences* might be able to occur, not by abandoning any set of beliefs presently adhered to, but by having (at least in this peculiar space) all beliefs as though one did not have them. Books do not talk to each other. Persons do. Sometimes the conversation occurs within the mind of a single reader. Here the line distinguishing *intertextual* from *intratextual* readings itself begins to blur. If nature is all that there is and the book of nature exhausts all of creation—moreover, if every person is an enormously complex sign that takes the form of a narrative gradually unfolding in time—then how does one stand *outside* of such a book or story in order to place it in conversation with something else?

I think that this kind of reading is what Peirce intended when he recommended the practice of musement. It is by no means the recommendation for doing a purely "natural theology" in the way that such an enterprise is typically conceived. As adults, we cannot simply take flight from our religious traditions and communities in the process of inquiry. We cannot shed our cultural, social, and linguistic habits like we do our clothes in order to "skinny dip" in the book of nature. These habits are by no means external to who and what we are. The key is to find a cognitive space in which play becomes a real possibility. Our biological and cultural constraints also define a world of possibilities. When the music begins to play, we should wish neither to abandon our human bodies nor somehow to elude the force of gravity in order to begin to dance—nor should we stop listening to the music. All of these factors are essential. It is hardly their elimination, but only the gentle softening of their grip, that makes dancing a genuine possibility. So, too, with our philosophical theologies. In reading the book of nature, our religious beliefs, doctrines, and scriptures, as well as the structure of our human brains and bodies, will supply many of the rules for a game that we must then decide how we will choose to play.

6 / Rules for Discernment

I

When Peirce encouraged the reader of his Neglected Argument to be fully awake to what is "about" or "within," he introduced a semiotic distinction that merits careful consideration. Assume that to be awake in the sense that Peirce recommended is a matter of paying disciplined attention to the signs that continuously present themselves in human experience. In a world filled with signs, much of this attention will be directed outward, to the various persons, places, and things that one happens to encounter, to events as they occur. At the same time, since one's own thoughts, feelings, and habits have been shown also to be signs, a good deal of attention will be focused on what lies "within" a person. This latter type of attending, along with the acts of interpretation that it enables, is central to the task of what is here being called "discernment."

The reader of *this* book will be well aware by now that such a distinction between what appears as outside and what lies within the self is hardly a rigid one. The semiotic self, as portrayed in the philosophies of Peirce, Royce, Mead, and others, is thoroughly porous and essentially relational. The linking of philosophical pragmatism to contextualism in the earlier discussion of theology as therapy served to underscore how a broader framework is required for the effective analysis of any individual's feelings and behavior. Moreover, traditional theological talk about the "discernment of spirits" muddies the water to an even greater extent. Even if their effects are wrought within the heart and mind of a religious devotee, these spirits—both good and evil—are often believed to exist as real and as really independent of the person affected by them.

There can be no possibility for success in discernment conceived as some form of unmediated intuition or introspection, as if it were a simple act of "gazing inward"; however it might be described, discernment is always a matter of interpreting signs—as with any other event of meaning, an essentially semiotic phenomenon. Even signs appearing to be located internally as thoughts, feelings, memories, imaginings, etc., if properly interpreted, can illuminate a spiritual landscape that embraces but dramatically transcends the individual who experiences them. By contrast, the failure to interpret accurately can represent a significant obstacle as one attempts to navigate such a landscape. The adoption of a third-person perspective on oneself will be important for discernment, a task often best facilitated by communication with others. Even if pursued in solitude, acts of discernment will expose the vital importance of our relationship to others *in community*.

No matter how muddy the water and blurred the distinctions, nevertheless, it will be expedient here to think of discernment as a form of reading that has oneself as the primary text, as the principal even if not the exclusive subject matter. It is self-reflexive because it is guided by questions the answers to which can dramatically impact the self: In a world filled with signs, is there any evidence of a purpose relevant to my life? Which path in life should I choose? Am I being deceived or am I self-deceived? What then must I do? This kind of reading is shielded from solipsism because it ideally takes the form of listening to and for the voices of others, not as a casual bystander eavesdropping on some conversation, but as someone being addressed and straining to listen.

Discernment requires attentiveness (how could one read effectively otherwise?), but what is achieved with success also always involves skill—beyond the perfecting of a certain habit of attention, skill in performing some act of interpretation. Faithful to its pragmatic inspiration, theosemiotic inquiry will never presume that simple attention, no matter how focused or intense, can suffice for the purposes of discernment. Every perception, including self-perception, will involve an element of judgment. Indeed, the primary role of attention here is to facilitate judgment. Moreover, this will require a special form of attention. Not only is intensely focused attention—a steady, unwavering introspective gaze—inadequate, it is also inappropriate for the goals of a discerning inquirer. A different sort of mindset is to be preferred, a certain vigilance or readiness, a commitment to being awake in the manner that Peirce himself recommended.

Discernment is a form of judgment, to be distinguished from other kinds of judgment in terms of its nature and purposes. In the present context, its nature will be understood as primarily self-reflexive and its purposes as being religious in character. It is possible to give the word a broader meaning, of course, as when we speak of someone having a discerning taste with regard to fine wine or clothing. Judges as well as juries should exercise discernment in courts of law. And we hope that parents will display discernment in raising their children. All of these instances can be analyzed in semiotic terms. But the special form of semiosis being considered here will be regarded as religiously meaningful. The signs that Jonathan Edwards explored with such detail and rigor were taken by him to be either reliable or unreliable indications of divine grace working in the heart and mind of a Christian devotee. Similarly, the rules formulated by Ignatius of Loyola were intended to be useful for analyzing specific feeling states, perhaps as indications of God's grace, but also quite possibly as the work of the devil (with whom Edwards was equally concerned). In either case, it is the presence and the purposes of something greater than oneself that one hopes to discern, even when this is best achieved by a careful consideration of one's own feelings and behavior.

Self-reflexivity should not be confused with self-preoccupation. It is worth belaboring this point. Once again, that which one struggles to identify or recognize in the process of discernment transcends the self even as its effects are visible there. I can look in vain for my lost keys in a messy room, suddenly stop, retrace my recent behavior in memory, then look again (a method that tends to be quite successful). In both cases (before and after stopping), the purpose is to find my keys, but it is the latter case that more closely resembles an act of discernment. This is an admittedly trivial example, although it does underscore the extent to which an attentiveness to the self and its experiences (thoughts, feelings, memories, etc.) can enhance our ability to interpret the world around us with greater accuracy and reliability. Consider then a less trivial example.

Anyone guided by the principles and perspectives distinctive of theosemiotic inquiry will recognize the fact that a theology of liberation must be very closely linked to and informed by an ethics of attention. Poverty, suffering, and oppression must first be *seen*, must be recognized as such, before they can be meaningfully addressed in praxis. This seeing is the work of semiotic, precisely in the sense that Peirce's logic of abduction must be understood in at least one of its modalities as a logic of recognition. Any judgment about our moral failure to address the reality of poverty and suffering presupposes that it is a state of affairs that we have already clearly perceived. But our failure to perceive is itself a moral failure, hardly an excuse for why we did not act in response. Paying attention is always our first deliberate reaction to the things that we encounter in the world, our attending to one thing rather than to another constituting a fundamental act of volition. Even if one insists that ethics is limited to the evaluation of what we ought to do, it must be conceded that what we do with our attention is of immeasurable moral significance, a feature of our moral lives and behavior that is all too readily overlooked. Our responsibility to act in certain other ways presupposes an obligation to perceive and interpret situations with honesty and accuracy. This act of interpretation is hardly neutral, then, for the one who performs it. In every case of discernment, questions will arise about how one ought to be disposed toward the persons and situations under consideration. These questions are clearly self-reflexive. What do I see or fail to see? How do I evaluate what I see? What must I do?

This is the deeper sense in which self-analysis is not to be confused with an unhealthy form (both morally and psychologically) of self-preoccupation. Take as yet another (and closely related) example the Ignatian emphasis on examination of conscience as a regular practice, especially early on in the first week of the exercises.[1] On any given occasion, to be sure, this practice can degenerate into a form of self-preoccupation, a type of scrupulousness that blinds an individual to the significance of anything or anyone other than the self. As a form of meditation perfected in practice, however, it becomes a way of attending to the self that illuminates how the self is *disposed* in its relationships to a complex myriad of other persons and things. Since relationships can be problematic (sinful), this example illustrates how broadly a genuinely pragmaticistic theory of inquiry ought to be conceived. That is to say, this is a case where the purpose of inquiry or examination is to generate problems where perhaps none had been previously discerned (I may be unaware of or only dimly recognize the presence of some deeply rooted disposition having a negative effect on my behavior and relationships), rather than immediately to find a solution to some problem that motivated inquiry in the first place. This example, it seems plausible to assert, can be generalized in a way that all acts of discernment might be accurately perceived as "examinations of conscience," liberally construed.

Both of the theologians being considered here—but Ignatius in particular—were eager to identify methods for discerning how God's will might be prompting an individual to act in one way rather than another, to choose this rather than that path in life. It would be important in the long run then to place Ignatius in conversation with Josiah Royce in order to supply a distinctively theological perspective on what the latter referred to as a life plan. In addition to being focused on one's own self as the primary text for interpretation, acts of discernment will be connected to praxis in the rather intimate way that all properly pragmatic forms of inquiry must be portrayed. Here the praxis is also self-referential, involving the making of choices about what one should do in a particular situation and more generally about how one should live one's life. While I have consistently argued that inquiry does not always begin with doubt and with some problematic situation, it almost always begins with a question (or very soon results in asking one). Those questions most relevant to the special kind of inquiry that constitutes discernment are about the choice of ideals, and also about how one wishes to be disposed, the habits (virtues) that one decides are worth cultivating, and those (vices) that need to be uprooted.

This inquiry about the self will inevitably trace a path back to some community and culminate with a question about "what then must *we* do?"[2] Since the self is always already a being-in-relation, no proper examination of its experiences should isolate it from community. Moreover, given a theosemiotic point of view, what we do together (and in the long run) is of far greater significance than the path that any single individual might pursue in solitude. Finally, most of those dispositions, first discerned and then judged to be harmful or sinful, will be social in origin. This is most certainly the case with various forms of bigotry. Bigoted families and communities will almost inexorably tend to produce bigoted individuals within their midst. Rather than serving as a moral excuse for such individuals, this observation amounts to the recognition that vice and sin have a powerful social dimension, often involving the risk of contagion. While we are all vulnerable to disease, the mature and discerning individual is responsible for taking measures to insure the preservation of health—in this case, moral and spiritual well-being.

All of these preliminary observations are consistent with and characteristic of the project that Ignatius himself initiated in the sixteenth century with his terse enunciation of "rules for the discernment of spirits" and with remarks scattered throughout his manual intended to instruct the devotee about how he should be properly disposed when engaged in acts of prayer and meditation.[3] Indeed, dispositions are crucial to the spiritual practice that Ignatius described. Not only are these exercises designed to facilitate a certain kind of habit formation, moreover, the habits thus formed will be essential if any insight is to result from the devotee's self-inspection. Such habits are numerous and subtly interconnected. In the first place, one should be disposed to *listen*, not in order to hear only a specific, determinate message, but as a readiness to perceive the divine will precisely in the manner that it is communicated, whether it manifests itself as confirmation of one's expectations or as a complete surprise. This requires that the exercitant should be like "a balance at equilibrium," leaning neither in one direction or another, but truly detached and free from prejudice or distorting inclination.[4] Once again, this listening is self-reflexive because it is always a listening *for* what is being addressed to *oneself*.

It will be important to examine how such a habit of detachment, its formation prescribed in the manual's preliminary observations, can be linked to the habit of love alluded to in the contemplation with which these exercises culminate. Throughout these deliberations, I have been exploring the hypothesis that the latter habit can be regarded as the ultimate logical interpretant of any human self-conceived as a sign, the desideratum for what a self should come to mean, at least insofar as it forms the fragment of a universe of meaning. Peirce's agapism, with its roots in Christian scriptures and theology, has helped to shape this hypothesis. But my intention is to articulate and defend it in a way that is neither narrowly nor exclusively Christian. The experience of love and an inclination toward benevolence are hardly private Christian property. Not only do these phenomena appear to be universally human (which explains their relevance to theosemiotic inquiry as a form of philosophical theology), but a wide array of religious communities and traditions have explored them, both theologically and symbolically, and also celebrated them.

Ignatius's rules, appended to the main body of his manual of exercises, were designed to assist the religious practitioner in the task of self-examination—in particular, to determine how feeling-states of both "consolation" and "desolation" might be interpreted as signs of either spiritual progress or regress. Two centuries later, Jonathan Edwards published his remarkable *Treatise on Religious Affections*, most immediately in order to help facilitate the process of evaluating the experiences of individuals participating in the Great Awakening, a religious revival that had been sweeping across the British colonies in America for more than a decade. Edwards delineated twelve signs that he argued were reliable indicators of the presence of divine grace after rejecting a number of others that he judged to be potentially deceptive.

How might Peirce's semiotic theory be adapted for the purpose of exploring these two theologies of discernment? For both theologians, as for Peirce, one's knowledge of oneself is never intuitive, simply available upon introspection, but rather always a matter of inference, of the disciplined interpretation of certain signs. This common link has been carefully identified and then emphasized in the earlier stages of my discussion.

In addition, such interpretation is rule-governed, not random or undisciplined, but deliberate in some important sense. How, then, might we identify these rules for discernment?

For both Ignatius and Edwards, the task of discernment is to determine the spiritual authenticity of certain signs. In any given instance, does the sign in question genuinely signify the presence of divine grace in the heart and mind of a religious devotee, or is it something counterfeit? The general question raised by each theologian is pretty much the same, but they each take somewhat different approaches to the problem. Ignatius restricts himself to one type of sign, distinctive feelings of consolation or desolation, and then asks under what conditions a benevolent Spirit might reliably be considered as the source of such feelings. In his treatment of the question, by contrast, Edwards surveys a vast array of potential signs—feelings of various kinds, but also bodily gestures and actions, patterns of thought, and modes of behavior—in order to determine which can be classified as reliable and which should be deemed unreliable signs of the operative presence in the soul of what he calls "gracious and holy affections." Both men were thoroughgoing fallibilists with regard to judgments of reliability. Any act of interpretation is potentially falsifiable—with respect to the type of sign being examined here this is emphatically the case, given what they perceived to be the cunning of evil spirits, as well as the extraordinary human capacity for self-deception.

Consider Ignatius of Loyola's much briefer and theologically less well-developed account first. The experience of consolation is of a certain kind of joyfulness, a confidence that one's spiritual exercises have been effective and that in the process of pursuing them one has drawn closer to God. For Ignatius, the label applies to "every increase of faith, hope, and love, and all interior joy that invites and attracts to what is heavenly and to the salvation of one's soul by filling it with peace and quiet in its Creator and Lord."[5] Feelings of consolation might very well be a sign of the health of one's spiritual life, of God's gracious response to the believer who earnestly seeks to develop a relationship with his or her Creator. As such, it would be a positive and encouraging sign, perhaps spurring even greater effort and devotion on the part of one who interprets it in this fashion. Yet it might also be a false sign, implanted in the heart by an evil spirit who wishes to generate false confidence in the mind of the devotee. Consolation can be a good or a bad sign, then, recognizable either as God's gift or as the work of the devil designed to produce in the devotee corresponding feelings of complacency, sometimes resulting in spiritual pride.

Feelings of desolation also require careful interpretation. In this condition, "the soul is wholly slothful, tepid, sad, and separated, as it were, from its Creator and Lord."[6] It is a "darkness of soul" resulting in a certain "restlessness" and an increase in "temptations." Such desolation might be caused by God, and for multiple reasons: as an appropriate punishment for one who has been lax in spiritual exercises; or as a test of one's spiritual mettle intended to reveal how well one will persist in prayer despite such distraction; or, finally, as an important reminder that true spiritual joy is gratuitous and not something produced by spiritual recipes or technologies. In other instances, feelings of desolation may be the work of the enemy, seeking actively to discourage someone who is struggling in the practice of prayer. In all of these cases, the meaning of some feeling as a sign can be discerned only if the devotee is attentive to what has preceded it, placing it in a narrative *context*. In the special case of a consolation not preceded by any discernible cause, the most reliable interpretation is that it is a divinely imparted gift pure and simple.[7] Yet even in such an instance, the appropriate context for interpretation will be a narrative one. For Ignatius, much as for Peirce, meaning is understood not as something attached to a discrete sign but only as emerging in a dynamic process, as the product of ongoing semiosis. This is fundamentally a triadic process, the mediation of a sign between its object and an interpretant continuously recurring to form a series. As with all semiosis, the ordering of items in the series is not accidental but essential, displaying the growth of meaning but sometimes also its erosion.

Recall from the account recorded in Chapter 1's brief history that the triadicity of semiosis is reflected and reinforced in the exercises by the invaluable presence of a spiritual director, with whom the exercitant regularly consults, and whose role can be described as one intended to assist in the determination of meaningful interpretants. Since, according to the basic and by now well-rehearsed principles of pragmaticism, we come to know ourselves by means of interpretive inferences quite similar to the ones that enable us to know other persons, someone else (in this case, a spiritual adviser) could happen to know certain things about us of which we are not ourselves aware. To be sure, some of these things might prove to be complementary to what we already know. Yet it could also be otherwise. We might be blind to certain troublesome facts about ourselves or even mistaken, perhaps mired in self-deception. Here our dependence on the perspective of others can be of a rather dramatic sort.

This bracing truth is semiotic at its core. The interpretant is itself a sign that "explains" the relationship between some previous sign and its object. A sign will determine interpretants both in the form of subsequent thought-signs internal to consciousness and as supplied by some other person with whom one is engaged in conversation. Even the stream of thought-signs internal to consciousness takes the form of a conversation. As Peirce observed and announced, all meditation, indeed all human thought, is essentially dialogical in nature (N3: 258–59). This insight is confirmed by Ignatius's manual of instructions, which not only incorporated regular consultation with a spiritual director for the duration of the exercises, but also emphasized within many of the individual exercises the technique of engaging in frequent "colloquies" (with Christ, or his mother, or perhaps one of the saints, and as one might best imagine such a conversation taking place under various circumstances).

The "first principle and foundation" of the spiritual exercises as a whole, articulated at the conclusion of Ignatius's "introductory observations," expresses a conviction that the basic end for which humans were created is "to praise, reverence, and serve God our Lord."[8] This end acts as a final cause to which all of the specific choices that a devotee will make—at various times and in diverse situations—are essentially ordered. Those choices yield results qualitatively different from the ones that they would produce were such an end not to be held in mind. The end as final cause illuminates and empowers those choices, gives them their own causal efficacy, even if from an external third-person perspective the actions taken do not always immediately or transparently display their guiding rationale. Once again, this is how Peirce understood the essence of freedom as self-control. One's behavior in the present has a gently shaping influence on future versions of oneself, the causal power of such behavior (or, in semiotic terms, its significance) consisting in its having been guided by some basic ideal, conducted at least in partial conformity to what Josiah Royce called a life-plan. (There are plenty of nonreligious examples illustrative of the point about how an ideal or guiding rationale is determinative of meaning. The cutting of someone's flesh with a sharp instrument, for instance, could be interpreted as either cruel or compassionate, depending on whether the end to which such an act is ordered was to be recognized as interrogation by torture or as life-saving surgery.)

Such a life-plan, formed in commitment to specific ideals and goals, becomes embodied in the person who adopts it as a set of habits deliberately cultivated. That process begins in childhood, on Royce's view, and continuously unfolds over time. The task of discernment is very much a matter of making explicit those habits and tendencies that may thus have been formed but may not now be clearly perceived. Once discerned and evaluated, they supply the interpretive context within which the experiences of some individual can be more accurately assessed. None of this can be done in a way that is value-neutral or free from uncertainty. A belief in some ideal will be as hypothetical as any other belief, just as vulnerable to correction, and always something that needs to be tested in practice. This is the whole point of Peirce's Neglected Argument: to test for the presence of certain basic instincts and dispositions, to correlate them with those ideals toward which they incline the muser to lean, and then to test the latter as hypotheses in the crucible of ongoing human experience. That is to say, ideals are among the beliefs that need to be submitted to pragmatic scrutiny. All of this begins with the contemplation of signs.

Now, a sign can be perceived as such only to the extent that one prescinds from the reality of the sign vehicle as a "thing." It is relatively commonplace for our attention to become entrapped in a world of things, both the things in our head that display themselves as thoughts, feelings, and beliefs and those that we bump up against continuously in the world revealed by our physical senses. This regular, ongoing, and inevitable commerce with things can actually blind us to the relations among them, obscure their significance. I would suggest that both Peirce's practice of musement and Ignatius's cultivation of an attitude of indifference were designed to counteract that effect, to illuminate the nature of things as signs, thus, to facilitate discernment. One can be so overwhelmed by feelings of consolation and desolation that one fails to discern what such feelings might actually mean with respect to the goals of the spiritual life. Similarly, one can be powerfully drawn to various riches, treasures, and honors in the world without ever recognizing the end for which they were created and to which our interactions with them should be properly ordered. Only by regarding them with a certain indifference can such recognition be facilitated.[9]

Ignatius was trained as a soldier, and his talk about the necessary cultivation of indifference can sometimes appear cold and demanding. This perception is undermined, however, by his joyful description of the "contemplation to attain the love of God," appearing at the end of the exercises. Within that contemplation, this practice of indifference culminates in a mystical awareness of how "God dwells in creatures," including oneself, and of how all created things are to be regarded as "blessings and gifts" (thus as the signs of their divine Giver).[10] Transformed by such an awareness, the devotee now moves about, not merely in a world filled with things, but in a world, as Peirce memorably described it, that is thoroughly perfused with signs.

There is a practical and playful strategy for training in indifference that Ignatius sketched in his brief discussion of the "three methods of prayer," included in the material appended to the four weeks of exercises. The second of these methods (which will be revisited in Chapter 7 of this book) involves pausing over each word of some traditional vocal prayer for as long as one "finds various meanings, comparisons, relish, and consolation in the consideration of it."[11] Here prayer is to be regarded not simply as an act of recitation but as an opportunity for cognitive play. Like a bee that, in order to make honey, will linger at a particular flower blossom for as long as it is fruitful to do so, the devotee will linger at prayer, playing with all of the possible meanings associated with each word that is uttered.[12] The resonance between this particular method of prayer and Peirce's prescription for musement, once again, is impossible to ignore. Musement, as Peirce conceived it, is a cognitive exercise that takes the form of pure play, bound by no rules other than the law of liberty: "It bloweth where it listeth" (*CP* 6.458). Yet it is in the midst of such play that self-transformative habits can be formed, most especially if engagement in play takes the form of a deliberate practice, a regular exercise.

Once formed, these habits are themselves meaningful signs, embodied in persons who constitute their sign-vehicles. Whatever else theosemiotic has been shown to mean, clearly it incorporates the insight and affirmation that each person is a living symbol or legisign, a complex bundle of habits, some of which take the form of beliefs about values and purposes. The character of a person will be displayed in dispositional patterns of feeling and conduct, not in flashes of feeling or in random thoughts and actions. Once again, it takes time to "read" a person's character, even as it does for that person to self-read and deliberately form such a character. Reading in all of its forms is obviously a semiotic process. Habits-as-signs will gently determine the kinds of relationships that a person will be able to enter into and then sustain. On Ignatius's view, the primary relationship to which all others must be essentially ordered is always one with God. Once properly established and understood, however, this relationship grounds all others, enabling the devotee properly to interact with all creatures, each now fully recognizable as one of God's "blessings and gifts."

Our primary concern is with Ignatius's method and rules, not with his theological presuppositions or conclusions. Contemporary theosemiotic should be invested in a Peircean analysis of the theologies of Ignatius, Edwards, and others. That basic human moods and feelings are the promptings of "spirits" either good or evil is a hypothesis that may be revealed as false upon extended consideration; if not completely false, it might appear adorned in symbolic clothing that a contemporary religious practitioner could judge to be less than felicitous. It is precisely because Ignatius's method is itself remarkably consistent with Peirce's that his theological biases are not fatal to inquiry. Whereas Peirce warns in his argument about setting out in musement with any particular goals established in advance, admittedly the entire purpose of Ignatius's exercises is to discern the will of God as it is manifested in one's life and experiences. Yet here the contrast can be softened to the extent that one recognizes how the law of liberty in Peirce's account is mirrored by Ignatius's talk about indifference. The primary rule for discernment is that one must be like a balance at equilibrium. The signs under consideration are always multivalent, their meaning never to be determined in advance, on any given occasion available only to one who truly and skillfully listens. Once discerned, the "divine will" may move the exercitant in directions that she never would have anticipated. Ignatius, much like Peirce, registered the significance in experience of what the latter called "secondness," something that "pushes back" when one attempts either to control or to ignore it. Meanings discerned in meditation are always vulnerable to correction in the form of future experiences that they simply fail to illuminate. The empirical method that seems operative here is less like gathering data in support of a claim and more like modifying a narrative as new details emerge that need to be integrated. This narrative is autobiographical, not purely fictional, no matter how much (abductive) creativity might be needed to trace its thread and link its episodes.

II

Jonathan Edwards's painstaking analysis of religious affections represents a much more elaborate theological inquiry than what Ignatius supplied, yet one also remarkably "Peircean" in important and comparable ways. "True religion," for Edwards, "in great part, consists in holy affections."[13] Contrary to the way that this word is sometimes used, these affections are not to be regarded merely as passions, but instead represent powerful inclinations of thought, will, and emotion; they give a decisive shape and orientation to the religious life of persons who embody them. Religious affections are thoroughly dispositional in character—real tendencies that can only reveal themselves with any clarity over a certain period of time. That they do, in fact, reveal or express themselves in human experience is a fundamental presupposition informing Edwards's treatise. If true religion consists in having such affections, what are the particular "signs" that most clearly manifest their presence to a discerning interpreter? The priority of a third-person, interpretive perspective as the key to knowledge of the self is also clearly presupposed by Edwards throughout these deliberations.

Before turning to the discussion of twelve "distinguishing signs of truly gracious and holy affections," Edwards reviews but then dismisses a range of phenomena often regarded as significant by others.[14] On his account, for example, the intensity of an affection is no reliable sign of its divine origin. Evil as well as good spirits can elicit within the believer a powerful emotional response. Dramatic bodily effects produced by affections—such as trembling, grimacing, groaning, weeping, panting, or fainting—are likewise to be dismissed as unreliable signs. The ability to speak eloquently about religious matters is rejected by Edwards as uninformative; such talk is cheap, as is the kind of speech that takes the form of audibly and continuously praising God. Surprising or unexpected experiences, as in having passages from scripture spontaneously come to mind or suddenly hearing mysterious voices, also fail to qualify as reliable indicators. To be clear, none of these signs, if present, acts to falsify the claim that truly gracious affections are operative in the life of the believer. Rather, they have no positive value and can be easily interpreted as counterfeit.

It should be made equally clear that perceiving evidence of the twelve distinguishing signs to which Edwards then devotes the bulk of his attention is no guarantee of the presence of the divine spirit dwelling in an individual's heart and mind; whether in judging others or in the process of self-examination, the quest for certainty in evaluating religious affections is misguided. That is to say, an unreliable sign does not falsify nor does a distinguishing sign verify the presence of God's grace in the person who manifests it. This is just to repeat that Edwards, like Peirce, was a thoroughgoing fallibilist in matters of interpretation. Even in the case of those signs that are considered as being reliable or authentic, the human capacity for discernment is limited and flawed. Reading the character of a person as displayed in her conduct is a good deal more challenging than reading the ingredients of a particular soup posted on the soup can's label.

Like any good pragmatist, Edwards also valued the experimental method as a means of determining the accuracy of particular interpretations. Now, remember that Peirce himself once claimed that his pragmatic maxim was only "an application of the sole principle of logic which was recommended by Jesus: 'Ye may know them by their fruits'" (CP 5.402, note 2). Edwards's religion was experimental in precisely this sense: that his search for distinguishing signs was an attempt to evaluate religious affections in terms of their fruitfulness. William James took very much the same approach in determining the significance of those religious experiences that he described with such great care in his Gifford Lectures. In a straightforward but nevertheless important sense this is another basic rule for discernment, just as it is the leading principle for pragmatism: we must judge ideas and feelings in terms of their long-term consequences displayed in behavior. If these ideas and feelings are already properly to be regarded as signs, their most reliable interpretants will be located in praxis. These interpretants are also signs so that, once again, the relationship between fruits and roots should be understood as that of sign to object, even if it is thoroughly mediated by numerous other signs in the flow of semiosis.

Establishing that relationship in theory constitutes the abductive and deductive phases of inquiry, a task to which the pages of Edwards's lengthy treatise on religious affections were devoted. Further establishing in any given case (albeit without certainty) that these signs are actually discernible as evidence of a specific person's saintliness is an inductive process; such is the case whenever one gathers data or performs any kind of experiment. The treatise on affections supplies the rubrics for such an experiment, but the actual gathering of data, its inductive phase, is a project executed in some of Edwards's other writings.[15] Those writings were narrative in form, in one case an edited diary, with others being devoted to supplying a "faithful" account of the New England revivals in which Edwards himself participated. What is being inductively tested in Edwards's experimental religion is not some sort of abstract, ahistorical claim, but rather, the proposed meaning of lived events and experiences.

Not all of the signs that Edwards described in an analysis extending for more than 250 pages can be treated here, nor are all of them equally relevant to the purposes of this discussion. The second and third signs are noteworthy to the extent that they emphasize how genuine affections will manifest themselves in a love for divine things, but only because those things are admirable in themselves (and so to be regarded with love apart from any self-love or self-interest). It is the great loveliness or beauty of the divine that proves itself to be the primary source and ground of true affections. Edwards's remarking on the aesthetic dimension of religious experience was later echoed by Peirce in his Neglected Argument when he insisted that it is the great beauty of the idea of God that would tend to cause anyone who contemplates it in musement to fall in love with that idea and rapidly to embrace it. (Recall how this emphasis on the aesthetic core of authentic religious experience was identified very early on here as a defining feature of theosemiotic.) Moreover, this kind of love, for both Edwards and Peirce, is most perfectly manifested in or signified by *deeds*. Peirce suggested that the muser will be inspired to pattern her life and design motivations for action in "conformity" with the God-hypothesis. For Peirce, the best evidence signifying the truth of this hypothesis will consist in its "commanding influence" over the thought, feelings, and behavior of those who believe in its truth (*CP* 6.490). Likewise, for Jonathan

Edwards the most reliable sign of authentic religious affections was "their exercise and fruit in Christian practice."[16] Experimental religion is a testing of embodied ideals (habits) in practice.

As noted earlier, the analysis of this sign, the twelfth and last of those considered by Edwards, occupies more than twice as much space in his treatise than that devoted to any of the others. Moreover, he explicitly and emphatically identified Christian practice as "chief of all the signs of grace," as "the greatest sign of grace," and thus as "the principal sign by which Christians are to judge, both their own and others' sincerity of godliness."[17] The use of this sign for self-judgment is most important on Edwards's account. Jesus's reference to "fruits" as evidence was intended to help his disciples distinguish true from false prophets. But for Edwards, the third-person perspective that I adopt in interpreting my own experiences and behavior takes precedence over my judgment of others. In part, this is because "Christian practice" is a category that embraces but is not restricted to publicly observable behavior. It also includes certain "immanent acts" of the soul, the movement of the will toward God in acts of contemplation or prayerful exercise, for example.[18] These inward actions can affect outward behavior, shaping it in distinctive ways, but they need not do so directly or immediately. I would suggest that Edwards's insight here mirrors Peirce's understanding of musement as an exercise and an experiment, so that some of the most significant effects of contemplating the God-hypothesis are wrought within the heart and mind of the muser, in the process of meditation itself.

Whether attention is directed to inner or outward actions and exercises, the key to their functioning as a reliable sign is the *consistency* in practice that will characterize the life and behavior of a true saint. Random acts, occasional feelings, and unusual experiences have very little evidential value from Edwards's point of view. Since religious affections are dispositional in character, they will be most readily displayed in regular forms of behavior and manifested in general patterns of thought and feeling. This requires the kind of "long run" perspective that was of such great importance in Peirce's mature thinking, a perspective that also distinguished his pragmaticism from what he regarded as cruder forms of pragmatism. Anyone can persist in practice for the short run. Edwards was fond of distinguishing counterfeit spirituality from true saintliness, metaphorically, by contrasting the ephemeral flash of a comet with the steady brightness of a star visible in the night sky. In any event, all of the actions that combine to form a consistent practice are to be regarded in decisively semiotic terms. Recall how Edwards observed that "there is a language in actions, and in some cases, much more clear and convincing than in words."[19] (Here, once again, we are confronted with a decision about whether it makes more sense to extend broadly the range of possible kinds of "language" or simply to insist that semiosis cannot be reduced to its linguistic forms. Following Peirce, the latter seems like the more comfortable option.)[20]

At first inspection, Edwards's approach to the discernment of spirits seems to contrast sharply with that of Ignatius, at least insofar as we focus attention on his account of religious practice as the twelfth and most significant of those signs to be considered as distinguishing marks of the presence of grace. True to his American roots and heritage (or more accurately, in anticipation of his nineteenth-century American successors), the theosemiotic insights of Edwards seem more firmly grounded in the spirit of pragmatism than those of Ignatius. Yet to jump to this conclusion would be something of a caricature. It is true that Ignatius's rules for discernment supply a disciplined method for sorting out the meaning of certain powerful moods and feelings. In this sense, one might argue that inner states of consolation and desolation, rather than publicly observable actions performed by the religious devotee, are the primary signs with which he suggests we ought to be concerned. On further analysis, however, this simple contrast begins to melt at the surface, revealing core insights that link Ignatius to Edwards in interesting ways. It will be useful before developing our own contemporary perspective on these issues to explore that link in somewhat greater detail.

The mere fact of feeling either consolation or desolation itself mattered very little to Ignatius.[21] Consolation can be good news or bad news, reward or seduction, a sign of grace or the work of the devil. Similarly, with desolation—but here the challenge for any interpreter is even more complex. Not a straightforward choice between test or punishment, God's motivation for causing the devotee to slip into this "dark night" might be a good deal more subtle, a way of undermining the false belief that any experience of religious insight is simply or straightforwardly the result of interpretive skill. For Ignatius, the only capacity needed for this purpose is a kind of listening skill, and such insight when it comes is always best conceived as a gift, the gift of meaning. Ignatius was as wary as his eighteenth-century Calvinist counterpart of presuming that God's grace is something that humans can discern and then control if they develop the appropriate semiotic sophistication. Such a presumption ignores not only the gift-like character of religious meaning but also the extraordinary human capacity for self-deception.

To put it baldly—and this is a point that I think will need to be further developed as a part of our contemporary deliberations—what we *feel* is of very little consequence for the spiritual life. What we then *do* with our feelings, how we interpret them, respond to them, the habits that we consequently choose to cultivate—these will all prove to be of enormous significance. But the feelings themselves do not matter all that much. This needs to be qualified and further explained, to be sure. At this point it is sufficient to observe that Ignatius was just as much of a pragmatist as his American counterpart in matters of discernment. The ultimate purpose of his spiritual exercises was to enable the exercitant to choose a way of life. His preoccupation with consolation and desolation is more an indication of how untrustworthy such feelings can be, the semiotic challenge that they represent, than it is a testimony to their importance as reliable signs. (The sole exception here may be Ignatius's rather remarkable discussion of "consolation without a cause." While other types of consolation may be mediated by events and experiences that could be portrayed in a narrative, in this special case consolation manifests as an indexical sign of God's direct and gracious causal influence—at least that is a Peircean way of understanding Ignatius's theological claim.)

The emphasis on doing or practice, pragmatic to the core, is a feature that links Ignatius's account to Edwards's, initial appearances notwithstanding. After all, some of Edwards's distinguishing signs are feeling states as well—feelings of love or delight, for example—but the feelings themselves are relatively uninformative. It is not what love makes us feel, but rather what it causes us to do that is most decisive for both theologians, not just in a vaguely ethical sense, but from an explicitly semiotic perspective that looks for patterns of behavior as the key to genuine discernment. Moreover, patterns of feeling, a consistency in feeling, will be more illuminating than any temporary, isolated mood. In the final analysis, it is the discernment of certain *habits* with which both theologians are primarily concerned. Feelings and actions can be perceived as having semiotic significance insofar as they provide evidence of or signify the operative presence of such real dispositions.

A pragmatic emphasis on *doing* is consistent with the judgment that what we do, not only in response to but also specifically *with* and *about* our feelings and moods, is of great importance. One can learn to feel affection for someone who now draws one's contempt, or compassion for an individual who presently elicits only anger. It might take time and a considerable amount of practice. There may be a certain wisdom in suggesting, however, that the first thing we ought to do in response to having a certain powerful feeling or being overwhelmed by a mood is carefully to lean in and listen to whatever it is that such anger, sadness, joy, boredom, anxiety, peacefulness, or whatever has to tell us and to teach us. This is the presupposition for being then able to know the best thing to do. Such feelings will not speak to us all at once as a voice booming from out of the whirlwind. There must be a narrative thread connecting feelings and actions over a period of time, if patterns of each form a separate subplot, an intratextual reading that illuminates their meaning in our lives. Even with the awareness of such a connection, what we eventually come to hear as spoken to us may sound more like a whisper than a booming voice. Something like this is how both Ignatius and Edwards understood the task of discernment.

There is the need for yet another caveat or cautionary note at this point in the discussion. The attention to design or pattern, a search for consistency, can never become obsessive or fanatical if discernment is to be successful. This warning might be regarded as something of a negative rule, corresponding to the already frequently articulated positive rule emphasizing the semiotic importance of those aspects of experience. Since meaning is a relation, nothing in absolute isolation can have any real meaning. Nevertheless, if meaning is to be lively rather than stale, if the semiotic path that it marks is to remain open rather than closed, then the teleology made visible in human thoughts, deeds, and feelings must be one that is truly developmental. Habits and virtues grow or, at the very least, are capable of growth. This is a crucial pragmatic insight, one that theosemioticians can hardly afford to ignore. Patterns change, and sudden discontinuities may enable some process to reach a whole new level of development. A habit does not rigidly insist that we always do exactly the same thing *even* in the same circumstances. (This is a stronger claim than the one made earlier about the flexibility of the joint connecting habit and behavior.) On the contrary, complex habits are flexible and can yield, under similar conditions, a great many different forms of behavior. To adapt an example employed earlier here, the habit of love established for my son more than thirty years ago does not require that I treat him in adulthood precisely as I did when he was an infant; nor does it demand that I treat him today exactly as I did yesterday. Even if the circumstances today are quite similar to what they were previously, their temporal position in the narrative about our relationship as it unfolds and evolves may suggest that a different response on my part would be more meaningful.

This last example points to the need for an additional distinction if the rules for discernment are to be carefully and properly articulated. The contrast between what we feel and what we do with our feelings, underscored rather forcefully earlier, needs to be reformulated with a bit more nuance in order to be useful for present purposes. When Heidegger wrote about boredom, for example, he described it as appearing in three forms.[22] The first of these was rather insignificant, a being bored with this or that, and only for the duration of time that I encounter it. Yet in its deeper forms, boredom is a more pervasive quality of experience, not something that arises only on an occasion, but a way in which one becomes *attuned* to whatever one happens to encounter. At this level or in this form, as a fundamental human attunement, our boredom is potentially revelatory. Differently from, yet also somewhat like the habit of love that may help to shape a relationship over many years, this deep boredom has an entrenched, dispositional quality. It is more akin to Edwards's religious affections than it is to Ignatius's feelings of consolation and desolation. Examining specific feelings or behavior for the purpose of discernment amounts to an attempt to find evidence of the presence of such a disposition. This is fairly explicit on Edwards's account.

That this distinction might appear to emerge less clearly in Ignatius's exercises, once again, is a potentially misleading observation. The attention to discernible "movements" in the soul (toward consolation or desolation) is evidence of the operation of certain "spirits" there (both good and evil). That they are personified in this way by Ignatius, identified as having agency and certain purposes, does not negate the fact that they are manifested as specific tendencies to feel or act in one way or another. One should acknowledge that Edwards's religious affections are also the direct result of God's grace working in the mind and heart of the saint. While different in other respects, here the theologies of discernment developed by both thinkers are actually quite similar.

For the purposes of a contemporary theosemiotic, talk about good or evil "spirits," if it were ever to appear useful, would need to operate at a fairly high level of vagueness. That one's deeply rooted tendencies and dispositions can sometimes move one in directions other than where one consciously intended to go—with consequences to be judged either positively or negatively in retrospect—is a somewhat mysterious fact about human nature and behavior that can be analyzed with theological or with purely psychological categories and concepts. It is not altogether clear that these are mutually exclusive. That my unconscious racial bias may result in racist conduct that seems inconsistent with how I would tend to describe the sort of person that I am—even despite my attempt to be honest with myself and others—is a feature of the human capacity for self-deception that has already been subject to some analysis in these pages. Earlier analysis was focused on the proposal that the self is no simple subject, but rather a complex set of relations, a living legisign engaged in the continuous process of reading and rereading itself. Reading, like any act of interpretation, can result in error, in partial or total falsehood. This is precisely why one of the several tasks of theosmiotic must be an essentially *critical* one; moreover, the execution of such a task can quite often take the form of self-criticism.

Here the focal point for analysis is slightly different. The self-as-semiosis is always already in relation, not only to itself but also to others. That a certain tendency to behave one way or another, an operative disposition or habit, would be something sui generis, arising altogether independently of one's relations with others, seems highly unlikely, given the sort of theological anthropology being developed here. On the contrary—and to remain with the example just supplied—that racist tendencies *within* the self originate or come *from somewhere else* and represent the influence *of someone else* appears to be a reasonable enough hypothesis, even if the choice is made not to frame such a hypothesis in terms of talk about good and evil spirits. (Recall the earlier remarks about "contagion.") Indeed, it is not even necessary in every case to talk about the influence of "someone" else; not all relations vital to a person's self-interpretation are with other persons, so that sometimes the source of a certain tendency can be perceived as the need to adapt to particular environmental forces and factors. Finally, nothing in this line of analysis is intended to suggest that individual selves lack agency, that they have no ability to generate highly original self-interpretations or to resist the shaping influence of others or of their environment. Nevertheless, it will be an enormous challenge for someone nurtured by a racist family, living his entire life in a deeply racist community, surrounded by institutions poisoned with racism, *not* to develop discernibly racist habits of thought, feeling, and behavior.

This reasoning indicates that discernment must involve a critical strategy that extends first to oneself—since in acts of discernment the self is recognized as being the primary text requiring interpretation—but then also to others with whom the self interacts, as well as to the various structures, institutions, and environments within which the self is embedded. The line separating these interpretive strategies (to repeat again for emphasis) will be as fuzzy as the one already identified as distinguishing between (without dichotomizing) theology as therapy and as political/social praxis. One's own self, other persons, relationships, communities, institutions, and environments all need to be subjected to regular theosemiotic scrutiny and criticism. Yet one can speak with a prophetic voice in a manner that will be truly effective in one's interactions with others only to the extent that one has engaged first in the most rigorous sort of *self-criticism*. This is more a matter of being able to see clearly, a claim about what is required for validity in interpretation, than it is simply a matter of appearing as humble and therefore plausible to the other members of a community. The inability to read oneself with any clarity and accuracy can have disastrous consequences in terms of its effect on one's interactions with others.

Edwards, like Ignatius, seemed to embrace a hermeneutics of suspicion with regard to the practice of discernment. The confident feeling that one's behavior is governed by virtuous dispositions ought never to be immediately trusted but always needs to be put to the test. Our daily lives are laboratories, and discernment is a rigorously experimental process from the perspective that Edwards articulated. That process may begin with certain direct observations about the self; but Peirce would classify these in any instance as perceptual judgments, their status as such being hypothetical, thus always in need of further explication in order to determine their full meaning, while also needing to be evaluated inductively in order for these meanings to be tested. (Is my joy a gift of God or the devil's temptation to self-complacency? In choosing either option, what evidence would be relevant to its evaluation?) In almost every case where Edwards rejects a possible sign of God's grace as unreliable, it is because of its multivalence. Consistent Christian practice is chief among the twelve reliable signs because, while an isolated deed might seem virtuous and yet be wrongly motivated, a narrative that strings such deeds together in a meaningful flow cannot be so readily interpreted as false. This is nothing other than the scientific method, its object being the assessment of human dispositions and its laboratory equipment consisting in the crucible of those daily trials and challenges "in which our hearts are weighed."[23]

Not only individual persons, but also communities of persons, are properly to be regarded as "embodied experiments" in this sense, a testing ground in which the primary data of relevance will be the character and conduct that they regularly display.[24] While the signs that Edwards identified and then described with considerable care were manifested in the feelings, thoughts, and behavior of individual Christians, the context for his inquiry was supplied by the "awakening" that occurred both in Great Britain and the colonies in the 1730s and 1740s. And so while the inquiry may have focused on what it means to be a saint, fully awake to the promptings of the Spirit and displaying the signs of someone embodying "truly gracious" affections, the context for inquiry was communal, the forces that shaped these frequent and very public revivals thoroughly social in character. Edwards did not anticipate Peirce or Royce in talking or thinking about communities as "greater personalities." Yet any future theosemiotic would need to extend his search for salient signs to include those that reliably mark a particular community as being disposed in ways that could be judged as spiritually felicitous or infelicitous. This is just another indication of the need to combine for theosemiotic purposes intellectual resources gleaned from all of the social sciences, including psychology, sociology, and political theory. Indeed, Edwards's emphasis on the relevance of Christian practice as a trustworthy sign might be productively examined against the background supplied by a capacious (rather than a dogmatic or rigidly narrow) theory of behaviorism, especially of the sort described earlier that informs recently developed cognitive behavioral therapies.

III

Rules for discernment are of relevance to this Peirce-inspired project that I have called "theosemiotic" because they are most readily to be understood as rules for the accurate interpretation of certain signs as being *religiously* meaningful. In an even more fundamental sense, they are rules that enable the recognition of something as actually (or virtually) *being a sign*, rather than merely a thing (feeling, object, event, or whatever) that signifies nothing beyond itself. I have tried to suggest here also, in yet another respect, that these rules might most appropriately be regarded as rules for *reading*, since reading is a kind of interpretive activity that occurs over an extended period, rather than in some sudden flash of comprehension or recognition. The requirement of a *narrative* context for the discernment of religious meaning is something that was emphasized in the theologies of both Ignatius and Edwards, as well as being implied by Peirce's dialogical semiotic. My reading of the next chapter of a novel can dramatically change the way that I come to interpret the one that I have just concluded. On the other hand, it may simply confirm and deepen the understanding that I already have. Finally, however, the type of text of special interest for present purposes is autobiographical in character—that is to say, discernment is to be further distinguished by its *self-reflexivity*.

Consistency in practice involves a necessary element of repetition. Sometimes reading takes the form not of movement forward to a new sentence, paragraph, or chapter of the text, but rather, of movement back, of reading over or reading again. My preferred etymology for the word "religion" traces its linguistic roots to just such a concept—that is, to *relegere*, the verb that designates this mindful act of rereading. Such an act will be governed by some rule that stipulates a necessary detachment from the practical goals and purposes that typically shape our attention, restlessly moving it ever onward in the constant search for new signs, for additional sources of meaning. By contrast, whatever special depth of meaning or religious insight emerges in the process of rereading is discovered by standing still in one place, by recollecting and reviewing signs already present to consciousness.[25] It was suggested earlier that this is the kind of meditative reading occurring each time that we carefully review a poem that we have come to admire or in the reconsideration of a person that we have come to know quite well, discovering fresh meaning in each, providing the occasion for knowing more deeply. The precondition for such a possibility will be the achievement of a certain openness to new experience, even in the encounter with someone or something that has grown quite familiar. Ignatius's *indiferencia*, the purposeless play that Peirce prescribed for musement, and the disinterested benevolence that Edwards attached to the saintly delight in divine beauty are all articulations of this particular rule for discernment.

To reread as a disciplined practice is not merely to interpret a series of signs, but in doing so also to embody the interpretants of those signs in appropriate habits of thought, feeling, and conduct. Certainly, emotional and sometimes even energetic interpretants will be produced in any act of reading. Rereading is distinguished, however, by the element of repetition that characterizes it, a feature conducive to the process of habit formation—that is, to the production of *logical* interpretants. Consequently, this repetition itself is another important rule for discernment, a regularity in behavior (of the kind encouraged both by Ignatius and Edwards) that will tend to result either in habit development or in habit change. Recall that the reader as discerning self is best conceived as a symbol, one of the "living realities" to which Peirce referred, an embodiment of meaning and purpose, working out results in the world. Even as what we thereby come to mean is, in some sense and measure, "determined" by the signs that we interpret, we likewise can partially determine the meaning of those who interact with and read *us* as complex living legisigns. Such determination surely needs to be conceived as a "soft" or "gentle" mode of causation, more akin to the operation of a formal or final than an efficient cause. That some general type of meaning will be determined through such personal interaction does not preclude the possibility of a broad range of different outcomes.

Importantly, rules for discernment always also function as rules for attention, both for how we direct our attention and for the quality of attention that we strive to maintain. We have already noted and need to recall here the very serious and deliberate attention that Peirce directed to the practice of paying attention itself, especially in the development of his phenomenology (or phaneroscopy), but also in his writings about semiotic and the logic of inquiry. The discernment of religious meaning, as Ignatius and Edwards so clearly understood, requires that one pay attention properly. This is no simple matter, but rather, it can represent an enormous challenge. The contemporary world may be characterized as one littered with distractions, making such a challenge even more formidable. Without anticipating either late capitalism or the Age of the Internet, nevertheless, these two theologians were convinced of the vicious reality of Satan, a supernatural enemy hell-bent on distracting us from whatever matters most, while also determined to erode the quality of our attention even when it is facing in the right direction. They were convinced that to avoid the devil's snare requires discernment, a special interpretive skill, the development of which demands fidelity and persistence. Even with no devil in the picture, Peirce recognized that cultivating real skill in musement would take considerable time and training. The risks and rewards associated with this task are serious ones. They have to do ultimately with what we will gradually come to mean as living symbols, a meaning that represents our most precious gift to anyone else with whom we engage and interact in a world best conceived as a complex web of semiotic relations.

For theosemiotic purposes, the word "discernment" designates that subset of interpretive judgments the goal of which is to identify whatever might be judged religiously meaningful in a person's life and experience. Nevertheless, to perceive anything as religiously significant is not to limit the extent to which it might be judged meaningful in other respects.[26] The human love that characterizes a marriage or friendship could also acquire a religious connotation. Judging right from wrong in acts of moral discernment can involve but may not be reducible to reasoning that is framed or motivated by religious beliefs and concerns. And as it was observed at the very beginning of this discussion in our brief history of theosemiotic, religious experience is often represented as also having a powerful aesthetic dimension.

I may be experiencing strong feelings of desolation for specific reasons that might in some instance be readily identified, involving something that has happened in the world or in my relationship to someone else (some tragic event or the loss of a loved one). The rules for discernment do not require that I must ignore the world or other persons in making interpretive judgments about such feelings. They do not stipulate for feelings that take on a religious significance that they must now be regarded as having no other meaning at all. In following those rules, I will be motivated to pursue a reading of my life for possible traces of religious meaning that is sensitive to the complex levels of intratextuality that such a reading might entail.

Oddly enough, if not properly oriented and regulated, the search for meaning can have a deleterious effect on one's capacity to pay proper attention. (This is a reversal of the concern articulated earlier about becoming lost in a world of things.) Discernment involves the ability to recognize a thing not only as it presents itself to an observer, as having a certain structure and characteristics, but also as being imbued with significance—that is, as being not simply a thing but also a sign. Consequently, in the encounter with anything that one recognizes as a sign, the attention will be to some extent divided. If I ask you to observe and carefully describe a particular object, your attention will be focused entirely on that object. If, instead, I invite you to contemplate it as a symbol, your attention will flow not only to the actual presence of that thing but also to whatever is absent but represented by it. The rush to abandon the former in order to secure the meaning that it signifies is a real and dangerous temptation for the discerning intellect. A divided attention, despite the human capacity for "multi-tasking," will prove to be problematic for purposes of religious discernment. One must be able to perceive meaning in and through the thing as symbol, as something that manifests *within* it as a depth of meaning. The sort of sign-interpretation being prescribed for such purposes is not a game of "hide-and-seek" with elusive meanings. It is a matter of fixing attention on the object-as-sign, sometimes patiently waiting for meaning.

Now it might appear that the particular type of empiricism that theosemiotic endorses, one in which all meaningful experience is always already conceived as semiosis, must work to undermine the distinction between perceiving something as being merely a thing on the one hand and as a sign or significant thing on the other. From this Peircean perspective there is no recognition of anything at all, even vaguely understood, that does not take the form of sign-interpretation. Recall that this is the implication of Peirce's argument that all perception involves some perceptual judgment in the form of an abductive inference. The relevant distinction here is not one being made between a form of perception without signs (there is no such thing) and another involving semiosis. Rather, it is a much more subtle contrast, already drawn at earlier points in this inquiry, between thinking *with* signs and thinking *about* them, between perception as semiosis and discernment as a form of meta-semiosis. In acts of discernment, one moves beyond the recognition of anything as a particular mood, experience, place, person, etc., to the perception of it as a sign of something *more*. This something more includes but is not limited to whatever might be identified as *other* than the sign—that is, as its object. It also extends to the more revealed about whatever is now recognized as a sign, as in the case when something is discerned to be a gift and so to signify a giver; its very character as a gift was not perceived earlier. Since there is a real and continuous semiotic relation between object, sign, and interpretant on the account being developed here, to reflect on anything as a sign is necessarily to consider it in its various relationships. The fundamental task of discernment is to evaluate with special care the relation of sign to interpretant, to consider *oneself* not in isolation but in relation to some sign as an interpreter of its meaning.

What then are the limits of or the challenges to discernment? At the outset of this inquiry, it was asserted that the universe in which we live, while it may be filled with signs, does not consist exclusively of them. Moreover, it soon became apparent that the discussion here was more directly focused on semiosis as a dynamic process than on the identification and classification of signs. Simply stated, if there is real growth in meaning, then there is room for meaning to grow, limits to meaning, times and places that seem to mark the absence of meaning. In the search for meaning that constitutes the work of discernment, the awareness of such an absence will typically be marked by distinctive feeling states. Boredom is one of these states. Melancholy is another. The latter can be related to the experience of boredom, and it has shades of meaning that also link it to complex emotions, like what the French label as *ennui* or the Portuguese *saudade*.

Three observations seem immediately relevant here. In the first place, such emotions, especially to the extent that they are deep and pervasive, effectively mark one of the limits of discernment. They suggest that in some instance there has been a breakdown in meaning, a disruption in the semiotic flow. The person engaged in a continuous process of self-interpretation can in these periods become exhausted, much as meaning seems to have been exhausted, evacuated, leaving the reader with no words but only a blank page. With certain experiences of boredom, it is as if the reader is now confronted with a blank white page. In other moods, it is as if all of the words have merged together and become indistinguishable, now swallowed in darkness. Whether the signs themselves have vanished or the meaning has been drained from them, the consequences for anyone engaged in the act of reading are pretty much the same. As Ignatius suggested in his advice for devotees, during such periods of time the only reasonable strategy may be to persevere in one's exercises and patiently wait for the rebirth of spiritual insight and consolation.

Interestingly, however, and somewhat paradoxically, a second observation follows upon the first: these feeling states or moods can themselves have meaning, sometimes complex "shades of meaning," as was indicated in the remark about melancholy just recorded here. A Peircean perspective that understands feelings to be vague thoughts and analyzes emotions as taking the form of judgments will have to conclude that even such responses to the dearth of meaning can themselves be meaningful. While at one level there is only a feeling of meaninglessness, as one moves to another meta-cognitive or meta-semiotic position, it becomes possible to contemplate and then interrogate such a feeling as if it were a sign. The challenge of discernment then becomes one about how to read such emotions, how best to engage them, not to put down the text but to look at it with new eyes, to pay attention to it in a different sort of way than one had been doing previously.

For the Daoists, spiritual exercise constitutes a strategy of "return" to some earlier stage of existence.[27] Jesus admonished his disciples by reporting that unless persons become like little children they cannot enter the kingdom of heaven. Emerson and Peirce argued that the way in which we must learn to see the world anew is in some sense the recovery of an old way of being and seeing. And Gutierrez advocated in his liberation spirituality for the cultivation of a "spiritual childhood" as a necessary "requirement for commitment to the poor."[28] Theosemiotic honors all of these insights. The task of discernment is a relearning of what it meant to have no tasks, to be like a child in a perpetual state of playfulness. There is a level of seriousness, however, that distinguishes discernment in adulthood from our experiences in childhood. The former involves moving boldly into meta-cognitive spaces where a child may be incapable of going. What exactly does this mean?

The child experiences a broad range of feelings, has emotional responses of various kinds to persons encountered, situations endured, and the activities in which she is engaged. While the child may be an "expert" at play, a number of these feelings can thwart or abort playfulness, can altogether stifle the spirit of play (as when a sudden fear or fit of anger proves sufficient to end the game being played). What the adult spiritual devotee brings to the practice of discernment is an ability lacking in the child, one that allows or enables her to play with the very emotions that tend to overwhelm the less mature individual, to render the child passive and helpless. It is not as if discernment is completely devoid of an element of passivity. But it is the "active passivity" celebrated by Daoists, a choosing to be passive in the very same way that often characterizes our play behavior.[29] This state of mind is not one of helplessness pure and simple. One might not be able always to choose what and how one feels, but the discerning individual will be able properly to identify what she feels, then to choose what to do about and with those feelings. What one does with one's feelings is a mode of activity that can only occur in a space cleared through disciplined meta-cognitive or meta-semiotic practices.

This observation about what one chooses to *do*—that is, about one's *conduct*—is the last of the three mentioned just now. A theosemiotic emphasis on praxis is not to be construed as a license to ignore the traditional theological concern about what one thinks and believes or to neglect the fact and nature of authentic religious experiences. It is to insist, however, that an analysis of behavior may be the key to interpreting beliefs and feelings. Even while focusing on feelings as being especially central for the project of discernment, it may be appropriate to conclude, once again, that our feelings are less significant than what we choose to do with them. The possibilities for such doing are multiple and complex. One of these involves making a decision about how one will interpret a particular feeling as it arises. Whether identified as anger or anxiety or joy, what does it mean to now be feeling this way? One's feelings are also signs in a semiotic stream, themselves the interpretants of other signs. On any given occasion, unless their meaning is transparent (as when one's anger is an obvious response to a gross injustice just observed) these feelings will need to be carefully examined, their meaning discerned. It might be a flash of feeling, as with sudden anger, or a more pervasive mood, a lingering boredom or sadness. It may prove to be much more difficult, not always but often, to identify the meaning of the latter than the former.

Now this observation about the importance of behavior is a slippery one for a pragmatist because the distinction between thought, feeling, and action is never perfectly rigid or clear from a pragmatic perspective. The decision to interpret a feeling as it arises may take the form of cognitive behavior, a "doing something" with thoughts that results in some interpretation. Nevertheless, there are other ways and forms of doing in response to feelings discerned, equally qualifying as interpretations of what those feelings mean. My being moved by sympathy in the encounter with some person's intense suffering to act in order to alleviate that suffering is the embodiment of meaning in conduct. How I behave in this instance is no less an interpretation of what my sympathy means than if I attempted to describe for someone else—a therapist, perhaps, or a friend—what I was experiencing and why I felt as I did. Given the pragmatic and liberationist emphases already frequently identified here as characteristic of theosemiotic, the act of alleviating suffering ought to be conceived as having greater hermeneutical value than any verbal account that I might supply of what I was feeling or doing.

To fine-tune this observation even further, what one does in response to an experience, if done purposefully and deliberately, can prove to be self-transformative in crucially important ways. This conduct can take the form of consciously working to develop habits of thought, feeling, and behavior deemed appropriate for situations just like or similar to one presently being experienced or imagined. It should be easy to recognize at this point how Peirce conceived of self-control as typically operating in this way. If I affirm, perhaps given some set of ideals that illuminate the kind of person I hope to be, that what I am thinking, feeling, or doing on a given occasion is morally and spiritually felicitous, then this becomes a matter of strengthening some habit that is already in the process of being formed. On the other hand, if my judgment of how I have behaved is decisively negative, it will shout for a habit change. Either way I will be engaged in the work of discernment.

This theosemiotic analysis suggests that a nuanced exegesis is required of the biblical passage in which Jesus warned that a man who regards a woman with lust, prior to any other action, is already guilty of adultery "in his heart" (Matthew 5:27–28). This warning seems excessive if it is intended to suggest that one might be able to control every feeling as it arises in response to something experienced. On this account, one would never feel jealousy or anger or sexual desire, even episodically or as a flash of feeling, in a way that could fail to be evaluated as blameworthy. Yet this is to presume a kind of moral and spiritual perfection as a baseline rather than to chart a path toward the goal of achieving it. Moreover, it is not altogether clear what such perfection would look like. Is one to be condemned for *having* the feeling or for what one *does* with, about, and in response to the feeling?

It is one thing to say that we are to some extent responsible for what and how we feel, that it is not acceptable for us to wallow in any kind of feeling as long as we are able to control our outward behavior. Indeed, if it *were* acceptable, I could be as angry with you or as envious of you as I please, so long as I did not convey those feelings to you in the way that I act—that is, so long as I am hypocritically successful in *deceiving* you about how I feel. Such an account would be problematic in a way that Jesus's teaching was intended to expose. It is quite another thing, however, to suggest that the mere fact of having such a feeling is itself deserving of condemnation. On any given day, most persons will be likely to feel a great many different things: happy, sad, angry, irritated, grateful, jealous, bored . . . perhaps even sexually attracted or aroused. It does not seem reasonable to assume that such a person could ever exercise complete control over these momentary flashes of feeling. In some sort of imagined, science-fiction, futuristic scenario, it might be possible to program sophisticated androids who would meet these standards (assuming that it would be possible for androids to feel anything at all). But flesh-and-blood human beings can never hope to achieve such an absolute level of self-control. It would require automatically experiencing in any given situation only the feelings deemed appropriate in advance for that set of circumstances. This would further require a complete knowledge of the circumstances, as well as demanding that one's habits be rigidly fixed, set once and for all in a pattern that would not be subject to change or open to growth.

The Peircean concept of self-control adapted here for theosemiotic purposes conceives of agency not as something that happens right on the spot or in the moment but as extending over time. Evidence of its operation can only be captured by some form of meaningful narrative. A spark of anger or jealousy or lust is hardly definitive of the sort of person that I am. What I *do* with that feeling, how I evaluate it, whether I choose to celebrate and cultivate the feeling or work actively to undermine its present or future hegemony—this, and not the fact of having such a feeling, is what registers as both spiritually and ethically significant. Surely, when Jesus spoke about adultery as something that one can do in one's heart, he was talking about cultivated habits of feeling rather than discrete episodes or uncontrollable flashes. The Gospel narratives do not paint a picture of Jesus as being a characteristically angry man, but there *is* a suggestion on a number of occasions that he may have lost his temper.

Here is another important rule for discernment, already discussed at some length and within various contexts, but now needing to be identified clearly and explicitly as a general rule: the attempt to interpret any feeling or emotion as one presently experiences it needs to be placed in a broader context (narrative and conceptual) in order for its meaning to be accurately gauged. There is a clear link in this regard between the strategies formulated by both Ignatius and Edwards and the theory informing certain contemporary psychotherapeutic practices. From a contextualist point of view, the broader the context examined, the greater the likelihood of properly evaluating any given feeling or behavior. A theology conceived as therapy will be most illuminating and useful to the extent that it is rooted *both* in these contemporary practices *and* in the traditions of spiritual direction and discernment of the sort that Ignatius and Edwards established.

There is another point on which psychotherapy and theology might be expected to converge. From neither perspective will it be assumed that the human interpreter can ever have perfect control over determining the meaning of some experience being subjected to scrutiny. Consequently, even as one moves forward in the process of discernment to interrogate such an experience, to narrativize and contextualize it, there can be no rush to meaning. Contemporary psychotherapeutic talk about mindful acceptance (partially Buddhist in its inspiration) is intended to suggest that waiting and "listening" supply the crucial foundation for any act of interpretation. Traditional theological discourse portrays human agency as being in complex interaction with other spiritual forces and factors. For Ignatius, what my desolation *means* is less a matter of what I intended than of the intentions of either evil or good spirits in causing me to feel that way. When it is God who is making me feel that way, either to test my spiritual mettle or to detach me from false confidence in my own ability to manufacture spiritual joy, then attentive waiting will be the most appropriate response available to me.

This is a claim that can be easily misunderstood. The kind of waiting being proposed here cannot be merely passive, the beginning and end of what one does in response to such a negative feeling state.[30] Indeed, on Ignatius's account, if my desolation is the work of Satan, intended primarily to discourage me about my progress and to distract me from my spiritual exercises, then what I ought to do in defiance and resistance is to renew my efforts in the pursuit of those exercises. This seems like a very different strategy from waiting pure and simple. Yet that contrast will appear exaggerated to the extent that one understands waiting itself (of a certain disciplined kind) actually to constitute a spiritual exercise. From such a point of view, waiting is a form of vigilance, not focused on this or that particular thing, but of the sort that Peirce associated with musement. This waiting is also a listening.[31] One can neither hear the voice of another nor possibly hope to identify the speaker without first carefully listening.

A philosophical theology conceived as theosemiotic will *not* need to presuppose the existence of a host of good and evil spirits, their voices competing to transcend a cacophony of noise in order to command an individual interpreter's attention. We need not embrace either Ignatius's or Edwards's religious worldview in order to enact their theological method. Indeed, deep listening is best enabled in the absence of distracting beliefs and biases, which is why we sometimes listen least effectively to persons whom we know well and for whom we have considerable affection. To be sure, one cannot simply choose to listen in a vacuum, pretending that one has no idea about who is speaking or what they might be likely to say, when in fact just the opposite is true. Nevertheless, Peirce, Ignatius, and Edwards are all in agreement that we must hold that idea loosely and lightly, with a certain sense of detachment, rather than cling to it tenaciously and impose its hegemony on any interpretation that we produce.

There are different possibilities here. One might be listening to the voice of a particular human interlocutor. Alternatively, one could be listening to no one in particular—that is to say, listening pure and simple. And so one might be listening *to* the voice or *for* the voice of another, the latter as in the case of an Ignatian retreat, when one actively waits to discern the promptings of the spirit, hoping to learn the will of God as it applies to the disposition of one's life. Yet, whatever one's initial inclination, it will be checked by careful observance of the rules for discernment. Prominent among these, once again, is the call for detachment, as when Peirce directed the muser to begin inquiry with no determinate purpose, or when Ignatius counseled that the exercitant should be like a balance at equilibrium, inclined neither in this or that direction, and so ready to learn whatever God is prepared to reveal.

In a very straightforward sense, since discernment is a form of inquiry directed to the goal of achieving greater self-knowledge, another quite general but important rule for discernment will be embodied in Peirce's warning that one should do nothing to block the road of inquiry. The rapid embrace of some conclusion or the ruling out of alternatives in advance are among the ways that such roadblocks are typically erected. Setting out in musement with the goal of arriving at belief in God would violate the principles that ought to guide theosemiotic inquiry. Peirce was quite clear on this point. At the same time, if one's careful, meditative reading and rereading of the book of nature illuminates something vaguely personal as nature's source or at its depth, it would be problematic to dismiss such a reading as some sort of anthropomorphic projection *onto* the text resulting in a distortion of its true meaning without first reading again, while also checking the reading experiences of other persons with whom one enters into conversation.

There is a certain common sense to what is being stipulated by any rule that takes the form of a cautionary tale like Peirce's warning about unnecessary roadblocks. If one wants to become more confident that one has read a text correctly, one should read it again. And if one fails to hear under certain conditions what someone else claims to have heard, then one should listen again and more deeply. This should *not* represent an attempt to hear exactly what another person has reported having heard. That report may be inaccurate, perhaps even self-deceived. Here it is the element of repetition that is most crucial, not some adjustment of one's inclinations or expectations. To the greatest extent possible, the latter should be more or less neutralized, at least in the earliest stage of inquiry, to be regarded as playthings.

Why does identifying a particular stage of inquiry supply the salient context for making a judgment about "more or less" in such matters of discernment? All initial readings are hypotheses and as such fallible and subject to correction on rereading. As one engages in that practice, induction gradually plays a more prominent role in inquiry; now attention will tend to be focused on certain aspects of things deemed relevant for the inquiry in progress, and specific expectations will inevitably be formed. It was argued earlier, however, that there should be no rigid, mechanical movement from one stage of inquiry to another, no forced separation of one from another. The dazzling explosion of fresh insight on the occasion of rereading a text that one has encountered many times previously suggests that the abductive phase was never completely left behind. A brand new or dramatically revised hypothesis is always a possibility, even in cases where one's primary purpose may have been simply to repeat an experiment or to gather additional data in support of a hypothesis already formed.

This is a reversal of the perspective on inquiry articulated earlier. It was suggested that even in the cognitive play of musement some proto-deductive clarification of certain ideas will take place as soon as they are entertained, as well as some vaguely inductive appeal to remembered experiences that might be relevant to the further evaluation of those ideas. Yet just as deduction and induction are already involved at this initial stage, it is also the case that the play of inquiry is never reduced to pure mechanical labor; even in the sweaty process of testing hypotheses that already seem entrenched in their plausibility, fresh insights may emerge, new directions suddenly grow attractive.

This discussion is intended to suggest that the rules for discernment do not differ in any remarkable way from the rules that ought to guide all inquiry. A careful reading of both Ignatius and Edwards shows that they were thoroughgoing fallibilists and experimentalists. The detachment that discernment requires is of the same sort that any scientist would hope to achieve in conducting an investigation. Moreover, there is an ongoing appeal to community in each case, to intersubjective checking, a criterion taken to a rather extreme level in Ignatius's exercises with the articulation of another set of principles, this time his "Rules for Thinking with the Church."[32] Finally, both theologians were empiricists in the complex sense that Peirce's pragmaticism mandates as normative. "Experience" must encompass both what we perceive and what we then choose deliberately to do: our practices. These should be easily recognizable by now as the two "gates" through which Peirce insisted that every good idea must enter and then exit consciousness. For the specific purposes of spiritual discernment, the tricky business of *self*-perception receives the lion's share of attention—that is, the ongoing assessment of one's beliefs, feelings, moods, and actions. In the text devoted to identifying his "rules," Ignatius emphasized an awareness of feelings. In evaluating the most important of "distinguishing signs," Edwards concentrated on purposeful action. Yet neither in Ignatius's manual nor in Edwards's treatise is either aspect of discernment ignored; both theologians were pragmaticists.

Contemporary theosemiotic should build on the model that these thinkers have provided. A deep sensitivity to the nuances of human feeling and emotional life can serve to spark rather than to prevent the recognition that what we feel matters a good deal less than what we choose to do with and about our feelings. That the love of God given birth in musement can be a powerful force shaping human conduct on Peirce's account is a significant fact precisely because of its dramatically self-transformative consequences. We understand such a life of feeling; we evaluate its authenticity, most especially by attending to such consequences.

Now, feelings like love and gratitude appear to have a special teleology that might be interpreted as supplying evidence for some form of vague theism; this was a hypothesis proposed in Chapter 3. Perhaps "evidence" is a misleading word to use here, insofar as it raises suspicion that some kind of "argument from design" is being sneaked in through theosemiotic's back door. Discernment is a semiotic process, an attempt to construe the meaning of certain signs, but not one that should be pushed in the direction of that sort of evidentialism. (Peirce himself was clear that anyone choosing to move in such a direction would arrive at a dead end.) The need to accumulate evidence in support of a hypothetical claim is an inductive project. Here attention is still being focused on discernment in its abductive mode. What does such love mean? What is the source of this gratitude, and what is it gratefulness for?

No answer to such questions will be found simply by providing a thick phenomenological description of the feelings themselves. In the first place, and to make a point consistent with everything that has been argued here, the attempt to understand the meaning of some episode of feeling will have very little theological value. It is to the nature of a certain *habit* of love/gratitude that the philosophical theologian will want to attend. It is only in tracing the effects of such a habit made visible in behavior that a distinctive teleology will be displayed. That was the whole point of Jonathan Edwards's insistence that Christian practice is chief among all of the distinguishing signs of truly "gracious and holy affections." Once again, it is not some discrete sign but rather semiosis in the form of a narrative that will be the conveyer of religious meaning. Moreover, precisely insofar as they function as signs, such habits of feeling will be self-effacing, pointing beyond themselves to something else. From a semiotic point of view, love is important not because of how it feels, but both because it gestures toward some beloved and because of how it causes one to act. It is only in relation to its object and to the conduct that it determines as its interpretant that love can be construed as a sign having any meaning.

In the religiously interesting case where love is directed toward some divine reality, its meaning as a sign must be regarded as extraordinarily complex. How can such a reality be the object of a sign when it is not in any clear sense an "object" at all? Peirce's "strictly hypothetical God" is the creative source of all things without being identified as one among them. How does one fall in love with such a God? How does this God even make an appearance in musement? Part of the answer to this last question, at least, is obvious: never directly as in the sense of an unmediated presence, but always through the mediation of certain signs. For Peirce, the "book of nature" played just such a mediating role. Depending on the form of naturalism that one embraces and the concept of "nature" that one endorses, this text may in fact include all of the signs that it is possible for one to consider—an entire universe of signs.

7 / On Prayer and the Spirit of Pragmatism

I

Peirce seemed to regard musement as an activity that might "flower" into some form of religious meditation, rather than as an act of prayer pure and simple (*CP* 6.458). Yet the continuities between musement and prayer are more relevant to this discussion than any specific feature of either practice that might be targeted for emphasis here in order to *distinguish* them. Even the portrayal of musement in the Neglected Argument as the wellspring of scientific inquiry serves to expose rather than obscure these continuities. In Peirce's view, every true scientist was a person of faith, and the pursuit of science was perceived by him, just as it had been by his father, Benjamin, potentially and ideally to constitute a religiously meaningful vocation (*SS*: 75).[1]

That prayer, properly understood, is both the first flower and ripened fruit of the religious life is a hypothesis that deserves careful consideration from the perspective that theosemiotic articulates. The religious goal of transforming all of life into prayer needs to be understood against a background supplied by the claim that human experience is always already a form of semiosis.[2] The genuinely pragmatic character of prayer also needs to be established and illuminated. This will require explaining how prayer is experimental in a manner that the earlier discussions both of musement and of Jonathan Edwards have been designed to suggest. The result will be a reading of Peirce's Neglected Argument that construes it in a way that he himself intended it to be understood: as an a posteriori, experimental version of the ontological argument. This reading will bring

Peirce into conversation with Simone Weil. It will also establish his 1908 essay as the table of contents for a contemporary theosemiotic, not primarily to be conceived as some new form of religious "evidentialism," but first and foremost as a theology of the spiritual life.

Musement is a species of cognitive play. All play occurs in the fertile space that arises between that which is determinate and a vague indeterminacy. In this sense, play is always parasitic on some determinate thing; it is the play of "this or that," never free play pure and simple. There is no game without rules, no dance without gravity, no music if the bow of the violin slides over unfastened strings. Sometimes the source of determinacy is *someone* else, so that play becomes interplay, a "playing with" (now there is both gravity and a partner to help shape the dance). This social dimension of play is more pervasive than it might first appear to be. The self, conceived as semiosis, can never be a perfectly solitary player. We carry our playmates with us in our hearts and minds. Their actions and voices blend with ours so that their presence often remains invisible.

So too with inquiry. The solitary inquirer is always already a member of some determinate community of interpretation. Yet inquiry can begin as musement only to the extent that the determinate puts on indeterminacy.[3] The specific beliefs, perspectives, and purposes shared by an individual with her community do not vanish but rather hover in the space provided by the play of musement. While something more than zero gravity, the force of gravity is reduced for this playful inquiry, like dancing on the moon. Purposes grow quiet in obedience to the one general principle that advocates purposelessness—what Peirce described as the "law of liberty." The content of belief is not annihilated; rather, the manner of believing (not identical but akin to make-believing) changes; one has beliefs now as though one did not have them. Finally, the muser sees the world, not as if from nowhere, but from multiple perspectives, shifting easily from one to another and in a way not narrowly driven by some objective, but with "eyes open, awake to what is about or within." Despite this emphasis on open eyes, musement is also, perhaps even primarily, a form of deep *listening*. Moreover, being awake in this fashion is an important precondition for initiating either the process of inquiry or the practice of prayer. (Indeed, it is even possible to conceive of prayer itself as a form of inquiry.)

Since Peirce was anxious to distinguish musement from any kind of state of mind that could be characterized as "vacancy" or "dreaminess," this play of thought should not be portrayed as a casual surrendering of attention by the muser to whatever stimuli may present themselves to consciousness. The contents of playful thought cannot be regarded as mere flotsam and jetsam on the surface of a turbulent ocean of sense impressions. Conceived in such a fashion, musement would be neither deliberate nor self-controlled, thus not properly to be regarded as a form of inquiry. Rather, play is a vigorous exercise of certain faculties, a deliberate activity but not one guided by preestablished purposes extrinsic to the exercise itself. This exercise (recall the etymology) is a "bringing into play." Whatever form such play takes, however it evolves, its teleology is thoroughly developmental. A summons to training in musement, as in phenomenology for Peirce, is an invitation at least initially to attend to the material quality or the suchness of things, not in order to undermine their significance, but in order to refresh our relationship with them by loosening the grip of well-established and sometimes weather-worn habits of interpretation.

While there are many different types of religious meditation, those characterized as "prayer" will be explicitly dialogical in form. Now, it is not immediately clear that meditation can appear otherwise. If the pragmatists are correct, human consciousness itself always takes shape as an inner dialogue; semiosis is by its very nature conversational, with every sign "introducing" its object to an interpretant, thus bringing them into relation.[4] Whether or not a religious tradition is explicitly theistic will certainly have some bearing on the question about how the nature and purpose of meditation ought to be understood within such a context. Yet even the sort of mindfulness advocated for the Buddhist practitioner sitting in *zazen* can be conceived in such a way that it takes the form of a conversation with oneself. That the goal of such a conversation might be to move consciousness toward a certain state of silence or stillness in no way alters this fact. Indeed, it is crucial here to consider the semiotic significance of silence, both in religious and in nonreligious contexts, to determine what it can mean or might communicate. In our conversations with other human beings, moments or periods of silence can be pregnant with meaning. It would be a dramatic mistake to conclude that such moments always fall outside of the act or process of conversation itself, that they represent the limits of dialogue (although they might) or somehow circumscribe or undermine its progress and purposes. This is not to deny that a certain stubborn silence can be antithetical to the goals of communication, that it can represent a refusal to enter into any kind of meaningful exchange. It is merely to observe, rather, that we can continue to convey meaning both in and with moments or stretches of silence.

Both of these two characteristics of prayer just now observed—that it can be characterized in some sense as playful and that it is conversational in form—are features emphasized in the manual for instruction about spirituality that Ignatius developed for his fellow Jesuits. Normally, a person engaged in these spiritual exercises would devote on each occasion an hour to prayer and meditation. What one does during that hour will depend upon the particular subject matter for meditation. Yet in almost every instance Ignatius structures these meditations so that they include—and often culminate with—a colloquy. As indicated earlier, the interlocutor will vary with different meditations, so that sometimes Christ will be the primary conversation partner, in other instances the Virgin Mary or one of the saints. The voices audible in our minds can be multiple, diverse, and competing. Here Ignatius is asking the devotee to focus attention on a selected subgroup of religiously meaningful voices, to choose carefully her conversation partners. Here is yet another way of employing the power of volition for the purpose of shaping semiosis, molding the continuous dialogue in which the self-as-sign participates in an ongoing fashion.

Any given colloquy can itself be conceived as playful, an *interplay* between interlocutors that is in no way carefully regulated so as to determine exactly how the conversation must unfold. There is no script provided by Ignatius for these exchanges. Occasionally there are general suggestions about subject matter but no additional instructions about how one should proceed, so that any prayer of this type will be carefully distinguished from the sort of frequently recited vocal prayer that also constitutes an important practice for someone pursuing these exercises. In the latter case, the words to be used in prayer are supplied in advance, committed to memory, their performance consisting in a recitation. And so the classical theological distinction between "vocal" and "mental" prayer might be thought to consist in a contrast that leans heavily on concepts like playfulness and developmental teleology in order to be drawn clearly.[5]

That contrast *might* but perhaps ought *not* to be drawn in such a fashion. Whatever the meaning and purpose of vocal prayer, mindless, habitual recitation hardly seems likely to produce spiritually felicitous results. It seems more reasonable to assume that there could be an element of playfulness involved even when praying in such a fashion—not the free play of musement, to be sure, nor a colloquial interplay in the explicit sense, but a prayer-as-play nevertheless, with its own special form and rules. How might this be so?

In examining the series of notes on "The Three Methods of Prayer" that Ignatius attached as an appendix to his Spiritual Exercises, his remarks on the second and third methods have already received some consideration here.[6] Note that these methods are portable and can be applied to any prayerful activity, not just to those meditations that occur within the course of an Ignatian retreat. On any given occasion, Ignatius recommends setting aside a certain amount of time for prayer in advance. The second and third methods describe different ways of using that period of time. While the third consists in a form of Roman Catholic breathing meditation, employing the use of the breath to regulate the pace of reciting the words of some vocal prayer, the second method offers a markedly different approach. With the space of an hour still designated as the standard amount of time set aside for prayer, during the course of that hour the pace of prayer will be determined by semiotic progress. That is to say, the devotee will linger over a single word of prayer for as long as it is possible to draw meaning from the contemplation of it—to recollect the lively comparison made earlier, much as a bee will linger at a flower gathering nectar for the making of honey. Only when meaning has been temporarily exhausted will she move on to the next word of prayer, considering it in a similar fashion, playing with all of its possible connotations. Pursuing this method, the pace of prayer *just is* the natural unfolding of semiosis. While the completion of an hour arbitrarily interrupts this stream of semiosis, the exercitant will continue where she left off on the next occasion when she returns to prayer. Here is a form of prayer in which the attention is somewhat focused (on one word at a time) and yet not rigidly fixed (either on a single meaning for each word or on a specific word when the contemplation of it seems to have grown stale).

Simone Weil conceived of the essence of any form of prayer as attention. Even earlier, William James had considered volition to be essentially a matter of attention. Earlier still, Duns Scotus rounds out this particular set of insights by identifying love as an act of the will—not a single act, but a well-established habit of volition. Any theosemiotic of the spiritual life, guided by these insights, will need to understand prayer in terms of the relationship between attention, volition, and love. Moreover, given our conception of the nature of the self as semiosis, all kinds of prayer, and not just the special kind designated as *lectio divina*, will be shown to involve acts of reading and rereading. Since the verb "to read" is also one characterized by a certain vagueness, typically applied to a great many different forms of interpretation or information-processing, it will be necessary to isolate the precise sense in which the one who prays can be said to be engaged in reading.[7]

When Peirce encouraged his own reader to become a reader also of God's great poem, it was the disciplined practice of musement that he had in mind. Even as a teenager, and long before he invented the word, Peirce had already offered a reasonably clear description of the state of mind for which it serves as a label (W1: 10–12). Peirce's encounter with

Schiller's aesthetics seems to have played a dominant role in shaping his early thinking about this topic. In his correspondence with Lady Welby decades later, he explicitly identified Schiller as the original source for his idea of musement.[8] During the intervening period of time, Peirce's own work on the logic of abduction, combined with his attempt to outline a comprehensive phenomenology (phaneroscopy), were the primary catalysts for the further development of this idea. Toward the end of his life, however, it was not for the purposes of aesthetics or logic or phenomenology, but rather in an argument for God's reality that this development would culminate.

A good deal has already been said here, much of it repeated at various points for emphasis and clarification, about Peirce's Neglected Argument, an essay that was identified as supplying much of the table of contents for my attempt to articulate a contemporary theosemiotic.[9] As this discussion draws to a conclusion, it becomes especially important to ask the question about exactly what sort of experiment Peirce was proposing to his readers in that 1908 essay. This will involve further repetition, at the risk of boring my reader, but now with the explicit goal of drawing all of these strands together in one unified interpretation of the Neglected Argument, subsequently, in one final portrayal of a theology conceived as theosemiotic. It will be necessary to invoke once again the insight about how the various stages of inquiry cannot be perfectly segregated, so that Peirce's initial "Humble Argument" already involves elements of deduction and induction. At the same time, the later stages of inquiry described in Peirce's essay reflect back on and are of enormous relevance for understanding the logic of this Humble Argument. It needs to be made clear that Peirce conceived of musement as a disciplined practice involving both reading and rereading (*relegere*) the book of nature,[10] toward the end of gradually transforming one's habits of feeling, perception, thought, and conduct. It is both an experiment intended to test for the naturalness or instinctiveness with which humans will be inclined to entertain the hypothesis about God and an exercise designed for the purpose of developing the skill needed to perform this experiment effectively (thus, an "instinct... purified by meditation"; see *CP* 5.496).[11]

Deceptive in his presentation of it, this experiment is even more complex than the description just provided would indicate. The inductive repetition of musement as a regular practice functions as a test not only of the instinctiveness of the God-idea, but also of the effects that, once it arises, it is likely to produce in the consciousness of anyone who considers it playfully. Its irresistible quality—that is, the fact that in contemplating it under the conditions prescribed for musement one will be virtually incapable of doubting the reality of such a being—helps to explain why Peirce regarded this as a version of the ontological argument. As with Anselm's proof but following a very different line of reasoning, for Peirce, to think about the idea of God carefully is to render oneself incapable of doubting God's reality. Consequently, any attempt to propose that Peirce was inclined in his metaphysics to appeal to God as the "ultimate explanation" of natural phenomena, in the form of something like a traditional cosmological argument or argument from design, is clearly misleading.[12]

In addition to the effects wrought immediately in the heart and mind of the muser (at least some of these being aesthetic in character), Peirce was also interested in extending inductive analysis to the long-term effects of believing in such a God on the general conduct of one who embraces such a belief. Moreover, since Peirce was not all that terribly interested in what *individuals* do, it stands to reason that such inductive analysis must be applied to specific communities of inquiry, in this case to religious communities that have adopted belief in God as a guiding principle.

There is nothing startlingly new in the general approach that Peirce took in 1908 to thinking about how religious knowledge is possible. Written almost half a century earlier (and in a period shortly after his initial exposure to Schiller's letters), Peirce's 1863 Cambridge High School Reunion Lecture on "The Place of Our Age in the History of Civilization" reads like a nearly perfect prolegomenon to the Neglected Argument (W1: 101–14). There, what he described as the poet's "affinity for nature" inspires religious hypotheses that the young Peirce was confident would someday be scientifically explored. His 1908 essay was an attempt to show how such an exploration might best proceed (certainly not with the requirement that the God-hypothesis must be true but as a way of testing its merits). Benjamin Peirce's conception of the universe as a "book written for man's reading" is one that shaped his son Charles's religious thought from its youthful beginning until the very end of his life. Both father and son understood the practice of science to constitute a religiously meaningful vocation, as a form of "communion" with the author of the book of nature.[13] Both embraced metaphysical perspectives organized around a belief in the ideality of nature. And both regarded evolutionary theory (although not in any narrowly or rigidly Darwinian formulation of it) as being consistent with certain basic religious convictions.

Now, it may very well be the case that Peirce was a bit "naïve in assuming that prejudice can be so easily avoided and in claiming that the products of his musings may be taken as an indication of where those of other people would end up."[14] It is certainly plausible to imagine that someone who accepts Peirce's invitation and attempts to engage in musement might experience very different results from the ones that Peirce claimed ought to be anticipated.[15] But it is also assuredly the case that anyone hoping to evaluate such results would need to know a great deal about the exact nature of such an attempt. Assume that the argument made here and elsewhere is valid: claiming that musement ought to be regarded as both an exercise and an experiment, and that a key element for success in either case will be redundancy. As an exercise, it is one that would need to be repeated with great regularity in order to have any real effect on the habits and sensibilities of the muser. As an experiment, it would also need to be repeated on numerous occasions in order to have any significant value as an induction. These two aspects of musement are not separable but related. The skill that one needs to perform an experiment successfully—in this case, the requisite sensibilities and habits of perception—are honed in the very act of performing the experiment itself, not on a single occasion but with a certain kind of regularity and devotion. Like many types of religious meditation and contemplation, musement is an exercise in which one is encouraged to engage ritualistically, a practice that also constitutes a form of experimentation with oneself. Consequently, one does not simply set out on some random Tuesday evening to take a walk at sunset and devote oneself to musement with the expectation that in doing so one will gather the data needed to verify or falsify Peirce's claims about this practice. Once again, we would need to have sufficient knowledge with details about the nature of anyone's attempt at replicating Peirce's experiment in order to evaluate their results.

There is a sense in which the truth about belief in God could be revealed only in the Peircean "long run," so that an assessment of that truth "would involve the gathering of data ranging over the entire scope of human history."[16] To imagine that testing the God-hypothesis must take such a form is to focus on conduct, on meaningful patterns of behavior, rather than only on feelings arising out of musement, and to concentrate attention on the history of communities rather than on the biographies of individuals. This is certainly not to deny that musement itself as a kind of test, with the results produced in musement to be regarded as relevant to a thorough assessment of the God-hypothesis. Yet the experiment that begins in this fashion is extended by Peirce in order to determine the "sustainability" of any ideal that arises in musement when the muser then adopts it and chooses to shape her conduct and to live her life in conformity with it.[17] One is a test of the instinctiveness of the God-idea. The other is a test of the pragmatic value of this idea as a hypothetical ideal for guiding action. These are not unrelated inquiries. For Peirce, its naturalness or instinctiveness is what first recommends the God-hypothesis as an ideal for praxis.

Now, it can no longer be the case that *only* the time set aside for musement is to be considered as experimentation. Everyday activities, interactions, and experiences become the living laboratory for any person who is genuinely devoted to some religious ideal, with the "fruitfulness" for life of such an ideal to be thus measured by the quality of those experiences and the outcome of those activities and interactions. Criteria for fruitfulness will have to be established with great subtlety and care. The worldly suffering and poverty of great mystics and saints do not preclude by other, religiously meaningful standards a judgment of success. Given the nature of Peirce's pragmaticism, long-term fruitfulness will matter more than anything achieved in the short run, with one's contribution to the flourishing of a greater community to be deemed more important than any individual achievement.

If this sounds like a difficult experiment, it most certainly is, whether one is talking about the discipline and skill that would need to be cultivated in musement in order that it might yield religious insight for any given individual *or* one is considering the sample size that would be required in order to evaluate any religious ideal in terms of the observably developed character of human lives lived in conformity with it. Indeed, with regard to the latter, we would need to examine the behaviors displayed by a great many individuals, from diverse cultures and different historical periods, in order for theosemiotic inquiry to proceed with confidence.[18] Is such a standard of evidence something that might be regarded as "obsessive"?[19]

It *might* be so regarded, especially if, following Peirce's own lead to make the point, one were to consider as a counterexample the testing of some "hypothesis concerning the properties of gold."[20] If we have no significant doubt about the purity of a specific sample of gold, then this one small quantity would be adequate for testing purposes, to be taken as representative of all other samples of comparable purity. Yet here I want to insist emphatically that hypotheses concerning "God" and "gold" are separated by a much wider gap than what might be signified by a single letter. Actually, the relevant hypothesis here is not about God in the abstract but about human beings in the flesh who might believe in God. It concerns their instincts and their character, not some physical property that might be attributed to them in the way that we identify the properties of gold. One cannot read a person's character in a single encounter or discern the real nature of some community, its own character, and its commitments, by immersing oneself in it for a brief period of time. And while we might be able to assume the purity of a gold sample, I cannot even begin to imagine what talk about "purity" would mean with regard to psychologically complex, culturally and historically conditioned human beings and their communities.

It is probably wise to agree with those who argue that Peirce did not think we are destined to converge on the truth about any given question only in some final opinion, to be formulated in the indefinite long run.[21] About some things we can feel confident that we know the truth right now. I suspect that an understanding of the basic physical properties of gold represents just such a case in point. Nevertheless, chemistry and philosophical theology are very different fields of inquiry. About God's purposes, working themselves out in nature and in the human effort over time to embody religious ideals in practice, Peirce was inclined to think that we can catch only a "glimpse" of their meaning (*CP* 5.402, note 2). To think otherwise would be to embrace the doctrines of a particular community or the ideas prominent in a particular historical period as constituting the whole of religious truth. It would also represent a dramatic underestimation of both the vagueness and complexity of those divine purposes (which, I might add, if they could be so readily gleaned, would provide ample support for the traditional design arguments that Peirce clearly regarded with suspicion).

The testing of religious ideals in practice is continuous with the experiment already enacted in musement. This is just another way of stating the now oft-repeated claim that abductive reasoning—even in its earliest "playful" stages—will already involve the initial clarification of ideas that suggest themselves as attractive hypotheses, as well as comparing the results of such clarification with remembered past experiences. In some limited sense, deduction and induction must already be occurring in this abductive phase. Moreover, the extended inductive testing of hypotheses through observation and experiment will generate new habits of thought and perception that will function as premises for future hypothetical inferences. Of great relevance to this discussion of pragmatism and prayer, one should note how Peirce included among those effects of the God-idea that would need to be evaluated for the purposes of inquiry those "produced by searching out and by finding the hypothesis itself."[22] Peirce was clear that the meaning of that idea was embodied in the "adoration" as well as in the conduct that it inspires (*CP* 8.262). All of this is to say that inquiry—which always takes the form of semiosis—is a typically gradual process, also a living process. When it flourishes, it involves the ongoing development of a diversity of habits (habits of feeling and belief-habits of various kinds, as well as habits of action), thus also the continuous growth of meaning.

What Peirce described as musement is not an initial, isolated act of reading God's "great poem" that first launches the inquiry described in the Neglected Argument but then is somehow left behind. It is the disciplined practice of continuously *rereading* that poem, as Peirce himself recommended, its value enhanced by any increase in the regularity of such an exercise. Not only is the muser gradually transformed by this practice, but the accumulated experiences of a life lived in conformity to the God-hypothesis as an ideal will also have a gradual but powerful effect on future practice. Consequently, each rereading involves playing a slightly different game than the one that preceded it, with (perhaps subtly) different rules for playing.[23]

Once again, the results achieved by one person's self-experimentation are of very little value here. Wish-fulfillment, cultural bias, genetic predisposition, etc., could all help to explain why some person or small collection of persons might tend to gravitate toward belief in God. The larger the sample size, the greater the value of the evidence in support of such a belief. Yet belief in God's reality represents only one particular reading of this universe perfused with signs, an interpretation tested continuously in the lives and experiences of those who share it; in another sense it will also be tested, or contested, by those who read the world differently.

Peirce's sketch of the Neglected Argument makes it appear much simpler than upon careful examination it reveals itself to be. Just as prayer can take on a great variety of forms and manifestations, so too can the process of thought portrayed by Peirce in his essay. Before turning attention in a different direction, it is worth considering here the range of possibilities that Peirce considers. Some of these have already been surveyed in an attempt to make sense out of the three stages of inquiry that Peirce described as unfolding in the argument. This is familiar territory for anyone who has examined either the essay or the various commentaries devoted to it.[24] What I have tried to underscore here is the continuity of those stages, their quasi-circular or, perhaps better, spiral arrangement, so that we might think of abduction as the starting point, with induction as the upshot of inquiry, but since induction is also an exercise and a process of habit formation, in another sense it lays the groundwork for each new rereading of the book of nature.

What has not yet been stressed sufficiently, however, but appears obvious upon a careful inspection of Peirce's essay, is that there are stages within musement itself, subtle but definite distinctions that allow one to understand musement as a developmental process. Peirce does not elaborate on these "stages" (or even label them as such), but his description suggests that a "passive" drinking in of impressions will rapidly give way to attentive observation that results in musement proper, and finally to interplay, "a lively give and take of communion between self and self" (CP 6.459). Here the continuity is even greater than that which characterizes the relationship between abduction, deduction, and induction. Yet the distinctions ought not to be neglected, as one can imagine, for example, that with "attentive observation" there is a movement away from being simply awake and ready for whatever might appear and toward a more selective or muscular form of attention, one focused now on this, now on that aspect of the phenomenon under investigation, still playful, but already anticipating the later work of deduction and induction. All of these forms of attending and thinking are taken up in musement itself, which begins as something of a soliloquy but evolves into a lively conversation. Since musement as Peirce described it is an exercise in which one engages in solitude, the "conversation" here could be imagined in two ways: as an interior dialogue or as a communing with the Mind made visible in nature, with the "author" of this extraordinary text. (The latter seems like the more plausible meaning that Peirce intended, although it does not preclude the former.)[25] In any event, these various ways of attending, thinking, and conversing all qualify as forms of musement, despite their differences, because of the meta-habit that governs all of them, a lightness of touch or spirit of playfulness, a freedom from all of the rules that typically govern inquiry except for the one law of liberty.

Even more subtle is the shift between one kind of thinking that occurs at the outset of musement and another that arises in the process.[26] This shift occurs at the point when, as Peirce predicted, the hypothesis of God's reality would be likely to suggest itself (CP 6.466–67). At the outset, musement is an act of contemplation with the book of nature as its subject matter. At the point now in question, attention is shifted to the *idea* of God, not as an about-face, but just as that idea naturally or instinctively tends to emerge in the meditative interaction with nature. Nevertheless, there is a turning here, a focusing now on one particular hypothesis, a falling in love with that idea and then the cultivation of that relationship. If attention remained focused on nature, the beauty or growth evident there, then there might be support for the tendency to characterize Peirce's essay as a defense of the teleological argument. Rather, much like Anselm (although also quite differently) at this turning point Peirce's contemplation is now organized around the God-idea. It is not the beauty or order of nature but the "irresistibility" of this idea that motivates Peirce to declare that God is real, indeed, that it has now become impossible to doubt God's reality. As he indicated in his letter written to William James a few years earlier, no one could contemplate the beauty of that which is most admirable, the perfect ideal, and yet fail to believe that it has "necessarily a mode of being to be called living" (*CP* 8.262).

Not only does Peirce explicitly identify this line of reasoning in his letter as a form of the ontological argument, but his description of it very closely resembles Simone Weil's brief outline of an "experimental" version of that argument. Here it is no longer a question simply of how the idea of God might happen to arise for any individual. One might already "believe" in God, perhaps in the form of an acquired belief inherited from some religious community, and yet still choose to evaluate such an idea in musement, not setting out to demonstrate its truth, but simply contemplating it as such. Such contemplation would involve the same playful movement back and forth between pondering how such an idea illuminates experience and imagining how admirably it would serve to shape human life and behavior. (The more deeply one becomes immersed in any process of musement the more one will tend to emphasize the latter sort of consideration. At least this seemed to be Peirce's hunch as a pragmaticist.)

How should one go about filling in some additional details of Peirce's sketch? Given its brevity, it has proven important to examine and reexamine (read and reread) his essay with painstaking care. Note, first, another line of continuity, this one between musement and religious forms of meditation or prayer. Peirce was confident that the former would flower into the latter, in much the same way (indeed, for precisely the same reason) that he thought the God-hypothesis was likely sooner or later to suggest itself to the persistent muser. So although it may begin with no particular purpose set out in advance, at a certain point in time—that is, the turning point when the muser turns to the contemplation of the God-idea—this exercise that Peirce is describing has actually become a form of prayer. (Whether it was prayer in some *virtual* sense prior to this turning point is an intriguing question, but one that I will not pursue here.)

Note, also, the language that Peirce used to describe the idea about God's reality. It is in the first place a hypothesis, one that will be instinctive for anyone who reads the book of nature under the appropriate conditions and in a proper state of mind. This idea, moreover, is also an *ideal* (as both the 1908 essay and the earlier letter to James make clear), one to be admired for its beauty but then also one, pragmatically speaking, to which one's conduct ought to be conformed. Finally, it is not to be regarded as an abstract ideal or a purely formal hypothesis, but as "living" and beloved. Although quite different in terms of how it unfolds—primarily because Anselm restricted himself to thinking primarily in the deductive mode—Peirce's version of the ontological argument is every bit as prayerful as that of his medieval predecessor, very much a communion with divinity that results in the desire to understand more deeply the nature of such a relationship.[27]

If my own argument here has been successful, that relationship will now be easily recognized as one that is semiotic in nature, something that Peirce alludes to in the essay but never makes as explicit as he could have. There can be no unmediated "communion" between self and self, any more than any individual can possess direct introspective access to herself or himself. This coming to know a person (either oneself or another, either human or divine) is always mediated by signs and always occurs over time. It involves patient, careful rereading. Every one of my own rereadings of Peirce's 1908 essay has deepened my conviction that this is exactly the sort of practice that Peirce intended musement to be, a prayerful exercise that also serves as a theologically useful experiment. If this insight is a valid one, it also helps to establish the agenda for any future theology conceived as theosemiotic.

II

It may seem like an abrupt change in topic to move from a discussion of musement and its role in the Neglected Argument to offer an account of the role that the human body plays as an instrument of attention. Yet despite the apparent disconnect, all of these issues are relevant to a pragmatic consideration of prayer and to the eventual articulation of a theosemiotic of the spiritual life. Here an account of how the body might be disciplined or mobilized to shape attention will gradually morph into a consideration of the religious significance of attention more generally speaking—that is to say, of how the exercise of attention can become an act of prayer.

I have argued that the self is a living legisign and that the human body is its primary sign vehicle. Moreover, the meaning of this sign is to some extent determined by the self's capacity to direct attention. In some traditional schools of prayer and meditation (Hindu yoga, for example), the disposition of the body, both in terms of posture and breathing, is given extended and meticulous consideration. Even where it receives less emphasis (as in Ignatius's exercises), it is never completely ignored. Ignatius has rules for eating, talks about the pragmatics of posture in prayer, and, as already explored, develops a rudimentary form of breathing meditation. Moreover, in Peirce's description of musement, while the focus is very much on the frame of mind and subject matter ideal for the practice, he frames it as a form of walking meditation. Now *both* pragmatists and liberationists are disinclined to create a gap in their accounts of the human person between body and mind or body and spirit. Poverty is such a central concern for the latter because of the very real bodily suffering that it can cause for those who are oppressed, deprived of what they need physically to flourish or even just to live. For all of these reasons, as well as others not directly stated here, no theology of prayer can be complete or informative unless it supplies a detailed account of the role of the body in such a discipline.

As with "self" and "body," the pragmatic argument here suggests that our capacity for attention and the condition of our physical bodies are inextricably linked, without one being entirely reducible to the other. My controlling your body is a significant factor contributing to my ability to direct and shape your attention, but it is no guarantee of success. Every teacher who has struggled with the boredom of students knows that required class attendance does not result automatically in real pedagogical engagement. And a highly disciplined individual can endure even physical torture by continuing to maintain self-control over thoughts and attention. Indeed, William James's portrayal in the *Varieties* of the ideal moral warrior invoked the image of "a sick man" unable to engage in bodily combat, but trained in "indifference" and so able to "willfully turn his attention."

This general observation notwithstanding, our ability to use the body as an instrument to regulate attention is significant and deserves consideration. On a very mundane level, one typically turns one's gaze in the direction of whatever it is that one wishes to contemplate or turns away and averts one's gaze from whatever is regarded as unpleasant or a distraction. If it is a sound, such as music, that forms the object of attention, I might actually close my eyes to facilitate concentration. If I am engaged in acts of meditation that require attending to internal or imagined states of affairs, I may find it useful both to close my eyes and to place my body in a space free from noise.

As noted earlier, the breath and breathing are used to regulate attention in a great variety of spiritual practices developed by practitioners from a wide range of religious traditions. Buddhist *zazen* and the extraordinarily sophisticated breathing exercises cultivated by individuals devoted to the discipline of Hindu yoga are prime examples already identified. Less well known are some comparable examples from Western religious traditions, like the third method of prayer described by Ignatius. Recall how Ignatius proposed that one recite any frequently recited vocal prayer with the use of the breath for pacing, so that each word uttered is correlated with the rhythm of a single inhalation/exhalation. In this instance, attention is not fastened to the breath in order to facilitate the circulation of *ch'i* or *prana* throughout the human body, as might be intended in certain Daoist or Hindu practices conducted against the background supplied by a complex internal alchemy. As with Buddhist *zazen*, for Ignatius one uses the breath and breathing primarily as a strategy for avoiding distraction; attention carefully focused there has already been successfully detached from other possible objects of concern.[28] For Ignatius, such detachment (*indiferencia*) and control of attention are understood in martial terms as being a prerequisite for success in the spiritual combat. Evil spirits will first try to control my attention in order then to shape my thoughts, feelings, and behavior.

An enemy's control of my body, as suggested earlier, need not preclude my ability to maintain control over my attention, thus in some sense, over my "self." Nevertheless, breath and breathing are regarded as the vital core of the self in many cultures, as manifesting the spirit that animates the human body, a belief no doubt traceable to the observation among early hominids that the sudden absence of breath signaled death and the dissolution of selfhood. And so if the enemy's control extends to my breathing, self-mastery will be seriously threatened. (This is a key reason that "waterboarding" is an especially effective form of torture, and also why it is so morally problematic.)

Regulation of bodily posture is a crucial component of many spiritual exercises; even apart from such exercises, the link between posture and attention is one readily observable. Soldiers are commanded to "stand at attention," while children are admonished to "sit up straight and pay attention." In Hindu yoga, ancient and extended experimentation with posture (*asana*) and its effects on human consciousness has resulted in the development of an elaborate system of practices. Yet even St. Ignatius, once again, understood the importance of posture for success in prayer and meditation, as he recommended that devotees should sit or kneel, lie on the ground either prostrate or face up, or walk back and forth . . . whatever is most conducive to eliminating distraction. The Zen Buddhist master Shunryu Suzuki affirmed with confidence that "the state of mind that exists when you sit in the right posture is, itself, enlightenment" and to be contrasted with a mind that is "wobbling or wandering about."[29]

If the self is a sign, one can "interpret" other persons by attending to their breathing or posture, even as one's own bodily posture can constitute a powerful means of communication with others. (I can greet another person with either a welcoming or menacing stance.) Yet the reading of the self as a stream of signs requires attending to the body in motion and over a period of time. Moreover, the interpreter herself will need to develop the skill of paying attention, not only when sitting or standing still in a meditative posture, but also when moving about in the world. When that movement is regular and cadenced, it might actually facilitate concentration, as is the case with various forms of walking or running meditation. In the Daoist discipline of *taijiquan*, the slowness of practiced movements is intended to have the effect of also slowing down the practitioner's stream of thought and reducing distraction. In all of these movements, moreover, the head is carefully aligned with the core of the body (*dan tian*); there is no such thing as "looking over one's shoulder" in taiji. As the body moves, so too one's gaze and attention are directed to wherever the self now faces and to whatever it confronts. To develop such a habit of movement reduces the possibility of a divided self, with the body oriented toward one set of interactions, but the attention being drawn elsewhere.

Consider briefly two martial arts exercises that are explicitly designed for training the practitioner to interpret with her/his body the movements and intentions of someone else: "pushing hands" as a part of training in taijiquan, and *kokyu dosa* in the Japanese martial art of aikido. In each case, the exercise is performed with a partner, with some gentle contact between the two: the back of one person's wrist touching the other person's forearm in pushing hands, both partners kneeling in *seiza* as they alternate holding each other's wrists in *kokyu dosa*. The purpose here is not to win a wrestling match (although pushing hands can take the form of a fairly lively competition), but rather to develop what the great taiji master *Zheng Manquing* called "listening" or "interpreting energy."[30] This is a wordless semiotic interaction, both a speaking and listening with the body, and one that requires an extraordinary capacity for attending to the most subtle details of movement. Here the sense of touch is even more important for reading the signs embodied in one's partner's movements than the sense of sight, so that attention is sometimes heightened when the exercise is performed with eyes closed. The key to success is not to "read into" another person's intentions one's own projected anxieties or fears, but with calm breathing and gentle responses to achieve a condition of readiness for whatever might occur. This "soft" or "empty" attention (*mushin*) is quite different in nature from the narrow concentration that, for some specific purpose, might become focused on a single object of concern.

In these examples, the body is perceived as relevant in a number of different ways. In the first place, the self-controlled body is used as an instrument of attention. Moreover, such attention is directed to the bodily posture and movements of others as tangible signs with decipherable meanings. The interpretation of meaning is one made by the body of the interpreter, not represented primarily in thoughts or feelings about the other, but in the interpreter's own active response, in the adjustment of her own bodily movements and disposition toward the other. While the self is open and ready for whatever might occur, it is also centered; anything encountered as external, even hostile to the self, is by discipline and skill to be brought into harmony with that center (the *hara* in Japanese disciplines, *dan tian* for the Chinese).

It is important here to offer a pragmatic evaluation of the strategy quite commonly utilized in aikido of moving *tenkan* (literally, "turning") in response to an attack, whether it takes the form of a push, a strike with hands, fists or weapon, or a kick. The person attacked (*nage*) will quickly pivot and turn 180 degrees, like a door swinging on its hinges when pushed. At the moment of encounter, the attacker (*uke*) and *nage* will be face to face, attention directed toward each other. *Nage* must swiftly read *uke*'s intentions and measure his hostility. In executing the movement *tenkan*, she will no longer be in confrontation with *uke*, but will now be standing alongside and slightly behind. In that temporarily safe space, a number of aikido techniques might be utilized in self-defense. More significantly, however, the entire situation has now been transformed, indeed, *reinterpreted*. No longer in confrontation with each other, perceiving a distinctive horizon but blinded to what each other sees, suddenly they are shoulder to shoulder facing in the same direction; *uke* and *nage* now share a world. If there is a possibility that this hostile encounter can be defused without violence, such a conversion—facilitated by the habits of movement and response that *nage* has carefully cultivated—will have provided the grounds for it. Instead of a clash of forces, there is now, as aikido's founder Morihei Ueshiba would have described it, a blending of two persons in harmony brought about by the power of love.

Moving *tenkan* in aikido is a strategy that can be extended metaphorically to a great variety of interactions that occur between embodied selves-as-signs. To effect such movement skillfully requires the capacity to control how one attends to and interprets any given situation; at the most advanced level of achievement, it also presupposes the ability to supply an alternative interpretation, to redirect the attention of others and so creatively to transform the nature of that situation. Ueshiba was correct to link such a capacity to the habit of love. Not all acts of attention are loving, but one can hardly claim to love that to which one does not direct a certain amount and a certain quality of attention, the cultivation of which requires time, effort, and discipline. Ueshiba understood the extraordinary power of such a habit once entrenched, as did William James; recall how James announced that the "love of enemies" represents such a dramatic "breach with our instinctive springs of action as a whole" and thus generates a force so extraordinary that "it might conceivably transform the world."[31]

It is easy to slip into speaking about attention as something that one does, so that "attend," like "love," becomes mischaracterized as an action verb that takes a direct object—that is to say, as something that I *do* to the object of my attention. Much of the discussion in this book has tended in that direction, since attention was identified as the essence of volition, with my decision to pay attention to this rather than that as the exercise of a certain kind of freedom. This can be a useful way to think about human agency—more useful than various alternatives, especially from a theosemiotic perspective that follows Peirce in construing the meaning of any self-sign as a function of what that self attends to and the manner in which it does so. This makes one's decisions about how one will pay attention very significant ones, both spiritually and ethically speaking. Nothing said thus far should be now recanted in a way that might undermine or mitigate that significance.

Instead, it seems felicitous to emphasize again certain observations made earlier about mutuality as the corrective to a somewhat restricted and simplistic way of thinking about human love. Part of the challenge here is to recognize, once again, that "attention" is yet another vague label for a broad range of phenomena. To compare a decision to pay attention, metaphorically, with the act of shining a flashlight on some object in the corner of a dark room is not so much false as it is grossly inadequate. Sometimes paying attention takes precisely this form. Yet even on this highly simplified account, a good deal is missing. The flashlight does not register or recognize what its beam of light illuminates. It is not in any way affected or transformed by that object. Without the hand of a human agent to guide it, the light shines at random. Nothing elicits it as a response. Nothing demands its performance.

The case is quite different with a human self-as-sign. Its attention will quite typically be drawn here rather than there, thus taking the form of a response to something already given in experience. What it then perceives in attending does not result in some neutral state but will be mildly or dramatically self-transformative, perhaps something in between. Even the mere act of recognition is a kind of response, the assignment of meaning to whatever one observes. Failure to recognize at all when we attend will also produce changes in the observer, perhaps shock or surprise serving as a stimulus to inquiry in the way that one of the main story lines in pragmatism has so frequently described. We consume by eating, but seeing and listening are also modes of consumption; it would be naïve to imagine that either could take place without the one who consumes being somehow significantly transformed.³²

Consequently, a more refined and fully satisfactory account of attention must portray it as essentially relational, involving call and response, an exchange of gifts, giving determinate shape to some stream of semiosis. That such a relation often displays mutuality was observed in the earlier discussion of loving attention. Yet attention need not be loving. I can direct my contempt to another in a way that will have a profound effect on both myself and the other. The effect is heightened in both directions if that contempt is returned in kind. One can imagine this occurring even when the "other" is not human—a pet dog or cat, for example. The transformative possibilities are most extraordinary, however, in the mutual attention shared by human beings. (These are the possibilities that William James must have been imagining when he treated the love of enemies as something like a contagious habit of attention with the power to reshape the universe.) This is less a matter of something that we do, like shining a flashlight, than it is a state of affairs in which we participate, an entering into relation.

Most of our attention is expended, to be sure, in ways that appear to lack this element of mutuality and may be a bit simpler to describe. The sleeping infant whom I monitor with my watchful gaze, the sun rising over the Atlantic as I walk along the New England shore, leaves turning color in October on the oak tree in my backyard. Even here, however, there is a call and response; and from a certain philosophical perspective it will seem entirely appropriate to say that these things *give* themselves to us for our attention.³³ The quality of such attention will have the capacity to modify the nature of our relationship in all of these cases. The same two things will exist in very different relationships depending on how attention is formed or comes into being—its direction, its intensity, its general quality, and its persistence. Attention makes all the difference in the world concerning how we will be in relation to everything that we encounter (or even imagine, since we can also choose the objects of our imagination).

Attention grows quiet, perhaps even lapses altogether, when we sleep. And many a saint and sage have capitalized on this observation in order to identify by metaphorical extension the sleep-like spiritual state in which we spend a good deal of our lives and from which we desperately need to awaken. In a dreamless sleep, attention seems to have no object. When populated with dreams, by contrast, the mind will attend to many things, but without agency, with no discernible purpose. The first of these experiences has been judged in some religious traditions to be spiritually felicitous, so that the ability to achieve while fully awake a state of mind in which the attention is directed to nothing in particular can become the goal of spiritual exercise. The latter experience, on the other hand, has very little to recommend it, its analogue in conscious existence representing a state of enslavement, not only because of the lack of self-control displayed, but because those things to which one's attention are drawn may prove to be harmful distractions.

The suggestion that attention can have "no object" seems absurd on the face of it. We can attend to one thing rather than another, but what could it possibly mean to attend to nothing at all? Hopefully, the seeds for a possible answer to this question have been planted in the earlier chapters of this book and are already beginning to germinate. Simone Weil, most probably influenced by Nicolas Malebranche, linked attention to prayer as constituting its essence. Recall that, unlike William James, she distinguished attention from volition;[34] my attempt to soften the contrast between their perspectives involved observing that attention displays itself in various forms. The kind of attention that constitutes a form of *waiting* for Weil is of special relevance for these theological considerations. It has also been identified as something akin to the sort of attention that Peirce deemed as necessary for his Humble Argument, in contrast to the narrow fixation on some selected feature of experience or on some isolated hypothesis that characterizes induction and deduction respectively. Such waiting is a waiting for nothing in particular, a readiness, not for something already conceived and anticipated, but for whatever might appear.

As both Weil and Malebranche were well aware, there is a passive quality to such attention, a responsiveness in prayer to the presence and will of God as it is manifested in the life of the one who prays. Yet this passivity is not of the sort that would cause anyone who advocates it to be described as endorsing some species of "quietism."[35] The indifference that distinguishes attentive prayer can never be an indifference pure and simple. If prayer is always a type of conversation, as Ignatius stipulated and even Peirce himself suggested (since musement was intended to become a lively conversation in the hope that it might flower into prayer), then an emphasis on this passive element corresponds to a recognition of the importance of listening if any encounter is to be genuinely conversational and to yield insight. Prayer-as-conversation is distinguished from many other types of exchange by the presumed asymmetry between conversation partners. Waiting, readiness, listening will always take precedence over whatever active role the devotee then proceeds to play in the dialogue.

Nevertheless, a careful consideration of what all of these thinkers are proposing as ideal for the life of prayer would tend, more than anything else, to suggest that a hard distinction between activity and passivity is yet another false dichotomy that an enlightened pragmatist might want to see softened or even dissolved. To be ready in this fashion, to be able to wait in the way prescribed, can take enormous effort and skill. It involves developing a carefully modulated habit of attention that will need to be refined and redeveloped continuously, even as the circumstances under which one enters into prayer are constantly shifting and evolving. So the first thing to be said about the passivity being recommended for prayer is that it must be of a very special sort, a disinterestedness that is not equivalent to a simple lack of interest, a purposelessness (to use Peirce's preferred term) that is very far removed from the eradication of all sense of purpose in one's life. Once again, the concept of playfulness goes some distance toward the end of explaining exactly what is required here. The seriousness with which one can enter into play, even as and precisely because one is not rigidly bound to a specific course of action, shaped by a determinate set of expectations, distinguishes the passive element in prayer from that associated with the most radical forms of quietism.

In the "lively give and take" of prayerful conversation, listening will be one moment in a dialectic that includes the gift of oneself, the gift of whatever meaning is embodied in the self-as-semiosis, extended to the other in the full mutuality of authentic love. Love as quiet listening gives way to praxis whenever this is something that love itself requires. There is no determining in advance exactly what it is that will in fact be required. This is why the habit of love must be as refined and carefully developed as the habit of attention to which it is most closely linked in the coordinated bundle of habits that constitute the self as living legisign. By virtue of how it attends and what it loves, the meaning of the self is established and continuously grows. That living, growing sign then determines the meaning of others with whom it interacts—in a sense so gentle that it does not belie the claim that such determination is better understood as an act of giving rather than of "making" or "causing." Whatever it does come to mean will best be embodied in praxis. Whatever gift it offers will best be communicated through actions. This pragmatic/semiotic ideal of the self, albeit rooted in a deep listening, offers a portrayal that is as far removed from pure passivity as one might imagine. Moreover, it is a theological account entirely consistent with the goals and requirements of a theology of human liberation.

Such an account is merely the attempt to employ philosophical resources borrowed from Peirce and pragmatism in order to make sense out of an Ignatian spirituality that blends contemplation with action. It is important to note that the Dominican Gutierrez embraced such an Ignatian perspective as crucial to the development of his own liberation spirituality.[36] Now, it would be a gross misreading to identify liberation theology as being committed to anything other than the most socially and politically engaged form of praxis. Yet it is also worth observing here how the spirituality that Gutierrez described was rooted, first and foremost, in the utter *gratuitousness* of divine love. Even in the midst of vigorous activity, one needs to be reminded that meaning is a gift, that the seeds of human liberation have already been planted so that what is required on our part is the effort and commitment to ensure that they might grow and bear fruit. The image of a gardener nurturing flowers with a cherishing love is one that has already been explored here; it is an image that anyone seriously attempting to understand the nature and purpose of prayer might be advised to keep steadily in mind.

III

What would a theosemiotic of the spiritual life look like if one were to develop it at least in outline here? What special perspective on practices such as prayer, meditation, or acts of asceticism might such a theology afford? Moreover, how is an emphasis on the significance of praxis—an emphasis distinctive of theosemiotic and already discussed at some length here—crucial for understanding those specific practices that one associates with spirituality and the spiritual life in traditional discussions of religious behavior? A very different sort of question may then be added to this list: Is it necessary to adopt some form of hypothesis about the reality of a personal deity in order to make sense out of the kind of spiritual life that theosemiotic describes? Does talk about prayer entail in some pragmatic sense talk about a divine person to whom such prayer is directed?

At this point in the discussion, all of these questions have to some degree been broached or anticipated. The reader should not expect that answers to any of them will now be supplied in full. Yet it does seem appropriate to conclude this book with an emphasis on religious practice, in particular, on the logic embodied in such practice, especially given the account supplied here about how the various persons and communities that engage in such exercises are best to be understood. If the self is a living legisign, moreover, if any community is always already a community of interpretation, then spirituality in many of its forms will be best conceived as a continuous act of reading and rereading; in the act of reading and being read, meaning is both something discovered and something given. That has been one of the central arguments of this book.

The background for such an argument is supplied by the twin convictions, both of them Peircean in inspiration: first, that all experience is interpreted experience or semiosis; and, second, that the universe that we inhabit is not merely a world of things, but a world in which many things actively function as signs.

The emphasis on praxis in this discussion has moved beyond any simple declaration that there is an important continuity between theory and practice—in this instance, between theology and the conduct that it both shapes and illuminates. It has moved beyond the claim that this continuity is most visible when theology is recognized as itself being a kind of practice and not merely a prolegomenon to the latter. Even more emphatically now there is a need to consider again—but here with a special emphasis on spirituality—how theology *follows* practice, in the sense of being a reflection on it, but also by being deeply and firmly rooted in it. This is a lesson already learned from a careful analysis of Peirce's stages of inquiry, these hardly constituting a simple progression from first to last, but rather, a spiraling through phases that involves a continuous return to the behavioral bedrock on which all inquiry ultimately rests. Theosemiotic will call for a truly experimental spirituality, a testing of meanings by the way that we live them. This testing eventuates in the living embodiment of meanings by the selves who read and discern them. What a person eventually comes to mean, not all at once but in the gradual unfolding of a narrative over time, is most especially revealed by the logic and pattern of her practices. When her conduct displays a distinctive kind of purpose or purposes, then that meaning might properly be interpreted as religious. Such a person is transforming life into prayer.

What would warrant the interpretation of a life as religiously meaningful? Any description of what a person means necessarily will remain quite vague, much more like the account of what a great novel "means" than like what a stop sign means or the meaning of directions recorded in the instructions for assembling a piece of furniture. The purposes that give shape to human behavior can be multiple and conflicting. What would qualify any one of them as "religious"? Here is the germ of an answer. There has been recurring mention in these pages of the habit of love that constitutes, from certain religious perspectives, the ultimate logical interpretant of persons-as-signs. Despite the lingering vagueness, something determinate can be said theologically about such a love. That it is essentially volitional in nature, presupposes a certain quality of attention, delights in the beloved, involves the cultivation of gratitude for the being of things, naturally manifests as a compassion or care for the suffering, and can also be analyzed in semiotic, triadic terms; even without the elimination of vagueness, these are all claims about the nature of love that can be articulated from a theosemiotic perspective. Much more can be said, however, about the kind of behavior that this habit of love will tend to elicit. A thick description of love's practices, even with the recognition that love's teleology is developmental and partially shrouded in darkness, is an entirely realistic agenda item for theosemiotic inquiry. Once again, theosemiotic is both preoccupied with and culminates in praxis.

This observation about praxis has already been used to establish a link between theosemiotic and various types of liberation theology. Yet it was intended, as insisted earlier, to be more than a merely formal link. That is to say, the affinity to be noticed here is more than one about shared methodology, more than a common inclination toward a certain kind of pragmatism. It is being argued here that theosemiotic is always already a theology of the spiritual life. The same is true for theologies of liberation, as Gutierrez made so clear, insofar as they must be grounded (if they are to have any legitimacy whatsoever) in a vibrant liberation spirituality. This in itself is still a purely formal resemblance unless it can be further argued that the substance of such a liberation spirituality is also one that theosemiotic requires, given its own particular assumptions and purposes. Only the basic outline of such an argument can be presented here, but it will nevertheless be important in concluding to do so. It must be an argument about what love requires, about how best to understand what it means to suggest that the ultimate logical interpretant of God's "great poem" would be the habit of love cultivated in the minds and hearts of its attentive readers, not regarded individually, but only insofar as they constitute a truly unlimited community of interpreters.

Although some liberation thinkers may have actually been influenced by philosophical pragmatism,[37] my argument thus far has been grounded in an observation about similarities: the common emphasis on community and praxis, the rejection of certain conceptual dichotomies, a clear recognition that human thought and feeling are always thoroughly *embodied*, and so on. Beyond the formal outline of such a comparison, what more can be noted? I have also suggested that what theosemiotic might most helpfully contribute to the future development of liberation theology is a clear conviction that the latter must be firmly grounded in an ethics of attention.[38] Alternatively, a theosemiotic organized around the principles of Peirce's pragmaticism can learn from liberation thought that there is no single issue that is more compelling, pragmatically speaking, than the suffering produced by human poverty. Theoretically speaking (think of Simone Weil), this is a conclusion that theosemiotic should be able to reach even without the nudge supplied by liberation theology. It is all simply a matter of seeing clearly and interpreting correctly (at least according to the argument that I am presenting here). The cultivation of a habit of love as the ultimate logical interpretant of what it means to be a self—combined with a cenoscopic analysis of what is revealed in ordinary human experience—together should supply an adequate motivation for embracing a "preferential option for the poor." I want now to suggest that the careful consideration of both of these topics (that is, the grounding of theology in an ethics of attention and the gradual focusing of such attention on the ubiquitous presence of poverty) is crucial to understanding the relationship between prayer and the spirit of pragmatism. One upshot of such extended consideration is achieving the insight that all prayer to some extent must take the form of a *lectio divina*.

From a theosemiotic point of view, how we attend, and subsequently, how we then read or interpret the signs that we encounter in experience, are fundamental to everything else that we do, to every other form of praxis. Yet it is crucial to reemphasize here that attending and reading are themselves always already forms of doing. The rules that ought to govern such practices are by no means preethical; rather, they are by their very nature fundamentally moral principles, ethical at their core. In certain instances, there is a clear sense that we ought to attend to one thing rather than another (the suffering of a grief-stricken friend as he shares his pain with me rather than the cell phone on the table between us that is vibrating with trivial text messages), as well as a clear sense about how we should read or interpret (if the pain is real it would be morally reprehensible for me to trivialize it as histrionic). Not every situation is as clearly defined as the example proposed. In some other instances it might require considerable moral skill—considerable discernment—for one to know how best to direct attention. This is to suggest that our habits of attention are morally meaningful habits, capable both of being developed and of serious atrophy. The practice of prayer seems crucial to their development. It is a practice deemed necessary in order to recover a way of seeing and listening, of carefully attending, that might have been natural in childhood but somehow later has been lost. This insight, shared by Jesus, Emerson, Peirce, and Gutierrez—also by Daoists—takes on a special relevance for the purpose of exploring an ethics of attention.

Indeed, one of my earliest empirical confirmations of this insight occurred when my son was a young boy, no longer a toddler, but certainly no older than seven or eight years of age. My wife and I decided that it might be exciting to take him on a day trip from eastern Pennsylvania where we live into New York City, just about eighty miles away. Our excitement was about observing his reaction to the lights, the crowds, the noise, and especially the tall buildings, whether standing at the base of them and looking up or poised atop one of them with a panoramic view of the city. After a full day of activities, we found ourselves exhausted and on a commuter train heading into New Jersey toward home. What about the city had interested him the most, what was most memorable? With quiet concern, a somber demeanor that I can remember vividly even though decades have passed, he queried us about the homeless people that he saw living on sidewalks and sleeping in subways. "How do they live and what do they eat?" he wanted to know. "When it snows or rains or becomes very cold, what do they do?" To be sure, my wife and I had observed these same individuals, but after having lived in the city early in our marriage, a certain jading had occurred, and they were now less noticeable. In order to see them clearly again, we needed to see with the eyes of our child. This was for me an important lesson in the ethics of attention.

My son's ability to see the suffering of other human beings clearly was not the result of his having engaged in the practice of prayer, but for me to recover such an ability (not just on this occasion but as an entrenched habit of attention), such a practice might prove to be essential. This, at least, is what theosemiotic presupposes. I *can* develop certain powerful dispositions as a result of some extraordinary encounter or experience, but if I am deliberately to do so, in a way that conforms to specific ideals and purposes, then it will be necessary for me to identify and pursue some sort of practice. Training in awareness (whether explicitly "prayerful" or not) can occur in meditative and sedentary seclusion. It can also take place during *either* a walk in the wilderness or along the busiest and grittiest of city streets. Indeed, except on the principles defended by a truly impoverished naturalism, my reading of the book of nature must include all of these possibilities.

Once again, it is not as if a theosemiotic perspective adds to the agenda of liberation theology anything that otherwise was completely missing. The widely circulated liberationist formula, "see, judge, act," clearly stresses the importance of being able first to perceive some suffering or injustice before it can be evaluated or addressed. Yet there is a special and singular clarity to the emphasis that Peirce and other pragmatists placed on the overall significance of paying deliberate attention, the way in which it shapes our inferences, and consequently, the manner in which it determines the meaning of our very selves. With his diligence in monitoring how every idea is first formed by attentive perception and then tested and refined in purposeful action, Peirce's pragmaticism is ideally suited for the task of supplying liberation theology with important philosophical resources for its articulation and development.

I have proposed that the substance of Simone Weil's philosophy—not specifically indebted either to pragmatism (originating in the decades preceding her own life and work) or to liberation theology (which was to emerge into clear view several decades after her death)—indicates that there may be a quite natural link between any carefully and consistently developed ethics of attention and the affirmation of a preferential option for the poor. In a remarkable way, Weil appears to have identified and woven together most of the strands of thought here judged as crucial for theosemiotic. She acknowledged both the importance of cultivating a profound sense of detachment and the cardinal insight that "attention taken to its highest degree, is the same thing as prayer."[39] For Weil, as decisively as for Schelling, Emerson, Peirce, or Royce, "the world is a text with several meanings."[40] While far from advocating a "religion of science," nevertheless, she echoed Peirce in concluding that "a science which does not bring us nearer to God is worthless."[41] Weil also knew that our human interactions quite typically take the form of readings, that "we read, but also *we are read by*, others."[42] On her view, this all requires training, the arduous work of prayer, and necessarily eventuates in suffering. She recognized that the object of our love can be something absent, but that if we are transformed by that love it cannot be something imaginary.[43] This is the gist of Weil's "experimental ontological proof." If we direct our love to an ideal perfection and are really moved, lifted up by it, "then this something is real. No imaginary perfection can draw me upwards even by the fraction of an inch."[44]

Like the liberation theologians, Weil was influenced by Marx and Marxism in the way that she thought about the social, economic, and political conditions that create poverty, as well as about the mechanics of oppression.[45] Of primary importance here, however, is the manner in which such elements of Weil's thought blended with and were transformed by her theosemiotic perspective. Of all of the injustices to which the working poor have been subjected, she announced, "the worst outrage . . . is violation of the workers' attention"; this Weil judged to be a "sin against the spirit" and so "unforgivable," one that "destroys the faculty of soul which is the source of all spiritual action."[46] It is the loss of a capacity for true prayer. If paying attention to the condition of the poor is the first important thing that I can do in response to them, the key to my establishing any real solidarity with them, it must include an awareness of those respects in which their condition prevents them from full participation in the process of human selving. In an even more fundamental sense, however, the key to Simone Weil's theosemiotic is her insight about how when the attention is most perfectly fixed on anything at all, it will reveal the "contradiction" at the very depth of its being.[47] It will reveal the emptiness, the poverty that lurks everywhere, at the heart of everything that exists. Our link with the poor is not merely some feeling of sympathy or compassion; it is metaphysical, a real continuity that binds all things together, visible only to one who attends with the utmost vigilance and care.

The intention here is not to offer a detailed interpretation of Weil's thought, but rather to think *with* her for theosemiotic purposes, even if doing so runs the risk of obscuring the very real differences between her religious vision and that of other individuals treated in my brief history. Without exhausting the meaning embodied in this concept of contradiction, I want to suggest that it highlights the curious sense in which every sign is both a presence and an absence, something given and something signified. The iconic aspect of signs may cause us to linger over them a bit more, with their indexical features directing our attention rapidly and forcefully to something else. Yet all semiosis involves something (a sign) drawing attention to itself, even as it gestures elsewhere toward its object and even as it pays the gift of meaning forward to some interpretant. If deliberate, it involves the continuous sacrifice of what is now present to that which is just coming into being in the flow of time. This is the natural asceticism that lies at the heart of semiosis as a process of growth. Weil clearly grasped the meaning of such asceticism. "Except the seed die," she recalled from the Gospel of John. "It has to die in order to liberate the energy it bears within it so that with this energy new forms may be developed."[48] The seed must die in order to bear fruit. This is the gradual loss of intensity that corresponds to the growth of concrete reasonableness as described by Peirce's law of mind, a principle that here has been shown to be indissolubly linked to his agapism.

Asceticism is not something different from prayer, but only one way of understanding what it means to live a life of prayer, the kind of suffering that it must involve. This is not to suggest that all suffering must be embraced. (Some of Weil's sharpest critics suggest that she may have leaned dangerously in that direction.) Love's attentiveness should reveal both when suffering must be patiently endured and when it must be assuaged, its causes forcefully resisted. That is the ongoing task of discernment.

What is it that we expect a life of prayer to reveal? What is it that might be discerned at the heart of nature if one contemplates it in musement as Peirce suggested? Is it something personal as he concluded, or rather something cold and indifferent? Might it be both? Can these readings in any sense be complementary? Recognizing that self-deception can be motivated by wish-fulfillment may seem like a compelling reason to reject any idea of a God that seems to arise in the midst of our contemplation of a world of things. It seems so perfect a match for our needs and desires that such an idea would be affirmed as true. It seems uncomfortably close to what finite and often helpless creatures rushing toward death might wish to be true. What is the evidence of its truth or even of its plausibility?

On the other hand, is it possible that our needs and desires could constitute an odd form of evidence in support of just such a belief? Augustine seemed to think so. I suspect that Peirce did as well. Our deepest desires, our most basic needs and instincts, if also universal—that is, not yours or mine but *ours*—may tell us something fundamental about what it means to be human, to have been created as such, or (from the perspective that Peirce established on this topic) to have evolved as such. In contemplating what lies hidden in the icon, the meaning of what is revealed is at least partially rooted in ourselves, typically hidden in our "occult natures," but under the appropriate conditions made accessible. (Creating such conditions is also the task of discernment.)

If there is some merit to this way of thinking, then perhaps we need carefully to evaluate our understanding of *petitionary* prayer. On this issue, Peirce may not be our most reliable guide.[49] Musement for him could flower into a form of prayer, a communing with the divine Mind in nature, that he regarded as being very different from petitionary prayer. Yet if our basic desires and anxieties, indeed, if our *poverty* (in all of the forms in which it displays itself), are fundamental markers of who and what we are as human, then petitionary prayer speaks to this reality in a way that no other form of prayer can. The communion of self with self must always, at the very least, involve a recognition of who and what we are, our poverty and our basic human needs.

In pragmatic terms, human poverty is most assuredly a problem to be solved, but within the context of Peirce's intricate and capacious theory of inquiry this observation can be only a part of the story that needs to be told. It has repeatedly been urged here that one of the key purposes of inquiry, especially of the sort pursued in the humanities generally—and certainly for any theology conceived as theosemiotic—is the rendering problematic of what previously had not been recognized as such. This is always the first task of an ethics of attention. What then needs to be established in addition to such recognition is the real continuity of all persons with those who are poor, a continuity that in liberationist terms is most typically described as constituting some form of *solidarity*. The nature of solidarity might also be productively explored and illuminated within the context supplied by Peirce's synechism. If we are, metaphysically speaking, always already existing in continuity with one another—indeed, if it is the most vulgar of delusions to believe that "I am altogether myself and not at all you"—what more must it take to achieve a meaningful solidarity? I am suggesting that the catalyst in this movement from the metaphysical to the ethical is the formulation of a powerful habit of attention conceived as love. This is the habitus, the practical skill, that gives to cenoscopy as a mode of inquiry the determinate shape and efficacy that it must have in order to be useful for theosemiotic purposes. (To make such a point, of course, is nothing more than to echo Duns Scotus once again.)

H. Richard Niebuhr indicated his indebtedness both to Mead and to Buber when he affirmed that the self "has a social character; it can know itself and be itself only as it confronts another knower who knows the self. 'I' and 'Thou' belong together."[50] That persons exist only as *being toward* one another in this sense is just one way of parsing Peirce's much more radical perspective, his semiotic realism, anchored in the affirmation that "the very entelechy of reality is of the nature of a sign," thus also to invoke his anthropomorphism. Even if the universe does not consist exclusively of signs, nevertheless, everything is at least potentially significant, capable of being made meaningful. On Peirce's view, there is something personal and purposeful at the very heart and in the depth of nature; so too, as already shown, for Josiah Royce. This is but one way of reading the nature of things, of course, by no means canceling or precluding other possible readings. Among the central preoccupations shaping these deliberations has been the need to evaluate the plausibility of such a reading.

That goal cannot be accomplished in a book, even if the book were to be conceived as a kind of argument attempting to fill in the details of the sketch that Peirce himself provided in 1908. It could be accomplished to some extent by a life devoted to prayer, to *lectio divina*, a reading of oneself, of others, and of the world in which strands of religious meaning gradually become woven into a meaningful narrative and the self as living legisign comes to embody that meaning. To be cautious in evaluating such an outcome, this would by no means demonstrate the truth or accuracy of such a reading, its superiority to other readings—both those with which it might be regarded, in semiotic terms, as complementary and, more significantly, those with which it stands in open conflict. (Even here there is a need for judgment. Might it be possible at some level of vagueness to affirm the semiotic complementarity of personal and nonpersonal symbols of the ultimate reality?)[51] The question here is only about *plausibility*, and that question will be further resolved and the possibility of an answer much better established by a vast community of readers, sharing their interpretations, comparing and contrasting each with others.

Such is the work of theosemiotic. Once again, it is continuous with and flows naturally from out of the spiritual life of those who take up this particular form of labor. It stands in relation to the reading of our world and of our lives as literary criticism does to the reading of poems, plays, and novels—as an extension, clarification, and sometimes even a critique of such acts of reading. As a science, theosemiotic can hardly be a private exercise. The experiences of others, their readings and rereadings, will have as much value as one's own, even if access to the richness of their details is a bit more limited. Consequently, theosemiotic is inevitably comparative, just as it is always in some fundamental sense a theology of the spiritual life. That it is also preeminently a theology of praxis suggests that our finest and most articulate readings will take the form of meaningful behavior, of what we do, especially together in solidarity, the patterns of meaning that are woven into our conduct and our communal lives, bearing fruit in concrete relationships of love.

If the world is a text, then our first readings of it, while still perhaps in some vague sense a part of who we are, will long ago have faded from actual memory. Our ongoing experience of the world consists primarily of continuous acts of rereading. That we must engage in this continuous process is inevitable. That in doing so we will be guided by specific ideals, committed to a distinctive trajectory traced by love's teleology, is not so much a necessary state of affairs. Moreover, different religious traditions and communities will interpret love's purposes in different ways, since this teleology is thoroughly developmental, perhaps also differently at different times. Nevertheless, the *continuities* among such diverse readings have proven in some cases to be both remarkable and numerous, and it is the ongoing task of any theology as theosemiotic to expose and illuminate them.

Niebuhr's extended meditation on faith is again useful here. Faith is a complex notion, multifaceted, involving both belief and trust, but under Royce's tutelage, Niebuhr fastened most especially on its character as *fidelitas*. It is in "keeping faith" with others in community—while also continuously affirming and so renewing those ideals and purposes that we value as beloved—that the self exercises an important kind of freedom. Indeed, "selves are beings that are under the necessity of exercising this freedom if they would be selves."[52] The continuity of our commitment can become a living symbol of the continuity of all things. Now, it is true that the individual self and its commitments must eventually fade and vanish; but still, meaning grows.

Postlude: The Play of Musement

"Enter your skiff of musement, push off into the lake of thought, and leave the breath of heaven to swell your sail" (*CP* 6.461). With eyes open, fully awake, begin a conversation with yourself. Do not be alarmed if you discover that your mind is filled with questions. Do not judge it odd that it might be difficult to know how even to ask some of these questions. And do not be concerned that anyone else should join the conversation. Your ruminations echo with voices from even the distant past, and each thought's momentum anticipates communion *in futuro*. Many others are present as soon as this conversation begins.

It is the continuity of things that I want especially to observe, things linked in space or over time and in a great variety of ways. They are causes and effects, or resemble one another, or display a tendency to turn toward each other like lovers reaching for embrace. Yet they are separable by a concerted act of will, much more typically when attention fails, so that the real bond between one thing and another, the real significance of one thing for another, rapidly fades from view. How is it the case that signs so easily become reduced to things, empty and opaque, the gift of meaning offered again and again to one unable to receive it?

Must I begin as a reader with the book of nature writ large and the consideration of whole universes of experience as they relate one to another? No such constraint upon musement seems to be required. Obey only the law of liberty. Any nook or cranny of nature can launch the inquiry about to unfold. "The gorilla, the lion, the fish, the polyp, the tree, the crystal, the grain of dust, the atom" (*W1*: 114), each or any may serve as my starting point, equally well as the night sky filled with stars. One thing is continuous with another. One thing signifies another. Begin anywhere, but linger there only as long as the spirit of play allows. Take care not to be intrusive or to wear out your welcome.

So consider the lilacs just now coming into bloom. Consider lakes and rivers and oceans, ocean breezes and the rock or sand that forms a shore. Contemplate mountains and sky. Regard the animals that inhabit these various places, a great diversity of species, some so tiny that they themselves are hidden and no eye can see them. Acknowledge human beings, persons, their ideals and commitments, their kindness and their cruelty, their genius and their ignorance. Children and elders, but do not neglect the middle-aged. Fields and farms, cities, towns, and neighborhoods, houses and rooms, some remote, some nearby, as well as the place now present at hand. Consider machines and factories. Human waste and magnificent works of art. Traces of memory and whatever has not yet existed but might be imagined. Listen carefully. Attend to what can only be heard, like a whisper, or like a breath barely audible, with eyes closed or in the darkness. In this same darkness, attend to what is neither seen nor heard but can be felt, like an object soft or hard, smooth or rough. What about the presence of something that is known only by its aroma or its taste, perhaps subtly discerned? Become a cosmic *sommelier* with the universe perfused with signs as your wine cellar. Begin with a simple drinking in of impressions, clinging to none of them, and so always ready for whatever might next appear.

It is the playful letting go of things and of purposes that permits me to begin to see them in their deepest reality, also to recognize the purposes that actually shape and move them. This is not easy. What I want and think and believe will intrude on my musement constantly. Allow all of these a place in the conversation. But gently push them to the edges of consciousness and beg them for now to be silent. Their business will come later. This is a time for play. Once they fall silent, I no longer find myself looking for those things that interest me or that I prefer, those things and places and persons that I love. This is a peculiar habit of heart and mind quite difficult to establish. Do not look for anything in particular, but be open and ready for everything as it appears. Love what you happen to find. Even when contemplating the things that you know the best and love the most, be mindful to love what you find. This can be a disconcerting experience, but it should not be unnecessarily painful if my looking and finding is gently cushioned by the spirit of play.

How quickly, if at all, does such a love manifest itself as gratitude? Test and see. To whom should one be grateful? How much must one know or understand about the giver of a gift in order to experience genuine gratitude? Must there be a giver at all? Suppose that what is perceived as a gift lovingly given is nothing more than the froth or foam on a sea of serendipity. How does one meaningfully distinguish the serendipitous from the gratuitous? What causes me to perceive anything as a gift, therefore as the sign of a giver? By what luck or skill or chance or grace does the thing that stands before me first blossom into such a sign?

I can resist the notion that it is a sign altogether, contemplate it simply as a thing, perhaps linger in the warmth of its radiant beauty, or feel repulsed by its ugliness, or simply become bored by its everydayness. Nothing becomes a sign without my cooperation. Nothing bursts forth with meaning if I greet it with an empty stare. Perhaps this is the most natural way to be. Perhaps this is true indifference. Why project a world of meanings onto the brute suchness of this simple collection of things? Yet if anything is perceived as beautiful or ugly, must I not already have read it as a sign? Will it not already mean something? My boredom is a more complicated matter. Is this the only way to encounter with authenticity the simple fact of a thing as such? Or might even my boredom mean something by signifying nothing in particular, nevertheless, signifying after all?

Maybe the blank stare is not a true way of seeing, but rather a refusal to see things in their significance, their relationships. This way of looking might result from laziness, even from fatigue. Musement is a lively exercise of one's powers. It is a vigorous engagement with the world that can for a time leave one breathless. It is refreshing and a recreation but not necessarily restful, unlike daydreaming or sleep. Stay awake. Continue the conversation. Try to explain, in the clearest possible terms, what you are thinking and feeling, but do not limit yourself to expressing these with words. Feelings do not always need to be called by a name. Yet they supply a richness of meaning to the things that we encounter and experience. Pay attention. Even as your mind presses forward with new images and ideas, do not forget to listen.

Do I remember the conversation that marked the first moment of my falling in love? Did the falling occur only after a lapse into silence, or was it a part of the conversation itself? In musement, it seems natural to respond with love to the objects of one's attention. Everything can seem so fresh and new when engaged in this fashion. What is it that I love? This tree, this neighborhood, this idea, this person. Yet not in pristine isolation but as each speaks to each. To be sure, I love *this* one and not merely what it resembles or portends. But is it not the miracle of such a love that in this one thing, by looking deeply, I discover the world?

All things run their course and pass away in time. Sign yields to sign, defers to its successor in the constant flow of thought. Every sign is both a presence and an absence. The paradox of love is that it embraces both communion and sacrifice. Is this my love's circular movement, in steady rhythm alternating between harmony and otherness? Be careful. This is not *my* movement, nor the progress of another to whom I am beloved. It is love's movement. Is it possible for me to begin to trace such a circle as I contemplate a world of signs? Does each sign speak of it if I listen with extraordinary care?

Love crucified must experience the death of each moment, the constant passing into nothingness of everything that I now cherish and affirm. That is why the presence of my beloved always also signifies an absence, why the fullness of love always carries with it an ache and an emptiness. It is also why being drawn "into harmony" by love can sometimes be experienced as an immersion in mystery, a descent into darkness. Perhaps love is as strong as death because it knows death so intimately. Perhaps love is bound to death not because death is its dialectical "other," but rather, because death is its primordial essence, not a cold darkness (here an act of faith may be required), but a warmth without image or glow. Perhaps dying is itself a form of inquiry. Then what is the goal of inquiry thus conceived? Surely something more than doubt's removal, much more than the fixation of belief. ("Now, Lord, you may dismiss your servant in peace.")

And so in the process of musement "the idea of God's Reality will be sure sooner or later to be found an attractive fancy" (*CP* 6.465). Turn then toward a consideration of that hypothesis. Resist the temptation to evaluate its "truth"; that would be too "serious" a task for one engaged in musement. How should I go about the preliminary and more playful business of measuring its plausibility? That this hypothesis is a beautiful idea and one that I might have fallen in love with makes such a measurement complicated. In that condition, no question of plausibility would even be likely to arise. I can imagine how such a love might gently but persistently determine the way that I live my life, the choices that I make, and the manner in which I should respond to whatever or whomever life places in my path. In a more sober state of mind, when the time for play is over, I might evaluate what I imagine. Pragmatically speaking, this is all that the idea of "God" could possibly mean. Pragmatically speaking, choosing and responding in such a fashion would be the only way to test the plausibility of such a hypothesis.

Recall Ignatius's "two points" about love, points made before beginning the contemplation that brought his exercises to their culmination.

The first was that love manifests itself in deeds rather than words. This is the pragmatic point just registered, although in my own musement I want to consider the possible and powerful ways in which the human use of words can also be considered as deeds. The second point was about love's mutuality, its consisting in a mutual sharing of gifts. This is musement's teleology—that while it may begin with attention and delight, it achieves its consummation in "a lively give and take of communion between self and self" (*CP* 6.45). In what does such communion consist? Semiosis, to be sure, but not every exchange of signs will result in the achievement of communion. Is the trajectory discerned here inevitable for any exercise in musement, or is it specifically love's teleology, a possibility only in those cases where the muser happens to fall in love, or to fall in love again?

Why in order to describe such an experience do we talk about "falling"? Maybe because it is something that we both do and do not do, both a doing and a happening. Maybe neither. Falling in love is not something that I "do" (even if it later displays itself in acts of love). The birth of love is not something that just happens. These mysteries run deep. It is hard sometimes even to know how to ask the questions.

Look again for guidance. Ask with Augustine, "What do I love when I love my God?" And how is this love in me first awakened and then continuously renewed? What of mutuality? Is the gift of divine love one that can ever be returned? (If so, is death the only possible act of returning?) Or can it only be signified, at least a fragment of its meaning signified, and then extended to others? Is this the semiotic rationale for any theology that insists on the unity of love of God with love of neighbor? How could one hope to respond to the love of God in any other way than by turning oneself toward those others with whom one lives in communion?

Consider turning toward those others most especially, but then also toward everything or anything else that exists and might possibly serve as a sign. Call to mind all of the things that Augustine rejected at first as answers to his question, but then were returned to him as treasure when he had found an answer that satisfied. These are the very same things that Ignatius eventually celebrated as "blessings and gifts," even though at an earlier point in his meditations they could be regarded as dangerous distractions. (How is it the case that signs so easily become reduced to things, empty and opaque, the gift of meaning offered again and again to one unable to receive it?)

Imagine what may lie hidden in the icon. Signs function in various ways. They are most dramatically self-effacing when they move us with indexical force to pay attention to something other than themselves. They nudge us more gently toward a certain set of interpretations when they act as symbols. While the play of musement is not restricted to any one particular form of semiosis, surely it will tend to linger over the iconicity of things before moving onward to something else, inviting the muser to luxuriate in the presence of the signs themselves. What if this "something else" is not to be found by looking elsewhere? What if there is only darkness elsewhere, something real perhaps and an eventual resting place, but nothing in particular actually to be discerned? Do not rush to move on. Do not rush to abandon the play of signs as you watch its dance unfold. Stay and wait. (But only for just a while before playfully letting go, like a bee gathering nectar.) Watch and listen. Pay careful attention without expectation.

"God dwells in creatures," Ignatius proclaimed, not in some distant and ethereal realm to which these creatures point as signals, but in the very midst of them, the very heart of them. Consider what may lie hidden in the icon. Fix your attention there and exercise a self-control that allows for the purest form of play. Look for nothing in particular. Nothing may happen to arise during this playful contemplation from the depths of my "occult" nature. Something may happen to arise. Wait and see.

If indeed there is something meaningful that arises, it will be nothing that can be seized or grasped, firmly fixed in place and affirmed as the truth of the matter. It can, however, be celebrated. It is the gift of meaning first received and then shared. This sharing, the further development of meaning, its growth from the seed planted here in musement to full flowering, will take us beyond the space of play in order that we might do the work of love. Delight and gratitude will bear tangible fruit in compassion. It will sometimes be a sweaty business. It will inevitably involve suffering.

For this reason, but without need for a reason, it will be good to return to this space, for musement not to be sporadic but to become a faithful, regular exercise. It is in this fashion that the "freshness deep down things" might renew us when in our suffering we have become broken, or in our distraction we have become lost. The faithful reading again and again of a great poem still being written is the practice that might best enable us to catch a fragment of its meaning, a tiny fragment, nevertheless a gift of infinite generosity.

Consider myself as a sign. What do I signify? Where does my love gesture? What meaning do I serve? Why do the same kinds of questions keep presenting themselves to me with a stubborn persistence? Why is it so difficult to put them into words? What then must I do?

Acknowledgments

This book began as the germ of an idea in 1989; I turned seriously to the task of writing it in 2006. There have been distractions and delays along the way, some of them a source of pain and sadness, others the cause of unspeakable joy. But the overwhelming feeling that one has in finishing a project like this is profound gratitude for many gifts received during the task's execution—too many of them to be recorded within the brief space of these acknowledgments.

Tangible financial assistance can often double as moral support at a time when it is most crucially needed. In 2017, after several encounters and conversations at meetings of the Semiotic Society of America, Ray Zimmer sent me a very generous check—totally unexpected, actually quite astonishing—along with a note suggesting that, from what he had heard me say about my plan for *Theosemiotic*, I was going to need all the help I could get. He was right. I am eternally grateful. I only hope that I did not disappoint him with the result. The National Endowment for the Humanities supplied me with a summer research stipend in 2010 to support my work on this book when it was still in its early stages of development. A Faculty Research Grant from Lehigh University in 2019 was icing on the cake.

The late Helen Tartar, of Fordham University Press, was one of the first people to express enthusiasm for my project. She invited my proposal to the Press and both warmly encouraged and gently prodded me until her tragic and untimely death in an automobile accident in 2014. Richard Morrison graciously assumed responsibility for guiding this book to completion, with the capable assistance of John Garza. In the later stages of my work, Eric Newman and Aldene Fredenburg navigated my way through the book's editing and production. I owe all of them an enormous debt of gratitude.

During the last thirty-plus years, my conversations and correspondence with those individuals who populate the tiny but vibrant community of scholars devoted to exploring the religious significance of Peirce's ideas have been a source of continuous stimulation and often inspiration. Most of these individuals have been identified in an endnote attached to my Preface. For their generous and thoughtful comments written after the review of a complete draft of this book, I especially want to thank Robert Neville and Douglas Anderson. I first met Bob and Doug at the Peirce Sesquicentennial Congress at Harvard University in 1989, and my admiration for both of them has continuously deepened, as I have leaned heavily on their work and insights ever since.

I am surrounded by another small community of scholars at Lehigh University, where I have served on the faculty since 1985. To the members of the Religion Studies Department, both present and past, I want to express appreciation for their friendship and collegiality, as well as their commitment to the highest standards of scholarship. (This includes a few "honorary" members—you know who you are.) Gordon Bearn in the Philosophy Department has been my most important interlocutor at Lehigh regarding all things Peircean; teaching an undergraduate seminar on Peirce together in 2017 was as fun as it was foolhardy. Our conversations are treasure for me.

The greatest debt that I owe to any community is one to my family. As we lived together in Massachusetts during the last several months of our mother's life, in the late spring and summer of 2017, my sisters Connie and Kathy were patient and encouraging as I struggled to find fragments of time and psychic space to continue work on this project. My children Daniel, Elizabeth, and Rosemary are for me a great source of pride, still the "precious jewels" in my life that I celebrated in a book dedicated to them in 2003, but now also one of my most important communities of inquiry. No jewel shines more brightly, no partner in inquiry could be more exemplary, than my wife, Mary Ellen. As this project was in its final stages, we marked the fortieth year of a marriage that represents my life's greatest miracle.

This book is dedicated to my teacher Murray Murphey, who died in December 2018 at the age of ninety and shortly after the publication of a volume on Thorsten Veblen that culminated an astonishing scholarly career. His 1961 book on Peirce, of course, is and will remain a prominent intellectual landmark. I have learned little about Peirce that he did not teach me.

The book is also dedicated to my grandson Tobin, born earlier that same year in January. Less than two years old as I write these acknowledgments, he has already mastered the use of indexical signs and demonstrated an extraordinary capacity to shape the attention of everyone around him. My greatest satisfaction in completing this project is that I will now have more time and energy to pay that sort of attention, hopefully to catch just a glimpse of what it looks like to see the world through his eyes.

Some of the material in this book is adapted from articles and essays previously published elsewhere. None of this material is included here without significant revision for the purposes of the book, but in instances where it does occur, the earlier publication has been identified in an endnote.

Michael L. Raposa
August 24, 2019

Notes

Preface

1. Michael L. Raposa, *Peirce's Philosophy of Religion* (Bloomington: Indiana University Press, 1989).

2. Raposa, *Boredom and the Religious Imagination* (Charlottesville: University of Virginia Press, 1999), and *Meditation and the Martial Arts* (Charlottesville: University of Virginia Press, 2003).

3. I refer here, in particular, to Douglas Anderson, Charles Conway, Robert Corrington, Hermann Deuser, Anette Ejsing, Robert King, Felicia Kruse, Gesche Linde, Robert Neville, Peter Ochs, David Pfeiffer, and Roger Ward. More recently, a growing community of younger scholars have thoughtfully engaged my ideas about Peirce and theosemiotic as they have worked to develop their own philosophical and theological perspectives: Benjamin Chicka, Brandon Daniel-Hughes, Rory Misiewicz, Leon Niemoczynski, David Rohr, and Gary Slater.

4. I would contend, however, that Deleuze's Scotism is frequently misrepresented and should be regarded as interesting in its own right. Moreover, attention to Scotus and Scotism might provide a useful point of contact between Catholic and Protestant theology as each has evolved in the post-Reformation period.

Prolegomena

1. Rulon Wells made this argument in a cautionary tale published as "Criteria for Semiosis," in *A Perfusion of Signs*, edited by Thomas Sebeok (Bloomington: Indiana University Press, 1977), 1–21. I will argue here that a sign exists only when it can be shown to have both an object and an interpretant—such triadicity is essential for semiosis. My emphasis is on semiosis as a process rather than on the identification of discrete things as "signs" or "sign vehicles." Moreover, the being of anything is not exhausted by its also being regarded as a sign.

2. See Gerard Manley Hopkins's poem, "God's Grandeur," in *Gerard Manley Hopkins: Poems and Prose*, edited by W. H. Gardner (London: Penguin, 1953), 27.

3. For an extended treatment of this topic, consider my discussion in Raposa, *Boredom and the Religious Imagination* (Charlottesville: University of Virginia Press, 1999), most especially in Chapter 5, on "Boredom, Semiosis, and Spiritual Exercises."

4. I have previously explored how verbal artworks, in particular, can be conceived as cognitive toys inviting their readers to engage in interpretive play; see Raposa, "Art, Religion, and Musement," *Journal of Aesthetics and Art Criticism* 42 (Summer 1984): 427–37.

5. "Metaboly," like "perfusion," is a term that Peirce used metaphorically to describe semiosis as a *process*. Like the latter term, its literal or root meaning is biological, denoting the ability of some cells to transform, to alter their shape.

6. Edwards described the rubrics for such experimentation most carefully in *A Treatise Concerning Religious Affections*, edited by John E. Smith (New Haven, Conn.: Yale University Press, 1959). My proposal that Peirce intended the practice of musement to function as a kind of experiment is articulated in *Peirce's Philosophy of Religion*, 134.

7. The contemporary neo-pragmatist Robert Brandom, while admitting that he has some limited use in his philosophy for a properly rehabilitated concept of "representation," announced that he has none at all for the concept of "experience," the latter being a word that does not even appear once in his magnum opus, *Making It Explicit: Reasoning, Representing, and Discursive Commitment* (Cambridge, Mass.: Harvard University Press, 1998). See Brandom, *Perspectives on Pragmatism* (Cambridge, Mass.: Harvard University Press, 2011), 197.

8. In *CP* 5.402, note 2, Peirce made this reference to Jesus's advice, reported in Matthew 7:16, about how best to evaluate the authenticity of religious teachers and teachings.

9. For an illuminating account of the broad range of cognitive activities that can be designated as examples of "reading," consult James F. Ross, "On the Concepts of Reading," *Philosophical Forum* 6 (Fall 1972): 93–141.

10. The relationship between redundancy, habit formation, and interpretive skill is the topic of Chapter 4, on "Ritual, Redundancy, and the Religious Imagination," in Raposa, *Boredom and the Religious Imagination*.

11. Even when the emphasis is on self-transformation, from a properly theosemiotic perspective this will be understood, in Dewey's terms, less as a passive or simple "accommodation" to presently existing environmental circumstances than as a religiously active "adjustment" that permits the self to live in harmony with a continuously changing universe. See John Dewey, *A Common Faith* (New Haven, Conn.: Yale University Press, 1934), especially 15ff. (For more on how Dewey understood the complex relationship between self and environment, see the discussion in Chapter 4, section III, of this volume.)

1 / A Brief History of Theosemiotic

This chapter represents the significantly expanded version of an essay published earlier as "A Brief History of Theosemiotic: From Scotus through Peirce and Beyond," in *The Varieties of Transcendence: Pragmatism and the Theory of Religion*, edited by Hermann Deuser, Hans Joas, Matthias Jung, and Magnus Schlette (New York: Fordham University Press, 2016), 142–57.

1. William A. Clebsch, *American Religious Thought: A History* (Chicago: University of Chicago Press, 1973), xvi.

2. Clebsch tended to contrast the aesthetic concerns of this group of thinkers with the emphasis on morality, ritual, and dogma that was characteristic of much of Puritan theology.

3. Olaf Pedersen, *The Book of Nature* (Notre Dame, Ind.: University of Notre Dame Press, 1992).

4. Here my own use of the word "language" might be considered metaphorical. Not all signs were linguistic on Peirce's account, human languages representing only one among many possible forms of semiosis. To the extent that one insists that "texts" must be written in some kind of language, narrowly conceived, Peirce's description of the universe as a poetic text would, of course, remain metaphorical.

5. See the exchange published in *SS*, especially 77.

6. As reported in Joseph Brent's biography *Charles Sanders Peirce: A Life* (Bloomington: Indiana University Press, 1993), 45.

7. In an autobiographical fragment, Peirce actually indicated that one of his earliest memories as a young boy was being in the audience when Emerson delivered his lecture on "Nature." See *MS* 1606 for his brief report of this recollection.

8. Ralph Waldo Emerson and Henry David Thoreau, *Nature/Walking* (Boston: Beacon Press, 1991), 32.

9. Ibid., 29.

10. Ibid.; see Chapter 3 on "Beauty."

11. Ibid., 20.

12. Ibid., 7.

13. See Emerson's *Miscellanies* (Boston and New York: Houghton, Mifflin, 1904), 486.

14. The philosophical wrestling with this "problem" has a long history. Most recently, the discussion has been spurred by the atheistic conclusions presented by J. L. Schellenberg in *Divine Hiddenness and Human Reason* (Ithaca, N.Y.: Cornell University Press, 1993). Schellenberg's argument stimulated a flurry of responses, many of them published in two volumes devoted to the topic: *Divine Hiddenness: New Essays*, edited by Daniel Howard-Snyder and Paul Moser (Cambridge: Cambridge University Press, 2001); and *Hidden Divinity and Religious Belief,* edited by Adam Green and Eleonore Stump (Cambridge: Cambridge University Press, 2015). Michael Rea devoted his 2017 Gifford Lectures to this topic, later published as Michael Rea, *The Hiddenness of God* (Oxford: Oxford University Press, 2018).

15. In the Gospel of Matthew 18:3.

16. These notions that a "return" to the spirit of childhood is especially propitious for achieving religious insight and that a properly developed or adjusted relationship between what is "inward" with what is "external" to the self is crucial for discernment are themes that will be woven into the fabric of this discussion as it unfolds. See, especially, Chapter 6.

17. Emerson, *Nature*, 7.

18. Ibid., 31.

19. Consider Emerson's observation, recorded at the end of the essay on *Nature* (65), that prayer is "also a study of truth. . . . No man ever prayed heartily, without learning something."

For an interesting comparison of Emerson and Peirce, underscoring how for both thinkers knowledge results when "we subject ourselves to the discipline of nature," when we experience the "physical blow" of encounter with what Peirce would call the "dynamic object" of a sign, refer to Richard A. Smyth's account in *Reading Peirce Reading* (London: Rowman and Littlefield, 1997), 78–80. Note, also, Smyth's illuminating claim that "Peirce's child is simply an Aristotelian (and Emersonian) naturalist" (81).

20. This is the analysis that is presented with meticulous care in Edwards's treatise on *Religious Affections*.

21. Jonathan Edwards, *Images or Shadows of Divine Things*, edited by Perry Miller (New Haven, Conn.: Yale University Press, 1948).

22. Edwards, *The Nature of True Virtue* (Ann Arbor: University of Michigan Press, 1960).

23. Ibid., 28.

24. Ibid., 2.

25. Ibid., 3.

26. Ibid., 11.

27. For evidence of Edwards's idealism, examine his youthful notes on "The Mind," included in *Scientific and Philosophical Writings: The Works of Jonathan Edwards*, vol. 6, edited by Wallace E. Anderson (New Haven, Conn. Yale University Press, 1980).

28. Consider Peirce's assertion, in a letter written to Lady Welby in 1909, that freedom of the will consists essentially in the "Freedom to become Beautiful. . . . There is no freedom to be or to do anything else" (*SS*: 112). Such a claim resonates with Jonathan Edwards's talk about how saints transformed by God's grace radiate a distinctive kind of beauty.

29. See Mary Beth Ingham's discussion in *The Harmony of Goodness: Mutuality and Moral Living according to John Duns Scotus* (Quincy, Ill.: Franciscan Press, 1996), especially 22–24. For development of the idea that all beings are "essentially ordered" to everything else that exists, consult Duns Scotus's *A Treatise on God as First Principle*, translated by Allan Wolter (Chicago: Franciscan Herald Press, 1966).

30. As an especially clear example of the many places where Peirce indicated his indebtedness to Duns Scotus, consider *CP* 1.6. The classic early account of this relationship is John Boler's *Charles Peirce and Scholastic Realism: A Study of Peirce's Relation to John Duns Scotus* (Seattle: University of Washington Press, 1963). My own account, appearing in Chapter 2 of *Peirce's Philosophy of Religion*, is adapted from my earlier essay on "Habits and Essences," *Transactions of the Charles S. Peirce Society* 20 (1984): 147–67.

31. F. W. J. Schelling, *System of Transcendental Idealism (1800)*, translated by Peter Heath (Charlottesville: University Press of Virginia, 1978), 12 and 232.

32. For a more detailed analysis of Peirce's distinction between God as primordial no-thing and the text of nature that symbolizes the purposes of a mind, if not "supreme," yet certainly a "Deity relatively to us" (*CP* 5.107), see *Peirce's Philosophy of Religion* (Bloomington: Indiana University Press, 1989), 54–62, 70–71, and 117–23.

Robert Neville, in a brief discussion of Spinoza's thought, has also described the relationship between *natura naturans* and *natura naturata* in explicitly semiotic terms. See his *Philosophical Theology*, vol. 2, *Existence* (Albany: SUNY Press, 2014), 247.

33. Although he mentions Schiller but never refers explicitly to Spinoza as a resource in his development of the idea, Peirce's description of how the love of God arises in musement displays features that resonate with Spinoza's own portrayal of the highest form of blessedness as consisting in the "intellectual love of God."

34. Mauricio Beuchot and John Deely, "Common Sources for the Semiotic of Charles Peirce and John Poinsot," *Review of Metaphysics* 48 (March 1995): 539–66.

It should be noted that one of the medieval texts upon which Peirce drew heavily, Thomas of Erfurt's *Grammatica Speculativa*, was mistakenly identified (by Peirce and most others at the time) as a work of Duns Scotus. For a general assessment of these medieval influences on Peirce's theory of signs, consider Claudine Tiercelin's "The Importance of Medievals in the Constitution of Peirce's Semeiotic and Thought-Sign Theory," in *Semiotics and Philosophy in Charles Sanders Peirce*, edited by Rossella Fabbrichesi and Susanna Marietti (Cambridge Scholars, 2006), 158–84.

35. Consult John Doyle's translation of *The Conimbricenses: Some Questions on Signs* (Milwaukee, Wisc.: Marquette University Press, 2001), 89.

36. Dominik Perler offers a very clear evaluation of the relevance of Scotus's idea of essentially ordered causes for his theory of signs, in "Duns Scotus on Signification," *Medieval Philosophy and Theology* 3 (1993): 97–120. Scotus's primary use of the concept was in his understanding of the relation between God and creation, most notably in his articulation of an argument for God's existence. Such a deployment of the idea should also be regarded as significant for theosemiotic purposes. Moreover, it is important to emphasize further how—for Scotus but clearly also for Peirce—the efficient and final causes of a thing are perceived to be essentially ordered.

37. See Allan B. Wolter and Oleg V. Bychkov's glossary attached to their translation of John Duns Scotus, *The Examined Report of the Paris Lecture: Reportation I-A* (St. Bonaventure, N.Y.: Franciscan Institute, 2004), 606.

38. What Peirce sometimes referred to as a "pure index" might seem to represent an exception to this claim, a counterexample in the form of a sign that *does* seem to denote its object by a kind of "brute force" or "blind compulsion." But in fact, Peirce doubted that it was possible to find an instance of an "absolutely pure index" (*CP* 2.306), such a conception being arrived at only by prescinding from what we observe of the actual operation of signs.

39. Of all of the medieval scholastics, Duns Scotus defended the most strongly realistic theory of relations. See the analysis in Mark G. Henninger's *Relations: Medieval Theories 1250-1325* (Oxford: Clarendon, 1989), Chapter 5.

40. Perler, "Duns Scotus on Signification," 110ff.

41. See Doyle's introduction to *Conimbricenses*, 15–29; also John Deely's *Medieval Philosophy Redefined* (Scranton, Pa.: University of Scranton Press, 2010), especially Chapter 10.

42. Doyle, *Conimbricenses*. The assertion is quoted by Doyle on the bottom of page 18 of his Introduction, and the influence of this way of thinking about signs on philosophers from Poinsot to Peirce is briefly discussed in the pages that follow.

43. Augustine, *St. Augustine's City of God and Christian Doctrine: A Select Library of Nicene and Post-Nicene Fathers of the Christian Church*, vol. 2 (Grand Rapids, Mich.: Eerdmans, 1984), edited by Philip Schaff, translated by Marcus Dods, Book 2, Chapter 1:1. (Gesche Linde's generous comments in response to an earlier draft of this chapter helped me to appreciate the special relevance of Augustine for any presentation either of Peirce's theory of signs or of the history of semiotic. John Deely argued for such relevance in numerous publications, emphasizing Augustine's pioneering attempt to bridge the gap between nature and culture by formulating a truly general theory of signs.)

44. This is a conception of the "objective" that is *not* attained by means of simple contrast with subjectivity. For a useful discussion, consult Paul Bains, *The Primacy of Semiosis* (Toronto: University of Toronto Press, 2006), 50–53.

45. Ignatius of Loyola, *The Spiritual Exercises of St. Ignatius*, translated by Louis J. Puhl (Chicago: Loyola University Press, 1951).

46. For Ignatius's discussion of consolation and desolation, consult his "Rules for the Discernment of Spirits," in the *Spiritual Exercises*, sections 313ff.

47. I have explored the importance of the role played by *attention* in both intuitive and abstractive cognition, in "Poinsot on the Semiotics of Awareness," *American Catholic Philosophical Quarterly* 68, no. 3 (1994): 395–408.

48. Edwards, *A Treatise Concerning Religious Affections*, edited by John E. Smith (New Haven, Conn.: Yale University Press, 1959), 406. My earliest discussion of Edwards's theosemiotic appeared in "Jonathan Edwards' Twelfth Sign," *International Philosophical Quarterly* 33, no. 2 (1993): 154–62.

49. Jonathan Edwards, *The Distinguishing Marks of a Work of the Spirit of God*, in *The Great Awakening: The Works of Jonathan Edwards*, edited by C. C. Goen (New Haven, Conn.: Yale University Press, 1972), 4:238.

50. These arguments were developed in two important early (1868) essays, published in the *Journal of Speculative Philosophy*, where Peirce first laid the groundwork for his theory of semiotic. See Peirce, "Questions Concerning Certain Faculties Claimed for Man" and "Some Consequences of Four Incapacities," in *CP* 5.213–317; also *W*2: 193–242.

51. For an approach to American pragmatism that in a number of key respects is congenial with the one that I take here, consider Joan Richardson's *Pragmatism and American Experience: An Introduction* (Cambridge: Cambridge University Press, 2014). I refer the reader, in particular, to Richardson's portrayal of pragmatism as a form of therapy, one that promotes healing by the manner in which it directs attention, and to pragmatism's emphasis on meta-cognition, as a method or way of "thinking about thinking." (These pragmatic aspects of theosemiotic are treated most fully here in the discussion of this book's central chapter, Chapter 4, "Theology as Inquiry, Theory, Praxis.")

52. This brief discussion of Duns Scotus's pragmatism is adapted from my essay entitled "Pragmatism, Democracy and the Future of Catholic Theology," published in the *American Journal of Theology and Philosophy* 30, no. 3 (September 2009): 288–302. That essay was itself the development of some insights first articulated several years earlier in "The Uses of Pragmatism in Modern Theology," in *Theologie Zwischen Pragmatismus und Existenzdenken: Festschrift fur Hermann Deuser*, edited by G. Linde, R. Purkarthofer, H. Schulze, and P. Steinacker (Marburg: N. G. Elwert Verlag, 2006), 13–24.

53. John Duns Scotus, *Duns Scotus on the Will and Morality*, edited by Allan Wolter (Washington, D.C.: The Catholic University of America Press, 1986), 137.

54. Quoted by Nicholas Lobkowicz, in *Theory and Practice: History of a Concept from Aristotle to Marx* (Notre Dame, Ind.: University of Notre Dame Press, 1967), 79.

55. William James, *The Varieties of Religious Experience* (New York: Penguin, 1982).

56. See Edwards's *Religious Affections*, 422–23, along with my discussion in "Jonathan Edwards' Twelfth Sign," 155.

57. The Jesuit ideal of "contemplation in action," inspired by the theology of Ignatius of Loyola as founder of the Jesuits, suggests that, at least in this respect, Ignatius was the same kind of pragmatist as William James. Gustavo Gutierrez, given his warm embrace of such an ideal, also leans toward pragmatism.

58. In James's *Varieties*, Lectures 6 and 7.

59. I suspect that Deleuze's philosophy, among contemporary perspectives, represents one of the more promising resources for addressing this question, not exactly for the sake of enhancing "precision," but for the purpose of generating further insight. Not only are the boundaries of the self not clearly delineated for Deleuze, moreover, the background against which any kind of "selving" might occur seems to be one describable in semiotic terms. Consider the reference to "the constellation of voices . . . from which I draw my voice," in Gilles Deleuze and Felix Guattari, *A Thousand Plateaus: Capitalism and Schizophrenia*, translated by Brian Massumi (Minneapolis: University of Minnesota Press, 1987), 84.

Compare, also, Peirce's characterization of the self as a "bundle of habits" with the attentiveness in Deleuze to "not only the sensory-motor habits that we have (psychologically), but also, before these, the primary habits that we are; the thousands of passive syntheses of which we are organically composed." See Deleuze, *Difference and Repetition*, translated by Paul Patton (New York: Columbia University Press, 1994), 74.

60. Emerson, "The Poet," in *Essays and Lectures* (New York: Library of America, 1983), 456.

61. Most especially in Part II of Josiah Royce's *The Problem of Christianity* (Chicago: University of Chicago Press, 1968).

62. Royce elucidated his understanding of the human self in reference to the idea of commitment to a "life-plan" in numerous writings, but perhaps most notably in his book on *The Philosophy of Loyalty* (Nashville, Tenn.: Vanderbilt University Press, 1995).

63. For an illuminating treatment of Royce's philosophy of religion that concludes by evaluating it as superior to certain other approaches, examine Wayne Proudfoot's *God and the Self: Three Types of Philosophy of Religion* (Lewisburg, Pa.: Bucknell University Press, 1976), especially Chapters 4 and 5.

64. Royce, *Problem of Christianity*, 390n1. For an extended discussion of Royce's relation to Peirce's project, consult my two earlier essays, "In the Presence of the Universe: Peirce, Royce, and Theology as Theosemiotic," *Harvard Theological Review* 103, no. 2 (April 2010): 237–47, and "Loyalty, Community, and the Task of Attention: On Royce's 'Third Attitude of the Will,'" *American Journal of Theology and Philosophy* 37, no. 2 (May 2016): 109–22.

Several books have been published that deal with the Peirce/Royce relationship in much greater detail than I offer in these two essays. Frank Oppenheim is the author of two of these, *Royce's Mature Philosophy of Religion* (Notre Dame, Ind.: University of Notre Dame Press, 1987), and *Reverence for the Relations of Life: Re-imagining Pragmatism via Josiah Royce's Interactions with Peirce, James, and Dewey* (Notre Dame, Ind.: University of Notre Dame Press, 2005). For a book published more recently, and perhaps advancing the most provocative argument concerning the nature of this relationship, see Randall Auxier, *Time, Will, and Purpose: Living Ideas from the Philosophy of Josiah Royce* (Chicago: Open Court, 2013).

65. Niebuhr was influenced by Peirce's ideas as he encountered them in the writings of both Royce and Mead. Mead's understanding of Peirce, however, was very probably also largely mediated by Josiah Royce. See Hans Joas, *G. H. Mead: A Contemporary Re-examination of His Thought* (Cambridge, Mass.: MIT Press, 1997), 98–99. As evidence of the influence of all three thinkers, observe how Niebuhr conceived of the life of faith in triadic terms as involving the self, some other, and a common object of concern.

66. H. Richard Niebuhr, *The Kingdom of God in America* (New York: Harper and Brothers, 1956), 164.

67. Niebuhr, *Theology, History, and Culture: Major Unpublished Writings*, edited by William Stacy Johnson (New Haven, Conn.: Yale University Press, 1996), 21. The Cole Lectures, entitled "The Position of Theology Today," "Toward New Symbols," and "Toward the Recovery of Feeling," appear on pages 3–49 as the first three items in this collection.

68. Royce, *Philosophy of Loyalty*; and refer to my comments appearing in both *Meditation and the Martial Arts*, 140–43, and "In the Presence of the Universe."

69. Most important, for present purposes, are Niebuhr's *Radical Monotheism and Western Culture* (New York: Harper and Row, 1970); *The Responsible Self* (New York: Harper and Row, 1963); and the essays published posthumously both in *Theology, History, and Culture* and as *Faith on Earth: An Inquiry into the Structure of Human Faith* (New Haven, Conn.: Yale University Press, 1991). On the importance of the "Will to Interpret" as a precondition for establishing the community of interpretation, consult Royce's *Problem of Christianity*, 318.

70. Another important thinker to consider, also influenced by Royce in this regard, is the French Catholic existentialist Gabriel Marcel. See his *Creative Fidelity*, translated by Robert Rosthal (New York: Fordham University Press, 2002).

71. Simone Weil, *Gravity and Grace* (London: Routledge and Kegan Paul, 1952), 90. I want to suggest that theosemiotic is in one sense simply an elaboration and extension of this peculiar form of the ontological argument, the ingredients of which are also embedded in Jonathan Edwards's philosophical theology and elsewhere.

72. Although my interests and emphases are quite different from his, nevertheless, Christopher D. Tirres offers a useful comparison of liberation theology and philosophical pragmatism in the Americas. (For Tirres, Dewey among the pragmatists, rather than Peirce, represents the primary point of contact with liberation thought.) Consult Tirres on *The Aesthetics and Ethics of Faith: A Dialogue between Liberationist and Pragmatic Thought* (Oxford: Oxford University Press, 2014).

73. In particular, Gustavo Gutierrez, *A Theology of Liberation* (Maryknoll, N.Y.: Orbis, 1972), and *We Drink from Our Own Wells: The Spiritual Journey of a People* (Maryknoll, N.Y.: Orbis: 2002).

74. While Gutierrez is being singled out here for special emphasis, Enrique Dussel's philosophy of liberation also displays features consistent with a theosemiotic emphasis. Not only does Dussel identify the pragmatists—including Peirce specifically—as an important resource for his own work, in his writing he also thoughtfully engages the contemporary German philosophers Karl-Otto Apel and Jurgen Habermas, both influenced in important ways by Peirce and Royce. His work and writings help to expose the natural affinity between a liberation theology and any theosemiotic properly grounded in philosophical pragmatism. See Dussel's *Ethics of Liberation: In the Age of Globalization and Exclusion* (Durham, N.C.: Duke University Press, 2013). Apel is one of the individuals to whom this book dedicated. A brief discussion of Peirce's pragmatism in relation to the ethics of liberation appears on 160–66.

2 \ Signs, Selves, and Semiosis

1. The original idea that persons are complex signs is Peirce's, although the discussion here will not be totally confined to his elaboration of it. The classic analysis of this idea in Peirce's philosophy, one to which I am gratefully indebted, is embodied in Vincent Colapietro's *Peirce's Approach to the Self: A Semiotic Perspective on Human Subjectivity* (Albany: State University of New York Press, 1989). See also John E. Smith's important essay on "Signs, Selves and Interpretation," reprinted in *America's Philosophical Vision* (Chicago: University of Chicago Press, 1992).

2. For two very different but (I think) complementary perspectives on the nature of human beings as *homo symbolicus*, consult Ernst Cassirer, *An Essay on Man: An Introduction to a Philosophy of Human Culture* (New Haven, Conn.: Yale University Press, 1944); and more recently, Terrence W. Deacon, *The Symbolic Species: The Co-Evolution of Language and the Brain* (New York: W.W. Norton, 1997).

3. Peirce did on occasion refer to the "stream" of thought, as well as to the "train" of thought. The metaphor of a stream is probably more closely associated with William James's portrayal of consciousness, but fits Peirce's account as well.

4. Peirce himself supplied an alternative metaphor for the self when he portrayed the stream of thought that constitutes human reasoning not as a simple, single chain, but rather, as a "cable whose fibers may be ever so slender, provided they are sufficiently numerous and intimately connected" (*CP* 5.265; *W*2: 213).

5. Admittedly, James used this memorable phrase in order to characterize an infant's experience prior to the development of a certain ability to discriminate among sensations. Even in an adult's consciousness, however, there will be limits to this capacity, in any give instance, the experience of more or less "confusion," more or less competition for one's attention. See James's *The Principles of Psychology* (New York: Dover, 1950), 1:488.

6. Søren Kierkegaard, *The Sickness unto Death*, translated by Alastair Hannay (London and New York: Penguin, 1989), 43.

7. I am indebted to Robert S. Corrington's brilliant explication of this concept of "selving"; see especially throughout his *A Semiotic Theory of Theology and Philosophy* (Cambridge: Cambridge University Press, 2000). Corrington, in turn, has indicated his own indebtedness to Gerard Manley Hopkins as the original source of both the word and idea.

8. Consider, for example, Norbert Wiley's somewhat misleading claim that "Peirce is the first major philosopher to define human beings without including the body," in his book on *Inner Speech and the Dialogical Self* (Philadelphia, Pa.: Temple University Press, 2016), 121.

9. A number of Peirce's commentators (perhaps T. L. Short most notably) have argued that it is inaccurate to characterize Peirce as an "objective idealist" throughout his philosophical career. They contend that this label is most apt for certain cosmological speculations in which he engaged in the 1890s, but not particularly useful for understanding his thought before or after. I would reject such arguments, but would also suggest that "semiotic realism" may provide a more useful designation for Peirce's metaphysical perspective.

10. Some of these symbols can also be interpretants. We can interpret with our active bodies as a dancer does with music or a martial artist does in response to some attack; see Michael L. Raposa, *Meditation and the Martial Arts* (Charlottesville: University of Virginia Press, 2003), especially Chapters 1 and 2.

11. This Peircean distinction between the "body" and the "soul" of a sign might be fruitfully analyzed against the background provided by Duns Scotus's theory of a "plurality of forms," which allows for a distinction between the form of the body (*forma corporeitatis*) and the form of the soul that animates that body.

12. Clarence Irving Lewis, *An Analysis of Knowledge and Valuation* (LaSalle, Ill.: Open Court, 1946), 72.

13. Peirce consistently rejected such a reduction. Refer, for example, to SS: 112, where he declares that "language is only the extreme form of expression."

14. The nature of this special form of causality involved in a sign being "determined" by its object or one sign "determining" another as its interpretant was never made perfectly clear in Peirce's writings. As the analysis here will suggest, it involves a certain form of constraint, a delimiting of possibilities. While there may be an element of secondness, of efficient causality, that is operative in such instances of determination, the constraining force can also be a good deal gentler, especially in cases where the sign in question is an icon or symbol rather than an index.

15. The insight that "selving" involves struggle and risk supplied much of the rationale for my discussion of martial spirituality in Raposa, *Meditation and the Martial Arts*.

16. In an astronomical version of the metaphor depicting the self as a vicinity or neighborhood (appearing in an unpublished manuscript), Peirce once described a person as being "like a cluster of stars." For an insightful commentary, see Rossella Fabbrichessi, "A Person is Like a Cluster of Stars," in *Charles Sanders Peirce in His Own Words*, edited by Torkild Thellefsen and Bent Sorensen (Berlin: Walter de Gruyter, 2014), 165–68.

17. In *Peirce's Approach to the Self*, Colapietro provides the helpful description of another important difference between James and Peirce regarding the *privacy* of human consciousness, which James affirmed and Peirce vigorously denied. See especially 37–38, 62–63.

18. James, *Principles of Psychology*, 1:291.

19. An interesting account of what the author refers to as the "Peirce-Mead Synthesis" can be located in Wiley's *The Semiotic Self* (Chicago: University of Chicago Press, 1994), especially in Chapters 2 and 3.

20. Josiah Royce, *The Problem of Christianity* (Chicago: University of Chicago Press, 1968), 287.

21. Ibid., 253.

22. I allude here to the criticism made first by John E. Smith, in his introductory essay to *Problem of Christianity*, 28–30, that Royce conflates "comparison" with "interpretation" in a way that does not pay proper attention to the importance of time-order in the latter. But this does nothing to detract from the claim that Royce's represents the first serious attempt to develop Peirce's ideas for the purposes of theosemiotic.

23. George Herbert Mead, *The Philosophy of the Act* (Chicago: University of Chicago Press, 1938), 445.

24. Mead, *Mind, Self, and Society* (Chicago: University of Chicago Press, 1934), 136.

25. Mead, *On Social Psychology* (Chicago: University of Chicago Press, 1964), 204.

26. Josiah Royce, *The Philosophy of Loyalty* (Nashville, Tenn.: Vanderbilt University Press, 1995), 78–81.

27. Mikhail Bakhtin developed his dialogical theory of the self in numerous writings, perhaps most notably in Bakhtin, *The Dialogic Imagination: Four Essays by M. M. Bakhtin*, edited by Michael Holquist, translated by Caryl Emerson and Michael

Holquist (Austin: University of Texas Press, 1981), and in *Problems of Dostoevsky's Poetics*, edited and translated by Caryl Emerson (Minneapolis: University of Minnesota Press, 1984).

28. Bakhtin, *Speech Genres and Other Late Essays*, edited by Caryl Emerson and Michael Holquist, translated by Vern W. McGee (Austin: University of Texas Press, 1986), 91, 170.

29. T. L. Short makes this argument cogently in *Peirce's Theory of Signs* (Cambridge: Cambridge University Press), 53–56.

30. I owe this useful example about Peirce and his future interpreters to Colapietro; see *Peirce's Approach to the Self*, 74.

31. John Dewey, *A Common Faith* (New Haven, Conn.: Yale University Press, 1934), especially 17ff.

32. This distinction appears in Augustine's treatise *On Christian Doctrine*, in the first and second chapters of Book II.

33. In the first place, the contemplation of any self-as-sign could only hope to offer a glimpse of divinity. Moreover, it would not be the self as frozen image but as an entire life, a "role" played by the self in the "drama of creation." The playing of such a role is what Peirce described as "the utter swallowing up of the poor individual self in the Spirit of prayer" (*CP* 7.572).

34. See Short's commentary in *Peirce's Theory of Signs*, 26, 211–12.

35. Flannery O'Connor, *Mystery and Manners: Occasional Prose* (New York: Farrar, Straus and Giroux, 1962), 34. ("To the hard of hearing you shout, and for the almost-blind you draw large and startling figures.")

36. For attempts to trace the late development of Peirce's semiotic, in addition to Short on *Peirce's Theory of Signs*, consider also James Jakob Liszka, *A General Introduction to the Semeiotic of Charles Sanders Peirce* (Bloomington: Indiana University Press, 1996), and most recently, Tony Jappy, *Peirce's Twenty-Eight Classes of Signs and the Philosophy of Representation* (London: Bloomsbury, 2017).

For a brilliant attempt to apply one of Peirce's late classifications of signs (1905) to the task of understanding his religious ideas, consider Gesche Linde's essay on "The Semiotic Structure of Peirce's Humble Argument with Brief Remarks on Different Kinds of Abducent Signs," *Transactions of the Charles S. Peirce Society* 54, no. 4 (Fall 2018): 515–31.

37. A pragmatic analysis of how unconscious habits can fuel racist behavior, drawing mainly on the thought of John Dewey and W. E. B. Dubois, appears in Shannon Sullivan's *Revealing Whiteness: The Unconscious Habits of Racial Privilege* (Bloomington: Indiana University Press, 2006). I have commented on Sullivan's book, incorporating insights from Peirce and James, as well as from contemporary cognitive behavioral therapy, in an essay on "Theology, Racial Privilege and the Practice of Resistance," *Journal of Race, Ethnicity, and Religion* 1, no. 10 (September 2010): 1–32.

38. John Henry Newman was teasing out a very similar distinction to this one when he contrasted "real" with "notional" assent, in Part 1 of *An Essay in Aid of a Grammar of Assent* (South Bend, Ind.: Notre Dame University Press, 1992).

39. Thoreau makes this observation in the remarkable second chapter of *Walden*, entitled, "Where I Lived and What I Lived For" (New York: W. W. Norton, 1951).

40. In his phenomenological investigations, Peirce discovered three basic categories of human experience, the second of which is the feeling of brute resistance, the direct confrontation with something over and against the self.

41. The allusion here is to a series of much-discussed psychological experiments exploring selective attention and inattentional blindness. For a useful overview and provocative argument, see Arien Mack and Irvin Rock, *Inattentional Blindness* (Cambridge, Mass.: MIT Press, 2000).

42. This quotation appears at the end of a Pulitzer Prize–winning novel by Thornton Wilder. The relationship between love and memory that Wilder was exploring is related to but not identical to the one that interests me here. See Wilder, *The Bridge of San Luis Rey* (New York: Washington Square Press, 1939), 180.

43. There is perhaps a subtle but important distinction to be made between a sign's material quality and its identification as a "tone." Peirce's differentiation between general "types" and their embodiment in specific "tokens" is rather well known and often discussed. But in addition to types and tokens, Peirce further distinguished "an indefinite significant character" as a tone—for example, the tone of voice that someone may use in speaking (*CP* 4.537; see also *SS*: 83).

44. This phenomenon of "joint attention" has been the subject of considerable scrutiny by contemporary psychologists. While I contend that it is important as well for theosemiotic, especially for an understanding of religious community, it can be explored in only a very limited fashion here.

45. Most especially in both his *Outlines of Psychology* (New York, Macmillan, 1903) and his very early work on *The Religious Aspect of Philosophy* (Boston: Houghton Mifflin, 1885), Josiah Royce developed an elaborate theory concerning the role played by attention, volition, and love-as-loyalty in establishing the selfhood of persons. On that account, the love given by one person to another functions as a principle of selection; the beloved is individuated, then actually achieves individuality, only by first receiving and then responding to the other's loving attention. For a close and illuminating reading of Royce on this topic, consult Randall E. Auxier, *Time, Will, and Purpose: Living Ideas from the Philosophy of Josiah Royce* (Chicago: Open Court, 2013), 145–59, 166–73.

3 / Love in a Universe of Chance

1. St. Augustine, *Confessions*, translated by R. S. Pine-Coffin (New York: Penguin, 1961), 211.

2. That the human experience of love does have religious significance is a widespread assumption among both theologians and devotees representative of a great variety of religious traditions. While not identical in meaning, concepts like *agape* in Christianity and *karuna* in Buddhism display sufficient continuity in meaning to merit further consideration of this assumption.

3. Josiah Royce, *The Problem of Christianity* (Chicago: University of Chicago Press, 1968), 270.

4. In various ways, and to a different extent in each case, Spinoza, Edwards, Schelling, Emerson, Peirce, and Royce were all objective idealists who fit this description.

5. For a more detailed account of Peirce's adaptation and critique of Darwin's evolutionary theory, consult *Peirce's Philosophy of Religion* (Bloomington: Indiana University Press, 1989), 9–10, 72–74.

6. One commentator has suggested that "with agapism, Peirce adds a spiritual dimension to the notion of 'fit'" that Darwinians employ in their talk about the survival of the fittest; John Pickering, "Is Nature Habit-Forming?," in *Consensus on Peirce's Con-*

cept of Habit: Before and Beyond Consciousness, edited by Donna E. West and Myrdene Anderson (New York: Springer International, 2016), 105.

7. Henry James Sr., *Substance and Shadow: An Essay on the Physics of Creation* (Boston: Ticknor and Fields, 1863).

8. *Peirce's Philosophy of Religion*, 18–21.

9. Royce, *Problem of Christianity*, 297–319.

10. This is not to suggest that such a point of view must be regarded in every case as implying a rejection of religion. For an example of how the "serendipity of history" can be employed as a concept for specifically theological purposes, consider Gordon Kaufman's *In Face of Mystery: A Constructive Theology* (Cambridge, Mass.: Harvard University Press, 1993), especially chapters 19–20.

11. Jeremy Dunham, Iain Hamilton Grant, and Sean Watson have traced the history of idealism from its ancient roots in the thought of Parmenides and Plato all the way up to the contemporary period, including an extended treatment of Deleuze's idealistic philosophy. See Dunham, Grant, and Watson, *Idealism: The History of a Philosophy* (Montreal and Kingston: McGill-Queens University Press, 2011). For a comparable history of panpsychism, consult David Skrbina, *Panpsychism in the West* (Cambridge, Mass.: MIT Press, 2017). *Panpsychism: Contemporary Perspectives*, edited by Godehard Bruntrup and Ludwig Jaskolla (Oxford: Oxford University Press, 2016) offers just what its title suggests: a volume of essays exploring the continuing relevance of such a philosophy. Finally, dipolar monism (a theory explaining how the mental and the physical are aspects of a single reality) has been associated historically with various forms of process philosophy and religious naturalism. For a recent defense of this view, see Wesley J. Wildman, *Religious and Spiritual Experiences* (Cambridge: Cambridge University Press, 2011).

12. Although there is no evidence of actual influence, there are striking similarities between Peirce's agapism and Pierre Teilhard de Chardin's argument that love is a primordial force in the universe bringing about a process of cosmic personalization. Most relevant here are the essays collected in Teilhard de Chardin, *Human Energy* (New York: Harcourt, Brace, Jovanovich, 1971) and *The Activation of Energy* (New York: Harcourt, Brace, Jovanovich, 1971).

I would argue, in addition, for a close analogy between Teilhard's contention that personality intensifies rather than dissipates with the multiplying and strengthening of relations and Royce's "fourth conception of being," that to be is to be uniquely in relation to the whole. Once established, that analogy can be extended, albeit a bit more loosely, to Peirce's vision of a "universe of signs," also to the medieval understanding of relations as "being toward."

13. That is the central task of this book's Chapter 6.

14. I owe this insight to Murray G. Murphey, articulated in his important essay on Peirce, published as Chapter 10 in Elizabeth Flower and Murphey, *A History of Philosophy in America* (New York: G. P. Putnam's Sons, 1977), 2:615.

15. For a classic account of how the meaning of any experience will be shaped by contextual factors, examine Erving Goffman's *Frame Analysis: An Essay on the Organization of Experience* (London: Harper and Row, 1974).

16. *Song of Songs* 8:6.

17. Examine Peter Ochs's discussion in *Peirce, Pragmatism and the Logic of Scripture* (Cambridge: Cambridge University Press, 1998), 223–28.

18. John Duns Scotus, *Philosophical Writings*, translated by Allan Wolter (Indianapolis: Hackett, 1987), 4–8, 19–30.

19. Aristotle, *Nicomachean Ethics*, translated by Terence Irwin (Indianapolis: Hackett, 1999), Book I:3.

20. The link between Peirce's anthropomorphism and his naturalism is one that I first established in Michael L. Raposa, "Holy Nostalgia: Toward a Sympathetic Critique of Religious Naturalism," in *The Routledge Handbook of Religious Naturalism*, edited by Donald A. Crosby and Jerome A. Stone (New York: Routledge, 2018), 379–89. The discussion that follows here is an adapted version and development of insights first articulated there and in a subsequent essay on "Pragmatism and the Future of Philosophical Theology: A Conversation with Wesley Wildman," in *Religion in Multidisciplinary Perspective*, edited by Robert Neville and LeRon Shults (Albany: SUNY Press, forthcoming).

21. For a more detailed account, consult my essay on "Instinct and Inquiry: A Reconsideration of Peirce's Mature Religious Naturalism," in *Pragmatism and Naturalism: Scientific and Social Inquiry after Representationalism*, edited by Matthew Bagger (New York: Columbia University Press, 2018), 27–43.

22. Of special relevance to the present inquiry is Peirce's further claim that "we are conscious *habitualiter* of whatever hides in the depths of our nature"; moreover, "that a sufficiently energetic effort of attention would bring it out" (*CP* 5.441). Indeed, one of the primary tasks of theosemiotic is to bring such attention to bear on those instincts and habits that can significantly affect our behavior but are quite typically ignored. It might be productive, in framing such a project, to compare Peirce's theory of instinct with Calvin on the "*sensus divinitatis*," Edwards on the "sense of the heart," Newman on the "illative sense," and even Polanyi on "tacit knowledge," albeit without conflating such notions by assuming their equivalence.

23. Compare how the medieval scholastics defined relations as a "being toward" another. See Mark G. Henninger, *Relations: Mediaeval Theories, 1250-1325* (Oxford: Clarendon, 1989), and Paul Bains, *The Primacy of Semiosis* (Toronto: University of Toronto Press, 2006), for useful commentaries on this topic. Once again, I choose to read Peirce's claim here as one about the potential for anything to be/become a sign, about a world "perfused" with, but not consisting "exclusively" of signs.

24. In various writings, Paul Tillich formulated the classical version of a "ground of being" theology. More recently, Robert Neville and Wesley Wildman have extended and developed Tillich's ideas.

25. Sigmund Freud's famous critique of religion appears in Freud, *The Future of an Illusion*, translated by James Strachey (New York: W. W. Norton, 1989).

26. The example of such a foolish maiden is one that Freud employed to illustrate how an illusory belief with the support of no evidence could be sustained by simply wishing it were true.

27. Despite Peirce's vigorous defense of anthropomorphism, his philosophy has been identified in at least one study as a valuable resource for posthumanist thinking. See Ryan White, *The Hidden God: Pragmatism and Posthumanism in American Thought* (New York: Columbia University Press, 2015).

28. Two clear accounts of the relationship between Peirce's realism and idealism have been provided by Robert Almeder, *The Philosophy of Charles S. Peirce* (Totowa, N.J.: Rowman and Littlefield, 1980), and, more recently, Robert Lane, *Peirce on Realism and Idealism* (Cambridge: Cambridge University Press, 2018).

29. I intend this way of talking about belief to be heard as an echo of the sort of detachment that Paul recommended to his readers in anticipation of the Parousia, in 1 Corinthians 7:29-31.

30. Simone Weil's version of this argument, as well as the comparable claims of Peirce and Edwards, are treated in Raposa, "Peirce and Edwards on the Argument from Beauty," in *American Aesthetics: Theory and Practice*, edited by Walter Gulick and Gary Slater (Albany: SUNY Press, 2020): 59-74). I will revisit these arguments, briefly in the next, then again in Chapter 7.

31. With regard to the question about God's reality, Peirce proposed that "the only guide to the answer to this question lies in the power of the passion of love which more or less overmasters every agnostic scientist and everybody who seriously and deeply considers the universe" (*CP* 6.503).

32. Robert Neville, in particular, has worried consistently about the unreliability of religious icons, about their necessary falsehood, while emphasizing the importance of indexical reference in his philosophical theology. On Neville's account, even when a sign is iconically false it may establish a real causal relationship between object and interpreter by functioning indexically, thus transforming the interpreter in important ways. See Neville, *Philosophical Theology*, vol. 1, *Ultimates* (Albany: SUNY Press, 2013), 70-73.

33. Consider my brief meditation on "Love as Attention in Peirce's Thought," in *Charles S. Peirce in His Own Words: 100 Years of Semiotics, Communication and Cognition*," edited by Torkild Thellefsen and Bent Sorensen (Berlin: De Gruyter, 2014), 161-64.

34. The medieval roots that I allude to here run at least as deep as the voluntarism of Duns Scotus. That love is an act of will and one to be directed to the highest good and that the will is more noble than the intellect are Scotistic theses that distinguish his philosophy from that of some other medieval thinkers; see Duns Scotus, *Philosophical Writings*, 70-71, 144ff.

While the trajectory of philosophical voluntarism is being traced here primarily to its manifestation in classical American pragmatism and the personalism of Peirce and Royce, it would be valuable for theosemiotic purposes eventually to extend it even further—for example, by examining elements of it as they appear in the thought of individuals such as Emmanuel Mounier and Hannah Arendt (with the latter being directly influenced by Scotus's thought). Within the context of Mounier's personalism, volition exercises itself in love as "the one irrefutable, existential *cogito*: I love, therefore I am; therefore being is, and life has value. . . . Love does not reassure me simply as a state of being in which I find myself, for it gives me to someone else"; Emmanuel Mounier, *Personalism*, translated by Philip Mairet (Notre Dame, Ind.: University of Notre Dame Press, 1989), 23.

35. *William James: Writings 1878-1899* (New York: Library of America, 1984), 528-29.

36. Simone Weil's meditations on attention and volition are scattered throughout her corpus of writings, with the richest concentration of them to be found in the material collected under the title of *Gravity and Grace*, translated by Emma Craufurd (London: Routledge and Kegan Paul, 1992).

37. My meditation "On Waiting" was largely inspired by my reading of Simone Weil, published as the Postlude to *Boredom and the Religious Imagination*, 167-73.

38. Compare also Heidegger's description of "*Die Gelassenheit zu den Dingen*," a "releasement toward things" that manifests itself as passive, but conceals a "higher" form

of acting within itself, a kind of willing not to will. See Martin Heidegger, *A Discourse on Thinking*, translated by John M. Anderson and E. Hans Freund (New York: Harper and Row, 1966), 54ff. and 67ff.

39. Although it might seem like a peculiar observation, even musement involves an act of will, a "prescinding" from something—in this case, from any particular purpose that might tend to dominate one's thinking.

40. This theme of disinterested love is developed within an Ignatian context by David M. Stanley, SJ, in Chapter 5, "Love What You Find," in *A Modern Scriptural Approach to the Spiritual Exercises* (Chicago: Loyola University Press, 1967), 50–56.

41. Ignatius of Loyola's description of love as a "mutual sharing of goods" appears in his culminating "Contemplation to Attain Divine Love," in *The Spiritual Exercises of St. Ignatius*, 101, para. 231. Here Ignatius makes "two points" about love as a prelude to the exercise, one about love consisting in mutuality and another about love manifesting itself primarily in "deeds" rather than words (Ignatius's pragmatism).

The classic philosophical investigation into the distinctive nature of I/You relationships is Martin Buber's *I and Thou*, translated by Walter Kaufmann (New York: Scribner, 1970).

42. Oscar Romero supplied a moving portrayal of such suffering in his writings and sermons collected in *The Violence of Love* (Maryknoll, N.Y.: Orbis, 2004).

43. On gratitude as an essential element of love, see Neville's reflections in *Philosophical Theology*, vol. 2, *Existence*, 226–29.

44. As Will Barrett contemplates his beloved, Allison, at the end of Walker Percy's novel *The Second Coming* (New York: Farrar, Straus, Giroux, 1980), he muses, "Is she a gift and therefore a sign of a giver?"

It is well known that Percy was impressed and influenced by Peirce's philosophy. For an account of that influence that utilizes my conception of a theosemiotic, review John F. Desmond, *Walker Percy's Search for Community* (Athens: University of Georgia Press, 2004).

45. William James, *The Varieties of Religious Experience* (New York: Penguin, 1982), 283–84, with my brief commentary appearing in *Meditation and the Martial Arts*, (Charlottesville: University of Virginia Press, 2003), 124–25.

46. An accessible and representative sampling of Morihei Ueshiba's teachings about the philosophy of aikido are included in Ueshiba, *The Art of Peace: Teachings of the Founder of Aikido*, compiled and translated by John Stevens (Boston: Shambhala, 1992). Consult also *The Essence of Aikido: Spiritual Teachings of Morihei Ueshiba*, compiled and translated by John Stevens (Tokyo: Kodansha, 1993), as well as Stevens's own commentary and analysis in *The Philosophy of Aikido* (Tokyo: Kodansha, 2001).

4 / Theology as Inquiry, Therapy, Praxis

1. See my discussion in Michael L. Raposa, *Peirce's Philosophy of Religion* (Bloomington: Indiana University Press, 1989), most especially in Chapter 5 on "Musement."

2. William James's Berkeley lecture was first published as "Philosophical Conceptions and Practical Results," *University Chronicle* 1, no. 4 (September 1898): 287–310. It is included in *William James: Writings 1878–1899*, edited by Gerald E. Myers (New York: Library of America, 1984), 1077–97.

3. I was long ago influenced by my dissertation mentor, Murray G. Murphey, in my evaluation that "The Fixation of Belief" is one of Peirce's "least satisfactory" publica-

tions. See Murray G. Murphey, *The Development of Peirce's Philosophy* (Cambridge, Mass.: Harvard University Press, 1961), 164–65.

4. The judgment, after reading his *Monist* essays on cosmology, that Peirce must have been losing his mind, was one made by his former student, the logician Christine Ladd-Franklin. See the account in Joseph Brent, *Charles Sanders Peirce: A Life* (Bloomington: Indiana University Press, 1993), 214.

5. One of the most impressive alternatives to theosemiotic as a theology inspired by Peirce's theory of inquiry is the "rabbinic pragmatism" for which Peter Ochs laid the foundation in his magisterial study of *Peirce, Pragmatism and the Logic of Scripture* (Cambridge: Cambridge University Press, 1998). Ochs's Peircean strategy is strikingly original and very different from the one pursued here (see especially Ochs's address to "Dear Theosemioticians" on pages 281–85). Nevertheless, there are some important points of contact between his view and my own—for example, an evaluation of the great importance for theology of a disciplined practice of reading and rereading; an understanding of the logic of vagueness as also constituting a logic of dialogue; a recognition of the fact that a pragmatic theology has a distinctively therapeutic function so that it must represent a compassionate response to human suffering; and his account of how, in praxis, the muser becomes a "living symbol . . . of the divine presence" (243).

For a helpful comparison and creative extension of two of the very few attempts to adapt Peirce's philosophy for theological purposes—Ochs's rabbinic pragmatism and Robert Neville's "theology of symbolic engagement"—examine Gary Slater's *C. S. Peirce and the Nested Continua Model of Religious Interpretation* (Oxford: Oxford University Press, 2015).

6. Perhaps the best-known theological account of the essential role that doubt plays in the life of faith appears in Paul Tillich's *The Dynamics of Faith* (San Francisco: HarperOne, 2009).

7. The classic portrayal of boredom serving as a stimulus to creativity can be found in volume 1 of Søren Kierkegaard's *Either/Or*, translated by David F. Swenson and Lillian Marvin Swenson (Princeton, N.J.: Princeton University Press, 1959).

8. What Peirce envisioned was something closer to the sort of ambulation that Henry David Thoreau famously described as "sauntering" in his essay on "Walking." See Thoreau, *Nature/Walking* (Boston: Beacon, 1994).

9. For his recollection of being absorbed in a practice very much like musement, "from sunrise till noon," while never wandering from the doorway of his cabin, examine Thoreau's *Walden* (New York: W. W. Norton, 1951), 128.

10. Such an emphasis on endurance, however, should never be interpreted as a suggestion that liberation theology has taken the backseat to a theology of survival; liberation presupposes but cannot be reduced to survival. Moreover, liberation should not be conceived as a solution to some theoretical problem of evil, but rather is a response in praxis to some actual state of affairs.

11. As examples of a pragmatic argument establishing the need to make hypotheses vulnerable to correction in philosophical theology, see Robert C. Neville, *On the Scope and Truth of Theology: Theology as Symbolic Engagement* (London: T. & T. Clark, 2006), and Wesley J. Wildman, *Religious Philosophy as Multidisciplinary Comparative Inquiry: Envisioning a Future for the Philosophy of Religion* (Albany: SUNY Press, 2010).

12. George Herbert Mead early on and Terrence Deacon more recently have explored the manner in which language, construed as verbal communication, evolved from a more basic form of meaningful interaction involving the human body and

gesture. For the accounts that they supplied, consult especially Mead's *Mind, Self, and Society* (Chicago: University of Chicago Press, 1934), and Deacon's *The Symbolic Species: The Co-Evolution of Language and the Brain* (New York: W. W. Norton, 1997).

13. Wayne Proudfoot first used the phrase "ubiquity of inference" as an especially felicitous description of what he observed to be one of the distinguishing features of a pragmatic theory of interpretation (in contrast to European hermeneutic theories focused on texts and language), in his essay "Interpretation, Inference, and Religion," *Soundings* 61 (1978): 378–99.

14. This question was first raised for me in reading the manuscript for an insightful book that offers a provocative Peircean analysis of religious communities as "embodied hypotheses and living experiments." See Brandon Daniel-Hughes on "the ubiquity of inquiry," in *Pragmatic Inquiry and Religious Communities: Charles Peirce, Signs, and Inhabited Experiments* (New York: Palgrave Macmillan, 2018). Daniel-Hughes's argument is an extrapolation from Peirce's position, employing an interesting distinction between "active" and "dormant" inquiry. It may be the case that my anxiety about affirming the "ubiquity of inquiry" is addressed by his conceiving of inquiry in its dormancy. But I do not think that inquiry is ubiquitous in human experience in quite the same sense that semiosis-as-inference can be shown to be.

15. Peirce's commentary on the Neglected Argument appears in two letters written late in 1908—the same year that the essay was published in the *Hibbert Journal*—dated December 14 and December 23. See *SS*: 66–86.

Peirce also wrote several unpublished variants of the text of the argument that appeared in print, preserved in manuscripts that are of considerable interest for the student of Peirce's philosophy of religion. See *MS* 841–44.

16. William James concluded "that attention with effort is all that any case of volition implies," in *The Principles of Psychology* (New York: Dover, 1950), 2:561.

17. Here I use the word "looking" as shorthand for the application of any of the senses that might be deemed useful for the purposes of observation.

18. As an early indication of his suggesting the relevance of cenoscopy for theology, consider the youthful Peirce's claim that "God's wisdom and mercy" should be visible "in every event" of one's life (*W*1: 114).

From a contemporary perspective, compare David Tracy's appeal to our "common human experience" as the proper subject matter for theological reflection. See his *Blessed Rage for Order: The New Pluralism in Theology* (New York: Seabury, 1975).

19. In addition, phenomenology will be *experimental* in the same sense as here proposed for theosemiotic. Compare *CP* 1.286–87, where Peirce invited other inquirers to check his own observations of the phaneron, just as several years later he proposed to his readers that they should test his results in musement.

20. A full argument in support of this claim (for which this book supplies only the prolegomenon) would need both to demonstrate that poverty (in its various forms and manifestations) is indeed a ubiquitous feature of human experience *and* to explain how a certain habit of love functions as a "perceptual set" enabling the cenoscopic inquirer clearly to perceive poverty and its effects.

21. I developed this argument previously, in Raposa, *Boredom and the Religious Imagination* (Charlottesville: University of Virginia Press, 1999), 126–35.

22. John Duns Scotus, *Duns Scotus on the Will and Morality*, edited by Allan Wolter (Washington, D.C.: The Catholic University of America Press, 1986), 137.

23. For an analysis of practices organized around the pursuit of internal goods, consider Alasdair MacIntyre's influential account in *After Virtue: A Study in Moral Theory* (South Bend, Ind.: University of Notre Dame Press, 1984).

24. See the brief examination supplied by Steven C. Hayes in his essay on "Acceptance and Commitment Therapy and the New Behavior Therapies: Mindfulness, Acceptance, and Relationship," in *Mindfulness and Acceptance: Expanding the Cognitive-Behavioral Tradition*, edited by. Steven C. Hayes, Victoria M. Follette, and Marsha M. Linehan (New York: Guilford, 2004), 6–10.

25. Ibid., 5.

26. Ibid., 6.

27. Stephen C. Pepper, *World Hypotheses: A Study in Evidence* (Berkeley and Los Angeles: University of California Press, 1942), vii.

28. Ibid., 268.

29. Ibid., 232.

30. Ibid., 233.

31. Steven C. Hayes, Linda J. Hayes, and Hayne W. Reese, "Finding the Philosophical Core: A Review of Stephen C. Pepper's World Hypotheses; A Study in Evidence," *Journal of the Experimental Analysis of Behavior* 50, no. 1 (1988): 100.

32. Ibid., 102.

33. Skinner, as quoted in Hayes, Hayes, and Reese, "Finding the Philosophical Core," 102.

34. Anthony Biglan and Steven C. Hayes, "Should the Behavioral Sciences Become More Pragmatic? The Case for Functional Contextualism in Research on Human Behavior," *Applied and Preventive Psychology* (Cambridge University Press, 1996), 5:50–51.

35. Ibid., 51.

36. See the discussion in Hayes, "Acceptance and Commitment Therapy," 7–8.

37. Pepper, *World Hypotheses*, 243–45.

38. For a brief overview of Relational Frame Theory, consult Hayes, "Acceptance and Commitment Therapy," 10–12.

39. I have previously discussed the resonance of cognitive therapy with the pragmatism of Peirce and James in my essay on "Theology, Racial Privilege and the Practice of Resistance," *Journal of Race, Ethnicity, and Religion* 1, no. 10 (September 2010): 1–32.

For philosophical treatments of James that are especially sensitive to the importance of his work in psychology, consult James Pawelski, *The Dynamic Individualism of William James* (Albany: SUNY Press, 2007), as well as numerous writings by Eugene Taylor, including his important book *William James on Consciousness beyond the Margin* (Princeton, N.J.: Princeton University Press, 2011).

40. The most extended treatment of this topic is Donald Robertson's *The Philosophy of Cognitive Behavioural Therapy: Stoic Philosophy as Rational and Cognitive Psychotherapy* (London: Karnac, 2010).

41. James's phenomenology of healthy-mindedness, the sick soul, and the twice-born is presented in his lectures on *The Varieties of Religious Experience*, especially in Lectures IV–VIII. For a contemporary account of how stoic and pragmatic insights might be effectively blended, consider John Lachs, *Stoic Pragmatism* (Bloomington: Indiana University Press, 2012).

42. On the dialectical philosophy that undergirds DBT, see Marsha Linehan, *Cognitive-Behavioral Treatment of Borderline Personality Disorder* (New York: Guilford, 1993), 31-41; also, Clive J. Robins, Henry Schmidt II, and Marsha Linehan, "Dialectical

Behavior Therapy: Synthesizing Radical Acceptance with Skillful Means," in Hayes, Follette, and Linehan, *Mindfulness and Acceptance*, 32–35.

43. See the comments on distancing by Zindel V. Segal, John D. Teasdale, and J. Mark G. Williams, in "Mindfulness-Based Cognitive Therapy: Theoretical Rationale and Empirical Status," in Hayes, Follette, and Linehan, *Mindfulness and Acceptance*, 51–52.

44. Arthur O. Lovejoy, "The Thirteen Pragmatisms," *Journal of Philosophy, Psychology and Scientific Method* 5 (January 1908): 5–12.

45. James, *Principles of Psychology*, 1:402.

46. Ibid., 416.

47. Ibid., 447.

48. Ibid., 447–48.

49. James, *Varieties of Religious Experience* (New York: Penguin, 1982), 45–46.

50. Ibid., 47.

51. Ibid., 44.

52. Ibid., 231. (Compare Peirce's early definition of what the self as sign means at any given point in time, explored in Chapter 2.)

53. Ibid., 206ff.

54. Ibid., 195–97.

55. Ibid., 272–73.

56. Ibid., 208.

57. The word "exposure" in this sentence was placed in italics because this discipline of cultivating a bracing openness to whatever one encounters in experience—as well as one's feeling responses to such encounters—resonates with the development of extremely effective forms of "exposure therapy" as a treatment for anxiety in contemporary clinical psychology. The work of Edna Foa has been especially foundational for this development.

I would suggest but cannot argue here that Søren Kierkegaard, with a distinctly theological twist to be sure, anticipated some of these psychological insights. Consider his early work on *The Concept of Anxiety: A Simple Psychologically Oriented Deliberation in View of the Dogmatic Problem of Hereditary Sin*, translated by Alastair Hannay (New York: Liveright, 2015).

58. Hayes describes this "classic ACT defusion technique" in his chapter on "Acceptance and Commitment Therapy," 19–20. Walker Percy's version appears in his collection of essays *The Message in the Bottle* (New York: Farrar, Straus and Giroux, 1978), 12, but then consider the extended discussion that follows.

59. It is interesting in this regard to note that Aaron Beck claims to have developed his therapeutic approach as a result of conducting free association with patients in classical psychoanalytical fashion; when doing so he observed how they had been failing in therapy to report certain thoughts at the "fringe of consciousness," many of which triggered intense emotions.

60. For an insightful Buddhist analysis of the concept of "deep listening," consider Thich Nhat Hanh, *The Heart of the Buddha's Teaching* (New York: Broadway, 1999), 12–13, 86–89, 92–93, 197, and *Teachings on Love* (Berkeley: Parallax, 1997), Chapter 7 on "Deep Listening and Loving Speech," 73–84.

61. On the extreme fragility of all structures of meaning, examine the penetrating account provided by Robert Corrington in the development of his "ecstatic naturalism." The quoted material included here is borrowed from what I regard as his most

important work, *A Semiotic Theory of Philosophy and Theology* (Cambridge: Cambridge University Press, 2000), 207.

62. The reference here is to Archibald MacLeish's concluding declaration in "Ars Poetica" that "A poem should not mean / But be."

63. This is the argument made in Raposa, *Boredom and the Religious Imagination*, especially in Chapter 5 on "Boredom, Semiosis, and Spiritual Exercises."

64. I owe this phrase also, as well as the corresponding insight, to Corrington. See his *Semiotic Theory of Philosophy and Theology*, 249.

65. John Dewey, *Human Nature and Conduct* (Carbondale: Southern Illinois University Press, 1988), 222.

66. For an illuminating portrayal of religious "virtuosity" that has surely influenced the development of my own thinking, examine vol. 1 of Robert Neville's three-volume *Philosophical Theology*, entitled *Ultimates* (Albany: SUNY Press, 2013), especially Chapter 16, on "Mystical Engagement," 301–16.

67. Numerous scholars have defended such an interpretation of Peirce, but perhaps none more persuasively than T. L. Short. See Short, *Peirce's Theory of Signs* (Cambridge: Cambridge University Press), especially 172–74.

For a wonderful collection of essays on the full range of meanings attached to the concept of "habit" in Peirce's philosophy, including but not limited to it serving as the ultimate logical interpretant of a sign, see *Consensus on Peirce's Concept of Habit: Before and Beyond Consciousness*, edited by Donna E. West and Myrdene Anderson (New York: Springer International, 2016).

68. Even Peirce seemed to admit this when he qualified his argument by explaining that "the habit alone, *which though it may be a sign in some other way*, is not a sign in the way in which that sign of which it is the logical interpretant is the sign" (*CP* 5.491; emphasis added). Perhaps this "other way" of being a sign is not as just yet another interpretant within the flow of signs that constitutes the self-as-semiosis, but as a sign for *another person* who happens to read and be influenced by it.

Murray Murphey agreed that, for Peirce, habits can be signs. See Murphey, *Development of Peirce's Philosophy*, 316 and 366.

69. The ultimate logical interpretant of a self-sign thus conceived will constitute a "conditional determination of the soul," manifested as that individual's "character" (*MS* 288).

70. Robert Corrington, Donald Crosby, Michael Hogue, Robert Neville, and Wesley Wildman immediately spring to mind as exemplars of this kind of religious naturalism.

71. Consider how, in his discussion of asceticism, James called for a "moral equivalent of war," observing that "there is an element of real wrongness in the world, which is neither to be ignored nor evaded, but which must be squarely met and overcome by an appeal to the soul's heroic resources"; James, *Varieties of Religious Experience*, 362.

72. The most persuasive attempt to ground liberation theology in a theological aesthetic was made by Alejandro R. Garcia-Rivera, in *A Community of the Beautiful: A Theological Aesthetics* (Wilmington, Del.: Michael Glazier, 1999). Peirce and Royce both loom large in Garcia-Rivera's account.

Notice also the centrality of the category of the aesthetic to the study of how pragmatism and liberation thought intersect, presented by Christopher D. Tirres, in *The Aesthetics and Ethics of Faith: A Dialogue between Liberationist and Pragmatic Thought* (Oxford: Oxford University Press, 2014).

73. In his foreword to Gustavo Gutierrez's classic articulation of a liberation spirituality, Henri Nouwen described Gutierrez's approach as having a distinctively "inductive character." See Gutierrez, *We Drink from Our Own Wells: The Spiritual Journey of a People* (Maryknoll, N.Y.: Orbis: 2002), xix.

74. Although the deepest roots of the "see-judge-act" model for Catholic theology may be difficult to trace, official endorsement came in Pope John XXIII's 1961 encyclical *Mater et Magistra*, and it has since become something of a regulative principle guiding Latin American liberation theologians in their deliberations.

75. In Gutierrez, *We Drink from Our Own Wells*, see especially Chapter 7, "Gratuitousness: The Atmosphere for Efficacy," 107–14.

76. My allusion here is to Robert McAfee Brown's influential attempt to reimagine theology in general by introducing liberation concerns. I regard a liberation theology conceived as theosemiotic to be an extension of that project. Consult Brown, *Theology in a New Key: Responding to Liberation Themes* (Philadelphia: Westminster, 1978).

77. I am thinking especially here of the magisterial work of Enrique Dussel, in his *Ethics of Liberation: In the Age of Globalization and Exclusion* (Durham, N.C.: Duke University Press, 2013), with a discussion of Peirce presented on pages 160–66.

78. Peirce himself wrote several prayers that have survived in the manuscripts, one of them conjoined to a collection of thoughts regarding semiotic, phaneroscopy, and the existential graphs and including an early outline of the Neglected Argument (see *MS* 277). For a much briefer prayer, written nearly half a century earlier, that in its own way vaguely anticipates the argument for God's reality rooted in an appeal to instinct, consult *MS* 891.

79. This is an insight developed by Gabriel Marcel in his remarkable book *Being and Having: An Existentialist Diary*, translated by Katherine Farrar (New York: Harper and Row, 1965).

80. On the sort of imaginative skill needed to perceive the "more" in experience, consider Mary Warnock, *Imagination* (Berkeley: University of California Press, 1976), 202–3; her essay on "Religious Imagination," in *Religious Imagination*, edited by James P. Mackey (Edinburgh: Edinburgh University Press, 1986), 47; and my comments in *Boredom and the Religious Imagination*, 124–35.

Peirce himself distinguished between "looking" and "seeing" (*CP* 7.627), the former involving an act of attention and being primarily related to the perceptual judgment, with seeing being related to the initial percept and not including the same volitional element. I would suggest that there is a certain way of looking or paying attention that facilitates the formation of a different type of perceptual judgment, one that permits you to see more or more deeply. This would involve prescinding from those habits of judgment that typically shape our perceptions.

81. The most illuminating exploration of this concept, imaginative rather than scholarly, is to be found in Fernando Pessoa's *The Book of Disquiet*, translated by Richard Zenith (New York: Penguin Classics, 2002).

82. "Training for Loyalty" is the title of Chapter 6 of Josiah Royce's extended meditation on *The Philosophy of Loyalty* (Nashville, Tenn.: Vanderbilt University Press, 1995).

83. I use these examples—of hitting a nail with a hammer and giving and asking for reasons—because both have been used by Robert Brandom on a number of occasions. He represents the sort of neo-pragmatism, I would argue, that operates with a concept of "practice" furthest removed from what that concept meant for Peirce and his pragmaticism. Brandom has also boasted that he has no need for the concept of

NOTES TO PAGES 154–66 / 291

"experience" in his philosophy. See his *Perspectives on Pragmatism* (Cambridge, Mass.: Harvard University Press, 2011).

5 / Communities of Interpretation

1. I have pursued this question previously, in a more limited context, as it pertains to colleges, universities, and other educational communities, in Michael L. Raposa, "Troubled Diversities, Multiple Identities and the Relevance of Royce: What Makes a Community Worth Caring About?," *Educational Philosophy and Theory* 44, no. 4 (June 2012): 432–43.

2. For the development of this ideal of "loyalty to loyalty" by Josiah Royce, see *The Philosophy of Loyalty* (Nashville, Tenn.: Vanderbilt University Press, 1995), 48–69. This idea receives further treatment and becomes explicitly linked to the Christian concept of love in Royce, *The Problem of Christianity* (Chicago: University of Chicago Press, 1968). For a useful overview and insightful analysis of Royce's philosophy of loyalty, consult Matthew Foust, *Loyalty to Loyalty: Josiah Royce and the Genuine Moral Life* (New York: Fordham University Press, 2012).

3. On the relevance of Peirce's philosophy for thinking about the nature of democracy, see Robert Talisse, *A Pragmatist Philosophy of Democracy* (New York and London: Routledge, 2007). For a more limited account tied to an explicitly theological agenda, consider Raposa, "Pragmatism, Democracy and the Future of Catholic Theology," *American Journal of Theology and Philosophy* 30, no. 3 (September 2009): 288–302.

4. Randall Auxier has offered a compelling argument that Peirce's influence on Royce began at a period much earlier than some other scholars, most notably John E. Smith, have suggested—that is, long before the writing and publication late in Royce's career of the *Problem of Christianity*. Moreover, Auxier contends that the influence was mutual and that Royce shaped Peirce's thinking as well. See Auxier, *Time, Will, and Purpose: Living Ideas from the Philosophy of Josiah Royce* (Chicago: Open Court, 2013).

5. To be sure, philosophical personalists might insist that, minimally speaking, the members of a community would have to share the characteristic of all being persons. Nonpersons (not to be conflated with nonhumans) could not be regarded as a proper object of the love/loyalty that forms the communal bond. This raises all sorts of questions about the logical extension both of a label like "person" and of the concept of community itself. Would it be accurate to say that bonobos live in communities?

6. The discussion that follows represents the heavily adapted version of a keynote address: Raposa, "On the Very Idea of a Virtual Community: Peirce and Royce Revisited," delivered at the Semiotic Society of America annual meeting in Pittsburgh, on October 1, 2015. Sections of material from that lecture were later included in "Loyalty, Community, and the Task of Attention: On Royce's 'Third Attitude of the Will,'" *American Journal of Theology and Philosophy* 37, no. 2 (May 2016): 109–22.

7. In the epigraph to a novel bearing the word as its title, Katherine Vaz defined "*saudade*" as "yearning so intense for those who are missing, or for vanished times and places, that their absence is the most profound presence in one's life." See Vaz, *Saudade* (New York: St. Martin's, 1994).

8. This is not to suggest that a proper understanding of the nature of attention has no metaphysical implications. I note—with interest but without comment here—that Vaz described *saudade* as "a state of being, rather than merely a sentiment." Moreover, the Vietnamese Zen Buddhist master Thich Nhat Hanh once observed that "the rite of

the Eucharist is a wonderful practice of mindfulness," in *Peace Is Every Step: The Path of Mindfulness in Everyday Life* (New York: Bantam, 1991), 23. The nature and quality of our attention do seem, at least potentially, to have some bearing on our judgments concerning the real presence or absence of persons and things.

9. Royce, *Problem of Christianity*, especially 314–19.

10. Ibid., 312–14.

11. Ibid., 270.

12. I have compared Peirce and Royce at greater length on this issue, in Raposa, "Loyalty, Community, and the Task of Attention: On Royce's 'Third Attitude of the Will.'"

13. See, especially, the material in Gregory Bateson, *Steps to an Ecology of Mind: Collected Essays in Anthropology, Psychiatry, Evolution, and Epistemology* (Chicago: University of Chicago Press, 2000).

14. Royce, *Problem of Christianity*, 356.

15. Moreover, the kind of language often utilized in technologically mediated communications is quite different from the ordinary language displayed in conversation, in letters, or in books—that is, significantly denuded, with meaning often attached to words or phrases by a code. Consider, as only one example, the use of an emoji in order to capture and convey a particular emotional response.

16. No one has explored this aspect of Peirce's thought more insightfully than the late Jesuit philosopher Vincent Potter did, especially in the pages of his book on Charles S. Peirce: Potter, *On Norms and Ideals* (Amherst, Mass.: University of Massachusetts Press, 1967).

17. Consider and compare Julia Kristeva's description of "an intelligence moving through love" as part of her meditation on Scotus's concept of *haecceitas*. Kristeva, *This Incredible Need to Believe*, translated by Beverley Bie Brahic (New York: Columbia University Press, 2009), 34.

18. As argued in Raposa, "Poinsot on the Semiotics of Awareness," *American Catholic Philosophical Quarterly* 68, no. 3 (1994): 395–408.

19. In order to examine Royce's discussion of provincialism, consult *Race Questions, Provincialism, and Other American Problems*, expanded ed., edited by Scott L. Pratt and Shannon Sullivan (New York: Fordham University Press, 2009), especially 69–91 and 25–63.

20. Gustavo Gutierrez, in numerous places and publications, has insisted that true liberation must always also include a liberation from sinfulness. That claim appears, for example, both in *A Theology of Liberation* (Maryknoll, N.Y.: Orbis, 1972), a foundational text in the development of Latin American liberation theology, and in *We Drink from Our Own Wells: The Spiritual Journey of a People* (Maryknoll, N.Y.: Orbis: 2002), Gutierrez's later attempt to articulate a liberation spirituality.

21. Enrique Dussel has proposed that the type of discourse ethics formulated by thinkers like Apel and Habermas needs to be supplemented and corrected by what he calls the "material principle." This principle asserts that, in order to act ethically, one "ought (as an obligation) to produce, reproduce, and develop self-responsibly the concrete life of each human subject, in a community of life." See his *Ethics of Liberation: In the Age of Globalization and Exclusion* (Durham, N.C.: Duke University Press, 2013), 104. Such a principle supplies for Dussel "the ethical content of all praxis." While he is clear that corporeality or materiality cannot be reduced to the bodily and physical, it must surely include the latter.

22. William James announced this proposal within the context of his Gifford Lectures on the *Varieties of Religious Experience* (New York: Penguin, 1982). For a very different yet still somewhat analogous contemporary approach to the scientific study of religious experiences, examine Wesley Wildman's *Religious and Spiritual Experiences* (Cambridge: Cambridge University Press, 2011).

23. Royce, *Problem of Christianity*, 318.

24. The example is not a purely imaginative one. I am considering the actual biography and thought of Fr. Robert Kennedy, SJ, here. Kennedy is the author of *Zen Spirit, Christian Spirit: The Place of Zen in Christian Life* (New York: Continuum, 1995), as well as *Zen Gifts to Christians* (New York: Continuum, 2004).

25. I have explored these contributions of James, Peirce, and Royce to the project of articulating a martial spirituality in the final chapter of Raposa, *Meditation and the Martial Arts*.

26. My attempt to make this argument forcefully is embodied in Raposa, "Troubled Diversities, Multiple Identities and the Relevance of Royce."

27. This concern about the dangerous hegemony of contemporary biosemiotics over other theories of interpretation, most especially textual hermeneutics, has been articulated by Gilad Elbom on numerous occasions, including a vigorous panel discussion in which I participated at the Semiotic Society of America Meeting in Berea, Kentucky, in October of 2018.

28. Jonathan Edwards, *Images or Shadows of Divine Things*, edited by Perry Miller (New Haven, Conn.: Yale University Press, 1948).

29. Consistent with C. I. Lewis's observation about language is Robert Bellah's much more recent assertion that the contrast between "experiential-expressivism" and a "cultural-linguistic" theory of religious doctrine is not so sharp as George Lindbeck presumed when he first labeled and defined these perspectives (in his well-known and highly influential 1984 book on the nature of doctrine). See Lindbeck, *The Nature of Doctrine* (Philadelphia: Westminster, 1984), and Robert Bellah's comments in *Religion and Human Evolution: From the Paleolithic to the Axial Age* (Cambridge, Mass.: Harvard University Press, 2011).

30. Consult also Walker Percy's distinctively Peircean analysis of what happened to young Helen in his collection of essays published as *The Message in the Bottle* (New York: St. Martin's, 2000), 34–45.

31. For another perspective not far removed from that of either Peirce or Buber, consider Josiah Royce, who described the only "right attitude" of the will as being "when we stand in the presence of the universe, and when we undertake to choose how we propose to bear ourselves towards the world"; Joyce, *Problem of Christianity*, 349.

32. George Lindbeck expressed such a hope in the very last paragraph of his book *Nature of Doctrine*.

6 / Rules for Discernment

1. Ignatius of Loyola, *Spiritual Exercises*, nos. 24–43.

2. The question first arises in response to the teaching of John the Baptist as recorded in Luke 3:10–14. As a fundamental question about the moral life, it has inspired a good deal of subsequent reflection, most notably by Leo Tolstoy, who raised it within the context of a powerful meditation on the poverty he encountered in late nineteenth-century Moscow. See Tolstoy, *What Then Must We Do?*, translated by Maude Aylmer

(Oxford: Oxford University Press, 1925). Subsequently, the question was revisited, from a Buddhist perspective, by Thich Nhat Hanh in *The Miracle of Mindfulness: An Introduction to the Practice of Meditation* (Boston: Beacon, 1999), and then was also embodied in the powerful performance by Linda Hunt as Billy Kwan in the 1982 film *The Year of Living Dangerously*.

3. The "Rules for the Discernment of Spirits" are appended to Ignatius's *Spiritual Exercises*, in nos. 313–36.

4. Ignatius of Loyola, *Spiritual Exercises*, no. 179.

5. Ibid., no. 316.

6. Ibid., no. 317.

7. Ibid., no. 330.

8. Ignatius of Loyola, *Spiritual Exercises*, no. 23.

9. Ibid.

10. Ibid., nos. 231–37.

11. Ibid., no. 252.

12. The image of a bee gathering nectar to make honey as an illustration in aid of understanding this method of prayer was one offered by St. Francis de Sales, whose own spiritual formation was thoroughly Ignatian in substance and spirit. See his *Introduction to the Devout Life*, translated by John K. Ryan (Garden City, N.Y.: Image, 1966), 88.

13. Jonathan Edwards, *A Treatise Concerning Religious Affections*, edited by John E. Smith (New Haven, Conn.: Yale University Press, 1959), 95.

14. Ibid., 127–90.

15. See, especially, Jonathan Edwards's version of *The Life of David Brainerd*, edited by Norman Pettit (New Haven, Conn.: Yale University Press, 1984), and the material collected in Edwards, *The Great Awakening: The Works of Jonathan Edwards*, edited by C. C. Goen (New Haven, Conn.: Yale University Press, 1972).

16. Edwards, *Treatise Concerning Religious Affections*, 383.

17. Ibid., 406–7.

18. Ibid., 422–23.

19. Jonathan Edwards, *Great Awakening*, 238. Once again, it is important not to reduce Edwards's insight to the cliché that "actions speak louder than words." Words can be used to constitute verbal actions, as in the taking of an oath, the making of a promise, or a confession of love. Yet in other respects, talk can be cheap, whereas our behavior, especially if it is courageous and consistent, can be eloquent.

20. In comparing the later "inferentialism" of a philosopher like Robert Brandom to Peirce's earlier perspective, it would be important to achieve as much precision as possible about how the former understands the nature and limits of human "discursivity." A broad conception of human discursive behavior (not restricted to verbal actions), to the extent that Brandom embraces it, would perhaps reduce to some extent the distance between his pragmatic perspective and Peirce's pragmaticism.

21. Compare the contemporary perspective in psychotherapy, discussed in Chapter 4, emphasizing that it is not the "form" of the feeling alone, but the feeling in "context" that constitutes the proper object of analysis.

22. Martin Heidegger's extended discussion of boredom as a basic human attunement appears in *The Fundamental Concepts of Metaphysics*, translated by William McNeill and Nicholas Walker (Bloomington: Indiana University Press, 1995). My

earlier commentary on this material is included in Chapter 2 of Raposa, *Boredom and the Religious Imagination* (Charlottesville: University of Virginia Press, 1999).

23. Edwards, *Treatise Concerning Religious Affections*, 433–34.

24. On religious communities as "living" or "embodied" experiments, once again, see Brandon Daniel-Hughes, *Pragmatic Inquiry and Religious Communities* (New York: Springer, 2018).

25. The wisdom of this sort of mindful rereading may be what the poet Robert Frost had in mind when he celebrated the fact that "Love by being thrall and simply staying possesses all." See his poem "Bond and Free," in the *Complete Poems of Robert Frost* (New York: Holt, Rinehart and Winston, 1967), 151.

26. Consider those elemental human experiences, like hope and laughter, to which Peter Berger applied an "inductive" method of analysis in the process of reading them as "signals of transcendence," in his *A Rumor of Angels: Modern Society and the Rediscovery of the Supernatural* (New York: Anchor, 1970).

27. For a brief discussion of this Daoist notion that spiritual practice facilitates the "return" to a more primordial state of being, consult Kristofer Schipper, "The Return" in *The Taoist Body*, translated by Karen C. Duval (Berkeley: University of California Press, 1993), 155–59; see also my comments in Raposa, *Meditation and the Martial Arts*, 43–46.

28. Gustavo Gutierrez, *We Drink from Our Own Wells: The Spiritual Journey of a People* (Maryknoll, N.Y.: Orbis: 2002); see Chapter 9.

29. Such a state of active passivity is one that Daoists refer to and celebrate as *wu wei*.

30. Raposa, "Postlude: On Waiting," in *Boredom and the Religious Imagination*, 167–73.

31. Raposa, "Musement as Listening: Daoist Perspectives on Peirce," *Journal of Chinese Philosophy* 39, no. 2 (June 2012): 207–21.

32. These rules are also appended to Ignatius's *Spiritual Exercises*, appearing at the very end of the manual in nos. 352–70.

7 / On Prayer and the Spirit of Pragmatism

1. See my commentary in "Scientific Theism," Chapter 1 of Michael L. Raposa, *Peirce's Philosophy of Religion* (Bloomington: Indiana University Press, 1989).

2. For an explanation of how individuals can transform their lives into works of art that I regard, in a peculiar but important sense, as something of a secular version of my talk about transforming lives into prayer, consider Gordon Bearn's remarkable book *Life Drawing: A Deleuzean Aesthetics of Existence* (New York: Fordham University Press, 2013).

3. This is a reversal of the cosmological story that Peirce frequently told, where the indeterminate becomes determinate, thus comparable in interesting ways to how the Daoists portray the spiritual life as a kind of "return."

4. The insight that all thought is essentially dialogical in form, already discussed at some length here, is one that Peirce arrived at early on and never abandoned. Consider his youthful meditations on "I, IT, and THOU" (W1: 45–46), as well as his 1891 definition of "tuism" as "the doctrine that all thought is addressed to a second person, or to one's future self as to a second person" (W1: xxix).

5. In traditional Catholic theology, vocal prayer, while it need not be recited aloud, consists of formally scripted words of prayer, as in the recitation of the rosary, whereas the teleology of mental prayer is truly developmental, not formulaic in this sense, but open and indeterminate as in a live conversation.

6. Ignatius of Loyola, *Spiritual Exercises*, nos. 249–57.

7. That the verb "to read" can be used in a great variety of different ways is the insight motivating the inquiry by James F. Ross that culminated in his publication of "On the Concepts of Reading" (*Philosophical Forum* 6 [Fall 1972]: 93–141). The spark for that insight was a meeting in which one of Ross's children was identified by his teachers as having a "reading disability," but without them being able to provide a clear sense of what that might actually mean.

8. Several years after the exchange with Lady Welby, approaching the end of his life, Peirce was still calling for the replacement of a "silly" conception of esthetics with a practice of "meditation, ponderings, day-dreams (under due control) concerning ideals" (*EP*2: 460).

9. The account of Peirce's Neglected Argument developed here is adapted from an essay entitled, "On Reading God's Great Poem: A Delayed Response to Christopher Hookway," *Transactions of the Charles S. Peirce Society* 54, no. 4 (Fall 2018): 485–95.

10. Throughout this book, I have associated the concept of "rereading" with the Latin infinitive in order to accentuate its religious significance. Although the more commonly accepted account concerning the etymology of the word "religion" is that it has roots in the Latin verb *religare* (to bind), it has also been linked, beginning with an ancient account supplied by Cicero, to the verb *relegere* (to read again). See the brief but informative early essay by Sarah F. Hoyt on "The Etymology of Religion," *Journal of the American Oriental Society* 32, no. 2 (1912): 126–29.

11. Toward the end of his first Cambridge Conference Lecture, Peirce suggested that both "meditation" and "adversity" can contribute to the "slow percolation" of instinct (*RLT*: 121–22).

12. On my evaluation, this sort of misreading of Peirce's Neglected Argument is commonplace. For two relatively recent examples, consider J. Caleb Clanton, *Philosophy of Religion in the Classical American Tradition* (Knoxville: University of Tennessee Press, 2017), and Michael Slater, *Pragmatism and the Philosophy of Religion* (Cambridge: Cambridge University Press, 2014).

For the example of an instance where Peirce clearly distinguished between the sort of ontological argument that he would endorse and a problematic theology of "evidences," see *CP* 6.395–97, *W*3: 306–7.

13. The religious meaningfulness of scientific investigation is a persistent theme in Peirce's writing. He encourages the scientist to "listen to the voice of nature until you catch the tune" (*N*2: 222). Nature is the "prayer book of an elevating worship" (*MS* 288), and the purpose of scientific discovery is to develop a new kind of mind ("answering mind") in order to "love God better" (*MS* 1334).

14. This was Christopher Hookway's judgment, as announced in his review essay "On Reading God's Great Poem," *Semiotica* 87 (1991): 156. That essay, a critique of my book on *Peirce's Philosophy of Religion*, was later revised and republished as Chapter 11 in Hookway, *Truth, Rationality, and Pragmatism: Themes from Peirce* (Oxford: Oxford University Press, 2000), 285–303.

15. Ibid., 161–62.

16. Raposa, *Peirce's Philosophy of Religion*, 134.

17. See Hookway, "On Reading God's Great Poem," 160, and Raposa, *Peirce's Philosophy of Religion*, 134.

18. While here they are being treated as continuous, note that there is a technical distinction between evaluating the effects of musement on the muser and evaluating the consequences of living one's life in conformity to the ideal contemplated in musement. One might choose to live such a life without ever having actually engaged in musement oneself, adopting an ideal that is articulated and proposed by others. But it is difficult to imagine that one could live in this fashion without *ever* contemplating the ideal in some fashion that would be considered comparable to musement.

With regard to the second of these forms of inquiry, compare Matthew Bagger's summary of the agenda for James's "science of religions": "Gleaning its data from the lives of generations of individuals venturing on their faiths, it offers provisional conclusions, at any given moment in history, about truth and falsity in religion, and it shapes the space of legitimate hypotheses at that stage of the inquiry"; Bagger, "Religious Apologetic, Naturalism, and Inquiry in the Thought of William James," in *Pragmatism and Naturalism: Scientific and Social Inquiry after Representationalism*, edited by Matthew Bagger (New York: Columbia University Press, 2018), 58.

19. Hookway, "On Reading God's Great Poem," 160.

20. Ibid., 160. Hookway is not alone in this assessment. In his book on *Peirce and the Conduct of Life: Sentiment and Instinct in Ethics and Religion* (Cambridge: Cambridge University Press, 2016), 125, Richard Atkins agrees with Hookway's criticism that I have set the bar too high here, so that "with respect to a test on oneself, the improvement of one's life as a consequence of heeding the call of one's Savior may provide at least a presumptive test in favor of the hypothesis." Whatever the relevance of such a test for one's personal life, however, in terms of its value for determining the *truth* of religious belief, I remain convinced that Peirce would have placed little value on the experiences of an individual inquirer, rather emphasizing what a vast community of inquiry achieves in its collective experience over considerable periods of time.

21. An especially lucid version of this argument is presented in Chapter 1 of Robert Almeder's book on *The Philosophy of Charles S. Peirce* (Totowa, N.J.: Rowman and Littlefield, 1980).

22. This observation by Peirce is recorded in an unpublished version of the Neglected Argument; see *MS* 843:70.

23. This difference will be greater to the extent that the text being reread has itself changed. Unlike a poem or a novel, the book of nature does not remain static from one reading to the next. Even more dramatic still are the transformations that other persons as living symbols undergo during a lifetime of our rereading and interpreting them.

24. There is now a vast secondary literature devoted to the consideration of Peirce's religious ideas, especially the Neglected Argument, most in the form of scholarly essays and many of them appearing in the pages of the *Transactions of the Charles S. Peirce Society*. John E. Smith (one of my most beloved undergraduate teachers) and Vincent Potter were early pioneers in this regard, between them publishing dozens of essays and chapters focused on Peirce's philosophy of religion.

In addition, there are several more extensive, book-length treatments of this general topic. Very early on (several years before I published my own book on Peirce), Donna Orange pioneered with her illuminating analysis of *Peirce's Conception of God: A Developmental Study* (Lubbock, Tex.: Institute for Studies in Pragmaticism, Texas

Tech University, 1984). Douglas Anderson's voluminous body of writing about Peirce is distinguished by the extraordinary clarity it displays and the insight that it embodies. For an important work that includes an extended commentary on the Neglected Argument, examine Anderson's *Strands of System: The Philosophy of Charles Peirce* (West Lafayette, Ind.: Purdue University Press, 1995). Finally, and most recently published, consider Roger Ward's *Peirce and Religion: Knowledge, Transformation, and the Reality of God* (Lanham, Md.: Lexington, 2018). Ward, like Anderson, supplies for his reader some useful details concerning Peirce's biography.

25. If, as Peirce opined, an Idea in the divine Mind can use me as a vehicle to "get itself thought," then such communion would necessarily be achieved. Indeed, real communion or successful communication always seems to take this form, whenever one person embodies as a sign-vehicle some idea that another person has shared.

26. This "shift" requires a redirecting of attention involving (I will suggest here without arguing) what Peirce described as "that wonderful operation of hypostatic abstraction," by means of which the signs that we use to think become themselves the objects of thought (see *CP* 4.549). That is to say, one moves from contemplating things to recognizing them *as being signs* of something. In the scholastic terms that Peirce quite frequently employed, theosemiotic is a discipline that involves the formation and consideration of "second intentions."

27. Jonathan Edwards's theology accommodates the possibility of both a teleological and the more traditional ontological argument for God's existence. Nevertheless, in his view, the primary and ultimate way of knowing God, at least for the saint, is to "see him . . . in images." This way of knowing is to be distinguished from any mode of inference based on what one observes of God's effects, thus, from any kind of design argument. What is perceived in nature is not, in this case, to be regarded as *evidence* for God's existence, but rather, as a *sign* of God's presence. For the saint, this involves the recognition as a symbol of "anything that being from him has resemblance of him, as the sun's majesty and green fields and pleasant flowers of his grace and mercy," as well as in "the soul of man that is made in the image of God." It is to recognize all of creation, using Peirce's language, as being "perfused with signs" and to read these signs as being religiously meaningful. Review Edwards, *The Works of Jonathan Edwards*, vol. 18, *The "Miscellanies,"* edited by Ava Chamberlain (New Haven, Conn.: Yale University Press, 2000), no. 777, 428ff. Consider also Perry Miller's commentary in his Introduction to Edwards's *Images or Shadows of Divine Things*, edited by Perry Miller (New Haven, Conn.: Yale University Press, 1948), 32–33.

28. I do not intend for this contrast to be excessively sharp. Forms of breathing meditation that presuppose an elaborate internal alchemy are also intended as strategies to resist the distractions embedded in everyday experience. In these practices, however, the objects of contemplation have myriad connotations. By contrast, for Ignatius (or in *zazen*), the breath functions almost as a pure index, channeling attention toward one object while detaching it from everything else.

29. Shunryu Suzuki, *Zen Mind, Beginner's Mind*, edited by Trudy Dixon (New York: Weatherhill, 1970), 28.

30. Cheng Man-Ch'ing, *Cheng Man-Ch'ing's Advanced T'ai-Chi Form Instructions*, compiled and translated by Douglas Wile (Brooklyn: Sweet Ch'i, 1985), 107, 112–13; with my commentary in Raposa, *Meditation and the Martial Arts*, 51– 52.

31. William James, *Varieties of Religious Experience* (New York: Penguin, 1982), 283–84.

32. The idea of "mindful consumption" extending far beyond simply the food that we eat has been carefully developed from a Buddhist perspective by Thich Nhat Hanh in numerous lectures and publications.

33. For an extraordinarily rich phenomenological account of the manner in which things encountered in experience can be perceived as "given," consider Jean-Luc Marion, *Being Given: Toward a Phenomenology of Givenness* (Redwood City, Calif.: Stanford University Press, 2002).

34. For Malebranche, unlike Weil, while prayerful attention is characterized by a certain passivity, it is nevertheless regarded as being clearly volitional in nature. See Nicolas Malebranche, *The Search after Truth*, translated by Thomas M. Lennon, edited by Lennon and Paul J. Olscamp (Cambridge: Cambridge University Press, 1997).

35. Malebranche was clear in his rejection of all forms of quietism.

In the concluding meditation "On Waiting" in my boredom book (*Boredom and the Religious Imagination* [Charlottesville: University of Virginia Press, 1999]), I was careful to insist that waiting is not utterly passive, but an engaged form of readiness, a rigorous spiritual exercise. Failing to do so would be highly problematic in light of the consistent attempt here to frame theosemiotic as a species of liberation theology.

36. Consider, as just one example, the endorsement of this type of Ignatian spirituality in Gustavo Gutierrez, *We Drink from Our Own Wells: The Spiritual Journey of a People* (Maryknoll, N.Y.: Orbis: 2002), 143n21.

37. Perhaps most notably Enrique Dussel, who, as I observed earlier, offers a brief commentary on Peirce's thought in his magnum opus while dealing at greater length with those contemporary German philosophers who have been significantly influenced by Peirce and Royce.

38. While it lies just beyond the scope of this project, it might prove useful to explore the resonance of what is being described here as an ethics of attention with similar proposals for a "semioethics" grounded in the semiotics of "listening." For an example of the latter, locate the remarks scattered throughout Susan Petrilli's *The Self as a Sign, the World, and the Other: Living Semiotics* (New Brunswick, N.J.: Transaction, 2013).

39. Simone Weil, *Gravity and Grace*, translated by Emma Craufurd (London: Routledge and Kegan Paul, 1992), 105.

40. Ibid., 118.

41. Ibid., 50.

42. Ibid., 121.

43. I think that it would be fruitful to compare Weil's meditations on desire without an object and love for that which is absent with Ignatius's rule concerning "consolation without a cause." Karl Rahner has made a compelling case for the argument that what Ignatius meant by the latter is an experience of consolation for which no object can be perceived as its cause. "What is decisive is not any particular suddenness of the experience but, to put it quite plainly, the absence of an object.... There is no longer 'any object' but the drawing of the whole person, with the very ground of his being, into love, beyond any defined circumscribable object, into the infinity of God." See Rahner's "The Logic of Concrete Individual Knowledge in Ignatius Loyola," included in *The Dynamic Element in the Church* (New York: Herder and Herder, 1964), 134–35.

44. Weil, *Gravity and Grace*, 90 and 99.

45. For readers who might judge my juxtaposition of Simone Weil with the liberation theologians as something of a "forced" comparison, I recommend examination

of a very useful study published by Alexander Nava on *The Mystical and Prophetic Thought of Simone Weil and Gustavo Gutierrez: Reflections on the Hiddenness and Mystery of God* (Albany: SUNY Press, 2001).

46. Weil, *Simone Weil: An Anthology*, edited and introduced by Sian Miles (New York: Weidenfeld and Nicolson, 1986), 255.

47. Weil, *Gravity and Grace*, 89.

48. Ibid., 30.

49. While Peirce did not dismiss petitionary prayer altogether, considering it in some forms to be natural and instinctive, he could also be disparaging of it. Consider his description of the distinction between "spiritual" and "mechanical" prayer in W_1: 503–4.

50. H. Richard Niebuhr, *Faith on Earth: An Inquiry into the Structure of Human Faith* (New Haven, Conn.: Yale University Press, 1989), 47.

51. With special reference to Hindu philosophy, Simone Weil observed that "God is at the same time personal and impersonal. He is impersonal in the sense that his infinitely mysterious manner of being a Person is infinitely different from the human manner." In *Letter to a Priest*, translated by Arthur Wills (New York: G. P. Putnam's Sons, 1954), 34–35, H. Richard Niebuhr, in a similar fashion, identified God both as the "principle of being" and as necessarily personal.

52. Niebuhr, *Faith on Earth*, 48.

Index

abduction, 5, 9, 88, 107, 116–18, 148, 152, 194, 205, 216, 224–25, 232, 236–38
abstraction, 8, 53, 77, 100, 177, 180, 298n26
acceptance and commitment therapy (ACT), 125, 127, 135, 288n58
ACT. *See* acceptance and commitment therapy (ACT)
aesthetics, 10–12, 15–16, 20–22, 93, 107, 145, 205, 232–33, 271n2, 289n72
affections, 203–6, 208
agape, 80, 83, 97–99, 104–5, 149, 159, 162, 184–85, 280n2. *See also* love
agapism, 77, 79–80, 91, 99, 106, 149, 159, 161, 184, 197, 255, 280n6, 281n12
agency, 12–13, 69–70, 74, 210–11, 222; attention and, 72, 170, 245; causes and, 26; in Edwards, 22; God and, 90; self-control and, 23, 221; theology and, 146
aikido, 105–6, 243–45, 284n46
analogy, 7
Anderson, Douglas, 298n24
Anselm of Canterbury, 109, 120, 233, 238–39
anthropocentrism, 45, 89, 92, 146, 164, 189
anthropomorphism, 87, 89, 92, 164, 188, 282nn20,27
Apel, Karl-Otto, 276n74, 292n21
apophaticism, 7, 16, 85–86, 89–90, 96, 112
Aquinas, Thomas, 7
Arendt, Hannah, 283n34
Aristotle, 45, 86, 272n19

art: beauty in, 22; in Emerson, 18; lives as, 295n2; saints as, 22; world as, 15–16
asceticism, 12, 249, 255, 289n71
atheism, 18–19, 76, 89, 93, 271n14
Atkins, Richard, 297n20
attention, 11, 44, 55, 71, 97, 280n44; abduction and, 116–17; agency and, 170; body and, 240–44; conversion and, 132; deduction and, 116; discernment and, 70, 193, 214–16; ethics of, 194–95; experience and, 118–19, 130; freedom and, 170; functional contextualism and, 125–26; inquiry and, 118; in James, 100, 130–31, 231, 241, 286n16; love and, 99–101, 103–4; meditation and, 34–35; metaphysics of, 291n8; musement and, 100; passivity and, 247; perception and, 290n80; persons and, 44; as relational, 246; self and, 35, 48–49, 134; and self-as-sign, 48–49; self-control and, 5, 11, 48, 134; volition and, 116, 231; in Weil, 99–100, 247, 254–55, 283n36
Augustine, 18–19, 27–28, 32, 56–57, 76, 93, 96, 109, 256, 263, 271n14, 273n43, 279n32
Auxier, Randall, 275n64, 280n45, 291n4

Bagger, Matthew, 297n18
Bain, Alexander, 67
Bakhtin, Mikhail, 54, 278n27
Bateson, Gregory, 169

Bearn, Gordon, 295n2
beauty, 21–24, 35, 40–41, 148, 205, 214, 238–39, 272n28
Beck, Aaron, 128–29, 288n59
behaviorism, 125, 127, 129–30, 135, 144, 213
Being and Having: An Existentialist Diary (Marcel), 290n79
Bellah, Robert, 293n29
Beloved Community, 39, 79, 165–66, 177, 184
body: attention and, 240–44; in Bateson, 169; in Duns Scotus, 278n11; language, 114; in Peirce, 45–46; posture, 45, 169, 204, 242–43; self and, 44–45, 51; self-control and, 243; self *vs.*, 44, 52; as sign, 44; as sign-vehicle, 165, 169, 178; as symbol, 45
boredom, 138, 209–10, 217, 285n7, 294n22, 299n35
Brandom, Robert, 270n7, 290n83, 294n20
breath, 180–81, 231, 241–42, 298n28
breathing meditation, 180–82, 184–85, 297n28
Brown, Robert McAfee, 290n76
Buber, Martin, 189, 257, 293n31
Buddhism, 47, 76, 85, 105, 123, 132, 136, 151, 178–80, 184–85, 190, 229, 291n8

Calvin, John, 282n22
Calvinism, 22, 176, 207
CBT. *See* cognitive behavioral therapy (CBT)
cenoscopy, 6, 118–19, 150, 152, 252, 257, 286n18
charity, 102, 186
childhood, 19–20, 41, 218–19, 271n16
Cicero, 296n10
Clebsch, William A., 271n2
coercion, 147
cognition, 27; abduction and, 194; as behavior, 129; interpretation and, 9; language and, 189; meta-, 62–63, 189, 275n51; psychoanalysis and, 126; as semiosis, 43, 45; in Skinner, 127
cognitive behavioral therapy (CBT), 128–29, 132–33
Coimbra, 27–28
Colapietro, Vincent, 277n1, 278n17, 279n30
Coleridge, Samuel Taylor, 24
community, 77–78; agape and, 184; Beloved, 39, 79, 165–66, 177, 184; in Dewey, 158–59; discernment and, 193; diversity and, 187; exclusion and, 156–57; family as, 182–83; freedom and, 258; ideals and, 157–58; inclusion and, 187; of inquiry, 8, 89; of interpretation, 37, 136, 147, 155–91, 228; interpretation and, 3, 37; "logic" of, 77–78; love and, 76, 79, 162–63; loyalty and, 79, 155, 161–62, 187; meaning and, 10; membership in, 77–78; neighborly love and, 175–77; in Niebuhr, 39; nuclear family as, 182–83; personality and, 49, 53; praxis and, 33, 146; in Royce, 38, 40, 159–62, 164–67; self and, 185–86, 196; similarity and, 156; solidarity and, 78–79, 156, 163; as symbol, 37; unlimited, 160–61, 165–66; "virtual," 161, 165–75; voluntarism and, 172–73
complementarity, semiotic, 179–80, 182, 185, 187, 257
consolation, 29–30, 35, 197–99, 201–2, 207–8, 210, 217, 299n43
contemplation, 5, 18–19, 34–35, 66, 69, 96–97, 113, 137, 186, 201, 231, 238–39, 274n57
conversation, 3–4, 36–37, 51–52, 71, 84–85, 133–35, 165–68, 199–200, 229–30, 292n15, 296n5. *See also* dialogue; speech
conversion, 123, 132–33
Corrington, Robert S., 277n7, 288n61
cosmology, 10, 16, 277n9, 285n4, 295n3

Daniel-Hughes, Brandon, 286n14, 295n24
Daoism, 85, 181, 218, 242–43, 252, 295nn27,29,3
Darwinism, 75–77, 80–81, 145, 280n6
DBT. *See* dialectical behavior therapy (DBT)
Deacon, Terrence, 285n12
deduction, 116–17, 120, 205, 224, 232, 238, 247
Deely, John, 273n43
Deleuze, Gilles, xii, 269n4, 275n59, 281n11
desolation, 29–30, 35–36, 197–99, 207–8, 210, 215, 222
detachment, 30, 100–1, 197, 222–24, 242, 283n29
developmental teleology, 53, 55, 64, 101, 164, 209, 229–30, 251, 296n5
Dewey, John, 33, 55, 124–25, 140, 150, 158–59, 162, 270n11, 276n72, 279n37
dialectical behavior therapy (DBT), 125, 129
dialogue: interreligious, 177; logic of, 84; prayer as, 229, 248; self as, 54, 65; therapy and, 124, 135; thought as, 51–52, 200, 295n4. *See also* conversation

dipolar monism, 80, 281n11
discernment, 18–19, 56; attention and, 70, 193, 214–16; challenges to, 217; community and, 193; in Edwards, 197–98, 203–4, 206–7, 209, 212–13, 225, 294n19; in Ignatius of Loyola, 29–30, 196–98, 209–10, 213, 222; as inquiry, 223; interpretation and, 221; in James, 204–5; as judgment, 194; limits of, 217; love and, 81, 143; musement and, 11–12, 201; narrative and, 213; passivity and, 218–19; praxis and, 196; psychotherapy and, 221–22; saintliness and, 206–7; self and, 29–30, 211–12; self-perception and, 224–25; of spirits, 192–93, 196–97, 207; theosemiotic and, 212–15
Dostoevsky, Fyodor, 54
doubt: Cartesian, 45; faith and, 285n6; inquiry and, 107, 109–10, 196; "paper," 117
Doyle, John, 273n42
Du Bois, W. E. B., 279n37
Dunham, Jeremy, 281n11
Duns Scotus, John, xii, 24, 40, 88, 122, 146, 154, 272n30, 273nn36,39, 278n11; apophaticism and, 85–86; causes in, 26–27; God in, 33–34; love in, 231; voluntarism of, 283n34
Dussel, Enrique, 276n74, 290n77, 292n21, 299n37

Edwards, Jonathan, xi, xii, 4, 20–22, 139, 142, 148, 176, 190, 270n6, 272n28, 280n4; affections in, 205–6; beauty in, 41; discernment in, 197–98, 203–4, 206–7, 209, 212–13, 225, 294n19; God in, 297n27; idealism in, 80; language in, 113–14; Niebuhr and, 39; pragmatism of, 30–33; saintliness in, 36, 206–7
Elbom, Gilad, 293n27
Emerson, Ralph Waldo, 15, 17–20, 96, 148, 218, 252; beauty in, 41; God in, 39; idealism in, 80, 280n4; nature in, 8, 31; Peirce and, 271n7; prayer in, 271n19; symbols in, 36; transcendentalism and, 24
empiricism, 5–6, 118, 128, 152–53, 216–17, 224, 252
enemies, love of, 105–6, 244–46
Eucharist, 166, 292n8
Euclid, 25
evil: in Ignatius of Loyola, 29; in James, 147; problem of, 93, 111–12, 285n10
"Evolutionary Love" (Peirce), 80, 102–3
existentialism, 140–41, 165

experience: attention and, 118–19, 130; cenoscopy and, 119, 252; empiricism and, 216; features of, 118; freedom and, 10; habit and, 20; induction and, 152; inference in, 70; interpretation and, 2, 5, 66, 69; in James, 34, 130; language and, 189; in Niebuhr, 38; openness to, 288n57; responses to, 219–20; secondness of, 153; as semiosis, 2, 5–6, 27, 141, 153, 188–89, 227, 250; signs and, 39, 62, 139; vagueness and, 39
experiment, 4–5, 81–83, 95–96, 119–22, 204–6, 212, 232, 234–37

fallibilism, 84, 91, 93–96, 112, 149, 152–53, 198, 204, 224
family, nuclear, 160, 182–83
"Fixation of Belief, The" (Peirce), 108
Foa, Edna, 288n57
Francis de Sales, 294n12
freedom, 9–10, 272n28; agency and, 70; attention and, 170; beauty and, 272n28; community and, 258; habit and, 3, 62–63; identity and, 72; interpretation and, 2, 62; in James, 99; self-control and, 62, 131, 200; service and, 23
Freud, Sigmund, 91, 282n25
functional contextualism, 125–26

God: beauty and, 23–24; in Duns Scotus, 33–34, 273n36; in Edwards, 297n27; in Emerson, 18–19; fallibilism and, 96; as hypothesis, 94; in Ignatius of Loyola, 201; in James, 88; in John, 77; love of, 75–76, 94, 263; musement and, 17, 205, 225; nature and, 16–17; in Niebuhr, 38–40, 300n51; in Peirce, 18–19, 34, 39, 272nn32–33; reality of, 150, 238–39, 283n31; as symbol, 95; vagueness of, 88, 92–93; in Weil, 300n51
Good Samaritan, 49–50, 186
Grammatica Speculativa (Thomas of Erfurt), 273n34
Grant, Iain Hamilton, 281n11
gratitude, 104, 106, 112, 163, 225, 260–61, 263
Great Awakening, 197, 212
Great Awakening (Edwards), 294n19
Gutierrez, Gustavo, xiii, 41, 149, 249, 274n57, 276n74, 292n20

Habermas, Jurgen, 276n74, 292n21
habit, 37, 62, 275n59; belief as, 67; change, 83; of detachment, 197; in Dewey, 140; in

habit (*continued*)
  Edwards, 142; experience and, 20; formation, 63–64; freedom and, 3, 62–63; as impermanent, 144–45; interpretation as, 2–3; love and, 83–84; love as, 142–43, 252; meta-, 71–72, 94, 134, 238; praxis and, 9; self-control and, 9, 63, 134, 145; teleology and, 225
"habituescence," 63, 145
Hayes, Steven C., 127–28, 287n24, 288n58
Hegel, Georg, 129
Heidegger, Martin, 138, 209–10, 283n38, 294n22
Hinduism, 178, 181, 240–42, 300n51
Hookway, Christopher, 296n14, 297n20
Hopkins, Gerard Manley, 269n2, 277n7
"How to Make Our Ideas Clear" (Peirce), 108
humanism, 87–88, 92
Humble Argument, 119–20, 232

iconoclasm, 89–90
icons, 55–61, 89, 95–97, 138–39, 255–56, 263–64, 278n14, 283n32
idealism, 12, 24, 45, 76, 80–81, 92, 129, 157–58, 281n11
Ignatius of Loyola, xii, 35–36, 154, 181, 184–85, 274n57; consolation in, 208; discernment in, 29–30, 195–98, 209–10, 213, 222; God in, 201; indifference in, 201–2; love in, 102, 262–63, 284n41, 299n43; prayer in, 181, 196, 201–2, 230–31, 241–42
illation, 114–15
"Illustrations in the Logic of Science" (Peirce), 107–8
Images or Shadows of Divine Things (Edwards), 20–21
indices, 55, 57–59, 96–97
induction, 9, 116–17, 120–21, 139, 152–53, 236–38, 247
inferentialism, 294n20
information inebriation, 173
inquiry, 140; abduction and, 117–18; active vs. dormant, 286n14; attention and, 118; community of, 8, 89; discernment as, 223; doubt and, 107, 109–10, 196; formal properties of, 113; musement and, 115, 133, 136–37, 224; praxis and, 41, 121–22; prayer and, 150–51; scientific, 115–16; theology and, 145; theosemiotic and, 108–9
instrumentalism, 110–11
Internet, 167–75, 215

interpretant, 6, 32–33, 48, 55, 61, 64, 78, 143–44, 199–200, 269n1, 277n10
interpretation: cognition and, 9; community and, 3, 37; community of, 37, 136, 147, 155–91, 228; discernment and, 221; experience and, 2, 5, 66; external forces and, 71; freedom and, 2, 62; as habit, 2–3; in Niebuhr, 38–39; of persons, 242–43; in Proudfoot, 286n13; in Royce, 37; self and, 51–52; symbols and, 3, 13, 182
intertextuality, 3, 82, 188, 190
Islam, 85, 178, 181

Jainism, 76, 89
James, Henry, Sr., 77
James, William, xi, 15, 33, 35, 44, 70, 87–88, 99, 108, 125, 128–29, 146, 274n57, 277n5, 278n17; asceticism in, 289n71; attention in, 100, 130–31, 231, 241, 286n16; coercion in, 147; conversion and, 132; discernment in, 204–5; evil in, 147; experience in, 34, 130; love in, 105; love of enemies in, 244–46; nominalism of, 34; poverty and, 151; pragmatism of, 34–35; "science of religions" in, 179; self in, 50–51
Jesuits, 25, 181, 184–85, 230, 274n57
Jesus Christ: children and, 19, 218; Eucharist and, 166; neighborly love and, 175; as pragmatist, 6, 204; service of, as freedom, 23
John, Gospel of, 77
John the Baptist, 293n2
joint attention, 280n44
Judaism, 85, 105, 190

Kierkegaard, Søren, 44, 53, 285n7
Kristeva, Julia, 292n17

language, 32, 47–48, 113–14, 170–71, 189, 271n4
"Law of Mind, The" (Peirce), 17
legisign, 46, 59–61, 64–65, 71–74, 79, 104, 106–7, 136, 143–44, 147, 150, 164, 185, 187, 202, 210, 214, 240, 248–49, 257
Lewis, C. I., 47, 126, 182, 293n29
liberation theology, 41, 147, 149–50, 152, 186, 251–53, 285n10, 289n72, 299n45
Lindbeck, George, 293nn29,32
Linde, Gesche, 273n43, 279n36
love, 12, 40; agapism and, 80, 97–99; anonymous, 102–3; attention and, 97, 101, 103–4; in Augustine, 263; community and, 76, 79, 162–63; death and, 262; deeds

and, 205, 263; discernment and, 81, 143; disinterested, 101; in Duns Scotus, 231; of enemies, 105–6, 244–46; of God, 75–76, 94, 263; as gratitude, 260–61; gratitude and, 104; as habit, 142–43, 252; habit and, 83–84; in Ignatius of Loyola, 102, 262–63, 284n41, 299n43; in John, 77; as loyalty, 40, 79, 154; neighborly, 175–77; in Peirce, 77; praxis and, 111–12, 149, 248, 251; reciprocity and, 104; as semiosis, 84, 97–98; suffering and, 255; teleology of, 75, 79, 91, 95, 97, 102–3, 122, 149, 251, 263; as vague term, 86–87. *See also* agape
Lovejoy, Arthur, 130
loyalty: community and, 79, 155, 161–62, 187; love as, 40, 79, 154; in Royce, 40, 154
Luke, Gospel of, 293n2

MacLeish, Archibald, 288n62
Malebranche, Nicolas, 247, 299n34
Marcel, Gabriel, 276n70, 290n79
Marx, Karl, 150, 254
Marxism, 140–41, 254
materialism, 45–46, 61, 126
Matthew, Gospel of, 220, 270n8
MBCT. *See* mindfulness-based cognitive therapy (MBCT)
Mead, George Herbert, 38, 51–53, 74, 84, 124–25, 130, 134, 285n12
meditation, 115, 180–82, 184–85, 200, 297n28
Message in the Bottle, The (Percy), 288n58
meta-habits, 71–72, 94, 134, 238
meta-semiosis, 65, 71, 74, 126, 136, 151, 216, 218–19
mindfulness-based cognitive therapy (MBCT), 125, 133
Miracle of Mindfulness, The: An Introduction to the Practice of Meditation (Nhat Hanh), 294n2
Monist (Peirce), 77, 80, 285n4
monotheism, 39
Mounier, Emmanuel, 283n34
Murphey, Murray G., 281n14, 284n3, 289n68
musement, 4, 8, 19, 110, 202–3, 215, 262; abduction and, 107, 117; aesthetics and, 16; attention and, 100; as conversation, 247; defined, 94; discernment and, 201; effects of, 297n18; as exercise of power, 119, 261; experimentation and, 235–36; God and, 17, 205, 225; ideals and, 236; inquiry and, 115, 133, 136–37, 224; interpretation and, 18; as meditation, 34; nature and, 233–34; in Neglected Argument, 232, 237, 240; play and, 228–29, 232–33, 259–64; praxis and, 285n5; prayer and, 240, 255–56; purposelessness and, 30, 48; and reality of God, 238–39; rubrics for, 121; Schiller and, 16; self and, 102; self-control and, 229; as self-experimentation, 120; stages of, 237–38; teleology of, 263; waiting and, 222

naturalism, 8, 76, 87, 89–90, 105–6, 180–82, 184, 226, 253, 281n11, 282n20, 288n61, 289n70
natural signs, 56–58
natural theology, 7–8, 188, 190
nature: beauty and, 22, 24, 76; "book of," 16, 31–32, 83, 95–96, 146, 188, 190, 223; contemplation of, 76; culture *vs.*, 8, 56–57, 188, 190; Darwinism and, 77; in Edwards, 20–21; in Emerson, 17–20; God and, 16–17; musement and, 233–34; in Peirce, 19–20; in Schelling, 24–25; signs in, 39; in Spinoza, 25
Nature (Emerson), 17–18
Neglected Argument, 8, 18, 38, 41, 80, 91, 96, 102, 110, 116, 192, 201, 205, 227, 286n15, 290n78, 296n12, 297n24
neighborly love, 175–77
Neville, Robert, 272n32, 282n24, 283n32, 284n43, 285nn5,11
"New List of Categories, A" (Peirce), 61
Newman, John Henry, 279n38
Nhat Hanh, Thich, 291n8, 294n2, 299n32
Niebuhr, H. Richard, xi, 38–40, 257–58, 275n65, 300n51
nominalism, 25, 30, 34, 89, 153
nuclear family, 160, 182–83

object, 6–7, 11–13, 26–28, 32, 46, 48, 52–55, 78, 81, 135, 149, 176, 216–17, 269n1
Ochs, Peter, 281n17, 285n5
O'Connor, Flannery, 59
On Christian Doctrine (Augustine), 28
"On Reading God's Great Poem" (Hookway), 296n14
Oppenheim, Frank, 275n64
Orange, Donna, 297n24

Parmenides, 281n11
Peirce, Benjamin, 17
Peirce, Charles S., ix–xi; beauty in, 22–23; body in, 45–46; cause in, 26–27; cenoscopy in, 6; cosmology in, 10, 16; Darwinism and, 76–77; Duns Scotus

306 / INDEX

Peirce, Charles S. (*continued*)
  and, xii, 24, 272n30; God in, 18–19, 34, 39, 272nn32–33; as idealist, 277n9; love in, 77; materialism of, 45–46; musement in, 4, 8, 16, 18, 202–3; Neglected Argument of, 8, 18, 38, 41; neighborly love in, 176; personality in, 53; Poinsot and, 25–28; pragmatism of, xii–xiii, 6, 107–8; Schelling and, 24; self-control in, 9, 23; self in, 49–50; semiosis in, x; on signs, 3; Spinoza and, 25; transcendentalism in, 17, 24; vagueness in, 7
Peirce and the Conduct of Life: Sentiment and Instinct in Ethics and Religion (Atkins), 297n20
Peirce's Conception of God: A Developmental Study (Orange), 297n24
Pepper, Stephen, 125–26, 128
Percy, Walker, 135, 284n44, 288n58, 293n30
Perler, Dominik, 273n36
personalism, 12, 40, 99, 283n34, 291n5
personality, 53, 95, 164, 281n12; community and, 49, 53; of God, 17–19
persons: as habits, 62; as multiplicities, 49; as signs, 12, 44–45; as symbols, 9, 36–37, 43, 48, 202, 297n23. *See also* self
petitionary prayer, 256, 300n49
phenomenology, 107, 118–19, 214, 225, 229, 232, 279n40, 286n19
"Place of Our Age in the History of Civilization, The" (Peirce), 233
Plato, 281n11
play, 2–3, 101, 115, 117, 122, 191, 202, 218, 228–30, 232–33, 248, 259–64
Poinsot, John, xii, 25–26, 28–30, 273n42
posture, 45, 169, 204, 242–43
Potter, Vincent, 292n16, 297n24
poverty, 112–13, 119, 149–52, 178, 194, 241, 251, 254, 256–57, 293n2
pragmatism, xii–xiii, 5–6; of Christ, 6; of Duns Scotus, 33–34; of Edwards, 30–32; as humanism, 87–88; of Ignatius of Loyola, 274n57; of James, 35; liberation theology and, 41; origins of, 107–8; rabbinic, 285n5; theory/practice dichotomy in, 33; third-person perspective and, 36
praxis, 8–9, 219, 251–52; beauty and, 148; discernment and, 196; in Dussel, 292n21; God and, 121, 235; inquiry and, 41, 121–22; interpretants and, 205; interpretation and, 33, 111–12; liberation theology and, 147, 150, 249; love and, 111–12, 149, 248, 251; musement and, 285n5; semiosis

and, 140; semiotic complementarity and, 179; as sign, 139, 141–42; theology as, 34, 124–25, 139, 145–46; therapy and, 127, 137, 139
prayer, 10, 71; asceticism and, 255; desolation and, 199; as dialogue, 229, 248; in Emerson, 271n19; in Ignatius of Loyola, 181, 196, 201–2, 230–31, 241–42; indifference and, 201–2; inquiry and, 150–51; musement and, 240, 255–56; petitionary, 256, 300n49; as reading, 10–11; vocal *vs.* mental, 296n5; in Weil, 231
Principles of Psychology, The (James), 131
privacy, of human consciousness, 278n17
Problem of Christianity, The (Royce), xi, 38
Proudfoot, Wayne, 275n63, 286n13
purposelessness, 100–1

qualisign, 60–61

"rabbinic pragmatism," 285n5
Rahner, Karl, 299n43
reading, 10–11, 16, 81–83, 190, 210–11, 214, 296n7
reciprocity, 104
Relational Frame Theory (RFT), 128
RFT. *See* Relational Frame Theory (RFT)
Richardson, Joan, 274n51
Royce, Josiah, xi, xii, 53, 74, 84, 87, 124–25, 129–30, 134–35, 172, 278n22, 280nn45,4; community in, 37–38, 40, 159–62, 164–67; discernment in, 195–96, 200–1; interpretation in, 37; love in, 76, 79; loyalty in, 40, 154; neighborly love in, 176–77; self in, 275n62

saints, 21–22, 36, 176, 200, 205–7, 210, 235, 272n28, 298n27
sameness, 4, 78, 141
saudade, 154, 166, 217, 291nn7–8
Schellenberg, J. L., 271n14
Schelling, F. W. J., 24–25, 37, 129, 254, 280n4
Schiller, Friedrich, 16, 87–88, 232, 272n33
science, 157–58, 227, 233, 254, 258, 296n13
scientific method, 4–5, 212
Second Coming, The (Percy), 284n44
self: attention and, 35, 48–49, 134; body and, 44–45, 51; body *vs.*, 44, 52; community and, 185–86, 196; continuity of, 54; as dialogue, 54, 65; discernment and, 29–30, 211–12; immortality of, 73; interpretation and, 51–52; in James, 50–51; in Kierkegaard, 44, 53; as legisign, 64–65,

136, 210; in Mead, 52–53; musement and, 102; opening of, 138; in Peirce, 49–50; play and, 228; as semiosis, 49, 65–66, 211; as sign, 46–47, 55, 61, 70–71, 178, 245–46, 264, 279n33; as symbol, 43, 67–68, 214; as system of relationships, 61–62; teleology and, 55; unity of, 50. *See also* persons
self-control, 23, 64–65, 145, 187, 220–21; agency and, 221; attention and, 5, 11, 48, 134; freedom and, 62, 131, 200; habit and, 9, 63, 134, 145; as meta-cognition, 62; as meta-semiosis, 71–72; musement and, 229; practice and, 9, 35; technology and, 174–75; thought and, 7
selfhood, 36, 59
self-knowledge, 43, 102, 223
self-perception, 193, 224–25
self-preoccupation, 194–95
self-reflexivity, 194, 213
self-sign, 50, 61, 68–69, 245, 289n69
self-transformation, 124
"selving," 44, 49–50, 63, 65, 123, 136, 164, 278n15
semiosis, x–xi; cognition as, 43, 45; in Duns Scotus, 27; experience as, 2, 5–6, 27, 141, 153, 188–89, 227, 250; language and, 32; love as, 84, 97–98; meta-, 65, 71, 74, 126, 136, 151, 216, 218–19; in Poinsot, 28; self as, 49, 65–66, 211; as temporal phenomenon, 44; thought as, 54–55
semiotic complementarity, 179–80, 182, 185, 187, 257
Short, T. L., 277n9, 288n67
sign(s): in Augustine, 27–28, 56–57; body as, 44; in Edwards, 30–31; experience and, 39, 62, 139; feelings as, 219; in Ignatius of Loyola, 29; illation and, 114–15; indexical force of, 58–59; interpretant and, 32–33; interpretant as, 199–200; legisign, 46, 59–61, 64–65, 71–72, 74, 79, 104, 106–7, 136, 143–44, 147, 150, 164, 185, 187, 202, 210, 214, 240, 248–49, 257; natural, 56–58; perfusion with, 1; persons as, 12, 36–37, 44–45; praxis as, 139, 141–42; qualisign, 60–61; self as, 46–47, 55, 61, 70–71, 178, 264, 279n33; thought as, 113–14
silence, 7, 132, 171, 229
sinsign, 60–61
Skinner, B. F., 125, 127, 129
Smith, John E., 278n22, 297n24
solidarity, 258; body and, 187; community and, 78–79, 156, 163; poverty and, 151, 254, 256

speech, 47–48. *See also* conversation; language
Spinoza, Baruch, 8, 25, 280n4
Stoicism, 128–29, 132
Substance and Shadow: An Essay on the Physics of Creation (James), 77
suffering, 93, 111, 123, 253, 255
Sufi Islam, 85, 181
symbol(s), 7–8; and acceptance and commitment therapy, 135; body as, 45; communities as, 185; experience and, 27; God as, 95; interpretants and, 55, 277n10; interpretation and, 3, 13, 85, 182, 263–64; meaning and, 2, 216; persons as, 9, 36–37, 43, 48, 202, 297n23; saints and, 298n27; self as, 64, 67–68, 214; thought and, 3; universe as, 10, 97; vagueness and, 4, 86–87; words as, 57–59

technology, 167–68, 170–75
Teilhard de Chardin, Pierre, 281n12
teleology: conversation and, 84–85; developmental, 53, 55, 64, 101, 164, 209, 229–30, 251, 296n5; habit and, 225; of love, 75, 79, 91, 95, 97, 102–3, 122, 149, 251, 258, 263; personality and, 53; of play, 229; of prayer, 296n5; self and, 55; of theology, 110
Tennyson, Alfred, 72
test, 61–65, 100–1
theodicy, 111
theology: apophatic, 112; in apophatic mode, 16; in Duns Scotus, 33–34; induction and, 120–21; inquiry and, 145; liberation, 41, 147, 149–50, 152, 186, 251–53, 285n10, 289n72, 299n45; natural, 7–8, 188, 190; as practical science, 154; as praxis, 139, 145–46; teleology of, 110; theodicy and, 111; as therapy, 135–36
theosemiotic: as apophatic, 85–86, 96; discernment and, 212–15; fallibilism and, 152–53; as inquiry, 107; inquiry and, 108–9; origin of term, ix; praxis and, 121; Royce and, 38; theism and, 39–40; Weil and, 40–41
therapy, 124–29, 132–36, 221–22
third-person perspective, 31, 36, 102, 123, 130, 193, 200, 203, 206
Thomas of Erfurt, 273n34
Thoreau, Henry David, 68–69, 110
thought: as dialogue, 51–52, 200, 295n4; as semiosis, 54–55; as signs, 113–14; symbols and, 3

Tillich, Paul, 282n24
Tirres, Christopher D., 276n72, 289n72
Tolstoy, Leo, 293n2
Tracy, David, 286n18
transcendentalism, 17, 24
Treatise on Religious Affections (Edwards), xi, 197
Treatise on Signs (Poinsot), 25–26
"tychism," 77

Ueshiba, Morihei, 105–6, 244, 284n46

vagueness, 4, 7, 12, 39, 84–87, 92–94, 97, 154, 171, 179, 210, 231, 250–51, 257
Varieties of Religious Experience, The (James), 131, 287n41, 293n22
Vaz, Katherine, 291nn7–8
volition, 100, 116, 131, 153, 231, 250
voluntarism, 169–70, 172–73, 283n34

waiting, 299n35
Ward, Roger, 298n24

Watson, Sean, 281n11
Weil, Simone, xiii, 40–41, 95, 131, 251, 276n71, 283n30, 299n43; attention in, 99–100, 247, 254–55, 283n36; God in, 300n51; liberation theology and, 152; prayer in, 231
Wells, Rulon, 269n1
What Then Must We Do? (Tolstoy), 293n2
Wilder, Thornton, 270n42
Wildman, Wesley, 281n11, 282n24, 285n11, 293n22
Wiley, Norbert, 277n8
Wittgenstein, Ludwig, 57
words, 47–48. *See also* language
World Hypotheses: A Study in Evidence (Pepper), 126

Zheng Manquing, 243

Michael L. Raposa is Professor of Religion Studies and the E. W. Fairchild Professor of American Studies at Lehigh University. He is the author of *Peirce's Philosophy of Religion* (1989), *Boredom and the Religious Imagination* (1999), and *Meditation and the Martial Arts* (2003), as well as of numerous articles on topics related to American pragmatism, philosophical theology, and the philosophy of religion.

www.ingramcontent.com/pod-product-compliance
Lightning Source LLC
Chambersburg PA
CBHW030434300426
44112CB00009B/997